I. David Welch has written six books and more than fifty professional articles on psychology and education.

Donald C. Medeiros has written more than a dozen articles on education and psychology.

George A. Tate has written a book on humanistic psychology and articles on religion and is a recognized authority on minority psychology.

All are active consultants to public schools, government agencies, and mental health centers.

BEYOND BURNOUT
How to Enjoy Your Job Again
When You've Just About Had Enough

WITHDRAWN

I. David Welch
Donald C. Medeiros
George A. Tate

A SPECTRUM BOOK

PRENTICE-HALL, INC. Englewood Cliffs, New Jersey 07632

Library of Congress Cataloging in Publication Data

Welch, I. David (Ira David), date
  Beyond burnout.

  "A Spectrum Book."
  Bibliography: p.
  Includes index.
  1. Burn out (Psychology) I. Medeiros, Donald C.
II. Tate, George A. III. Title.
BF481.W43   158.7   81-15401
                         AACR2

ISBN 0-13-074740-8

ISBN 0-13-074732-7 {PBK.}

Editorial/production supervision and interior design
  by Louise M. Marcewicz
Cover design by Honi Werner
Manufacturing buyer: Cathie Lenard

This Spectrum Book is available to businesses and organizations
at a special discount when ordered in large quantities. For
information, contact Prentice-Hall, Inc., General Publishing Division,
Special Sales, Englewood Cliffs, N. J. 07632

10 9 8 7 6 5 4 3 2 1

Prentice-Hall International, Inc., *London*
Prentice-Hall of Australia Pty. Limited, *Sydney*
Prentice-Hall of Canada, Ltd., *Toronto*
Prentice-Hall of India Private Limited, *New Delhi*
Prentice-Hall of Japan, Inc., *Tokyo*
Prentice-Hall of Southeast Asia Pte. Ltd., *Singapore*
Whitehall Books Limited, *Wellington, New Zealand*

To my wife Marie and to my sons, David and Daniel. Often the source of frustration and always the cure for my burnout.
I.D.W.

To Ruppert, who kept me from burning out.
D.C.M.

To my father and mother, Godfrey L. and Carrie E. Tate.
G.A.T.

Contents

Preface

In the past few years, much has been written about a phenomenon known as burnout. The literature describes what happens to a number of persons engaged in what may broadly be called "the helping professions." During this same period of time, the authors of this book began to notice changes in our own lives and in our attitudes toward work, our colleagues, and, in fact, life in general. We are all college teachers. Our interest in burnout is both academic and personal. It created a perfect blend for us, since our academic interest in burnout touched our personal lives directly. The combination of these two sets of circumstances led to the writing of this book.

Since we are psychologists, we were educated in the information which should have made us immune to the problems of burnout. However, we quickly realized that we carried no such immunity. If we were susceptible to burnout, might not other professionals be even more susceptible to this problem? Thus, the idea to write a book which would help others to become aware of the problem of burnout, its causes, its symptoms, and suggestions for relieving or reversing it. In this endeavor we hope we have been successful—for the reader's sake.

The literature we reviewed suggested that burnout chiefly affected persons whose professions involved working with others who had problems or other needs. In short, burnout seemed mostly to affect those in the helping professions. The thirteen professions discussed in this book were chosen because there was sufficient information on burnout to make some reasonably clear guesses about the particular causes within those professions. In no way does this imply that other professionals do not suffer from burnout or that they are less significant. In fact, it seems reasonable that members of other professions, such as athletes (coaches and players), politicians, actors, homemakers, and firefighters (no pun intended!) might all suffer from burnout and follow the pattern discussed in this book.

The research for this book led us to various definitions of burnout. Most dealt with the physical and social aspects of burnout. However, closer investigation suggested that these definitions were too narrow and limited. We found five areas of human functioning that are affected by burnout: the physical, intellectual, emotional, social, and spiritual. These areas are closely interrelated and, indeed, represent artificial divisions of experience. They are suggested only as guides to help clarify the symptoms of burnout and to organize the suggestions for preventing and relieving burnout.

The various chapters are each divided into three sections dealing with the causes of burnout, symptoms of burnout, and suggestions for prevention and relief. Again, this organizational scheme is a tool. It is designed to help readers analyze their lives, make comparisons, gain insight, and plan prevention or relief. It is used to help readers increase their awareness not only of their own lives but also of the vulnerability of colleagues to burnout. Our assumption is that increased awareness of causes and symptoms will allow changes to be made so that burnout cannot continue too long. The "cures" section in each chapter and all of Part Two contain practical suggestions for preventing and reversing burnout. It is our hope that readers will, through an awareness gained in this book, avoid burnout and its symptoms. Further, it is our hope that the reader will be able to help others avoid burnout as well.

The primary assumption which underlies this book is that people are responsible for their own burnout. Somewhere in their lives they have made decisions which facilitate burnout. To the extent that this is true, they are free to change those decisions and reverse the process. What they need is a recognition of their own role and alternatives to help them change their lives so that burnout is not as likely. That is the purpose of this book.

We sincerely hope that the work we have invested will prove useful to the reader. We feel confident that it will. The main reason for that confidence is that we have gained personally from the study and use the suggestions in our own lives. To the degree that we are reversing our own feelings of burnout, we are hopeful that our personal gains may be yours, too.

I.D.W.
D.C.M.
G.A.T.
Greeley, Colorado
1980

Acknowledgments

We gratefully acknowledge the following persons and publishers for permission to use their works: Dr. Loretta Jean Engelhardt for permission to use works from her dissertation. Dr. Gilbert M. Burney for permission to use works from his dissertation. Holt, Rinehart and Winston for permission to use works from *Interval Training,* by Edward Fox and Donald Mathews, A and W Publishers for permission to use works from *Understanding Yourself,* by Christopher Evans and Dr. Spencer Rathus for use of his Assertiveness Schedule.

We wish to acknowledge our colleague Dr. Wendell Osorno, who suggested references and provided ideas which contributed to this book. We appreciate the work of Daveda Hodges, who typed the rough draft of the manuscript. And we especially appreciate the contribution of Carrie Finke, who worked hard to complete the final manuscript on time.

Finally, our appreciation to the editors at Spectrum, especially Lynne Lumsden, who saw the value of this book and encouraged us to complete it.

1
BURNOUT

"These people aren't people anymore . . .
They are just mere bodies moving by me."[1]

---

[1]Reginald L. Smith, "Those people aren't people anymore . . . ," *Hospital Topics*, November/December 1979, p. 15.

1. The Dynamics of Burnout

"My candle burns at both ends;
It will not last the night..."
—Edna St. Vincent Millay

Donald David George is a young psychologist. He spent years preparing himself for a profession in which he could work helping others. In his first years in a mental health center, he was contemptuous of the hard and crusty professionals he met. He knew that if he could go back to school and get a doctorate, he could move into a position of authority in the mental health field and begin to hire people who really cared about other people and get rid of the ones who were just hanging on. He might even be able to help the people who seemed not to care about the clients in the mental health center where he went to work after his master's degree. Whether he could help those people or not, he knew that he would not be one of them. He couldn't understand how it came to be that people who didn't even like people could end up working in a mental health setting. Even worse, some of those uncaring professionals had ended up in charge of an entire center. He knew that things would change when he finished his doctorate and could begin to influence things.

His professors thought highly of Donald. He worked hard. He was obviously compassionate, dedicated, and scholarly. He would be a fine professional.

His first year in his new job went well. He was well thought of—if a bit naive. His enthusiasm, his willingness to put in long hours, and his desire to

3

serve on various committees were appreciated. His notions about a deeper involvement with clients, their families, and their lives was greeted with knowing nods by the "old-timers" at the center.

Dr. George's first problem in the mental health center came when he proposed that the center stop using the ordinary diagnostic labeling system, since he thought it demeaned clients. He was rebuffed. Shocked and saddened at the callousness of his colleagues, he was confronted with the same uncaring attitude he saw when he first entered the mental health field. His new credentials hadn't made any difference at all.

He has been a therapist for five years now. He became a team leader and now holds the position of director of out-patient services. He is not well liked by his colleagues. He drinks too much. The younger staff members consider him unapproachable. He hates his job, feels trapped by it, and sees no place else to go. He thinks the younger psychologists on the staff are idealists and simply don't understand the complexities of mental health work. "They'll learn," he says often. His marriage is in trouble. He is sick and tired of the human tragedies he sees every day. Sometimes he wonders why in the hell those people just don't get a hold of themselves and do something about their lives. They just seem weak. He is thirty-six years old. He is burned out.

What happened? A bright young professional has lost the capacity to feel concern and compassion for the very persons the profession is meant to help. Confronted with human misery hour after hour, day after day, week after week, and year after year, a career has been destroyed. Things just didn't go according to plan. The story might have been about a physician, social worker, police officer, homemaker, teacher, journalist, or factory worker. The job, the people, and sometimes life itself are just not worth it anymore. Some people hang on and some people just quit. All grapple with the problem of the loss of meaning in what was once a dream.

THE PROCESS OF BURNOUT

It is rare that a person enters a professional or life situation already tired. The name given to the phenomenon suggests that it is sudden. But, it is more likely that burnout is gradual. A crisis might result from a confrontation, event, or failing that signals burnout, but that is only the visible moment of history. It is the end of a beginning that had its roots in human caring, a desire to help, to make a worthwhile contribution, a yearning to create—in short, a dream.

Those who see themselves as helpers enter their life work with joy and enthusiasm. They genuinely care about the persons with whom they hope to work. Or, another side of the same caring attitude is that many enter their life work with a love of the task itself. A teacher may say that he or she loves children. A police officer may say that he or she cares about the law or even a principle—"to serve and to protect." A physician may love healing. Whatever the reasons, it is characteristic of the young to enter their work with enthusiasm.

If we may speculate on the motivations of the people who enter the helping professions, we would conclude that they are compassionate. Somewhere along the line, however, that compassion leaves them as they grow increasingly frustrated and thwarted in their desire to help. It seems as if the power to put dreams into practice never comes. Compassion turns to carelessness.

With their compassion blunted, they take less care in their relationships with those they are dedicated to help. They might listen less carefully to a welfare mother's plea for more subsistence money. They might yawn in the midst of an intelligence test for a youngster. They might let pass, just this once, an opportunity to protect a matter of principle.

Confronted with human adversities, it is impossible to be compassionate all the time. Yet all of the helping professions make that demand. How do people resist becoming careless? Many don't. In many, it goes even further. Carelessness turns to callousness.

Workers might begin to defend carelessness. "What the hell, nobody really cares. All anybody really cares about are the reports. The paper. They don't care what is in the reports so long as the report is filed. Put down anything. All that counts is the paper work. Cover your ass. That is what matters." Vocabulary changes subtly. Physicians begin to describe their patients in terms of symptoms. They might no longer refer to Mrs. Jones as Mrs. Jones, but as "the gallstone." Teachers may come to describe their job as "baby-sitting." It shows up in tragicomic ways, as in the now-famous story of the kiddy radio personality who, thinking he was off the airwaves at the end of his show, said, to his ultimate dismissal and to the embarrassment of thousands, "Well, that ought to hold the little bastards for another day."

Callousness reveals itself in cynicism. Many seem hopeless. They deride the hopeful. Since dreams and caring have been altered by frustration, disappointment, and exhaustion, they may even come to actively dislike the persons with whom they work as colleagues and as clients. Callousness turns to cruelty.

They no longer merely treat the persons with whom they work in simple mechanical ways. They actively work against them. Let us take as an example "Big Nurse" from the book and movie *One Flew over the Cuckoo's Nest*. She had passed beyond carelessness, and certainly she was hardened. But, she was also cruel. Her compassion had turned to contempt. She hated the "inmates" and actively worked to demean them. She treated them in depersonalized ways. She dehumanized them. How different is "Big Nurse" from other attendants in our institutions for the old, the intellectually impaired, the sick, the criminal, or the abandoned infants and other children of our society? How different from the teacher who insults or humiliates a child for the "good" of "discipline"? How different from the mother who locks her children in their room for hours? How different from the police officer who, at small provocation, goes too quickly to the riot stick? All of these things—and more—have happened to persons who entered their life work compassionate and now use their power, position, or authority to work against those they have sworn to help.

They have traveled a path that led them from compassion to carelessness, from carelessness to callousness, and from callousness to cruelty. There the path ends. Not every professional walks to the end. Some, whether by their nature or by chance or by the authority of their own will, never cease to be compassionate and helpful people. Others arrest their decline and remain merely careless or callous. There are degrees of burnout. Luckily, the process can be reversed, as the rest of this book suggests.

A DEFINITION

Since burnout has only recently received much attention, there is as yet no commonly accepted definition of this phenomenon. It seems to the authors that current attempts to define burnout have been too narrow and restricted. Such definitions seem to touch on one or two aspects of human functioning. For the purposes of this book, we will define burnout as a complex process which affects at least five major areas of human functioning: physical, intellectual, emotional, social, and spiritual.

PHYSICAL

This refers to the energy one brings to whatever one needs and wants to do. One of the first symptoms of burnout is fatigue, a general, all-around tiredness which carries over from work to home. There is ample evidence from physiology and medicine that exercise and nutrition are two key elements in general physical well-being. Recent research also suggests the importance of stress reduction in the maintenance of sound physical health. People experiencing difficulty in this area seldom engage in any systematic exercise, nutrition, or stress-reduction program.

INTELLECTUAL

This refers to the sharpness with which one thinks and solves problems. A common symptom of burnout is a general loss of sharpness in thinking and problem solving. Creativity may diminish, and this can carry over from work to everyday non–work-related matters. There may be a cynicism toward innovative or different approaches shown by burnout victims. Statements such as "That will never work" or "We've tried something like that already" reflect this cynicism. People experiencing difficulty in this area seldom have a hobby or other means of intellectual relaxation such as reading, chess, or music.

EMOTIONAL

This refers to the general positiveness or negativeness of one's emotional life. Is a person basically optimistic or pessimistic, happy or unhappy about what's occurring in his or her life? Is he or she even aware of what is going on emotionally? Does the person have emotional outlets other than work? One of the common emotional symptoms of burnout is the overinvestment of energy in one's job with very little interest in anything outside of work. When the job begins to go poorly, the person's life, which consists chiefly of work, necessarily begins to go poorly, too. With the loss of one's dreams and expectations come feelings of helplessness which can result in symptoms of a depressionlike nature. It is interesting and encouraging to note that people with varied outside interests appear to have a built-in buffer against the severity of burnout symptoms. When problems arise at work, they have other aspects of their life which can still offer satisfaction. Their loss and subsequent feelings of helplessness are diminished.

SOCIAL

This refers to feelings of isolation versus feelings of involvement. Do others understand a person's feelings of fatigue, frustration, anger, or disillusionment? Is a person free to share these feelings with others, or does such behavior seem inappropriate? What type of social support system does the person perceive as available? Is there someone outside of work who will listen—perhaps a clergyman, friend, or relative? People suffering from burn-out may not want to burden someone else with their problem; they may feel it is an imposition or they may fear rejection. The net result is self-imposed isolation.

SPIRITUAL

This refers to the degree of meaning one feels one has in one's life. Many people have noble expectations upon entering their profession. Quickly, they may realize these expectations will never be fulfilled. The result is a void in their lives. A large part of who they are and a large part of their dream are now missing. For what purposes are they now doing their work? How can they create new meaning for their lives? One way has already been implied, and that is to develop meaningful interests outside of work. A second approach is to ask, What will have to change in my job to make it more meaningful? The answers to this question provide a starting point for persons to begin creating meaning in their lives.

BURNOUT SYMPTOMS

As is evident from the description offered above, our definition is a definition of symptoms. It is not an explanation of causes. While we are about to offer ideas about two very broad causes, we believe that in general the causes are many, varied, individual, and in some cases, unknown. Burnout begins to look very much like the common cold. While the causes are many, the symptoms are remarkably alike regardless of the cause. This book will offer ideas about the causes of burnout, discuss the most common symptoms, and, finally, offer remedies—hopefully more effective than the ones we buy over the counter to combat the common cold.

Even those people who don't ever lose their compassion and begin the decline into cruelty might experience burnout. They might grow weary of the job, of the long hours, of the seeming intractability of the system. They might just be tired. They experience frustration for a short period of time. This short-term burnout is characterized as physical. Its effects are short-lived, and, except for momentary frustrations and an occasional hostile reaction or manner, the persons afflicted by it go about doing their jobs with relish and effectiveness. They might have to "check in" with colleagues and clients with a statement about being tired or run-down, but the "cure" for their "burnout" is a short vacation or even a day off. Often, the merest alteration in their job or workday is enough to bring back their enthusiasm. Such people are affected by boredom, and new challenges remove that. Persons affected by physical burnout probably work in jobs that they like and with people who are sensitive to their needs. They are also persons who are able to ask for what they need, and more often than not they get it. The day-in, day-out contact with humans in need wears them down physically, but they recover rapidly with time off and new tasks.

The second major symptom of burnout is the one which receives the most publicity. It is long-term and what is often characterized as psychological. For our purposes, this gross characterization was insufficient. We recognized that psychological functioning included different symptoms which we further identified as intellectual, emotional, social, and spiritual. Most people recognize the physical stresses of their job and learn how to cope with them in one way or another. It may be, however, that even those who recognize the psychological stresses of their jobs are sometimes unable to cope with them. That is when the decline in sharpness, empathy, sensitivity, and compassion described at the beginning of this chapter begin. The psychological weight piles up gradually so that it is noticed only when a crisis occurs, when the inability to cope with the psychological stresses has escaped the confines of their jobs and has begun to affect their relationships in all aspects of their lives. Their families struggle to tell them that they are treating them carelessly or callously. Their friends tell them that they are aloof, distant, uncommunicative. They go inside with their emotions and seem unable to get out their frustrations, disappointments, sadnesses. Recreation becomes mechanical and blunt as their ability to experience the positive emotions decreases.

Certainly, no one burns out except in a climate that encourages burnout. One of the reasons psychological burnout is difficult to detect is that, in many situations, it is a pattern followed by many persons in the same organization. Cynicism, distrust, bureaucratic organization, and resistance to change are descriptive of many of our human institutions. The loneliness and isolation of an attorney may be duplicated in industry, schools, or patrol cars. Given no one to point out the slippage, it goes unnoticed until a breakdown occurs. Separated from the kinds of services they are expected to give others, people sometimes become the very cases they are expected to treat.

Psychological burnout takes longer to happen and longer to reverse than physical burnout. A vacation is not enough. A day off is not enough. Going to a burnout workshop is not enough. It takes time, a generous application of all of the above, following some of the suggestions in this book, and a rediscovery of compassion.

Perhaps most difficult is the recognition that burnout is not a simple reaction to circumstances. In order to reverse the process of burnout, whether it be short-term physical burnout or long-term psychological burnout, people need to recognize their own contribution to their plight—they are part of the problem. That is the negative side. The positive side is that they are also part of the solution.

TWO REACTIONS TO BURNOUT

Burnout is an interesting term in that it reveals its meaning. *Burn* evokes conflagration, heat, anger, hostility, the reaction of a person who strikes out at others, an aggressor. Once, when one of the authors was visiting North Miami Beach, Florida, an older woman was going through the checkout line at a grocery store. The "bag boy" dropped a bottle of vinegar and it broke. The woman screamed, "I won't pay for that! You broke it! I didn't break it! You did it! I won't pay for it!" Her anger overwhelmed everyone around her. Seemingly, no amount of talking could help her. The manager's telling her that she wouldn't have to pay didn't help. She was striking out. She was still yelling as she left the store with a fresh bottle of vinegar. Here was a person whose anger was simmering just below the surface. The smallest aggravation would unleash it. She was, to our understanding, burned out. Her reaction to her burnout was anger and hostility. She sought subconsciously to ease her pain by making life painful for others.

There are many persons like this. They work in all kinds of jobs and make others' lives miserable. The result can be that they cause others to be like them because the natural tendency is to respond in kind: If they are going to strike out at people, then people tend to strike back at them. They end up justifying their actions because the very hostility they generate turns back on them, making them even more hostile.

We are not talking here about anger created by a situation. Situational anger is justified, as when an injustice occurs. If an adult is beating a small child, this demands a response. It is probably wise to worry about persons in society who do not feel anger at injustice. But here we are discussing the anger that boils and bubbles just beneath the surface, anger created by the feeling that life is not measuring up to one's expectations or dreams. Such sufferers perceive many others as frustrating these dreams; they become angry at their jobs, their colleagues, their boss, and their patrons. They hate everything, and their anger is directed at anyone they consider to be a suitable target.

Thus, one reaction to burnout is to burn. But that is only one reaction. There is another reaction. If some burn, others are just *out*—there is nothing left. If some strike out with anger and hostility, others are alienated and depressed. They sit back, sigh, and claim that nothing can be done. They are out, and they are simply not going to give any energy to help someone else. They hang on, put in their time, do their job, but expect nothing from it and certainly aren't going to give anything to it. There is a story of a teacher who, when asked if he thought the strife between students and teachers would end, said, "I'll tell you when it's going to end. It's going to end when I retire and get out of here. That's when." They are just waiting to retire. Then, mercifully, it will be over.

With nothing left to give, they live lives of interminable boredom. They are the ones in organizations who subvert any new program simply because they believe that they will be asked to do something. They simply don't have the energy to do anything. It is better to make their jobs as mechanical as possible because then they won't have to think about anything; they can just do their jobs. It is not their intention actually to hurt anyone, as in the first reaction to burnout, but they do just that by not doing anything. Their sin is a sin of omission rather than of commission. Whatever energy, compassion, desire, feelings of competence, integrity they once had are gone— they are out.

Both reactions to burnout are common enough. We are not certain if one type is better than the other. It is probably less taxing to be alienated and depressed; at least that way one doesn't have to fight. If a burnout victim is hostile and angry, every day is a battle of some kind or other. In either case, however, others' chances of becoming burned out are increased by their association with such colleagues. It might very well be that if some are aggressive, then others might end up being passive. If they are passive, then others might end up being aggressive. We don't know. Neither one is an attractive alternative.

People's reactions to burnout may simply reflect their style of life. If they are aggressive types, then perhaps they carry that into burnout. If they are passive, then their tendency might be to react with alienation and depression.

It does not appear that a particular reaction to burnout attaches itself more frequently to either type of burnout. For example, a person who is experiencing short-term physical burnout is not more likely to respond with anger than with depression. In the case of the authors of this book, one of us responds to stress with anger, another with withdrawal, and, unusually enough, the third responds with calm during the stress and then panics afterward! How people respond probably has as much to do with their personality as it does with job environment, colleagues, family, and so forth. It may be enough to recognize the symptoms—as either *burn* (anger/hostility) or *out* (alienation/depression)—to begin to reverse the process.

THE CAUSES OF BURNOUT

There are many causes of burnout, and they interact in unknown ways. The causes vary with the individual, with different factors assuming greater or lesser importance. However, two very broad causes seem almost invariably to be present. First, there is the problem of *expectation*. Second, there is the problem of *distribution*.

The problem with expectation has to do with the short life-story that began this chapter. Dr. George was a young man who entered his profession with high expectations about changing the way mental health services were presented to the public. He was unprepared for the resistance he encountered and depressed by his inability to bring about the changes in his profession that he wanted. He was caught up in an expectation of accomplishment rather than an expectation of striving. He saw only the goal, not the struggle it would take to make the accomplishment come to life. It seems to us that this is a difficulty with many young professionals—in fact, many young persons. While it is proper and good to dream, it is dangerous to dream without any understanding of the difficulties one may encounter in trying to make the dream a reality. Perhaps it is here that our educational system fails us more than in any other single area. Many educators fail to allow their students to touch with any real significance the realities of life. They allow them to go forth to attack the system without knowing in any real way that the system is going to fight back and that it is a damned tough adversary. They fail to acquaint them with the idea that persons already in positions of power are not going to "roll over and play dead" just because some new voice is striving to make itself heard. The powerful will try to hang on to their power. Many young persons have not been provided with the idea that there is more struggle in life, more sadness, more tragedy, and more pain than their young minds can imagine. Our educational systems, our television and movie industries, our advertising philosophies all seem dedicated to protecting young people from seeing with any clarity the tough part of life. No wonder then, when confronted with the toughness of systems, old ways, and dogmatic personalities, their compassion gives way.

The second expectation that seems to us to lead to burnout is what has been described as the "personal fable." Essentially, the personal fable is the belief that "it can't happen to me." All those other people may burn out, but not me. People believe they will somehow be among those who do not ever lose their compassion. They will be the effective ones. They will be the happy ones. They will be the ones who avoid the pain and tragedy everyone else is talking about. It is this belief in a protected life that shatters so easily when the crisis finally comes. To paraphrase Mark Twain, "Oh, the dreams of youth. How beautiful they are. And how fragile." It may be impossible to break through the personal fable of young persons. Certainly, we do not advocate making life unnaturally hard on young people just to teach them that life is not as they envision it to be. We are not advocating that educators become "killers of the dream." We would advocate, however, that persons be prepared with skills aimed at helping them avoid burnout on the one hand and coping with and reversing the process on the other.

These two expectations seem to us to set people up for burnout. We advocate, at the minimum, that job training or professional training teach young people that change is difficult and that no one is protected from the struggles of life. Then, it might be possible to avoid some of the problems of burnout that seem to be ever-increasing.

The second problem leading to burnout is distribution. Many persons seem to fall into a metaphor of life that might be characterized by one of two geographic phenomena: One is Death Valley, and the other is the Dead Sea.

Death Valley is a desert. It is interesting because it was once an ocean teaming with life. It supported vast societies, giving life to creatures and life forms no longer present on the planet. It gave all of that for untold eons. But something changed. Oceans need feeding. Water flows from somewhere to give life to the ocean so that it might in turn give life. Whatever fed the ocean that became Death Valley stopped. Although there was nothing coming in, the ocean still tried to feed the societies that depended on it for life. It gave so much that it dried up and became not an ocean but a desert. Death Valley is a phenomenon of nature in which there is an outlet but no inlet. It simply gave up what it had and, since nothing new was coming in, it died.

Think how that might describe some people. They are asked to give of themselves day in and day out. Teachers, social workers, ministers, and police officers all have demands made on them by others. If they believe that they can continually give without somehow being fed themselves, then they become psychological Death Valleys, unable to give anymore, unable to sustain life anymore. They become hollow, drained, sterile. They are the teachers without life in them. Their classrooms are infertile. They are incapable of creating a climate in which young things can grow. They are the fathers whose kisses are always dry; they are unable to give the warm, wet kisses of affection that enable their families to grow and develop. They are persons who have no sustenance coming in from outside themselves. They have dried up.

The Dead Sea is a body of water that is stagnant. The Jordan River flows into the Dead Sea. It was once a body of water that supported life, but it no longer does so. It has an inlet but no outlet. It collects the waters of the Jordan River, accepts life, and then doesn't let it out again, with the result that it is smothered and dies. Nothing escapes from the Dead Sea. It has nowhere to go. It takes everything in but lets nothing out.

There are people who, for one reason or another, are unable to let anything out. There are people who have more than they need. They have no ability to share the richness of themselves. They collect their emotions and hold them in. Never getting out, those feelings fester, become cancerous, and eat away, so that the persons again become devoid of life. They bloat with collected human expressions, experience, joys, and sadnesses. They don't know how to give. They are the physicians who are unable to reach out a hand to a dying patient. They are the athletes who forever pretend that they are on the playing field and never come to the rest of life. They are the nurses who tell little boys that cuts and broken arms don't hurt because all of their own feelings have been smothered in their own internal Dead Sea. They take everything, and they give nothing back.

Whether they never developed ways of sharing their feelings or, through time, developed a fear of sharing themselves, the result remains the same. The inability to share intimacy with some other person leads to burnout.

These two fairly straightforward understandings of why persons burn out can also provide some ways out of the burnout dilemma. It is not necessary to expect that dreams always succeed or that people lead charmed lives. It is not necessary to lead a life which is unsupported or unnurtured and in which there are not persons with whom to share hopes, fears, dreams, joys, and sadnesses. If people can avoid expectations that condemn them to failure and can avoid distribution systems that either drain them or prevent human contact, they will have gone a long way toward avoiding burnout in their lives.

HOW TO USE THIS BOOK

In this book, we have investigated many different professions. Each chapter deals with a different profession and is divided into three sections: causes of burnout in the particular profession, symptoms of burnout in that profession, and suggestions to prevent or relieve burnout for persons in the profession. We have termed this third section "cures."

Part Two of this book contains concrete activities which are suitable for persons in any profession. These activities are especially designed to help in the five major areas of human functioning which are affected by burnout.

To obtain maximum benefit from this book, one should read the chapter which deals with one's profession or the profession most similar to it. Think about the causes and symptoms. Decide if they fit. Then try and follow the suggestions in the "cures" section. Next, go to Part Two and read through the activities. Decide which would be the most appropriate or fun to do. Start with them. Try to do at least a few from each of the five areas in Part Two.

Even if persons don't feel they are burning out, the activities in Part Two can be reviewed as effective preventive measures against future burnout. Also, consider suggesting these activities to colleagues who appear to be burning out. Consider doing these activities with colleagues at work. The interactions generated by following these activities can do much to improve the climate at work and lead to a more productive professional life.

BURNOUT
AND THE SCHOLARS

2. Teachers

*"A teacher reflects eternity;
he can never tell where his influence stops."*
—Henry Adams

Have we got a deal for you! We have a job for a young person right out of college. The salary is about $13,000 a year. There are excellent fringe benefits. Short working days. Frequent vacations. Most summers off. Job security. And the best part of all is that the job involves working with children or young people. Sometimes the competition for this job is tight. Many people are drawn to it. BE A TEACHER! Yes, it is an ideal job.

Yet, in a recent poll of teachers in Chicago, fifty-six percent reported physical or mental illness as a direct result of their jobs. In 1979, some 110,000 teachers reported physical assaults. In fact, in this "ideal" profession, the National Education Association, one of the largest professional teachers' organizations in the United States, reported that fully thirty percent of American teachers would rather be doing something else.

WHAT WENT WRONG IN ACADEME?

It is hard to figure out what is going wrong in a job that presents so many benefits. The people who enter it are dedicated, sincere, and well educated. But there is a flaw somewhere in the scheme, because teachers are leaving the profession in record numbers; indeed, the supply of teachers with twenty or more years of experience has been cut in half since 1962. Those teachers are leaving for good reasons. Out of the confusing fog of information, a pattern is beginning to take shape. It is not a solid picture to which concrete proposals of change may be submitted to correct the problem immediately, but it isn't so vague that it can be ignored any longer. Teachers are burning out. What are the causes?

Teachers are people. Therefore, the causes of personal problems are individual. However, the patterns beginning to emerge are ones which characterize what has been written about teachers who are burning out.

THE PROBLEM OF MONEY

Teachers start work, after four or five years of college, at approximately $12,000 to $13,000 a year. (This can vary somewhat according to region, town size, and, sometimes, tax base.) It isn't much, but it is not bad. It is, however, the most-often-mentioned cause of teacher burnout. Before the American public criticizes teachers for being money-hungry, let us all consider that this is a primary concern for a good share of all working people. In business, salary increases have proven to be among the best motivators and the best morale boosters of the many incentive plans tried by industry, business, and management teams. Teachers are caught in the same cycle as everyone else. They have received yearly raises (most of the time), but those raises have not kept pace with inflation. It is an irony of modern life for teachers that they are making the highest salaries in history, yet the bills grow larger, their standard of living seems not to get better, and instead of advancing confidently in the direction of their dreams they seem to fall further and further behind each year. Their salaries are higher, but they have to skimp a little more each year to make it through.

The problem of absolute dollar amounts, while important, is not the primary cause of burnout in teachers. What underlies the frequent mention of money is a conflict that cannot be solved with a simple increase in salary. Every year, when teachers go to the bargaining table, they hear the same old jokes. "Why do you need a raise? You already have three months' vacation. Why not get another job in the summer?" If teachers take their families to the movies or a restaurant and they run into a school board member, then the teacher might hear, "Why do you need a raise if you can afford to take the whole family out to a movie?" Every year there is a battle for a raise that ends up being about half the inflation rate. One of the insults teachers have to bear is that they are nothing but baby-sitters and that anyone could do that job. Consider this: Baby-sitters are paid $1.50 an hour. What if we paid teachers baby-sitters' wages? Teachers work seven-hour days (often longer). On the average, they have about thirty kids in a class. They work 180 days a year. By simple multiplication: $1.50 per hour per child × 7 hours × 30 children × 180 days per year = $56,700 per year! If you are a teacher and you hear the old saw about being a baby-sitter, accept baby-sitters' pay as fast as you can! Teachers have come to believe that what they do is actively resented by the public. The overall feeling they have, and the primary cause of burnout, is that there is a lack of monetary appreciation for the job they do. Plumbers average $19,000 a year.

In the final analysis, this belief in the lack of appreciation, as reflected in the yearly battles over salary, takes its toll. The teachers, underappreciated, begin to doubt their own worth. They have taken a step toward burnout.

THE PROBLEM OF DISCIPLINE

In 1979, the National Education Association estimated that one of every twenty teachers in the United States was physically attacked. That figure represents an increase of approximately fifty-seven percent over the 70,000 attacks reported in 1978. The 110,000 teachers attacked in 1979 were attacked on school property. Another 10,000 were attacked by students off school property. Of the teachers attacked, 11,500 required medical attention. Another 9,000 required psychological counseling as a result of the attacks. Understandably, ten percent of the teachers responding to the survey reported that they feared being attacked in the near future. While fear of personal attack was a primary concern, twenty-five percent of the teachers told of theft of personal property at school, and another twenty-five percent reported that their personal property had been damaged at school.

These figures are frightening. Equally frightening are the figures indicating an increasing number of attacks by students on other students. And, sadly, an increasing number of attacks by teachers on students.

Teachers are confronted with what appear to be increasingly disruptive students, increasing numbers of parents who say they can't do anything about it, and a supervisory structure that tells them to "do the best they can" but has the reputation of doing nothing to help as the supervisors simply look the other way. The teachers report that there are simply too many students who will not do the work required to learn, too many students who will not complete homework assignments, too many parents who are disinterested or report that they cannot make their children do schoolwork, too many self-protecting administrators, and too many school boards who cut budgets and expect superior results. All of this, coupled with violence and vandalism, combine to drive more and more teachers from the profession or leave many of them with what many are beginning to call "combat neurosis"—read burnout.

THE PROBLEM OF RESPECT

"Those who can, do. Those who can't, teach." It is a widespread idea that anybody can teach. It is not uncommon, during a strike, for example, to hear many parents, even school board members, say something on the order of "Hell, let the teachers strike. We can get people off the streets to staff the classrooms." This general notion that the job teachers do is not very difficult reflects a feeling that teachers report as another cause of burnout. It is the belief on the part of teachers that there has been a gradual but profound devaluation of education by society in general.

Perhaps no other profession is so constantly criticized, so thoroughly held up to public scrutiny, yet so nearly devoid of prestige. To be a public school teacher in the United States is to work in the least respected of all the professions. This ironic situation has taken its toll on the morale of teachers. The effects of the feeling of disrespect contribute to teacher burnout.

THE PROBLEM OF WORKING CONDITIONS

Sometimes the problem of working conditions has to do with broken windows, too little equipment, or unsanitary environments. For most teachers, however, these are problems of the past. Occasionally, especially in schools of the inner city, such conditions may still exist. For the great majority of teachers, however, the physical working conditions are not a problem. The working conditions problem that is a cause of burnout is, in the main, psychosocial. A friend of one of the authors told him recently of her day in an elementary school. From the time she arrived in the morning until she left in the afternoon, she had no time that she was not in direct contact with students. In fact, in this elementary school the time was so regimented that no time had been planned for the teachers to go to the toilet! Since the rule in the school was that children could not be unsupervised, the teachers had worked out a system whereby one teacher would stand in the middle of the hall between two classrooms while another teacher ran for a toilet break.

The problem is that the student-teacher ratio in most public schools runs to about thirty to one. In many schools it is higher. Parents might consider this when they are having trouble controlling two or three of their own children and ponder what teachers face with thirty.

Many people talk about teachers' working a six-hour day. This is a myth. One of the authors of this book was a teacher in a public school system; all spent one day a week in a public school during the 1979–80 school year. Even the worst teacher in the school, a time-conscious, thoroughly burned-out cynic, spent an eight-hour day at school, with only twenty minutes in the morning and twenty minutes at lunch without direct contact with students. The hours in the public school are long and physically exhausting. A colleague of the authors used to get up every morning at 5:30 A.M., drive to pick up a baby-sitter, get to work by 7:30 A.M., put in a day's work, drive the baby-sitter back home, and arrive home after dark. He finally took a $6,000 pay cut to teach at a university where, though the pressures are many, the physical demands of the job are less severe and there is a greater degree of control over his time. His comment: "I know I'm losing money, but at least I'm not leaving home when it's dark and getting home when it's dark."

Both teachers mentioned above were involved in extra-curricular activities as sponsors of clubs or special activities at their schools. After getting up at 5:30 A.M. and getting home after 6:00 P.M., it meant a hurried dinner in order to be back at school by 7:30 P.M. to supervise the club or activity. In fact, the hours of a public school teacher are long. If it is the dedicated who burn out, then the hours are even longer for them. The student-contact hours are too great, with very little time set aside to talk to colleagues, to take a break, or just to have some private time. It is especially this inability to withdraw voluntarily from a situation that produces stress and compounds teachers' problems. Many of us, when confronted with a tense situation, can walk away for a time to collect our thoughts. Teachers cannot leave the classroom. They are trapped—victims of a structure that demands that they be present all the time.

More than the contact time itself is the kind of contact demanded by teaching. Teaching requires that decisions be made immediately. Certain decisions a teacher makes can sometimes ruin a career. In less critical situations, the teacher is still judged by the students, the principal, fellow teachers, and parents. One teacher reported to the authors that he sent a note home reporting some misbehavior by a student in his class, and the parents came to school and threatened to beat him up! Such immediate demands create pressure.

THE PROBLEM OF STUDENT ATTITUDE

It may very well be possible that, since time began, adults have pointed to their own childhood and determined that the youth of the day just didn't measure up to the past. Regardless of whether it is true that today's children are somehow different from the children of the past, the belief that they are contributes to burnout in teachers. In an effort to make the complex simple, it seems that there are two distinct types of students confronting teachers today that make the job appear more difficult than it used to be. Teachers feel that they are dealing with a new type of student who is somehow the product of a counter-culture that does not see the value of traditional education. These students are the ones who are challenging the efforts of teachers because they do not see the importance or relevance of what is being taught and have other things that they wish to study. Essentially, they see the teachers as getting in their way and actively preventing them from learning what they want to learn. The second group of students also does not see the value of traditional education, but these students are not really interested in anything else, either. The first group wants to be at school but to have more to say about their education; the second would rather be somewhere else. The first cares about learning and education; the second doesn't care. They are both disruptive. They both make the teacher's day miserable. Neither will do the work necessary to learn the subject matter considered necessary by the teacher and the school.

In the shifting attitudes of modern youth, many teachers are considered by the young to be beyond help! They are viewed as hopelessly antiquated. In their turn, teachers consider the youth impulsive, undisciplined, and disrespectful. In this adversary relationship, both suffer. For the teachers, this is another factor in burnout.

THE PROBLEM OF ISOLATION

It is a puzzle why, in a profession of ideas, teachers find themselves isolated from one another. It is a rare teacher who thinks it important to make time for discussion of educational ideas with colleagues. Indeed, it is a rare teacher who has a group of colleagues to whom the discussion of educational ideas and ideals is important. Certainly, the structure of the school system does nothing to promote teachers' getting together to talk over educational issues. It is another puzzle why, in a profession of human relations, so little effort is extended to train and promote sound human relations among colleagues, students, and supervisors. Teachers find themselves in classrooms with thirty children and occasionally one other adult. They are more than alone. After the school day, most go their separate ways, and the concerns of the day, the pressures, the problems, and the joys are left undisclosed. It is a sad fact that many do not have a single teacher colleague whom they trust enough to share the frustrations and joys of teaching.

Rather than reporting a climate of mutual concern for education and children, most teachers talk about the political intrigues that exist in any given school. Who is next to the principal? Who will be the department chair? Who will teach the "gifted and talented" class? Which requests for equipment will be accepted? The list is practically endless. Such political jockeying and infighting make it extremely difficult to develop a spirit of sharing which could help teachers overcome the pressures of their job. Instead, their isolation drives them even more toward a decision that separates them from their profession.

THE PROBLEM OF CHANGING
PHILOSOPHIES OF EDUCATION

America is a nation of people who love technology. We believe that all our problems will eventually be solved by the invention of some thing. If it isn't some thing, then it is some new idea or gimmick that will make difficult things easier. Education has not been immune to such desires. The American educational system is swept from fad to fad approximately every ten years. We have been through new math, open classrooms, teaching machines, programmed instruction, behavioral objectives, performance contracting, management by objectives, the workshop way of learning, individually guided instruction, mastery learning, prescription teaching, discovery, learning centers, and more. Teachers who have spent any time in the classroom at all start developing techniques to protect themselves from the often silly theories of education and simply go on teaching. However, the pressures to accept and practice whatever the hot new fad is are great. No one wants to be thought of as old-fashioned and closed-minded.

The difficulty is that while many theories are silly and unproductive, some are important and helpful. The problem becomes how to tell the difference. The hours spent learning new techniques, attending classes and workshops, and taking in-service training can leave teachers agog as each new educational consultant tries to convince them that this or that new method will prove to be the cure to all their ills.

Aside from the problem of techniques, there is the problem of a gradual movement during the 1960s and early 1970s toward the greater involvement of students and parents in the educational decisions of the schools. Teachers are no longer in control of the curriculum of the schools (if they ever were). The curriculum, the textbooks, and frequently policies are the work of committees often dominated by persons who are not educators. This increasing involvement of persons from outside the school may be viewed by teachers as an attack on their authority. If many teachers feel that they have lost control of students, many more feel they are losing control of their profession.

Teachers who are caught in the constant innovation, the problem of keeping up in their subject matter or educational methods, and the feeling of a loss of control of the profession are easy targets for burnout.

THE PROBLEM OF BEING USED

Many teachers who reported the symptoms of burnout related that they started with high ideals and somehow lost them in the process of teaching. Those values seem never to have been supported by the other teachers, supervisors, parents, or students. They have feelings of being used by the system, by students, and by their own ideals. Teachers are caught in a way of thinking that leads them to believe that someone ought to appreciate what they are doing. If such praise is not forthcoming, teachers begin to doubt that they are worthwhile as professionals and as persons. Teaching is an occupation in which there are often no tangible rewards. Students pass from one class to the next, graduate, and enter the world of work or college. Teachers rarely know what happens to the students with whom they spend a year. They lose contact, and a whole new bunch comes in. It is easy to come to believe that nobody cares. For many teachers, school is a factory, an assembly line: they plug in their respective part at the fourth grade or the eleventh but never get to see the final product.

If they should leave, they believe it wouldn't make a difference. The system would go on, and the school would simply hire another technician to fill the vacancy. It is easy to become disenchanted and disheartened from such a viewpoint. To dedicated, young, creative people, any suggestion that they are cogs in a wheel, if believed, leads them to burnout.

THE PROBLEM OF RED TAPE

Some say that educational institutions, like the mill of God, grind slow but sure. It is a saying that means that the process is slow but the results are good. By and large, it is a lie. It is more accurate on the side of the slowness of change. An institution as large as the educational endeavor in the United

States, involving more than 2 million teachers and 41 million students, does not change easily. Even small systems are caught in a tangle of federal and state regulations that make change difficult. The size of classes, the quality of instruction, racial balance, per-pupil costs, food programs, and school procedures all have elements of control that exist outside any given community. All are compounded by the paperwork necessary to remain a part of any bureaucratic structure.

If one were to follow a request for something as simple as calculators for elementary math, one would find that a school committee might have first to recommend them. Then, the school principal would have to approve the request. It would be forwarded to the assistant superintendent for elementary education, who would approve it and forward it to the assistant superintendent for instruction. It would then be sent to the purchasing department for a purchase order. If the cost exceeds $100, the item would be sent out for bids. The bids would have to be approved by purchasing. After the winning bid was approved, the items would be shipped to the school district warehouse. Payment would then be made to the supplier. The school would be informed that the item was in and that they could send a request for delivery. The principal would send a request to the assistant superintendent for elementary education, and so on. It sounds like a joke, doesn't it? It isn't, and it is a factor in the burnout of some teachers.

THE PROBLEM OF STRUCTURE

Teachers who are young, dedicated, and creative enter the teaching profession with enthusiasm. They hope to make a difference in the lives of students. They have ideas to help students learn and to change some of the things they thought were wrong when they went to school. What they discover is a system in which the curriculum has been predetermined, the classes already designed, the content established, the books selected, the tests already made up, and the hours of instruction set. In fact, they discover a structure in which every detail to which they thought they could contribute has already been arranged. The situation is such that they cannot use their own ideas in any but the most superficial ways. Certainly, their style may be superimposed on the curriculum, but what, when, and where they teach is already an established fact. The next year won't be any different, nor will the year after that. Indeed, not only is the curriculum locked in, but the teacher will also most likely have to teach the same grade time after time and the same content over and over and over. While the children might move up and study different content, the teachers are stuck. They might spend twenty-five or thirty years in the first grade, teaching the alphabet, phonetic sounds, math preparation, and reading, over and over again.

We have, without doubt, a highly structured public school system. Certainly, this is a condition that insures that the system will survive. It is not a condition that insures that the teacher will survive. Evidence suggests that the greater the amount of structure in a profession, the greater the chance of burnout.

In addition to the curriculum, there is a fairly strict line-and-staff organization in most schools. Students are subordinate to teachers, teachers to principals, principals to superintendents, and superintendents to school boards. Ideally, school boards would be subordinate to citizens. It is difficult to be told on the one hand that one is a professional and on the other that one is an employee answerable to any number of higher-placed employers. As one teacher phrased it, "How many personalities can you have in one day? I was one personality for the principal. Another for parents. Another for children. Another to the reading supervisor. Another for the other teachers. I couldn't be that many different people in one day. I had to quit."

What happens to people when they face the problems of money, discipline, respect, working conditions, changing student attitudes, isolation, changing philosophies, being used, red tape, and rigid structures? One thing that happens is that teachers burn out. What does a burned-out teacher look like?

SYMPTOMS OF TEACHER BURNOUT

For the purposes of this writing, the symptoms of burnout have been separated according to physical, intellectual, emotional, social, and spiritual concerns. These are artificial separations, but they provide a structure for discussing the problems that burnout can cause for teachers.

PHYSICAL

The physical demands of teaching have already been discussed above. The physical symptoms of burnout are the first to appear and the easiest to remedy. Burnout results in a feeling of physical tiredness. It is the kind of tiredness that doesn't go away with a night's rest or a weekend's rest. It is a tiredness that lasts all day and carries over into the night. The teacher doesn't want to go out at night. It is a tiredness that might be alleviated somewhat by a summer off. The problem is that many teachers have to go back to school in the summer.

So, they trade one kind of pressure for another. One of the reasons that their tiredness isn't relieved by a night's rest is that victims of burnout stay up nights trying to figure out what to do with their lives. Their profession is failing them and they are failing their profession. They worry themselves into exhaustion.

It is no mystery, then, that burnout carries other physical symptoms as well. Physical exhaustion, even the bone-weary kind, will respond eventually to rest and vacation, but some of the symptoms of burnout are more serious. The symptoms of tiredness may lead the teacher to a concern with physical well-being. If it lasts over a long period of time, that concern might become excessive. Teachers may lose the ability to recognize when real sickness is attacking the body. Since they feel sick all the time but go to work anyway, they set themselves up for profound illness because they do not respond to slight symptoms.

Burned-out teachers are often victims of headaches. They may be persons who have colds and flu often. Stomach upsets and chronic pain may give way to peptic ulcers. And occasional problems with breathing may lead to other respiratory illnesses and eventually to cardiovascular disease.

These are not symptoms that are used as excuses to avoid work, although absenteeism does increase; they are real, painful, and serious diseases that are attacking the body. It is just that their cause lies primarily in the psychological trauma of stress. Eventually burnout is the result.

INTELLECTUAL

Teachers are people who make their living by using their intellect. It is no surprise, then, that burnout affects the intellectual functions of teachers. It was mentioned that teachers have to make immediate decisions every day. Teachers have to deal with a wide variety of people, ranging from students to parents to superiors to custodians. They have to deal with problems of learning. The pressure of all these variables begins to break them down. Burned-out teachers start to lose the ability to carry a number of variables in mind at once. They begin to forget what tasks they must do, what has been taught, who has been given information, even what class they have taught in a given day. One educator with a number of different classes to teach each day, after years on the job, discovered one day about ten minutes into a class that he was teaching math to his science class.

Essentially, there are four indications of intellectual burnout in a teacher. Foremost is a loss of clarity. This means that the teacher evidences an inability to understand problems and continually gets stuck or confused on sometimes simple issues. This inability to think clearly may lead to two other symptoms. It may lead to an inability to make decisions. For example, the school might ask the opinion of several teachers on which reading series to select. In times past this may not have been a problem, but for a burned-out teacher it may be insurmountable. While the other teachers are ready to select and move on, the burned-out teacher may ask for more time or throw up objections to every series, thus preventing the rest of the staff from moving on. Or, the burned-out teacher may evidence a lack of flexibility in thinking. The teacher may insist that the series that was used last year be used again this year, even though the other teachers believe that the new series is better. To change means more work, and the burned-out teacher is already used up. The result of the loss of clarity is diminished job performance. These four symptoms spell intellectual burnout for teachers: loss of clarity, inability to make decisions, loss of flexible thinking, and deterioration of work performance. It is as if they can no longer solve their own problems because the tools they need to think their way out of their dilemma are missing. Many simply hang on to the job and perform their duties mechanically. Many quit and spend months until the pressures are gone and they are capable of making some decisions about their life again.

EMOTIONAL

What may first call attention to burned-out teachers is their apparent lack of zest. They may seem to be depressed all the time. This emotional deadness, punctuated occasionally by an explosion of temper against a fellow teacher or a student, is one symptom of emotional burnout.

Emotional burnout results in an active dislike of the job and the people associated with it. A sign of it is what might be called "high-IQ whining." The teachers seem not to like children anymore. They complain constantly about the children's behavior. They begin to discuss children in psychopathological terms. Teachers may begin to call kids "schizy" or "sick." They may begin to make comments incorporating psychological terms, like "that kid must be suffering from a character disorder" or "I bet that kid's mother is a real neurotic." The whining may take the form of a constant criticism of the administration, school district, parents, or socioeconomic conditions of the neighborhood. Finally, it may take the form of criticizing the motivation and intentions of colleagues. In a school recently, one of the authors listened as one teacher was highly critical of another teacher who was active in such things as the school council and the sponsorship of clubs. The first teacher said, "The only reason he does it is because he is bucking for a principal's job." Such reading into the intentions of another can be more than mere gossip. In the context of constant criticism and an inability to find anything good in the behavior of colleagues, it can signify burnout.

Burned-out teachers begin to refer to students in increasingly negative ways. They begin to use jargon and refer to increasing numbers of students as slow learners, disrupters, and "brain-damaged." Seldom do burned-out teachers have much that is positive to say about students. An interesting exception to this is when a burned-out teacher continues to say how much he or she cares for the kids but it is the other teachers, administrators, and parents who have caused him or her to sour on teaching. All of that compounds on such teachers, causing them to be depressed, frustrated, and disappointed. They are depressed because they know they are not doing their job. They are frustrated because they cannot see any way out of their dilemma. They are disappointed because they are not realizing their dreams. Finally, burned-out teachers stop blaming others and begin to blame themselves. They take on guilt, shame, and a real loss of self-esteem. They begin to consider themselves failures and start to think seriously about leaving the profession.

SOCIAL

It must be obvious that such emotional upsets will disturb social relations. Burned-out teachers adopt two positions in response to social change. First, they don't care. They will be loners, withdrawn and increasingly isolated from their colleagues. Or, they will adopt a superior, know-it-all attitude which usually results in their being opposed to any change. They will be cynical and negative to change and will respond to attempts to discuss issues with defensiveness. While it may not be possible to have a discussion with a burned-out teacher about educational issues, it will not be difficult to talk about the upcoming vacation. In fact, it may be all he or she wants to talk about. Some people call it "vacation hypermania." Such teachers don't like their jobs, but they are often interested in fantasy vacations and other occupations.

Because of a growing discontent with the profession of teaching, such teachers are often absent from work. Sometimes physical ailments, real or imagined, are used as excuses. Whether the person actually has physical symptoms or not, this is often the only excuse that a school system will recognize.

A final social symptom is a decline in interpersonal relationships, not only at work, for many of the reasons listed above, but also away from work. Family and friends may begin to notice that the teacher is growing more and more distant, is less and less fun to be with. Such teachers seldom accept invitations to go out and thereby place severe strains on friendships and marriage. Deteriorating interpersonal relationships mean that important needs and wishes go unmet and unfulfilled.

SPIRITUAL

Spiritual, as used here, means that persons affected by burnout have lost a sense of meaning in their lives. They question the value and meaning of teaching. They begin to see it as hopeless; they refer to the horrible conditions from which children come, the crummy society in which we live, the rotten world situation, and they believe that the world is worse off than it used to be. They may react with physical symptoms such as overeating, alcoholism, drug abuse, including both prescription and over-the-counter drugs such as sleeping pills, tranquilizers, and aspirin. Such physical symptoms may represent a loss of respect for their own bodies or an inability to confront the loss of meaning in their lives. Whatever the cause, burned-out teachers are teachers who no longer have the ability to give themselves to their profession. They are commonly viewed as teachers with two main characteristics: the benign characteristic of apathy and the malignant "kids be damned" attitude. Some burned-out teachers are actually doing more than hanging on; some are actively trying to hurt children. Their cruelty is sometimes disguised behind demands of high expectations or high standards as they humiliate, ridicule, or insult children while explaining such behavior as strict discipline or a return to traditional values. Burned-out teachers can sometimes be characterized by disoriented values in which they think they are doing good by practicing the harshest educational techniques they know. It represents a real search to rediscover the lost meaning of their lives and their job.

These symptoms range from mild to severe. Some are easy to correct, and others are very difficult. Physical symptoms are, by and large, the easiest to deal with, and those listed under spiritual symptoms the most difficult to "cure." The section that follows provides suggestions that the authors believe will be helpful to teachers seeking to prevent or reverse the process of burnout.

CURES FOR TEACHER BURNOUT

The recommendations that follow are not foolproof, nor are they guaranteed, but they might be helpful. They are presented in the categories used above: physical, intellectual, emotional, social, and spiritual. The authors recommend them as ways teachers might avoid or reverse burnout. Part Two contains others that may be helpful, too.

PHYSICAL

Perhaps the most demanding part of a teacher's job is the constant contact with students. In order to make the time teachers spend with students more enjoyable, try to reduce the amount of time spent with them. This is easy to say but difficult to do unless teachers in a school decide to help each other with this idea. It need not be every teacher in school, but it would be better if it were. Contact other teachers in the school and make a deal that you will take their class for thirty minutes sometime in the day if they will take yours for thirty minutes. If the entire school is involved, it may be possible to have even more time available during the day for private noncontact time.

Here are three suggestions about how to "buy" noncontact time. First, show a movie that is appropriate for every child in a particular grade level. That means that only a single teacher need be present during the showing and possibly the discussion following the film. Second, invite a guest speaker at least once a week, at which session only one teacher need be present. Third, make a deal with other teachers that you will teach your favorite lesson or unit or subject, combining sections, if they will do the same for your class. These are only three suggestions. Get together with colleagues and brainstorm on others. The point of this is to provide some time during each day when teachers can be away from students. When contact is already high, the less time spent with students, the less pressure the teacher feels and the more enjoyable teaching is.

Do not try to do too much at school. Do not allow yourself to become overextended; if you already are, cut back on your activities. Remember, teachers need a life outside of school. As a rule of thumb, do not spend more than two afternoons or nights a week in extra-curricular activities. Second, do not attempt to assign more work than you can correct in one hour. If children have homework assignments, make sure that they are essential either to practice a concept or to teach a new concept and that you can check them quickly. Third, and most important, tell the children in your class what the limits on their behavior are as clearly as you can. Tell them the consequences of misbehavior and stick to it. Do not be mean, but be firm and consistent. Do not shout, but use some gimmick to gain attention—a bell, a hat, or a signal if in elementary school; a bell, a whistle, or flicking the lights off and on in secondary school. Count to five or so before starting or repeating the signal.

Some teachers work two jobs. Some are volunteers in mental health centers, some deliver "meals on wheels," some are volunteer firefighters, some act as sponsors for the Boy Scouts or Girl Scouts, and so on. Part of their physical tiredness comes from their working hard both in and out of school. As a rule of thumb, commit only one afternoon or night a week to a volunteer activity outside of school. Many teachers feel they must hold a second job for financial reasons. However, if this must be so, it is advisable that it be a job that is enjoyable as well as financially rewarding. Seek out a job with flexible hours in an area of interest. For example, real estate lends itself to part-time and weekend participation. A teacher interested in electronics might seek a job in an electronics or hobby store. Avoid any job that might cause a conflict with teaching or invite ridicule or sarcasm from students or other members of the community. In essence, leave at least two nights a week for social activities and entertainment, time spent with family or friends. Plan to spend at least one afternoon a week in some vigorous physical activity that will firm and tone the body. Teachers who live within running distance of school might consider jogging home after work every day. Teachers who work at schools with track or sports facilities may be able to use them before going home after school. Think about organizing a weekly staff basketball or volleyball game. It does not matter what the exercise is as long as one does it at least twice a week. Three times a week would be even better. The important thing is that it be a regular plan. Run, bike, swim, walk, or play a sport, but do some regular exercise at least twice a week.

Food is important because it provides energy. Unfortunately, it also adds weight. So far as energy is concerned, take a little time to consider what most teachers get for food at school. First, they either take their lunch or they buy cafeteria food. Second, they buy the stuff in machines like cola, candy, and coffee. It seems reasonable that there is enough information around to teach that those are not especially good energy foods. All three have the effect of creating either nervousness or lethargy. It might be better to skip lunch and instead eat four or five small snacks during the day. Keep a supply of healthful snack foods in a desk drawer for energy throughout the day: Peanut butter and crackers, oatmeal and raisin cookies, and raw vegetables are all good snacks. If it is possible, keep fruit and fruit drinks in the school refrigerator. Fruit juice is a better energy drink than coffee or cola. If you have a good nutrition plan, follow it; otherwise, the advice above is straightforward, nonfaddist, nonfanatical, and easy to follow if you want to keep your energy up throughout the day.

As stated before, food also adds weight. Find out what an appropriate weight for you is, what feels comfortable. Then get there and stay there. The authors are not experts on diets or on how to lose weight. But we can tell you how we do it. We are different ages—thirty-six, forty, and fifty-five—and all reasonably skinny. We all enjoy eating and drinking—sometimes to excess! What we also enjoy is feeling good and not looking sloppy. All of us are weight-conscious without being obsessive about it. We weigh ourselves every morning. If we are at our ideal weight, we don't do anything special. If we are over our desired weight, we eat lightly all day. We do that until the day we reach our desired weight. And every day, we keep our sugar and salt intake low. That's it. It works for us; try it for yourself.

Rest is of major importance. The first rule of getting rest is to learn to take a nap at the end of the working day. Whatever the schedule teachers keep, it is usually possible to move everything back thirty minutes so that after work they can lie down for a half-hour nap. Those thirty minutes may buy a teacher an entire evening. The second rule is to learn how to use a five- or ten-minute break for actual rest. The secret is to sit down in a comfortable chair and *not* do schoolwork. Read a novel, newspaper, news magazine, or professional journal but do not grade papers, engage in teacher-lounge gossip, or discuss school problems. For five or ten minutes, just rest. If you want to do those other activities, do them after you rest. Recognize that physical exercise, food, and rest are all related to the energy teachers have to do their job.

Classrooms are stressful places in the best of times. Some people have learned to handle it. They use many techniques, but the most important one is that they have learned to relax even in the midst of tension. Here are three ways to relax—and people won't even know you are doing it.

1. Do not respond quickly to stress-producing situations. Quickly, in this case, means within a tenth of a second. It seems silly that we would respond that fast to situations, but we do most of the time. Teach yourself to wait a full second or even to a count of five. What you will discover is that things are not as tension-producing as at first thought.
2. When something is really getting to you, do this (it may seem silly, but it actually works). Breathe in through your nose to a count of four, then breathe out through your mouth to another count of four. Take the time to do this four times. If you really have time, do it eight times. Tension and anger will be lessened.
3. When you get home, take a warm bath or a shower that hits you on the top of your head and then square in the middle of your shoulders. Both places carry a good bit of tension, and the warm water will relax you.

Every teacher knows that there are times in the day when everyone is weary. Right after lunch is a terrible time for energy. Most of us have a real slow time right after lunch. Here are three quick, easy ways to get energy into the class and into teachers. They sound crazy, but they really work.

1. Have the class shout, whoop, bay at the moon like coyotes. The louder the better. They will all feel silly, but they—and the teacher—will be awake.
2. Breathe very rapidly through the mouth. When you breathe in, lift your shoulders up until they touch your ears. Then breathe out and lower your shoulders. Do this very rapidly ten times. Again, crazy but effective.
3. Have the students clap their hands together. Then have them slap their own backs. Then pat their arms very hard. Then their legs and thighs. Then their chest. Then their face. Hard but not hard enough to hurt. And finally the top of their head. This brings blood to the surface and energy back to an otherwise dead classroom. It is good for teacher and students alike.

Part of leading a relaxed life is to have time that is unplanned. If you have your usual drama club on Tuesdays and the jeep club on Thursdays, and then you add the Girl Scouts on Monday, dinner with Bill and Sue on Wednesday, a play on Friday and a fishing trip for the weekend, you can end up just as hassled as if all your activities had to do with school. Leave a little time in every week that has nothing planned. Then use it for a walk through a shopping mall, a trip to the park, fixing the bike, browsing in a bookstore, or anything you like that is nonscheduled, tension-free, and undemanding.

INTELLECTUAL

Teachers who lead interesting lives make interesting teachers. If you do interesting things, then you will be an interesting teacher. You will be able to share the interesting things you do with other teachers and with students. Many teachers have hobbies that occupy a good part of their lives. One may be a history teacher in high school and an expert in bottles or cans. One teacher we know is an expert in southwestern pottery. Another has one of the most complete collections of comic books around. A third is a movie historian. A fourth makes jewelry. A fifth shows horses. Of the authors, one works with wood, one engages in a variety of sports, and the third reads for enjoyment.

Another way to keep an active mind is to enroll in classes. Those classes may range from the ballet to auto mechanics. The point is to extend a base of knowledge and get away from school for awhile.

It is also possible to enroll in professional classes. In most states this is required by law. A teacher may choose to work toward a degree or just to add hours to his or her B.A. In either case, if a teacher picks both class and professor well, it can be an enriching experience.

One of the neglected aspects of teacher preparation is human relations training. In some states, students are required to take one class in human relations training. In others, nothing is required. In any case, one way to continue to be intellectually alive is to learn what does and what does not appear to be effective in working with other human beings. Some people are good at it "naturally." Certainly, the rest can learn to get along better. Enroll in a human relations class and begin to practice what is taught there.

While it is important to sponsor clubs and student activities, it might be worthwhile to divide your time between one club and one faculty activity. If teachers can participate in the policy and decision making activities of their individual schools, then they can have a voice in the policies and decisions they will be expected to follow. If there are rules that are creating pressure, they will be in a position to do something about them other than complain. They can make changes.

Another way to involve oneself in the policies of the school is to volunteer to coordinate an in-service workshop for your school. Pick something that is an area of interest of yours and invite someone you know who is *really* good to come and do it. It might be an especially impressive college professor or someone you have heard before. Remember, the guest should be *really* good. What this will do is create a climate in which you will be able to do more in the future, and it will give you an opportunity to work with adults as well as children or teenagers.

Learn to seek out other people to discuss problems encountered at school. Find out who the willing teachers are and create a time to sit down to brainstorm for answers to problems that are troubling. You will learn that you are not an isolate in school when you actively seek out other teachers to help you. You can learn to be an active agent in your school rather than a pawn who is pushed around by others or by circumstances.

Find out what the stress-producing aspects of the job are and learn to avoid them or create ways to deal with them. Learn what causes burnout in teachers and start a plan to make sure it doesn't happen to you. One way of doing this is to take a sheet of paper and draw a line down the middle. On one side put things you enjoy at work and on the other put things that cause stress. On the back side of the paper draw a line down the middle and put "how to get what I want" on one side and "how to avoid what I don't want" on the other. Then brainstorm to fill the four columns. Follow the resulting guide to see if it works for you.

One of the causes of burnout is having to do the same old stuff time after time. One way to avoid this is *not* to do things the same way time and again.

For example, it is within the power of most teachers to manipulate the schedule within their classroom. If they team-teach, they can arrange together to alter the schedule. If one has to teach math, there is no reason why it must always be taught at the same time. One day, introduction of a concept may be necessary; but the next day a game might help the students learn about the concept in practice. In one school district with which the authors are familiar, math in the elementary school is helped along by allowing the students to play Monopoly. Every ten minutes the tax collector comes around to collect seventeen percent in taxes. Each student has to figure up all their assets and pay seventeen percent of the total. The tax collector has to make sure the figures are correct. The kids enjoy it, and the teacher gets a break! So, then, one way to create variety is to vary the routine.

Another way is to work for flexible responsibilities on the job. It might be possible, for example, to spend part of the day teaching first grade and another teaching fifth. It may be possible to switch places with a guidance counselor, if the school has one. It might be possible to trade subjects with another teacher for a semester. In any case, it is worthwhile to investigate the possibilities of varying the schedule and job responsibilities, since it is one more way to avoid burnout.

One way to stay aware of any changes that take place in one's life is to keep a diary or a journal. It is a good way to get rid of the frustrations of the day, and it is also a good way to keep track of ideas, thoughts, and feelings that we have about ourselves and about teaching. It provides a running record from day to day to year to year about how well we are doing in moving toward our dreams.

This is, perhaps, the most important recommendation of all: Read through the recommendations of the physical, intellectual, emotional, social, and spiritual ideas, and form a systematic stress-reduction plan for yourself that keeps you physically fit and spiritually alive. Create it, follow it, revise it, make it work for you. It would involve physical activity, intellectually stimulating activities, emotional stability, social involvement, and the importance of what you are doing. Given such a plan, the chances of burning out are very slim.

EMOTIONAL

Decorate your classroom. This seems frivolous, doesn't it? It isn't. Think about it. Where do teachers spend almost all their time? In their classrooms, right? Then it follows that that classroom ought to be a place, an environment, in which a teacher likes to be. Many classrooms are dull places—intellectually and often physically. Making them bright, cheerful, and meaningful is a task for teachers. Make your classroom a place you want to be in. Bring flowers every day if you like. Invite the children to do the same. Bring something you especially like to look at and invite the children to do the same. Fill it up with things that are inspiring, beautiful, helpful.

If it is at all possible, finish all the schoolwork you have before you leave school. Stay a little after school, if necessary, but go home without things on your mind and without school-related tasks. Keep home for yourself. If it is not possible to leave all the work at school, set aside a particular time to do schoolwork at home and stick to it.

If you drive to work, find a five-minute detour that is scenic and quiet to drive along on your way home. Or, spend five minutes alone at school before you start toward home. Or, spend five minutes in the car alone before you go into the house. Do not think about school or business or family matters or bills or anything. These five quiet minutes belong to you. One simple technique is to hum a favorite tune or to hum nonsense. Just do anything that helps you forget the day's tasks.

Limit your activities at school and out of school. Learn to say no. Tell people factually the limits on your activities and why you are limiting them. Do not be hostile. Just tell people no in a straightforward, friendly way. Most people will accept that. Remember, one person cannot save the world. We can't even help the ones with whom we come into contact unless we have the energy to help them. We can't help anyone if we burn out. Learn to say no in order to be an effective helper.

Seek to have a personal day legalized as a part of the teacher's contract. Whether one is or not, when you feel the pressures starting to build up, take a "mental health" day from time to time, even if you must call in sick, just to get away. Take a long drive to a lake, the beach, or the mountains and spend the day alone, just to let the systems relax. Teachers deserve it!

It is nice to take a day off now and then, but it is not enough. Sometimes it is necessary to get completely out of town. In town, it is difficult to escape the teacher role. People treat teachers like teachers, talk to them about teacher things, and expect them to act like teachers. But on a trip where nobody knows who we are and on which there are no professional expectations, relaxation comes easier. It is a truly relaxing period when one is away from the job. The added benefit is that people who travel have something interesting to share with other teachers and students. It makes for better teachers.

Practice responsible selfishness. This means that people have the right to do things that they like to do. Other people may think what is done is crazy or stupid, but if they are enjoyable activities and hurt no one, do them. This advice is a bit different from the "do your own thing" philosophies of the '60s. What we're saying is, as long as you accept responsibility for what you do, it is probably OK to do it. Put aside personal time. Join the parachute club or the four-wheel-drive club, dress like a cowhand. People who spend their lives trying to please everybody put themselves under a lot of stress. Perhaps less dramatic but equally important is taking time to be alone. One person we know sets one hour a day aside for herself. Other people might try to call her during that time, but she won't answer the telephone. People try to make appointments during that time, but she won't make them. We have seen a number of people tell her she has no right to set that time aside, but she does, and she won't budge from it. It is her time. She is by herself. That is responsible selfishness.

If we know our own internalized structure, how we respond to situations and events, and if we know our own character make-up, then we are in a very good position to know what will bother us and what will not. If we have a clear idea of what bothers us, then we can take real steps to avoid things that will create stress. The way to find out about feelings about self is to talk to people we trust. Another way is to write the answers to a series of incomplete sentences. Here are five.

1. I am the kind of person who . . .
2. I really get angry when . . .
3. I really like people who . . .
4. I think the only thing in the world I wouldn't do is . . .
5. The kind of man/woman I am looking for is . . .

Another way to take care of emotional needs is to seek out counseling. One of the phrases that may help is one that developed out of humanistic psychology: "You don't have to be sick to get better." One does not need to be neurotic or psychotic to seek counseling. If a personal friend is unable to help with problems at school or life in general, go to a local mental health center and ask for a personal counselor. They are all fully trained and not overly expensive. If there is something in life that needs taking care of, then do it. Most things can take care of themselves. Sometimes we need people to share our private thoughts with, and that is what counselors are for.

SOCIAL

It seems most important that teachers not become isolated in their own school. In order to prevent this, it is important to take active measures to avoid it. Purposely seek out other teachers who share similar views and begin to build a support group for yourselves. Start by inviting one or two persons whom you like to dinner. During and after dinner it may be possible to talk over some of the things at school that are most enjoyed and most disliked. It may be possible to share activities, ideas, films, and teaching techniques. The goal, of course, is to be and feel supported during faculty meetings, budget discussions, and planning sessions. This at-school support group can also serve as a group for all members to ventilate their frustrations about school, teaching, or other things in their lives that might be bothering them. Certainly, it can result in teachers' understanding that they are not in school alone.

It is also important to try to establish an out-of-school support group. Sometimes teachers believe that the rewards of teaching will come from the classroom because of the interaction with students. In fact, while there are rewarding moments in the classroom, there is not enough pay-off from students to sustain teachers. They need to get their enrichment from sources outside the classroom. Their positive acceptance might very well be the source of the energy teachers take into the classroom. As a rule of thumb, spend at least one night a week meeting with, talking with, and socializing with friends.

Teachers actually spend little time talking with one another. It seems silly that so little time is allowed for teachers to get to know one another. Take one weekend, preferably at the beginning of the school year, to go off to the lake, mountains, or beach to do nothing but socialize with the faculty of the school. If possible, have everyone in the school go along—principal, secretaries, cooks, custodian, and aides as well as teachers. Spend the time actively building a community feeling in which trust is higher and support greater. It is a fine way to avoid burning out.

Seek out another teacher in the school with whom to team-teach. Experiment with a number of different teachers until a good, compatible team is formed. Share ideas, classes, units, and practices. Such a person becomes an ally not only in the classroom, but also when trying to promote suggestions, innovations, and goals at faculty meetings.

At least once during each grading period, have a faculty potluck social. Organize the faculty to have a potluck dinner every two months or so. If people do not want to come back to school or visit someone's home, organize a potluck meal during the school day every once in a while. It is difficult to be a highly competitive, backbiting or back-stabbing staff when a good bit of time is spent learning about one another in such informal gatherings.

This is much easier said than done, but spend some time building a friendship in which each party feels free enough to share intimate problems or joys. Having someone with whom to share turns out to be a very important part of psychological health. Make sure that about once a week such close friends get together for lunch, dinner, or a talk.

SPIRITUAL

It seems important that teachers spend some time every once in a while thinking over the reasons why they entered the profession. It is easy to forget the ideals with which many teachers start their careers. The daily grind may crush the memory of their original motivations and ideals. One way to recall these ideals is to establish a special diary or journal in which teachers write their reasons for entering the profession. It may be possible to write these and then amend them as the years progress. It is a good way to recall original goals and to watch progress and change.

It is important to establish a satisfying life style outside of school. If teachers devote all of their lives to school, they become real candidates for burnout. They will have nothing coming in to enrich their teaching and time at school. If one becomes a martyr to teaching, one may be good at the job for a few years but will shortly burn out. Adults need lives as adults. If teachers spend their days interacting with young students, it becomes even more important to spend time with adults. Many pieces of evidence indicate that good teachers are the ones who have a balanced life outside of school as well as a dedication to what goes on at school. Do this small exercise. List five things that are truly enjoyable. Then write beside each how much it costs, the last time you did it, with whom and when you plan to do it again. If, of those five things, you do not have plans to do one of them again within one week, plan immediately to do one of them. If all cost a lot of money, then make another list of inexpensive things that are enjoyable. If all either involve other people or exclude other people, make a balanced list of activities done with others and alone. Finally, end up with a list of five activities that is balanced according to costs, privacy, sociability, and frequency. That will be a list that will move teachers toward a more satisfying life style.

Make a list of your professional strengths. Then make a list of personal successes that you have achieved during teaching. Ask these questions: How can I use my professional strengths better at school? Further, how can I move in the direction of creating the conditions that led to past successes?

The most important question for anyone is, Am I doing what I want to do? If the answer is no, ask, What do I really want to do? If the answer is something other than teaching, than the courageous thing, the wise thing, is to get out of teaching. Often, however, the answer will be, Teaching, but . . . What differences reveal themselves when you ask, What would teaching be like if I could do it my way? Make a list of what you really want that would make teaching more enjoyable. Then start to make plans that will result in the kind of teaching experience you really want.

Always have something to look forward to. Have a summer vacation planned by Christmas. Plan the trip that would be most enjoyable. Or spend some time looking around at the summer offerings at colleges across the country. It is not necessary to go back to the state university to get the hours needed to be recertified. Check out other colleges for special programs that have personal appeal. Check out cruises for college credit. See if the district will allow credit for travel to Mexico, Canada, Europe, or Asia. See if work on a special project will count as recertification credit. These and more do count in many districts. In addition, plan some weekend trips throughout the year that are fun, inexpensive, and likable. Become involved in special projects. Remember, always have something to look forward to.

Practice detached concern. If this can be mastered, we guarantee that burnout can be avoided. Detached concern means that problems are put in their proper perspective. There are many problems associated with teaching. There are problems of colleagues arguing with one another. There are problems of too little equipment. There are problems of children not learning. Certainly, these are problems, but they are not personal problems. They are problems that lie outside the self. If one can learn this lesson, then teaching will be a less stressful profession. The concern is real. The effort is difficult. But the individual with detached concern is a person who can put away that concern at the end of the school day. The problems remain at school. Easy to say, hard to do.

3. Principals

"The Schoolmaster is abroad, and I trust to him, armed with his primer, against the soldier in full military array."
—Henry Peter, Lord Brougham

The dissatisfaction with schools involves its managers as well. Not everyone who drops out of education is a student or teacher. Principals are leaving in record numbers. It is a phenomenon much like the world of business in which the top managers seem to have developed strategies for dealing with burnout but the middle managers, in this case, principals, have not and are affected in a number of ways. Leaving the profession is a choice for many.

Principals are in an uneasy position in the educational organization. Their actual contacts with teachers and students may be many or few, but the expectation is that they should always be handy for any short-term emergencies and have a firm grasp on long-term goals and procedures. The role is often confusing so far as whom the principals represent. Are they the teachers' representatives to the higher administration, or are they the higher administration's representatives to teachers? Many principals never solve this dilemma. Many solve it by opting for one alternative over the other. Obviously, the solution has much to do with the pressures that are placed upon individual principals. Equally obvious is that the solution has much to do with burnout in principals.

There is, perhaps, no other profession in which a person has so many masters to serve. School boards, superintendents, teachers, students, parents, the media, and educational professionals in higher education all contribute to the pressures that are focused on the principal's office. It is a confusing, stressful, and often thankless job.

WHAT WENT WRONG IN THE PRINCIPAL'S OFFICE?

THE PROBLEM OF THE NATURE OF THE JOB

There are three primary aspects of the job of principals which make it a job that readily leads to burnout. First, principals are isolated from teachers, students, parents, and the higher administration. It is a job in which there are no natural allies. There are other principals who share similar problems, but these persons are located in other buildings and are under the same pressures. With no natural allies, principals have no natural outlets for the frustrations of their job. Any provisions for coping with burnout must originate with the individual principal. Contacts with teachers are often discouraged by the higher administration, which fears that the principal may become too much of a teachers' advocate rather than a representative of higher administration policy. This role conflict acts to prevent the establishment of close personal working relationships with teachers.

In high schools, the pressures from both teachers and the higher administration prevent the principals from becoming too close to students. The fear here is that the teachers will not have anyone to whom they can send severe discipline problems or use as a threat to maintain control over students. Principals seem to be caught in a job in which the expectations are that they maintain distance from teachers and from students. In fact, the expectation seems to be that they should not form close ties with anyone on the job. They are isolated not so much by the personal style of individuals who enter the profession as they are by the conflicting expectations of the job.

Second, principals put in an inordinate number of hours every week. Those hours are often after everyone else has gone home. One elementary principal of our acquaintance had a child injured on the playground shortly after school was dismissed. Unable to contact the child's parents, he drove the child to the emergency room for treatment. He stayed with the child at the hospital from 4:00 P.M. until 6:00 P.M., and, still unable to contact the parents, finally drove the child home. When he returned the child home the parents said, "Well, we wondered where he was." No thank-you. No expression of recognition of the extra effort the principal went through. He arrived home at 7:30 P.M. and hurriedly changed clothes in order to attend an international dinner at his school that evening! It is estimated that the average principal works fifty-six hours a week, fifty weeks a year, including three nights a week of school-associated activities such as attending football games, proms, school board meetings, parent conferences, principals' meetings, Parent-Teacher Organization meetings, student council sessions, homecoming, and a host of others. The hours are long, and many of them are unseen and unappreciated by staff, students, and parents.

Third, principals work in an organizational structure which is considered by many to be inefficient and ineffective. The organizational structure is such that it does little to protect the principal from burnout. In fact, it is a major cause of burnout for principals. While teachers work under stress, many of them at least have tenure, which provides them with job security. Further, teachers work under a contract which details their job responsibilities. It may come as a shock to many in the education profession, but, in many situations, principals do not have such protections. It is widely known that principals do not have tenure as principals. Many assume that they do as teachers. However, that is not always the case. Principals serve at the pleasure of the superintendent. If a principal is dismissed, either for cause or on whim, he or she may be retained as a teacher or not, at the discretion of the superintendent. Principals serve on a one-year contract every year. They don't have tenure to fall back on.

It is an even greater problem now that job mobility in principalships is severely restricted. It is a problem that plagues all of education at the present time. People in the educational profession, by and large, have to make it where they are. One of the reasons so many are leaving the profession is that there is little opportunity to change jobs. They have lost the option of changing jobs as a way of handling stress. It is not a frozen profession, but it is very tight. Even within a particular school system, a principal may not have a choice of schools in which to work. A principal may have established a sound working relationship with one staff only to be transferred to another school the next year. Such involuntary transfers provide another source of frustration for many. It is evidence of the feelings of helplessness that will be discussed below.

Finally, the nature of the job is that it involves innumerable routine tasks, many of which could be performed by someone less educated, less trained, or less busy. It is another reflection of a poor organizational structure that insists, for both teachers and principals, that routine tasks be performed by highly educated persons.

THE PROBLEM OF RESPONSIBILITY

We have already discussed how busy principals are. They put in a lot of time. Characteristically, that time involves decisions. Principals carry the responsibility of the school. If a problem in a particular school is called to the attention of the superintendent, the superintendent refers it to the principal or calls the principal in for a talk. If a problem occurs with a teacher in the school, a parent goes to the principal. It is no understatement to say the expectation is that no matter what problems occur at a school, the principal should handle them. Those expectations now encompass an incredible array of responsibilities. Principals are expected to be accountable for the safe passage of children from home to school and back, for breakfast programs, for hot lunch programs, for the needs of special students, for minimum achievement standards, for moral education, for health education, for sex education, even for the performance of the athletic teams! Principals work in a job in which the demands are growing and the resources are declining. The job demands are greater than they have ever been in the history of American education. These demands are voiced in the face of growing public dissatisfaction with the educational endeavor. While the demands are growing, the willingness of the public to finance the growing costs are diminishing. Principals are faced with the problem of doing more with less.

A mounting frustration for principals is that these growing responsibilities are being demanded while individual autonomy is decaying. While principals seldom have input into new policies, they must carry them out. Often, the unpopular policies of the higher administration are channeled through the principals to the staff. All of the anger, frustration, and disagreement are aimed at the principal who has little idea of the reasons behind new policies. Yet the principal is expected to defend and explain new programs, policies, and procedures. A growing feeling among principals is that they are powerless to interact with their staffs in effective ways since they have little input into the decisions that affect their schools.

The psychological outcome for many principals is that they blame themselves for the numerous problems of public schools. This internal blaming of self becomes a major force in the burnout of principals. While the public points with alarm to the public schools and the media seldom reports anything positive about schools, these external pressures are internalized by many principals, who see themselves as the agents primarily responsible for the conduct of their schools. Faced with too much to do, with declining resources and decaying autonomy, the satisfactions associated with being a principal are being eroded, with little to take their place. The result—burned-out principals.

THE PROBLEM OF NATIONAL TRENDS

Times change. The relative calm within which the educational profession worked for so long has passed. That is a revelation to no one. The schools have become a political football kicked around in the vested interests of any number of vocal groups. Depending on one's point of view, the schools are too strict or too lax, cost too much or do not receive enough money to do the job, educate for comformity or don't place enough emphasis on patriotism.

One national trend that seems increasingly a problem for principals is public attacks on schools. Given the pluralistic nature of American society, one expects differences of opinion among citizens. This is especially true in areas of large population. What is unexpected, however, is that persons of different points of view seem themselves unable to grasp that fact. Vocal special-interest groups seem to believe that their way is the only way that is acceptable in any public endeavor. They attack the schools for their particular cause, with little understanding that public institutions are charged with the problem of meeting *everyone's* needs. The result in practice is invariably a situation that offends someone all the time! Such public narrow-mindedness results in a general dissatisfaction with the schools. The target of the dissatisfaction is often the individual school. And the principal takes the brunt of that.

Another national trend is that education has become news. The media have played every educational crisis into a national event. We no longer have community problems. Increasingly, and possibly permanently, we have only national events, since electronic communication makes known nationally what was once strictly local. The problems of busing in Los Angeles are no longer discussed in that city alone, because busing is not a local problem, it concerns the nation. The hiring or firing of a big-city superintendent is national. Declining test scores, integration, discipline, grades, teachers' contracts, the political impact of the National Education Association, collective bargaining, violence, vandalism, costs, stress, and the competency of teachers have all been examined in the daily newspapers and weekly news magazines. In the main, these treatments have been negative. They "point with alarm" at the problems.

One example of an unintended negative impact has to do with the issue of principal burnout. In many instances, it is reported that the really good principals are dropping out of education. Consider for the moment what impact this has on the principals who stay in. They are confronted with the same pressures they have had to deal with for the last few years, but now they have to contend with publicity that says the ones who remain are not the best principals. They are now in a double bind. It is a dilemma.

Another national trend is the problem of budgets. In the last few years there has been a trend to limit educational spending. Yet, as mentioned above, there has been another trend to increase the responsibilities of the schools. This economic crunch is being felt everywhere, but it is a real problem for school personnel. It is not uncommon to read of districts having to take extraordinary measures to keep schools open. Such measures range from closing the schools during the peak winter months to save on energy costs to not replacing retiring teachers to actually reducing the work force in some districts to reduce costs. Further, budgets are examined with more detail than previously, and much time is spent in justifying budget requests.

Finally, since there is not as much job mobility as there once was, teachers have a tendency to stay where they are. This means that there are fewer new teachers coming into systems and schools. What that means for principals is having to work with teachers who may become increasingly set in their habits without the infusion of fresh ideas from new teachers. It also reduces the opportunity to use more experienced teachers in a greater variety of ways which would help principals reduce their own routine work assignments. The principal is the one who is responsible for the morale of the school staff. As we have already seen, the longer one stays in the same job, without much variation, the greater the chance of burnout. Without the influx of new teachers and new ideas, the opportunities for variation are reduced.

THE PROBLEM OF THE NATURE
OF INTERACTIONS WITH PEOPLE

In many ways the principal of a school is like the unfortunate employee who is assigned to the complaints desk in a large store. When customers are angry, they vent their wrath on the person behind the "complaints" sign. It is much the same in a school. More often than not, students see the principal when they are in trouble. Parents see the principal when they have a problem with the school or the school has a problem with their child. The principal might go to see teachers for any number of reasons, but teachers seldom go to see the principal except when they have a problem. In short, a principal's interactions with people are almost always negative. In fact, in most of their interactions, principals are in a no-win situation. So far as teachers are concerned, principals always bring the bad news. If we still lived in the days when the messenger who brought bad news was killed, we wouldn't have a principal left! The bad news may come in the form of a bad evaluation, news that the job has been eliminated, or a denial of tenure. Whatever the case, it doesn't make for very good working relationships when a single individual must do all the dirty work in an organization in which there is little positive reinforcement anyway.

The nature of the principal's contact with students is another example of poor organization. Every one of us who has been told to "go to the principal's office" knows that it isn't something to look forward to. Principal-student contact is in the main negative. It is planned that way. It is a rare principal indeed who has been able to overcome the negative reaction students automatically have toward being sent to the principal's office. For principals, the behavior of students called to their attention is more often than not unacceptable, antisocial, occasionally violent, and often destructive. In a word, principals don't have much opportunity to see students at their best. In large systems, there might be a vice-principal in charge of discipline, but in small high schools and in elementary schools it is the principal who handles it all. In having to deal with such problems, principals have been physically attacked and have even had their lives threatened. It is not uncommon to have principals caught in a conflict with their own values in dealing with students. It is the principal who must decide whether or not a student should be suspended, expelled, or allowed to continue in classes after a serious offense. Many principals have at heart a sincere concern for the education of young people. The last thing in the world they want to see is a student dismissed from school. Yet, if the student poses a threat to other students, teachers, or even the principal, they must take the position that the school cannot tolerate the presence of a dangerous student. The principal is trapped between personal educational values and the institutional values that insist on a particular kind of behavior.

In such situations, the principal is often the buffer between an angry teacher and angry parents. The parents want their child in school, and the teacher wants control so that classes may proceed smoothly. In such situations, it is no wonder that both teachers and parents see the principal as being of little help. In trying to please both, he pleases no one. But, that is the job as it is defined.

The higher administration judges a principal's performance by the lack of complaints about a school. If things are going well in the accountability area (test scores), then the principal is assumed to be doing a good job as long as there are no complaints from the community. Principals have a job in which they are expected to please everyone. And while trying to please everyone they are also expected to be decisive, innovative, and unfaltering. Is it any wonder so many principals are leaving the profession?

THE PROBLEM OF THE LACK
OF SUFFICIENT PROFESSIONAL TRAINING

The professional training we are talking about here does not involve the curriculum principals have to take in order to be certified as administrators in any given state—organization and administrative theory, school law, school finance, elementary or secondary organization, and the like. It is more the classes they do not take that lead principals to problems of burnout. It is the lack of training in human relations, for example, which contributes to personnel problems, the inability to handle disputes between parents and teachers, and the failure to have a firm grasp of discipline strategies appropriate for elementary and secondary school students. Often principals have no more guidance in human affairs than their own personal experience and upbringing. Such untutored assumptions work for a time. But in crisis situations, a lack of understanding of other human beings, their assumptions and their points of view, condemn the principal to at least partial failure all of the time. Classes in human communication, conflict management, human growth and development, and discipline might be more appropriate for a school principal than school law and school finance. Certainly it is not an either-or affair. Both are necessary. Unfortunately, only one group of courses is being provided.

Principals are also lacking in managerial skills such as time management and delegation of authority. It has already been indicated how many separate tasks a principal is expected to do in any given day. Any person who makes the assumption that those tasks must be done by a single person has obviously not had the benefit of a solid course in management. Good managers are those who are able to spread out the workload so that no single person is overburdened. Principals haven't yet seemed to get that idea firmly into their scheme of how to run a school.

Finally, principals lack skills in handling stress and preventing stress for others. It is as important for a principal to take care of himself or herself as it is to manage effectively the working of the school. Certainly the time is long past when people did not recognize the relationship between the two.

THE PROBLEM OF REWARDS

This problem has to do with the tangible and intangible rewards of being a school principal. There was a time in American society when a principal of a school could watch young people grow and develop. The principal could manage a school staff with autonomy, set educational policy, deal with personal problems in a personal way, and take some satisfaction for a job that lasted long enough for children to grow into young adults. There was satisfaction in that. Those of us who are educators, whether in administration or in the classroom, know that feeling. It subordinates a multitude of gripes. That satisfaction has disappeared for all but a few small-town principals. Our highly mobile, highly technological, highly structured, and highly centralized school organization put an end to such personal satisfaction. The rewards have diminished for school principals.

Such intangible rewards have been replaced in the world of business by money. Such has not been the case for school employees. A recent survey by the National Association of Secondary School Principals indicated that school principals earn on the average between $20,000 and $28,000 a year. More than one fourth earn less than $20,000 a year, and only three percent earn more than $35,000 a year. Such low pay for the job they do only exacerbates the pressure under which principals work.

SYMPTOMS OF PRINCIPAL BURNOUT

PHYSICAL

The physical symptoms of burnout are often nonspecific. This is the case for principals. If a person is under tension long enough and has no strategies for handling tension, then there will be physical symptoms. They are unavoidable.

These unavoidable, nonspecific symptoms range from low-grade infections to heart disease. It is no wonder that persons who work almost sixty hours a week feel tired and are susceptible to infections. As we have pointed out earlier, this is especially true if the person has not developed ways of coping with pressure that will relieve it or psychological attitudes that can reduce it.

Principals who have experienced burnout report symptoms such as loss of sleep, respiratory distress, chronic back pain, headaches, and irritability. They experience, in fact, all the physical symptoms of stress.

INTELLECTUAL

Principals seem to be most affected on their jobs by the symptoms of intellectual burnout. There are three areas in which their performance can be seriously affected.

First, there is a deterioration in the ability to plan. Principals show this inability through a lack of clarity which may take two forms. It might show up in their interactions with the staff. A principal with intellectual burnout might become increasingly unclear and indirect in giving information and instruction to the staff. Teachers leave staff meetings asking, "What are we supposed to do now?" Principals may lose the agenda, shuffle papers, forget the purpose of the meeting, or begin to block out the names of staff members. Such confusion deepens the criticism and isolation the principal experiences and pushes the principal deeper into self-blame and burnout.

Such behavior in public interactions reveals a loss of clarity in thinking which also hinders the principal in planning future events and in solving everyday problems. Diminished problem-solving ability not only affects the organization, but prevents the principal from coming up with alternatives for resolving personal dilemmas as well.

The second area in which intellectual functioning is affected is in taking action. Principals who are experiencing a loss both of clarity and of the ability to solve problems simultaneously exhibit an unwillingness to take action. They cannot seem to develop the insight necessary to see a course of action and take it. They develop feelings of impotency and powerlessness. The burned-out principal becomes convinced that there is nothing that can be done to save school or self. Such hopelessness dissolves into inaction. The staff deepens its criticism, school morale plunges, and the principal seems to be caught in a downward spiral of despair that leads out of the profession.

Given that a principal is caught in such a downward spiral, how are the daily affairs of the school conducted? A final sign of intellectual burnout is the degree of mechanical routine to which the principal adheres. It is a paradox. It is the routine, the day-after-day activities, that cause the boredom that precedes intellectual burnout, yet it is to these routines that the burned-out principal turns for safety. Burned-out principals point more and more to the rules and have less and less patience with staff members who want to go outside them. Naturally, different principals use different tactics to defend against the new ideas presented to them. Some take the tack of finding fault with every suggestion. Others complain about the new work that will have to be done or the increased paperwork or insist that no one appreciates the work they already do. Still others may take an agreeable stance in the beginning, only to subvert all efforts to actually implement new ideas. Whatever the approach, all these efforts are aimed at making the day-to-day tasks more and more routine and less and less demanding so that no new ideas will have to be dealt with. The loss of clarity that is a major sign of intellectual burnout becomes most apparent as the burned-out principal loses the ability to seek ways out of burnout. The final sign is turning to the very things that caused the burnout in the first place.

EMOTIONAL

The burned-out principal seems to be characteristically depressed. There is no joy in the job, and he or she is in a constant state of worry and tension. Such principals know that their performance on the job is poor, and they fear being found out. That is one reason for the retreat into routine. At least they will have the defense that they were following procedure. Yet the suspicion is strong that everyone knows they aren't doing their job properly.

Their frustration is that they do not have the energy to devote to doing a good job because they don't care about the job anymore. The joy that they might have once felt in creating a climate in which a staff could work effectively is gone.

Burned-out principals are increasingly aware of being isolated from other members of the staff. The isolation extends to their interpersonal relationships outside of work. Their irritability, loss of clarity, and lackluster job performance all serve to alienate others.

It is no wonder that principals caught in the symptoms of burnout see little that is funny in their situation. This lack of ability to see the humor in their situation becomes another factor in emotional burnout. Their serious approach to the job and life contributes to the pressures they have to confront daily. Their humorlessness causes tension not only to themselves but to others as well. Those others, sensing the coldness in the burnout victim, find little time to spend with the person, thus increasing his or her sense of isolation.

Finally, the emotional pressures on the job affect the principal's home life. Interactions with family members become less friendly, and events which previously caused no problem in family interaction become sources of argument, anger, and depression. The burned-out principal's enjoyment of loving family and friends becomes strained. The very persons needed to overcome the pressures of work are thus also alienated; the isolation on the job extends to home and friends, and the principal loses an important opportunity to escape the pressures of the job. The tension has become a part of the principal's life.

SOCIAL

When the tensions of a person's job become a part of one's pattern of living, it is no surprise that social encounters suffer too. Burned-out principals become self-absorbed and lose the willingness to relate to others. They become social isolates. Their spouse might suggest that they visit friends, go out to dinner, go to a movie, or even take a vacation. But, failing in their job, they may be afraid to take any time off. Burned-out principals may spend more time than ever preparing for the job. They can't take a vacation because they are losing effectiveness on the job and want to show the higher administration that they are developing new skills to do better or maintain previously reached standards. Of course, they do not profit from this increased "preparation," since no real energy is given to the experience, and they are once again just "putting in their time." They may half-heartedly take classes, attend workshops, or study at home, but their intellectual burnout prevents them from getting much of real worth from their experience. Burned-out principals turn increasingly inward, and their social relationships with staff, friends, and family suffer as a result.

SPIRITUAL

Educators are sensitive people. A retreat into routine, deteriorating social relationships, ineffective job performance, and intellectual incompetence are all felt and cause pain. We have already indicated that a characteristic of principals is to blame themselves for many of the criticisms of public education, and certainly this extends to their personal problems as well. This tendency toward self-blame, a symptom of burnout, ends up in feelings of worthlessness. The principal's self-image crashes. Some try to hang on for a while, but many who have lost faith in themselves come to see their job as meaningless or even impossible and ultimately leave the profession. Their years of preparation, commitment, and desire to help have all wilted under the pressures that a modern-day principal has to face. In an effort to rediscover meaning, they look toward some endeavor other than education. While the new work may not approach the satisfactions they expected to find in education, they no longer have to face the pressures created by the demands of society and by their own idealistic expectations.

CURES FOR PRINCIPAL BURNOUT

PHYSICAL

Physically there is a good deal principals can do about tiredness, health, and physical condition. The first thing to do is to create a physical stress-reduction plan. Such a plan must involve three aspects: food, exercise, and rest. For example, tiredness can be caused by the amount of work one has to do, but it can also be caused by a simple lack of food or by a lack of muscle strength.

Take a look at the food people eat every day. Lunch may be a nourishing meal, but the rest of the day all that is available is junk food. If principals find themselves feeling tired during the day, it is possible that a piece of fruit or a glass of fruit juice could provide the extra energy that could take them through the rest of the day without anger or irritability. It is possible to keep high-energy food in the office. It is even possible to take the junk food out of the teachers' lounge and stock it with high-energy food so that everyone in the school can profit from snacks that aid in overcoming stress rather than contributing to it. Substitute fruit juice for coffee. Substitute fruit for candy bars. Such a program will help in the fight against low-grade infections, colds, and flu, as well as preventing energy lapse during the day.

The second part of a burnout-resistance plan deals with exercise. It is a wonder of modern life that we have buildings well-equipped with exercise paraphernalia that go unused. We are thinking, of course, of school gyms. The first step in the plan is to legitimize the use of the school facilities by the school staff. It might be possible to start an after-school basketball league using elementary school facilities. A principal can invite the staff to join in an after-school jogging club. Or create a principal's tennis tournament. Finally, it is possible to exercise right at one's desk. Isometric exercises are fine for toning and maintaining physical condition.

Physically, weight becomes a problem for all of us as we grow older. It is especially a problem for those of us who work in jobs which require little physical activity. The solution is simply to find a comfortable weight and maintain it. This might require a visit to a physician to determine one's optimal personal weight; charts aren't of much help in this matter. It is easier to maintain weight than it is to lose it. Step on a scale every morning. If weight is creeping up, simply decrease food intake for a few days. Go to fruits and juices as recommended above. This plan may be easier said than adhered to, but weight maintenance is another of those physical accomplishments that affects all the other aspects of our being. Emotionally we feel better, intellectually we are sharper, and socially we are more confident.

A final recommendation is that a warm bath be taken right before bedtime. Wait until the house is quiet and take fifteen minutes or more of just soaking in a warm tub. Sleep comes quicker and is more refreshing, and waking is easier. With a good regimen of physical exercise, high-energy food taken regularly, and sleep, one is much better able to deal with the stresses of any day.

INTELLECTUAL

It is important that principals identify the sources of both stress and satisfaction on the job. It is a simple task to divide a piece of paper down the middle and title one side Stresses and the other Satisfactions. That list might provide some insight into solutions as well as problems. The next step is to move toward increasing the opportunities for more activities at work that are satisfying.

Another step in reducing intellectual burnout is for principals to develop an awareness of their own role in the production of stress for themselves and others. If principals are creating stress for themselves, that is something over which they do exercise control, and it can be reduced without assistance from outside. If they are creating stress for others, one way of making work a better place is to make a concerted effort to stop doing things that create stress for others. By reducing stress on others, the principal can reduce isolation and start a cycle of responses that can lower the chances of burnout or reverse it. We realize that this is not a simple task. One way to begin would be to ask teachers and other staff members to identify stressors in their jobs. Once this information is obtained, accept the challenge of designing a program which will lead to the elimination of the identified stressors.

A third suggestion for principals is to reduce boredom at work. Here are several suggestions that will help in doing just that. If it is true, as suggested above, that principals lack skills in conflict resolution, management, and human relations, then work can be a more exciting place if principals would seek out just those skills and begin to use them at work. Enroll in human relations classes (most important), conflict resolution workshops, and courses that teach and discuss management problems. This will do two things. First, the intellect will be engaged in new tasks and problems, and second, the skills learned promise to make school a better place to work.

Another suggestion is to plan at least two conferences a year that will take time away from work. If at all possible, schedule one of them out of town. This gives principals the opportunity to talk to other principals from other communities about similar problems, and it also takes them away from the day-in, day-out stresses of the school. It is a vacation as well as an intellectual stimulation.

Every principal should be involved in reading. Essentially, there are two kinds of reading. One is professional. It is important to keep up with issues in education and in the larger world. New ideas, techniques, and concerns can only aid in one's work. However, the second kind of reading is equally important. It is the one that is often neglected by busy professional people: reading for pleasure. This is reading for which one does not have to be accountable. It might involve mysteries, science fiction, or the latest best seller. It might involve one's interest outside professional work. For example, one school administrator known to the authors is an expert in Sherlock Holmes, and another is well-read in the area of the search for extraterrestrial life. Those concerns don't especially help them in their work, but they do provide them with many hours of reading pleasure.

By and large, jobs are boring because they involve doing the same things over and over. If that is the case, one can make the job more interesting by changing the job. Vary the daily schedule. Don't always do paperwork first; save it for last on some days. Eat lunch early some days and later on others. Don't make class visitations at the same time every day. Create variety in the job. Visit other schools. Enlist other principals in projects that involve more than one school. Refuse to let things fall into a rut. In other words, change things just to change things, and if anyone asks why, tell them it is a burnout prevention plan.

EMOTIONAL

Here are four suggestions to avoid emotional burnout. If one is a young principal, say in the first or second year, seek out a mentor among the older principals or higher administrators. Ask them questions, seek advice, discuss problems, and share planning and skills. If one knows that there is at least one other person to whom one can turn during high-stress periods, the chances of burnout are reduced.

Principals have the power to legitimize the need for educators to talk to one another. Principals can even plan in-service days devoted to discussion of professional problems of educators, just as they are planned for the new math program or the new reading series.

Principals can seek out groups which are designed for self-renewal, stress management, or burnout prevention. It is possible that such a group can be organized among the principals of a single district. Such groups do not have to be professionally run. A single principal can open up his or her house for a meeting once a week at which principals share their concerns and problems.

Principals can do something about their own emotional isolation by providing positive feedback to the members of the school staff. If someone in a school does something good, or does more than is expected, or just does a good job all the time, principals who take the time to notice that and to tell the staff member than they have noticed and appreciate it create a climate in which other members of the school staff will do the same for them. The creation of a positive emotional climate is no accident, and principals are in a position to create such a climate through positive feedback to staff members.

Finally, it is possible for principals to make taking a mental health day legal—for the staff and for themselves. A mental health day is a day on which one is not sick and has no physical reason for not going to work. In fact, feeling fine can be a good reason to take that day off for oneself! Use the day to relax, explore, visit, or engage in a hobby.

SOCIAL

Frankly, the way to avoid social burnout is to be selfish. Don't be shy about wanting to be liked and respected by people. The way to be such a person is to do things for other people. Such "altruistic selfishness" means building bridges to others in the school, in the community, and in the profession. It means taking the time to have the staff of the school over to the house for a spaghetti dinner. It means seeking out people in the school system who share similar ideas and philosophies in order to build a support group for one another. It might involve creating the time for several members of the school staff to have lunch together once a month or so.

If a principal does not like being isolated at school, then he or she must do something about the circumstances that lead to isolation. It may mean involving the staff in the decision-making processes of the school. It may mean learning skills that will help groups to change policies in the school district that they do not like. It means expressing appreciation for people more often. It means remembering that people have to support one another if they are going to avoid burnout.

SPIRITUAL

If one is to avoid burnout because of a loss of meaning, one has to be able to know clearly what meanings one was seeking in the profession in the first place. That may mean for persons late in their career that they will have to begin a process of identifying the ideals and goals that they had when they entered the profession. It may mean that the years of hardening may have to be deliberately softened to recapture the ideals of a younger time. The cynicism of years may have caused us to devalue the dreams of youth, but that same process is what has led some of us to lose meaning in our work.

Second, principals must remember that education is a people job. It is easy to forget that in the crush of paperwork. But it is those principals who emphasize the administrative details of their jobs that become the prime candidates for burnout as they discover such details routine and boring. People are naturally many things, but boring isn't one of them; they are sometimes contrary, unpredictable, irritable, unreliable, and incompetent, but they are not boring. If principals can come to understand that any efforts used in working with people will result in long-term gains, they could lose their fear of the short-term loss of efficiency found in initial people work. Rushing through decisions may lead to hostilities which, in the long run, will undermine and sabotage the very decisions reached so quickly and efficiently.

The feeling of powerlessness among principals is based in the increasing centralization of schools. The threat is real. However, it is not going to be counteracted by policy. It will only be counteracted by principals who *assume* autonomy. The demands for doing things in a standardized way are paper orders. Anyone who has ever worked in any large organization understands that nobody really cares that much how things are done so long as they are done and there are no complaints from outside the organization. In fact, principals do have autonomy. They can do things their own way. The way to avoid feelings of powerlessness is to act powerfully. Seize the initiative and run with it. Teachers are clear on this issue: They want a principal who will take charge and act in a firm, fair manner.

If a principal is going to avoid isolation and rediscover or maintain meaning in the job, such a principal will have to communicate with every staff member. The principal is charged with the morale of the school, like it or not. All of us recognize that a single disgruntled staff member can screw up an entire organization. Undiscussed anger, gossip, or rumor can destroy the effectiveness of any organization. However, principals with the courage to confront issues out in the open defuse any passive-aggressive staff members. Openly confronted, such staff members can begin to find more productive ways to use their energy in the organization. One way in which to quell a disgruntled staff member is to give that person meaningful work to do in the school. It is important to involve parents, teachers, and other staff members in decisions that directly affect them in the school. Finally, routine tasks should not be performed by the principal or by teachers who could more profitably use the time for more stimulating and exciting activities. It is possible that what might prove to be routine and boring for adults could be exciting and challenging for students or volunteers in the school. By removing routine tasks from the responsibilities of principals or teachers, burnout could be reduced for both groups.

Certainly, we must face the knowledge that many principals cannot be saved from burning out by the recommendations above. It may be that such persons will have to leave the profession. It may be well worthwhile to take a leave of absence for a year to think over one's goals and desires. After the year, a decision about staying in the profession can be considered again. It may be that the rewards and satisfactions simply do not add up to enough to remain. During a leave of absence other careers can be examined, and it may be more meaningful to opt for one of those than to stay in the profession of education. Clearly, a decision to leave the profession is one that would be more rational once burnout has been reversed and/or prevented.

4. Students

"From contemplation one may become wise, but knowledge comes only from study."

—*A. Edward Newton*

The late teens and early twenties are thought by many to be among "the best years of our lives." It is a time to experiment, test new ideas, try new things, and it is a time of intellectual, emotional, and physical strength. For many persons in the physical sciences, their best and most innovative work occurs in their twenties. For many athletes, their best performances are recorded in these years. It is a time of learning, growing, and developing. Many in this age group continue their learning by entering colleges, universities, and professional schools. Their competences, skills, and knowledge undergo profound changes during these years as they prepare themselves for the world of work and professionalism. They are years rich with learning and social development.

Yet for some of these youths there is a dark side to the college years. While on the one hand it provides the opportunity for significant learning and social development, on the other it also creates for many "life in a pressure cooker." The college-age young commit suicide all too frequently. It is the second leading cause of death among this age group.

Certainly, more is written about the problems faced by teachers, but students are affected as well. The "best years of our lives" are years that may be spent in dealing with more stress than necessary or reasonable. What causes the pressures of the student years?

WHAT WENT WRONG IN THE STUDY HALL?

THE PROBLEM OF FAILURE

The pressures inherent in college life are real. There are external pressures that come from individual classes, deadlines, and assignments, all real enough. However, it is not these pressures that take the major toll on students. The internal pressures are even more severe. Consider, for example, the pressure created for students who enter college to discover that the requirements are more demanding than anticipated. Their plans for the future—their dreams, hopes, and ambitions—are all threatened as never before. Certainly, there may have been doubts before entering, but now the students are faced with facts that may condemn their dreams to failure. A career in a highly competitive, respected profession may seem to be, for the first time, unattainable.

What does it mean in the life of persons when they learn that they are What does it mean in the life of persons when they learn that they are not up to a task? Their belief in themselves is challenged. They are less than they hoped they would be. They are failures. Self-esteem flounders in the face of such evidence.

Those dreams are not only the dreams of each individual student. They are the dreams of parents, friends, neighbors, and past teachers. For a student to let the dream crash is to dash the hopes of many people. The loss of a shared dream carries increased importance and can do increased damage to a student's self-concept. The strain becomes too much for many students. Even for those who remain and succeed, the pressures they have overcome are real, severe, and they exact a price.

THE PROBLEM OF NEW RESPONSIBILITIES

Among the pressures that students find when they go to college are new responsibilities that they have not often been asked to assume before. In many cases, friendships that lasted throughout the high school years disappear. Now the student must take reponsibility for finding new friends. No longer will the familiar social patterns of the past which provided the social glue for friendships be effective. The individual will have to create new social patterns.

The responsibilities of mastering knowledge and skills are different in college than in high school. The responsibilities of college fall squarely on the shoulders of students. (Their mothers aren't registered for class.) In college, one cannot "pass" if assignments are not completed. Perhaps, for the first time as a student, performance really counts.

THE PROBLEM OF ISOLATION

College provides a population of people different from those students are used to. For young people from rural settings, there are street-wise urbanities, and vice versa. For many, college may provide their first contact with persons from cultures other than their own. For persons of both the majority culture and minority cultures, it may provide the first real encounters with one another.

Most students face these new social realities alone. Their friends from high school may not be attending college or be going to college elsewhere. Often, even after a single semester, college students return home to discover, already, that their interests, concerns, and ideas have been altered so much that they have little in common with "old" friends.

That isolation may be compounded throughout the college years, since a college population is not a stable one. New friends move, drop out, stop out, get married, or find new friends. This transient state of relationships does little to provide a sense of permanence. Students discover that there is little in college life that can be depended upon to remain the same.

THE PROBLEM OF MONEY

The demands of money create many different pressures for students. Interestingly, some have too much, and that can be a source of embarrassment for them in light of those who have too little and scrape by from semester to semester. In the face of the contrast in affluence, they are sometimes frustrated into believing that they aren't really experiencing college the way it is for other students. This relative rarity is in addition to the more common struggle of students' trying to pay for tuition, room, board, books, and entertainment. Further, during this time of rising costs, these students are constantly reminded of the strain their education is placing on their parents.

THE PROBLEM OF ROLE

One does not need to be involved in higher education for long to realize that students have very little power. The sixties notwithstanding, to be a student in America is to be virtually powerless. Even while students are preparing for leadership roles in college, they are subordinate to the wishes, whims, and dictates of their professors.

Consider now that these are intelligent young people, and they are aware of their powerlessness. That awareness becomes too heavy for some. They are unable to tolerate their servile status. They leave, or they seek out programs in which they do not feel this powerless role so keenly.

There is a rating for estimating students' chances of surviving the social demands of studenthood. It is called the SQ. Students with a high SQ are more likely to survive college long enough to get a degree. Students with a low SQ are more likely to quit and find something else to do. SQ stands for "shit quotient"! In point of fact, some people are able to put up with more shit than others. There is an awful lot of shit at college.

THE PROBLEM OF INDEPENDENCE

Students are on their own, often for the first time, and yet are expected to make mature decisions. They are struggling for independence. In the midst of that struggle, they are confronted with incredible inconsistencies. First, many are going to college on money provided by their parents. It is difficult to achieve independence when one is the ward of someone else, yet most students' existence depends on money from home. More often than they wish to be reminded of it, parents point out this insulting fact to them.

Another inconsistency is that while they are being prepared for future leadership roles, they have little to say about the preparation they are receiving. The institutions are in charge of that. Students are striving for independence in the face of constant reminders that they are dependent!

THE PROBLEM OF SCHOLASTIC EXPECTATIONS

In many ways, students must be sensitive people. They must be able to size up a professor on very little information. Every professor in college has personal ideas about how his or her particular discipline must be mastered and how that mastery must be demonstrated. Some rely on tests. Some tests are multiple-choice, others are essay. Some teachers regard tests in about the same way many of us regard the common cold: while it is common, it is something to be avoided. Some professors encourage questions, others frown upon their lectures' being interrupted by inquisitive students. Some like students to drop by the office for a chat, others are busy and have no time for "idle chitchat." Some are friendly and some are cold. Some are demanding and some are not. Some promote student responsibility and some do not. The fact remains that it is the student who has to adjust to the professor and not the other way around. Often students carry five or more different courses. It is entirely possible that those five courses could be in five different disciplines, each with a different professor with a different style.

Yes, the demands on students are real. They leave home, go to a new place, leave their friends behind, struggle with financial concerns, and seek to find an identity, all in the face of having to master new competencies, skills, and knowledge while being told they are not mature enough to make decisions for themselves. Is it any wonder that some of them do not survive and burn out?

SYMPTOMS OF STUDENT BURNOUT

PHYSICAL

Students push themselves to meet the demands of college life. Those demands come from their professors and from their own desire to succeed. The physical symptoms of student burnout range from mild to severe. They are more than the simple physical tiredness caused by staying up late to study or for a party. The physical symptoms of burnout in students are related to other pressures in their lives, such as the social, emotional, and intellectual concerns discussed below. For example, their tiredness may come from a lack of sleep caused not by staying up to study but because they cannot go to sleep. This lack of sleep might more likely be caused by anxiety. They find themselves short of breath or have other difficulties in breathing. They may sweat for reasons not related to temperature. Given all that, they find themselves constantly tired, unable to study, to socialize, or to participate in the normal routines of college life.

It is not unusual, for example, to find college students who are plagued with a series of minor illnesses—colds, flu, mononucleosis. Sometimes illnesses are caused by accidents. In fact, accidents are the leading cause of death among college students. There are various psychological explanations for accidents, and among them are several which suggest that accidents are caused by the persons involved in them. It is not unreasonable to believe that persons under stress are less attentive to their surroundings than necessary to avoid dangerous situations.

Finally, students may experience bowel and bladder problems. They may find themselves unable to sit through an entire class without having to go to the bathroom.

The point of all of this is that, during a time of maximal physical strength, students with symptoms of burnout may be weak to the point of inability to continue their studies.

INTELLECTUAL

The intellectual symptoms of burnout are ones that seriously impair the students' ability to function as students. They may find themselves forgetting classes, assignments, or appointments. They may go to the library to study, only to spend their time staring off into space. They may discover that during a test they have lost the ability to concentrate on the test itself and instead become occupied by random thoughts. Their papers may be characterized by a lack of attention to detail. This may account for many professors' complaints regarding student work. The pressures of college life might be genuinely increasing. If that is true, then those pressures might be increasing student burnout and the intellectual symptoms of grammatical and mathematical sloppiness.

While these symptoms are serious enough, they are not the most damaging in intellectual burnout among students. Far more important is the loss of individual initiative. While students might be sloppy in their work, they might still be able to gather their resources and mount a counterattack. However, if their initiative is lost, they are trapped in a downward spiral that ends in the loss of their educational opportunity, for a while at least. Lacking initiative and interests, such students are led to boredom, uselessness, and cynicism. Little is left that would hold them to their educational pursuits.

EMOTIONAL

The emotional symptoms of burnout are exaggerations of normally occurring events. It is no accident that students are occasionally irritable with their parents or friends or that they are sometimes self-pitying or depressed or sad. It is a symptom of burnout when these conditions become ordinary rather than occasional. Students who are victims of burnout cry easily. They may go to their rooms or apartments and cry because the assignment in a particular class is too demanding. The assignment does not exceed work asked for in the past, but now it is just too much. Students suffering from burnout can be characterized as irritable most of the time and often have angry outbursts at their roommates, spouse, or friends.

They become suspicious of the intentions of their professors; one might hear a student talking about some professor's intention of plotting to fail them so that they will be forced to quit school. Or one might talk to students who have come honestly to doubt their ability to finish their course of study. Such feelings of worthlessness and depression can lead to more serious symptoms.

While the college years are years of experimentation with new ideas and new forms of social arrangements, they can also be years of sadness. Students are often known for their excesses. Perhaps one of the most dangerous excesses of recent years is the use of "mind-altering" drugs. While many positive benefits are claimed for such chemicals, their dangerous aspects are underplayed or ignored by the college population. It is not unusual for a student undergoing emotional pressure to turn to drugs at a college where they are reasonably easy to obtain and where there are a good number of advocates. Even such relatively harmless substances as marijuana can be abused. It is more dangerous when students turn to LSD, speed, angel dust, cocaine, or heroin. The chance of abuse is greater, and the consequences are far more dangerous. The problem is that in student burnout the ability to reason clearly and solve problems efficiently is reduced. The stresses compound to create more emotional strain, with a corresponding lack of intellectual functioning to help solve the problem. It is then that the chance of serious substance abuse is greatest.

SOCIAL

There are four major social symptoms of burnout. First, students become increasingly critical of themselves and others. It is as though they have ruled out all persons as being able to help. Neither students nor others can provide the climate in which the anxiety and pain can be alleviated. Second, because they have lost faith in their own abilities and in the ability of others, they tend to withdraw from the very persons and events that could serve to help them move out of their burnout. Third, they become less and less able to trust others, and as a consequence cut themselves off even more from people. Finally, their lack of faith and lack of trust turns to blame. They come to see themselves as victims of other people and as less and less in control of their own lives. As a result, they come to blame others for all of their troubles. They have become social isolates, trapped first by the pressures under which they live and second by their own attitudes which prevent them from reaching out to others.

SPIRITUAL

The word *spiritual* is used in this book to refer to a sense of meaning in what one is doing. Loss of meaning is the most serious aspect of burnout. For students, it means that their creative abilities to help themselves are seriously impaired. As seen above, intellectual functioning declines, and they are no longer able to creatively solve their problems. Instead, they may begin inflexibly to apply solutions that no longer work. Their rigid thinking leads students to see everything in terms of their past experiences and everything outside the college as being of more worth and more useful than that which they are learning. This past orientation prevents them from profiting from what the college has to offer. The student tries to use past learning to get by, rather than developing new skills, competencies, and knowledge. For some students, this means that they simply go through the motions. They attend their classes, do their assignments, complete the requirements, and receive credit. Yet they do not value their experience. They are little altered by it. As one student phrased it, "I came, I sat, I graduated."

Others find college life so useless that they drop out to pursue some other way of being in the world. They become true enemies of colleges and college life and use their energies from that point on to criticize and condemn higher education, never recognizing their own agency in the circumstances of their lives.

The ultimate spiritual decline for a young person is suicide. Unable to solve problems creatively, yet still faced with them, students find that not only college but life itself is useless, boring, frightening, and too tragic to continue. They commit suicide.

How shall such waste be prevented?

CURES FOR STUDENT BURNOUT

PHYSICAL

There are three recommendations to help avoid physical burnout. There is food. There is exercise. There is rest. If you eat well, exercise, and rest, the chances of burnout are significantly reduced.

If a student lives in a college-sponsored dorm, the opportunity for nutritious (albeit not very appetizing) food is good. All the student has to do is get up for breakfast, make it back for lunch, and get to dinner. If a student does not live in a dorm but lives alone, with friends, or with a spouse, follow these suggestions and your food consumption should be OK. First, have a high-energy breakfast. That does not necessarily mean an entire meal, but it might mean a specially prepared high-energy drink like this one: Blend vigorously eight ounces of milk, one egg, chunks of fresh fruit (strawberries, a peach, or any other), and two tablespoons of wheat germ. It takes very little time, and it is not expensive. It is, however, a good high-energy drink. It is certainly more nutritious than a cup of coffee, a carton of chocolate milk, or a cold drink. Second, eat a light lunch. A salad with meat and cheese followed by yogurt would be good. Finally, no matter what you eat for dinner, always have a salad with it. If you have another diet you prefer, follow that. Any sensible nutrition plan will work to help prevent physical burnout.

The next step is to be involved in an ongoing, mildly strenuous exercise program. It is entirely possible to participate in college intramural athletic programs. If not motivated by team sports, a one-mile run every day will do just as well, if you run hard for one hundred yards or so twice during the mile. Frankly, many people say that brisk walking will work fine. In fact, even such mundane advice as avoiding elevators would do wonders for some people! But the advice is important. Do something that involves the body in exercise frequently. Take an exercise class or see a friendly coach or P.E. major.

Finally, set a regular pattern of rest. Set a reasonable time to go to bed, and stick to it. Even if some students are people who love to party, our advice would be find time each day to rest before going out. Thirty minutes of rest right after dinner or right before "a night of drinking" will help. In the morning, always leave enough time to eat, dress, and get to class without rushing. Get up in time, even if the night before was long and hard, so that everything that must be done can be done. If you have had a hard night, then find some time the next day to rest. Even if it means not studying, find time to rest. In the long run, if a person can find the time to rest, his or her studies will be better.

INTELLECTUAL

In order to avoid intellectual burnout as a student, there is one thing more important than any other. Do things as they come up. Don't put things off until the last minute. Every piece of evidence we know of says that the better students are people who do things as they are required rather than all at once. If one has to read a textbook for a course, draw up a plan of how much will have to be read each day—and do it. If such a plan is followed, grades will improve and college will be a less stressful place. The easiest way to do this is to make a list of things to be done and check off each as it is accomplished. If anything is left on the list, it becomes the first thing on the next list. Try it. It actually works.

There are other things students can do to avoid intellectual burnout. Always take at least one course each semester in which there is a real interest. If one does not have a real interest, select a professor who is really good. It is also possible in every class to form learning teams that meet to review for tests, plan papers, or even just talk about the class. People who involve themselves in such learning groups are better students, make higher grades, and avoid burning out.

If one is concerned with substance abuse, sexual matters, or interpersonal relationships, there is no better place to find resources for help than a college campus. It is possible to enroll in a class, visit an expert, or drop by a student-run information center. The college might have a free university in which students hold classes to help others with personal problems and to teach studying skills, relaxation techniques, or any number of other student-interest courses. Participating in programs of this kind can help to prevent intellectual burnout.

EMOTIONAL

Essentially, emotions reflect the value we place on events. Many students have never had an opportunity to examine their own values. Sometimes they have come from home or school backgrounds that actively prevented them from looking in any serious way at their own value system. For some, the idea of examining them is frightening. It may be frightening because they sometimes discover that they have no personal value system, only the one they were given by parents or teachers, one which they have accepted without question. It may also be frightening for students to discover that they hold values in which they really don't believe. But the truth is, if students are ever going to bring their lives under their own control, they have to know what they value and what they do not. In order to do this, students have to find ways of exploring values. There are gimmicks for exploring values, but it is also possible to seek out classes in which it is appropriate to examine values, to obtain books that provide for clarification of values. (See Chapter 3 of Part Two for some values-clarification exercises.)

Another way to analyze one's values is to keep a "crisis log." Entries are made whenever one's emotional reaction seems out of proportion to an event or whenever one wants to preserve one's reaction to highly emotional events. There are three columns in a crisis log: 1) The event, 2) The reaction, and 3) The resolution. Such a log will provide a record of how an individual tends to resolve conflicts and how effective he or she has been. If it works, keep it up. If it doesn't, invent some other technique.

Finally, it is possible on college campuses, perhaps as nowhere else, to find the opportunity to join a group of other people who wish to explore their values and reactions to events. Such groups may be made up of friends or established by the college counseling center, but all provide the opportunity for students to learn to control their own lives more and thus avoid burnout.

SOCIAL

It is an irony of modern college life that there can be so many lonely students all gathered together in a single place and yet be unable to find one another. It is true, however, that colleges have tried to help students to make social contacts. The college counseling center could provide the opportunity for group discussions, encounters, or therapy. The center can also provide support groups for people who have difficulty in making social connections.

Such social connections can be made in other college-sponsored but less formal organizations. It is not an exaggeration to say that there is hardly an interest known that does not have a corresponding college club. Such clubs provide the opportunity for people of similar interests to get together to talk. They also provide the opportunity for friendship, courtship, and even scholarship.

In any case, there are formal and informal ways to avoid the social isolation of burnout on college campuses. Of course, seeking out such ways demands that the students have enough initiative to do so. What if students do not have that initiative? Colleges often provide the skills necessary to help students develop initiative. If a student is very shy, a class in "assertiveness training" can help develop the attitudes and skills necessary to seek relationships which can prevent burnout.

SPIRITUAL

The loss of meaning that characterizes burnout seems to take three very serious forms. First, there is boredom. Second, there is dropping out. Third, there is the threat of suicide. Of these, boredom is the most easily cured. Here are three techniques to make any class interesting. If students follow these suggestions, their academic work will take on meaning again. First, come to class every day with at least one question to ask the professor. Second, prepare an interview form in which the professor's attitudes, convictions, beliefs, and practices are explored. Drop by his or her office one day to make an appointment for such an interview. And finally, negotiate the requirements of the class so that they fit in with personal interests. The way this is done is to tell the professor what one's interests are and ask what aspects of the subject being studied match with those interests. We assure students that most professors are the kind of people who will respond favorably to such a request.

The second problem is one that lends itself to a clear-cut recommendation: instead of dropping out, stop out! Do not quit school just to quit. Drop out for a specific amount of time and for a specific reason. If a student wishes to drop out of school in order, say, to hitchhike across the United States, well and good. Plan to "do your thing," and plan on taking a semester to do it in. Have everything ready for reentry into college before the adventure is even begun. If students who are burning out do that, their leaving and reentry can both be accomplished without anger, and the goal of finishing school is not lost forever, it is just put off for a while. In fact, students who stop out appear to be superior students when they return. Some colleges even recommend it!

The third spiritual form of burnout is not so easy to make suggestions about. Suicide by a young person signals a loss of individual nerve and of imagination. Such deeply troubled students have already exhausted their creative abilities in trying to solve their own problems. It also signals that they have lost faith in the ability of their friends, parents, and perhaps spouse to help them. If a student threatens suicide, he or she should be taken seriously. A professional should be notified to talk to the student. We do not need the permission of potential suicides to seek out professional help for them. Do it and take whatever heat may be generated by the action. Friends, parents, and husbands or wives are usually not prepared to handle the serious effects of suicide or suicide attempts. However, the people at a college counseling center are. If you are a student thinking of suicide, do not be ashamed, do not hesitate, but go now to someone in your counseling center. It is free, and it will help. If you are the roommate of a person talking about suicide, call the counseling center now to get help for that person. You cannot help them, but the counseling center can. Failing the willingness to call or go to the counseling center, at least call a suicide prevention hot line to talk about it. It is most important to remember that the suicide of a young person is not an isolated act. It involves the rest of us as well. It is the responsibility of the rest of us to potential suicides to tell them that our imagination is not exhausted and that there are alternatives that can be imagined that will help. Only then can this most serious spiritual form of burnout be overcome.

BURNOUT AND THE ARBITERS

5. Attorneys

"And do as adversaries do in law,
Strive mightily, but eat and drink as friends."
—William Shakespeare

Attorneys share an interesting dilemma. Some are highly respected. In fact, our Congress has more attorneys than members of any other profession. It was once held that a law degree was a virtual requirement for political office. The dilemma is that, while some are highly respected and well placed, the general attitude toward lawyers is not at all positive. Lawyer jokes almost always involve cheating someone out of money. They are widely viewed as crooks in three-piece suits. It is this strong negative public bias that weighs so heavily on many lawyers.

It is especially burdensome for idealistic young lawyers who see the law as a means of righting so many of society's wrongs. While they hold high ideals and honestly want to represent the will of the people, the people they wish to represent distrust and vilify them.

The source of the dilemma is, of course, that every time a lawyer does violate the law, it is widely publicized. Take Watergate as an example. Partly, the emphasis on attorneys' being held more accountable to the law than others may be justified. It is a bit like a cook ruining the soup on purpose. Lawyers are the ones we turn to to interpret the law so that it is understandable for the rest of us. When attorneys break the laws they are meant to interpret for us, we—the public—feel violated.

It is no less so for attorneys themselves. They feel violated as citizens and doubly violated as attorneys. Here we strike a problem for them. To whom do they turn when the pressures of their profession become too heavy? If they are suspect because they are lawyers, what sympathy can they expect from others because being a lawyer is becoming too much? It is no wonder that many attorneys simply abandon the profession.

WHAT WENT WRONG IN THE COURTROOM?

THE PROBLEM OF UNFULFILLED DREAMS

Many energetic, dedicated, bright young men and women enter law school with a dream. They have ideas about helping people, perhaps saving an innocent defendant from the death penalty with a brilliant defense. Or perhaps the dream is of working for a corporation, handling cases which have a significant impact on the economic life of the organization. Or perhaps the dream is of conducting an antitrust suit against some giant corporation, thereby improving the quality of life for millions of ordinary citizens. Above all, there seems to be a belief that the respect of others in the profession and of the public will be their reward. Whatever the dream, for many lawyers it soon becomes apparent that their dreams are not going to be fulfilled and that they are engaged in a profession which is not at all as they imagined.

When young lawyers graduate from law school, it is unlikely that they have enough legal or economic experience and training to establish their own practices. Thus, many opt to become associates in an already existing firm. Important cases are reserved for the more experienced and presumably competent senior partners and associates. The new lawyers are often burdened with relatively uninteresting and unimportant minor cases. At times the senior lawyer may need assistance in researching an impending case, and this task may also fall to the new lawyers. In this instance, they may not even get to use the information they have worked so hard to assemble. The dream of handling a Supreme Court case or setting some legal precedent is shattered by the repetitive, dull, and boring work of handling minor cases and doing research work for others.

Some lawyers choose not to join an established legal firm but opt instead to work for some type of legal services organization, often supported by public funds. Their dreams seem to include helping less fortunate people, the poor and oppressed of society, as a major component. For reasons we will discuss later, they are often unable to make any significant improvement in their clients' lives. Even when they win a case, nothing much changes for their clients, and another case soon appears to eradicate the victory.

Clients come to lawyers with various motives, such as recouping losses or getting back at someone whom they feel has wronged them. They are emotional, and their goals are emotional. They may not even have a clear idea of what they would like the lawyer to accomplish for them. The lawyer, however, must be logical and deal with facts and points of law. At times lawyers experience frustration in obtaining information they need because the client doesn't see the relevance or importance of the information. The clients' emotional needs must take a back seat to legal needs. The client often wants something the lawyer can't give, and the lawyer's logical, rational use of the law may appear to the client as disinterest or lack of motivation. Thus, a state of conflict may exist between client and lawyer, resulting in strained relations and a mutual perception of lack of trust and appreciation.

THE PROBLEM OF VALUES CONFLICTS

Most lawyers are undoubtedly decent, law-abiding people. They have families, they experience joy and sorrow, and in most ways are like other people. Being like most people, they have values which include not hurting others when at all possible, being honest, and pulling for the underdog. These same values may clash directly with values that are taught in law school and rewarded by the profession.

One such value is total victory. The need to prove a point beyond any doubt, to make a point so strongly that it can't be disputed, to strive for total victory is learned early on in school. This may result in a witness's being humiliated, emotionally devastated, and psychologically shattered. At times, the witness may be the *victim* of a crime, as in rape trials. Yet the adversary system calls for total victory so that the defendant will have the optimum chance to escape conviction. Even though it is "part of the job" or "just business," harsh and even cruel treatment of witnesses conflicts with the human values of many lawyers. This conflict causes stress and may even be damaging to a lawyer's self-image.

Another manifestation of values conflict is the defending of a guilty party. The lawyer may know his client is guilty or strongly suspect it. Even so, the nature of our legal system maintains that clients are innocent until proven otherwise. The lawyer must work tirelessly to prevent the client from being convicted. This may further include preventing an injured party from obtaining material or emotional restitution. Again, the lawyer's *personal* sense of fairness and justice may be battered by the *legal* requirements for fairness and justice. Consider the case of a pedestrian or driver critically injured, perhaps paralyzed, by a negligent driver. The lawyer for the driver must strive to prove his innocence, to pull out all the stops, while knowing or suspecting that his client was intoxicated or driving recklessly. This may all happen with the injured party in full view of the attorney. Such a conflict will almost inevitably have emotional effects on the attorney and challenge his self-image as a caring, feeling human being.

Not all attorneys deal with individuals. Many represent businesses and corporations whose effects on individuals may be less noticeable. But the values conflicts are no less damaging. Perhaps a business is accused of violating some health standard or of producing a product that does not meet safety standards. Perhaps, the company is planning a campaign which will bring financial ruin to its competitors. Perhaps a client, individual, or corporation is seeking damages or restitution far greater than the loss. In all of these instances, the lawyer may know of or suspect the inequity. Yet the job requires full effort and total committment to a cause that is felt to be unjust, unfair, or wrong. The resulting conflict of values can be devastating to the lawyer.

Values conflicts may arise over legal fees. Lawyers may charge $300 per hour and more. It is not uncommon to charge $100 an hour. Receiving this much money for services bothers many lawyers. They take it, wondering if what they have done merits the amount. Privately, many lawyers don't believe their fees are equitable. When such fees are collected for cases that violate a lawyer's *personal* sense of fairness or justice, the problem is only compounded. The attorney's sense of self-esteem may further be damaged.

THE PROBLEM OF THE LACK
OF A SATISFYING PERSONAL LIFE

The personal lives of attorneys, which, as for all people, should be a source of renewal, inspiration, and balance, may come to add to the problem of burnout. Long working hours are a primary contributor to a restricted personal life. The average work year for associate lawyers is approximately 2,100 hours per year, or forty-two hours per week for fifty weeks. For lawyers in legal services offices, the workload may be even greater. Some studies suggest they handle anywhere from 250 to 500 cases per year more than attorneys in private practice. They may put in as many as sixty hours per week. Both associates in a legal firm and legal services attorneys find it necessary to bring work home and to work late at the office. As a result, they must spend too much time away from their families. It becomes difficult to plan activities with the family. Even as simple an event as dinner may become the source of friction between lawyer and spouse. Absence from home makes sharing child care a difficult problem, too. When the lawyer does come home, fatigue, irritability, and the need to concentrate on work-related matters may compound the problem. Vacations are difficult to schedule and short, with less than two weeks per year likely to be available to young lawyers.

Planning a night out with friends, going to dinner, a movie, or a ball-game can become rare occurrences. The chance to play tennis or engage in other recreational activities may also disappear under piles of paper and legal journals. A satisfying personal life fails to appear and, as a result, the attorney fails to get recharged and inspired.

THE PROBLEM OF CRITICISM

Most lawyers probably expected that they would receive respect and be held in high esteem by the public. They probably believed that the long hours of difficult study would in part be rewarded by the admiration of those who sought their services. At least their colleagues would appreciate their dedication and hard work. However, little of this seems to come true. Public criticism of lawyers can be traced back as far as Plato, who wrote of their "small and unrighteous souls." Thomas More apparently did not want attorneys in Utopia. Mark Twain, referring to a lawyer who kept both hands in his pockets while introducing Twain, said it was the first time he'd seen a lawyer with his hands in his own pockets! The role of so many attorneys in the Watergate scandal has done nothing to endear the profession to the public.

Professor Harry Cohen suggests that journalists are competing with attorneys for the role of "adviser of the masses and protectors of the public well-being." He further suggests that to many journalists, lawyers, either consciously or unconsciously, become "enemies." The accuracy of Professor Cohen's hypothesis may be questioned; what cannot be questioned is the increase in articles which are critical of the legal profession and which portray it as filled with ambulance chasers and whiplash specialists. The public reads such articles and so do lawyers. The effect on the self-image of lawyers can be devastating, and they may even begin to doubt their own sincerity and honesty.

Lawyers may also be unpopular with the public for other reasons. Attorneys often have to share negative information with clients, information the clients may not want to know. Servicing a deceased person's will may rekindle painful memories in the survivors. Lawyers may have to uncover unpleasant information in order to build a stronger case, information which can be upsetting to clients and family members. Part of an attorney's job is to interpret the law. Clients may not wish to abide by the law as interpreted. Clients may see the attorney as a roadblock to their getting what they want. Clients' lack of knowledge of the law and the single-minded pursuit of their goals may place them at odds with their attorney, who has to work within the law. The result is a further lowering of some citizens' opinion of members of the legal profession. Finally, the use of technicalities, subtle methods of interrogation and cross-examination, and witnesses who contradict the testimony of other witnesses confuses many people. The term "competitive lying" has been used to describe what legal procedures seem like to lay persons. Trials look like so much jockeying and maneuvering that "truth" and "justice" seem unimportant in the proceedings. Since lawyers play such a prominent role in the legal system, much of this "competitive lying" is attributed to them. Many believe the "trickiest" lawyer or the richest will be the one who emerges victorious. Many believe that the trickiest *is* the richest. Underlying this is the belief that dishonesty and lying are the tools of the successful attorney. The net result is further reduced confidence in the legal profession.

Lawyers have recently come under stinging criticism from within the profession itself. Chief Justice Warren Burger in 1977 suggested that forty to fifty percent of practicing American lawyers were not qualified to represent their clients adequately. Some studies suggest that a lower but still significant percentage of practicing lawyers are not qualified to do an adequate job. In spite of studies which show that most attorneys are well qualified, pronouncements like those of Chief Justice Burger seem to carry more weight. Perhaps because of his stature, his voice is heard most loudly. The result is another blow to the self-esteem of many lawyers who are hard-working and competent.

There is also a criticism which originated within the legal profession and is shared by the public. This criticism paints successful attorneys as elitists who fail to serve the masses. Instead, they serve the interests of prevailing social and economic interests. Successful lawyers are seen as working for the rich and as inimical to the interests of the average or working-class citizen. This view seems popular among many persons and can further reduce the self-esteem of an attorney who encounters it over and over again in dealings with people outside the profession.

THE PROBLEM OF LACK OF TRAINING

A complaint heard from many lawyers is that the training they received in law school is inadequate for the job they have to do. They do learn about legal theory, but they learn little about practical skills they will have to use on a daily basis. More important, they receive little, if any, training in human relations or communications. Consider for a moment what many lawyers must do. They are confronted by people who are emotionally upset. Clients may be enraged, anxious, depressed, confused, or scared. They may need reassurance and comforting. In fact, the lawyers' success in gathering information and planning strategy may depend upon the type of relationship he can establish with a client. The same holds true of witnesses. If a sense of trust and understanding is not established, the lawyer may be working under a serious handicap. Attorneys working for legal services organizations seem particularly susceptible in this area. Their clients are almost always poor, confused, frightened, and at the mercy of the legal system. Emotional intensity is high in many of these cases, and the lawyer cannot help being affected.

In addition to hampering work, constant exposure to human problems also can have a draining effect on attorneys. As we have seen in so many professions, this type of exposure leads to emotional exhaustion. If lawyers had the skills to practice "detached concern" they might avoid burnout. But a quick review of the law school curriculum shows little preparation in the area of human relations.

We have also found lawyers who complain that they received insufficient training in the organization and preparation of cases. Most time is spent on theory and landmark cases, the foundation for any practitioner of law. However, occasional mock trials are apparently insufficient to prepare young lawyers for working on real cases. Lacking these skills, new attorneys must spend inordinate amounts of time preparing their cases, reducing time for their personal lives and adding to the stresses of their work. Legal services attorneys, sometimes with double the caseload of private practitioners, are even more stressed. They want to do a good job and end up sacrificing too much personal time trying to keep up with their caseloads. As we have seen in other professions, the more that work cuts into personal time, the more likely a person is to suffer from burnout.

THE PROBLEM OF MONEY

Most lawyers undoubtedly enter the profession with the expectation that they will be paid handsomely for their skills and hard work. Once into the profession, however, the monetary rewards are discovered to be not as great as had been imagined. Because of a lack of training and legal experience, most new attorneys cannot establish their own practice. They also lack the financial know-how to do so. Therefore, most law school graduates attempt to join an established firm as associates. The experienced attorneys are partners in the firm. Recent studies suggest the *median* annual salary for partners is about $65,000, while for associates it is about $24,500. Some graduates of prestigious law schools may make up to $30,000 their first year out of school, but such jobs are relatively scarce. Half of the associates are making less than $24,500 a year. Although not a pauper's salary, it may be far less than the new attorney had hoped for. If the lawyer works for legal services agencies, the salary may be considerably lower than the figure mentioned for associates. It may take up to *eight years* to make $30,000 working for a legal services agency. Lack of financial rewards is a major factor in lawyer burnout.

Because of the financial nature of law firms. partners organize their business to maximize profits. This usually translates into having associates generate much of the money. The "rule of three" approach expects associates to generate three times their salary in billings. Thus, a $20,000-a-year associate would be expected to generate $60,000 a year in business. Partners, although eager to gain revenue, are less eager to add new partners, since this will cut into profits. Thus, the hope of achieving partner status is limited by economics. It is also limited by intense competition between associates for the few partnerships that might become available. With salaries low, prospects for achieving partnership and a higher salary are pretty dim. A current surplus of lawyers only adds to the competition and further reduces prospects for financial improvement.

THE PROBLEM OF POOR MANAGEMENT

A final cause of burnout for attorneys is the poor management practices encountered in many law firms. Young associates are eager to do well and attain the status of partner. However, it is not always clear to them what they are expected to do. At times, different partners may have different expectations, and the new associate may be caught in the middle. Lack of clear communication of expectations places a heavy burden on the associates' shoulders. Not wanting to appear too dependent or confused, they may muddle through six months or a year not knowing if their work is up to expectations.

Law firms may not have a formal program for evaluating the quality of associates' performances. The criteria upon which good work and thus progress toward a partnership is judged may be unclear or unknown. In some instances this may be intentional, so that associates may be dismissed and replaced with newer, younger, less expensive associates. The effects of this type of pressure, of having to be competitive yet not being told how one is doing, can be overwhelming.

A recent phenomenon reflects the reaction to the factors just discussed. There are increasing attempts to establish unions for lawyers and nonlegal personnel working in law firms. Lawyers can be terminated from a law firm for no apparent cause other than that their performance didn't meet some vague or undefined criteria. There is no recourse in such cases. Thus, the strength of the unionizing movement is a reflection of the lack of job security felt by many young attorneys. Not only are their salaries disappointing, but their fear of losing their jobs for no clear reason is a cause of worry and stress as well. It leads to more competition in a field which may be too competitive to begin with. The thought of losing one's job, always in the back of one's mind, can be a source of incredible tension. Knowing there may be hundreds of lawyers who would willingly take that job can only increase the pressure. Burnout becomes a likely result.

Poor management is reflected in other ways. Associates are often given minor cases to handle or asked to do research work on someone else's cases. The work soon becomes repetitive, dull, and routine. With very little actual responsibility for handling cases of importance, an associate may view his work as unimportant and insignificant. This may lead to low morale and may soon affect the accuracy and efficiency of his or her work. A feeling of being used may develop. All of these conditions can increase the likelihood of burnout.

Finally, there seems to be a lack of professional growth opportunities for many lawyers. Overworked, with too many clients and too many cases to prepare, believing their work is unimportant, many associates begin to spin their wheels. They begin to see law as a dead-end profession. Opportunities to develop new skills or to apply already existing ones seem not to exist. Associates are expected to fill their time and, if it isn't filled, to ask for more work to fill it. The chances to discuss cases, strategy, recent developments, or important decisions are limited. The opportunity to take courses which might aid professional growth is often not provided. The attorney may begin to feel stagnant. Without professional growth there is a likelihood of a decreased professional self-image among young lawyers and consequent feelings that they may not be keeping up with the competition, many of whom are after their jobs. They may begin to lose confidence in themselves as lawyers and to see themselves more as high-priced law clerks.

SYMPTOMS OF LAWYER BURNOUT

PHYSICAL

As we have seen in many other professions, the initial symptoms of burnout are fatigue and exhaustion. Long hours and intense concentration are physically demanding. But the fatigue under discussion here is not that caused by hard work. Rest does not cure this fatigue. A long weekend away from the job is not enough either. This fatigue starts in the morning upon awakening. The person begins to dread going to work, and even thinking about the job brings on the fatigue. The tiredness lasts throughout the day, the attorney having to push hard to get through tasks that were formerly much easier. At home there isn't enough energy to play with the kids or to go out to dinner or a movie. There is seemingly no energy available for any activity.

With depleted energy, the attorney becomes more susceptible to a wide variety of illnesses. Colds, flu, and headaches appear more frequently and last longer. Shaking a common cold becomes a struggle, and once the cold is over it may return quickly. Such minor illnesses are more a nuisance than a danger. After a while, however, more serious stress-related problems begin to appear. Coronary problems, respiratory infections, ulcers, severe headaches, skin disorders, and back pains become commonplace. Such psychosomatic disorders are real and are more likely to occur in an attorney who is tired and less able to tolerate the stressful nature of legal work. Current psychological thought recognizes an emotional component in all physical illness, and nowhere is this concept more clearly appropriate than in the physical symptoms of burnout.

INTELLECTUAL

Intellectual burnout has several distinctive symptoms which follow closely on the heels of the physical symptoms just discussed. One of the first signs is a loss of clarity in intellectual functioning. Partly because of fatigue, the mind does not work as efficiently or clearly. Decisions become more difficult to make. Does a particular point of law pertain to a current case? Will a particular judge respond to a certain type of argument? Such decisions were formerly arrived at with some clarity and feelings of confidence. Now both sides of the question seem equally plausible. The decision seems insoluble. Such indecision is not restricted to work but spills over into the attorney's private life as well. Where to go on vacation, whether or not to get the house repaired, and many other formerly routine decisions become major stumbling blocks. Part of the problem in decision making can be traced to slight slippages in memory. Information previously on the tip of the tongue can now be recalled only with effort and sometimes not at all. Forgetfulness may extend to appointments with clients or friends. The attorney may run errands and not remember what the main reason for the errand was. Memory becomes less effective.

A second intellectual symptom is the development of a cynical and negative outlook. At work this is displayed in various ways. Suggestions and proposed changes are met with skepticism. Instead of looking for positive parts of a proposal, the burnout victim nit-picks and concentrates on weaknesses and problems with the plan. Closed off to innovation and alternative approaches, the burned-out lawyer opts for the less demanding approach, maintaining the status quo. Opportunities for growth and improvement are lost. The mind is in neutral, and the burnout victim won't shift to move forward. The lawyer becomes negative not only to the ideas of others but also to self-generated ideas. One's own ideas also require energy and effort to develop. Rather than invest the energy, the attorney takes the easy way out and suppresses creativity and problem-solving skills. The result is one who functions at the lowest acceptable level.

The burnout victim has neither the ambition nor the energy for high-level legal work. So the attorney begins to go through the motions and stay with the familiar and comfortable. The quality of legal services to clients begins to drop as a minimum amount of energy is invested in each case. A form of categorization is used. Cases are viewed more in terms of their similarities and less in terms of their individual differences. Divorce cases become all alike, and the divorce-case "formula" is followed. It is as if the paperwork could be the same for every client, with only the name changed where necessary. The lawyer could as easily represent the husband or the wife, the plaintiff or the defendant, with no change in feeling or attitude. If cases are lost, blame is easily placed on the client for not cooperating enough or not being a "good enough" witness. Or the judge may be blamed for being obstinate, unfair, too conservative, or too liberal. Any excuse will do as long as it obscures the attorney's own lack of effort on the case. The burned-out attorney has become a technician and has lost touch with the challenges to creativity, intellect, and competence that once were motivators.

EMOTIONAL

Attorneys often meet with clients who are beset with emotional problems of severe intensity. Deaths, divorces, custody hearings, and law suits are often accompanied by intense feelings of guilt, hostility, fear, and embarassment. A natural human reaction when confronted by the emotions of others is to experience emotionality oneself. To exist in a state of continual emotional arousal is unhealthy. Fatigue and exhaustion are the first signs of such arousal. In order to protect oneself, natural defenses are brought into play. The attorney develops a psychological "insulation" against the client's feelings. One way this is accomplished is by ignoring or denying the feelings of the client. If a woman has been battered by her husband and is seeking a divorce, the burned-out lawyer will "choose" not to deal with the client's emotions. Rather, he or she will concentrate on the facts and figures of the case, the number of children, the husband's income, the value of the home, and so forth. Another technique is to view the client in legal terms. The divorce-seeking wife becomes "the plaintiff," an accused murderer becomes "the killer." At times, the attorney may become convinced that clients deserve the problems they have. If they were smarter, they wouldn't be in the trouble they're in. If the wife was smarter, she would have left her abusive husband long ago. If the renters had any sense, they would have read the fine print in the contract and would be getting their deposit back. By viewing them in increasingly negative ways, attorneys can justify their clients' suffering and minimize its effect on their own lives.

Legal-services attorneys are particularly susceptible to emotional insulation. Confronted by unreasonably high caseloads and clients who are poor and uneducated, the emotional intensity they face is constant and at extremely high levels. Time pressures and self-protection force the attorneys to adopt an assembly-line approach. No time for individual feelings of fear, anger, or hurt. Get the facts, throw together the best case possible in too little time, and see the next client. Emotional arousal is not only uncomfortable for the attorney, but it also takes time to deal with, time that is not available.

The burned-out attorney avoids the humanness of clients. Their hurt, fear, or anger is dangerous to the attorney, and all the techniques mentioned above insulate attorneys and keep them from becoming emotionally involved.

SOCIAL

Although insulated from the emotions of clients, the attorney pays a price for this protection. When work is over, the attorney has a family which has concerns and emotions, too. Johnny may have been in a fight and is hurt and frightened. Mary may be worried about a test at school. The attorney's spouse may be feeling neglected because of the lawyer's long hours at work and want some attention and affection. Unfortunately, the effective insulation techniques from work have become habits. They can't be turned off when the attorney walks through the door. Tired and emotionally exhausted from work, new demands are placed on the attorney's already depleted emotional reserves. It is no surprise that the same techniques are then applied at home. Listening to Johnny's fear and hurt would only lead to similar feelings in the tired lawyer. So the attorney plops down in front of the TV to "watch the news." If interruptions occur, the spouse is asked to "handle it." After dinner, there is the paper to read. If these don't provide enough respite, the cynicism and negativism from work may emerge at home. Johnny may be blamed for starting the fight or told to learn to handle his own affairs. Mary may be admonished to study harder or her feelings of worry minimized by saying, "You usually do OK." The emotional needs of family members are not dealt with, only the attorney's need to avoid emotional interaction. Many burnout victims bring work home or, worse, go back to work to finish what "must" be done. The avoidance of emotional involvement in this flight into work must be recognized.

The need for emotional insulation is mirrored by another problem. The role of the lawyer includes being competent and in control. This implies that attorneys should control their emotions. It would be a sign of weakness to admit that one was worried about a case or upset about what was happening to a client. In such a competitive profession, with so many competing for so few promotions, it is difficult to admit weakness to a supervisor or a competitor. Thus, attorneys not only shut themselves off from the feelings of clients, they also deny expression to their own feelings. Colleagues who undoubtedly share similar feelings and could be a source of support are not allowed to do so. The burned-out attorney keeps personal emotions private. Again, the habits developed at work are unwittingly carried home. The always-competent and in-control lawyer cannot admit weakness at home. Emotions are withheld from family members, and meaningful communication begins to dwindle. The idea of total victory which becomes important in the courtroom begins to pervade the lawyer's personality. Arguments and disputes at home are handled in the same way. Total victory is achieved by devastating the opponent's argument, whether the opponent is another attorney or one's spouse or child. Instead of seeking support and compassion, the lawyer becomes isolated and must live alone with fears, anxieties, and insecurities.

SPIRITUAL

The final stage of burnout reflects a loss of meaning in the life of an attorney. The dream of an exciting, important career which helps people begins to fade. The motives which led the young person to enter the legal profession become vague.

The first sign of spiritual burnout is an increased frequency of thoughts about the futility of the job. At first these may center around whether the hard work is worth the relatively low pay and heavy stress. Attorneys may question whether the time spent in law school and the struggling to become a partner with no guarantee of promotion is worth it. The more such questions are answered in the negative, the more likely burnout is to become severe. Thoughts may later turn to whether the attorney's work is even beneficial to clients. Is the work performed preparing a case really going to make such difference in the client's life? If this kind of question is answered negatively, burnout is complete.

If the attorneys' jobs hold no meaning, make no difference, this will be reflected in a lack of concern and respect for clients. They become insignificant cogs in the process which produces a paycheck for the attorney. Realizing the job holds no meaning, these attorneys simply go through the motions of caring and working. With so much time and energy invested in their careers, attorneys find it almost impossible to change professions. A career change would suggest failure and further damage the concept of a competent, in-control professional. So, they hang on, shells of the bright young idealists who first entered the profession.

Another sign of spiritual burnout is increased dependence on alcohol and other drugs. At first, alcohol may be used to ''unwind'' after a stressful day. It may even be a part of a working luncheon with a client or colleague. As burnout deepens, the use of alcohol and other drugs increases. The pain associated with the discovery that one's career and life do not have importance and meaning, that one has been struggling to get to the top of a profession which lacks personal meaning, is devastating. With family relationships not working, with colleagues seen as competitors and not allies, burned-out attorneys are alone with their pain. Alcohol and drugs are readily available ways to ease the pain, at least temporarily.

Many attorneys decide to leave the practice of law. They recognize their burnout and choose to deal with it by a career change. The more unfortunate ones lack the courage to take this step. They remain and are unhappy, hostile, and ineffective. They suffer, their families and clients suffer, and the legal profession suffers.

CURES FOR LAWYER BURNOUT

PHYSICAL

The techniques for reversing physical burnout are quite simple and will probably come as no surprise. They include sound nutrition, regular exercise, rest, and a consistent stress-reduction program.

With heavy caseloads, too many clients, and long working hours which include evenings, lawyers must often eat on the run. This means they may rush through meals. Our first suggestion is to make the time to eat and eat slowly. Try never to eat alone. Make meals social events that do more than just put energy into the body. Create the opportunity for emotional energy as well.

Another drawback to rushed meals is the high frequency of fast-food consumption. Relatively nonnutritious foods, while gaining time, do little to replenish the enormous amounts of energy expended during intense concentration. In addition, such foods do little to prepare the body to deal with the stresses discussed in the section on causes. It would be much more effective to keep highly nutritious foods in the office or one's desk. Small cans of juice could replace coffee. Fruit, seeds, nuts, or bars made of combinations of these can be stored easily and kept at hand. If a refrigerator is available, many other healthy foods can be made a part of every working day.

If lunch is usually eaten in a restaurant, try not to discuss business. Avoid drinking alcohol at lunch, as it saps energy and reduces the body's ability to tolerate stress. Limit coffee and sugar intake at lunch. Try to eat a light lunch to avoid afternoon fatigue. It would be better to eat a hearty breakfast and a lighter lunch.

Physical exercise is another suggestion which will do much to alleviate the physical symptoms of burnout. Regular exercise, on a daily basis, if possible, is crucial. Make it a part of your day, whether before work, after work, or during lunch. Any exercise which will improve cardiovascular functioning is fine. Swimming, jogging, racquetball, basketball, or walking are just several of many possibilities.

Lawyers, like many professionals, spend long amounts of time sitting.

This can put unusual stresses on the body; back pains are only one sign that something needs to be done. Stretching exercises are a simple and effective way to combat this problem. Make a point of taking five minutes every hour to get up and stretch. (Look in Chapter 15 of Part Two for suggested stretches.) In addition, isometric exercises can be performed while in the office or while sitting at a desk. (See Chapter 12 for suggestions.) The goal is to break up the long periods of sitting. Make these stretches a part of your day. Schedule them. It is really not very difficult to take control of one's schedule as opposed to letting the schedule do the controlling. If it is impossible to do the exercises, at least get up and walk around the office once or twice. Better still, go down the hall or up a couple flights of stairs. The main thing is never to stay seated for more than an hour at a time. Also, take the Sitting for Health test in Chapter 15 of Part Two. It will help to determine whether sitting is a problem.

If long hours and evening work begin to accumulate, be sure to plan rest periods into the workday. If a job requires three hours of overtime, take *at least half* of that time off the next day. Schedule it. Make sure it's taken. What may be lost in time the following day will be more than made up for by increased efficiency and productivity. A rested body can do more than a tired one. Plan into each day two fifteen-minute rest periods. Make it guilt free by making it policy. During these periods, don't work or think about work. If possible, close your eyes and relax. Visualize doing something relaxing and enjoyable. Take a vacation to a glamorous spot in your imagination. This suggestion may be recognized as daydreaming. We recommend it. Again, the benefits will far outweigh the small amount of time spent resting.

Finally, some form of relaxation technique can prove very beneficial during periods of stress. Many variations, such as deep muscle relaxation, biofeedback, transcendental meditation, the quieting response, and hatha yoga breathing, are all effective. They all have in common that they are easy to practice and learn and can be used easily during periods of high stress. One such simple procedure is described in Part Two.

INTELLECTUAL

One of the major causes of lawyer burnout is criticism and lack of respect from the public. To counteract these problems, we suggest that lawyers read some of the many articles which provide evidence and opinions to the contrary. One such article can be found in *The Solicitor's Journal* dated July 27, 1979, authored by Harry Cohen. Reading such articles will demonstrate to lawyers that they are held in higher esteem than is generally believed. Criticisms of lawyers from within the profession are also a problem and should be countered. Again, the suggestion is to seek out articles and stories which give a more balanced view of lawyers and their profession.

A major problem for lawyers in private firms and legal services organizations is the lack of training in interpersonal skills. When dealing with human beings who are beset with problems and emotionally upset, special skills are needed. Some persons have these skills naturally. Most can learn them. Our suggestion here is to build such skills onto already existing legal skills. Law schools don't usually offer such courses, but they can be found in most universities, community colleges, open universities, and free universities. If none of these is handy, seek out a community mental health center or social services agency. Workers in these organization use such skills daily and are often eager to share their knowledge. Contact the consultation and education director for information.

The complaint of boring, routine work can in part be addressed by varying the daily routine. Don't always do the same tasks at the same time. Do paperwork in the morning some days and in the afternoon on other days. Don't always do correspondence at the same time. Don't always interview at the same time. Organize the day for variety. When possible, collaborate on cases which fall outside of the usual range of cases. If one's specialty is real estate law, occasionally sit in on a criminal case or a divorce case. Again, the important thing is to take control of events that fill one's day instead of letting them take control.

The stresses that affect lawyers have been well documented. What is surprising is that so many lawyers are unaware, whether out of denial or apathy, of the particular sources of stress in their lives. Our suggestion here is to do a careful, thorough analysis of each day's activities for a week. Pay attention to the times when one is tense. Notice when unhappiness or anger is present. If sweaty palms, headaches, rapid breathing, or fatigue is experienced, make a note of it. What happened just prior to these symptoms of stress? What people were involved? Where did it take place? What was your role in creating the situation? Keep a record of such situations at work and at home for a week. Also keep a record of when you feel happy and relaxed. In what situation did this occur, with whom and where? Try to schedule some of these pleasant events into each day. (See Chapter 16 of Part Two for suggestions, especially the Stressful Habits Test.) Once sources of stress are identified, concentrate on changing those that can be changed. Those that are not changeable, over which one has no control, should be left alone. Don't worry about things beyond your control. Do spend energy thinking of ways to make changes in controllable areas.

Advancement in an organization, whether a private law firm or a legal services agency, depends in part on the skills one possesses and uses. Inquire of supervisors as to what is specifically expected on the job. Spend time making sure this is clear. Once this is determined, list the skills that are needed to meet expectations. Make plans to develop skills that are missing. Find courses, workshops, or seminars which will teach these skills. Seek out other lawyers who have these skills and learn from them. Again, the key here is to make time for these activities. Don't let the schedule prevent professional growth.

EMOTIONAL

Emotional symptoms may be countered in several ways. One suggestion is to use timeout periods. When stress is heaviest and efficiency seems to be lowered, walk away for a time. We aren't talking about scheduled breaks here. Rather, these are unplanned periods of relatively brief duration when stress is at its peak. Go to a quiet spot, maybe a bathroom. Take several slow, deep breaths. Close the eyes and just relax. Close off the rest of the world and for a few moments just be alone. The work will be there when the timeout period is over. The body, which is in a state of tension and going at full throttle, needs a break. Don't push it beyond its limits.

The inability to deal with the emotional intensity of clients causes problems for lawyers. Being confronted by persons experiencing stress produces stress in lawyers. The natural tendency of persons in such a situation is to insulate themselves from the feelings of clients by the various methods discussed under symptoms. One way to avoid this is to practice "detached concern." This approach recognizes the reality of the pain that clients are feeling, but it also recognizes that dealing with the pain is the responsibility of the client, not the responsibility of the lawyer. No one should attempt to take on the emotions of a client. It doesn't help either the client or the attorney. Psychotherapists and counselors who have learned this lesson are able to avoid both emotional insulation and burnout.

The other side of the insulation coin revolves around expression of the attorney's own feelings. While beginning at the office with clients, it soon spreads over into the lawyer's personal life. To counter this, one must do two things: regain awareness of what one's feelings really are and learn to express those feelings in an appropriate manner. The simplest and most effective way to accomplish these two tasks is to take a course in interpersonal communications or assertiveness training. Such courses are offered in workshops, at universities and community colleges, and in adult education programs at many high schools. The number of self-help books dealing with these topics is overwhelming and there should be little trouble in locating one. Reading the books is important, but practicing the skills is essential. Classes offer the opportunity to practice, but it is also possible to form groups of interested people with whom to practice. Two excellent books are *Parent Effectiveness Training,* by Thomas Gordon, and *Your Perfect Right,* by Robert Alberti and Michael Emmons.

A simple and extremely valuable technique is to develop and practice a "decompression" routine. Essentially this means to find time between the end of work and the resumption of family life to unwind and slow down. Great racehorses and world-class athletes, upon completing a race or a competition, keep moving to cool down their bodies slowly. In a similar manner, an emotional cooling down after a day filled with tension will be helpful. Don't leave for home right away. Sit at a desk or on a couch for a few minutes and do some visual imagery. Close the eyes and concentrate on breathing deeply and slowly. Think of the positive events that have happened during the day—a smile from someone, a good job done on a case, a joke shared between colleagues, whatever. Try to relive those pleasant experiences. Take a different way home, possibly a longer route. Notice new buildings, stores, shops, parks, et cetera. Make a point to discover three places or objects that haven't been noticed before. Don't rush home. Slow down and relax. Upon arrival at home, don't go right to the door. Walk around the block or sit in the car for a couple of minutes and listen to the radio. By following such a routine, the day's stresses can be dissipated and a more refreshed person will walk in the front door.

SOCIAL

Most of the social symptoms discussed earlier revolved around difficulties in maintaining satisfying and productive interpersonal relationships. Thus, our suggestions will center around remedies for this situation. For example, establish meetings with clients to discuss the pressures that are inherent in legal work. Let them know the large number of cases that are pending, the time pressures that are involved, and any other aspects of the job that are stress-inducing. It may sound like complaining or whining, but it can prove beneficial too. The lawyer will break down barriers and appear more human to the client. The level of trust generated by such self-disclosure, the view of the attorney as less than perfect and omnipotent will set the client at ease and establish rapport. It will also make it unnecessary for the lawyer to maintain the aura of total competence and emotional detachment which is impossible and so damaging. We are not suggesting that lawyers dump personal problems onto their clients. We are suggesting that they be honest with their clients and not play a role which is unhealthy.

Another suggestion is to form a "colleagues club." In private firms this might include associates; in legal services agencies, junior and middle-level attorneys. Schedule regular physical activities. Plan a racquetball tournament, bicycle races, running events, or a one-on-one basketball tournament. Better yet, plan a pentathlon with the above four events and one other. If physical activities aren't especially attractive, schedule bridge matches, backgammon games, or dart tournaments. Plan quarterly potluck dinners or picnics. Go to ball games or cultural events as a group. Have the club perform some public service event on a volunteer basis. The major goal is to bring colleagues together in a pleasant, relaxed setting. All of the above activities provide the opportunity for attorneys to get to know one another as human beings, persons who have joys, fears, worries, and dreams. Sharing human attributes is often easier in such informal settings, away from the office where humanness is hidden.

The colleagues club could also schedule regular meetings with partners or senior supervisors. These would be meetings called by the junior and middle-level attorneys to discuss concerns related to their jobs and the legal profession. Ask senior attorneys to participate in a program of in-service training. The expertise and skills of experienced attorneys can be shared with young lawyers, and at the same time a sense of comradeship can develop. The benefits of junior-level–initiated meetings are several: concerns of the junior attorneys can be addressed directly, senior attorneys can observe that the younger attorneys are interested in the firm and the profession, young attorneys can develop a sense of having some influence in the organization, and, by helping young attorneys with their concerns, senior lawyers can build morale and establish a sense of teamwork in the organization. The colleagues club can also meet to discuss any of the problems which are causing stress on the job. Stresses that lead to anger, fear, or envy can be dealt with in an open manner beneficial to many. Appoint a burnout "lookout" to be aware of early signs in colleagues. This person's job will be to notify anyone exhibiting symptoms and to alert at least one other colleague. The support network can begin its work. We have found that many victims of burnout held the idea that "it couldn't happen to me." With such attitudes, awareness becomes blunted and the role of "lookout" becomes more important.

Another suggestion is for attorneys to improve their relationships at home. The stresses at work and the resulting emotional insulation can spread to home life. As a result, marriages experience profound problems or even fail totally. Seek our marriage-enrichment workshops which are directed toward improving troubled marriages. Contact the Association for Marriage and Family Therapists to locate such workshops. Consider marital or family counseling. It means admitting there are problems and that the lawyer isn't perfect and does need help. It means admitting that the attorney is human. The interpersonal communications suggestions listed in the emotional suggestions section above can be followed with one's spouse, and beneficial results obtained. The first and hardest step is to recognize and admit that there is a problem. The rest is easier.

Much can be done to prevent problems before a marriage gets into trouble. Schedule time that is family time and remains so. This time should be inviolate. Part of the time can be for a spouse, part for children, and part for the whole family. Scheduling may seem funny, but it is most often people whose schedules control them who don't have time for the family. So use the schedule as an ally, and build in family time. The same principles that governed the junior-level–initiated meetings apply to family time. Let other family members initiate suggestions and voice concerns. (See Chapter 18 of Part Two for a model family meeting.)

Invite family members to the office and to court when appropriate. Let them see what a lawyer does, what some pleasant and unpleasant parts of the job are. Ask them to portray a jury and react to legal arguments and render decisions on a current case. Have them "prepare" an opposing case and present it. In addition to building closeness, it will be fun, and the legal profession is less likely to be seen as a source of negative feelings. Don't forget to schedule or include friends in this suggestion. Decide what persons are fun to be with and help one feel relaxed. Seek these people out and spend time with them. Avoid those who aren't fun or cause tension. Remove them from the schedule.

Spouses can also establish an informal or formal group. No one knows the problems faced by lawyers' spouses better than lawyers' spouses. Rotate the meetings from home to home. Go out to dinner and a movie as a group. Provide the opportunities to share the positive and negative aspects of being married to a lawyer. Create a support group which will help one get over rough times. Schedule a time for the group to go to the office and to court to see what those situations are really like. Invite the spouses of other professionals to come to dinner and share what their problems are like. More similarities than differences will appear, and the support group will enlarge.

SPIRITUAL

Spiritual burnout is the end of the line. When burnout reaches this stage, there is little that can be done. So these suggestions should be implemented as early as possible.

One of the easiest suggestions is to keep a journal which lists all of the positive things that occur during the workday. A compliment from a colleague on work well done, a thank-you from a client whose life has been helped, a favor done for a secretary or a co-worker—all of these and others should be listed. The goal of this exercise is to remind the attorney that the job is neither meaningless nor all negative.

Another suggestion to add meaning to the job is to develop a personal code of ethics. Think and decide what is important morally and ethically to oneself. Write these ideas down as clearly and as concretely as possible. Read this code every couple of months and stick to it. If instances at work occur where the code is violated, think about what else might have been done and why it wasn't. Stick to the personal code of ethics. The positive feelings generated by this activity will do much to eliminate spiritual symptoms of burnout. Once a year, write out the reasons for remaining in the profession. Decide what material and nonmaterial rewards one is seeking. Does the job in fact produce these rewards? If not, what needs to be changed to produce them? If changes are not possible, then a career change should be considered.

Teamwork has already been mentioned and this suggestion also deals with it. Team up with another attorney on a case that is exciting. Although requiring extra time, the excitement and enthusiasm that are generated can inject meaning back into the profession. Once a year, take a case outside of one's area of expertise. Seek help on this case and offer help to someone else on a particularly tough case of theirs. When not following these suggestions, ask questions of lawyers working on exciting cases or in other areas of the law. Try and follow their line of reasoning and seek out nuances in their presentation and strategy.

These will help keep contact with the profession as a whole and give a sense of belonging to a larger, more meaningful profession. Make time for such activities!

6. Police Officers

"When constabulary duty's to be done,
The policeman's lot is not a happy one!"
—William S. Gilbert

Ponder for a moment the idea that to show tenderness is to be viewed as weak. Consider for a while the assumption that every human encounter that is a part of your job could be a life-and-death situation.

What sort of life would that be? Well, it is the life that police officers have chosen for themselves. There is little room for sentiment (except for one another) in the life of a police officer. Even those the rest of us ordinarily turn to for comfort, our familes, are not often sought out. One reason is that they may be viewed as persons who should be protected from the daily horrors many police officers see, hear about, or experience themselves. Another may be that it is easy to take off a uniform at the end of a day. It is not so easy to take off the attitudes, values, assumptions, and beliefs that may ensure survival on the job but are inappropriate so far as family interaction is concerned. Many families complain because the police officer treats them like criminals!

Without the ordinary supports of family life, police officers tend to turn to one another and in the process reinforce a set of assumptions that prevent honest interaction and affection. The image of the tough male that is sterotypical for most of us is actively supported in police bars, clubs, and cliques. Tough cops are honored by cops. The problem is that tough cops burn out.

What happens in the lives of police officers that leads so many of them to suffer from burnout? Our investigations suggest that at least the following causes seem to be operating.

WHAT WENT WRONG IN THE PRECINCT?

THE PROBLEM OF SELF-ESTEEM

Perhaps the most important cause of burnout in police officers is a loss of self-esteem or self-worth. It is crucial for emotional health and effective functioning that people feel positively about themselves, see themselves as competent and capable. The absence of such feelings and beliefs is often the precursor of emotional difficulties and lowered levels of personal functioning.

Many of the police officers working today, as in the past, were motivated by the dream of protecting and serving. The double duties of protecting the weak from stronger, evil persons and providing assistance in various emergency situations motivated many persons into choosing law enforcement as an occupation. Their dream, to protect and to serve, is indeed a noble one. However, a series of factors, which we will describe below, work to prevent that dream from being realized. The result of these shattered dreams is a loss in self-esteem, a feeling that is reflected in officers' reports that the job they are doing is not meaningful or important and that they aren't doing the job very well.

A cycle is established where low self-esteem leads to a diminished ability to tolerate stress and frustration, which in turn leads to further loss of self-esteem, which in turn further lowers the ability to handle stress, and so on.

What are some of the factors that operate to diminish the self-esteem of police officers and prevent their dreams from being realized?

THE PROBLEM OF POLICE WORK ITSELF

Many police officers have described their work as boring. An estimated eighty-five percent of police activities are unrelated to criminal activities. Such tasks as dispensing information, and directions, dealing with minor disputes, handling family quarrels, and other service activities occupy most of a police officer's on-duty time. The dream of preventing crime is seriously thwarted by the nature of the job.

Such service activities can be important and helpful. However, officers are prevented from experiencing the fruits of their work. Because of the sheer volume of calls that officers must handle, they usually don't have the opportunity to see the effects that their intervention produces. If they intervene in a family quarrel, what happens to the family? If the family is referred to a social service agency, do they learn to handle their problems or do they continue to quarrel? Chances are that the officer will never know. If a juvenile is arrested, what happens? Does a stay in a corrections facility help or do the criminal activities resume after release? What evidence can an officer get that intervention made a difference? How can the officers know that their job was meaningful and that they did it well?

Sociologists have suggested that a role conflict exists for many officers. Their dream tells them that they should protect the weak and the less able. Their job requires them to arrest many minority and economically deprived persons, those so often engaged in street crime. At the same time, they are experiencing this contradiction. They know that white-collar crime, infinitely more profitable and damaging, is also occurring and that little can be done to stop it. Thus, the dream of protecting and serving is further shattered, and feelings of self-esteem are lowered. The cycle continues.

THE PROBLEM OF THE CRIMINAL JUSTICE SYSTEM

The dream of protecting and serving is blocked by the vary nature of the job of law enforcement. Another factor blocking the dream is the role of the criminal justice system. To many officers the attitude of the courts seems to be that the accused criminal has more rights than the victim. Only about twenty percent of serious felonies result in an arrest, at times because the police don't believe they have enough evidence to stand up in a trial "biased" in favor of the accused. Of the arrests made for serious felonies, only about five percent result in a conviction. Often, some technical point of law results in a case being dismissed and a criminal returned to the streets. Thus, about ninety percent of serious felonies don't result in convictions.

When a conviction is obtained, lenient parole and probation policies can place the felon back on the streets in a relatively short period of time. An amazing story is that two days after the arrest of the "Son of Sam" killer, David Berkowitz, a pretrial service agency for the city of New York recommended that he be released in his own custody because of a lack of family members living close by and a lack of any previous criminal record.

Corrections organizations just don't seem to be able to make much headway in rehabilitating convicted offenders. Budgetary problems, lack of proven rehabilitation methods, and overcrowding of institutions can result in unchanged criminals being released prematurely and returned to the streets.

The arrest process may then be seen as a senseless repetition of "paper pushing" whereby reports are filed and left to gather dust, with infrequent attention paid to them. Criminals are arrested and then either released or, if convicted, paroled or placed on probation. Is it any wonder that police officers can develop feelings of doing an unimportant, useless job?

THE PROBLEM OF PUBLIC APPRECIATION

Another severe blow to the self-esteem of plice officers is the perceived lack of public appreciation for their work. Press accounts of police activities, often rushed to meet publication deadlines, may be incomplete, leaving an impression unfavorable to the police. Surveys of officers have shown that many believe their coverage by the press to be unfair and biased. Some examples of attitudes:

Police do not have the respect of the people.
Police do not protect the interests of the lower class.
Police are mean.
Police pay more attention to minor crimes than to major violations.
Police have a separate way of handling blacks and other minorities.
Police are dishonest.
Police are cruel in the search and arrest of suspects.

These negative feelings were expressed toward the police by minority persons in a recent survey. With increasing political activity by minorities, more reports of police brutality and racism are being voiced. Needless to say, many officers see these accusations as unfair and at variance with how they see their own behavior.

The general public also shows unfavorable attitudes toward the police. One indicator is voters' rejections of propositions which could help the police do a more effective job. There are increasing reports of verbal abuse heaped upon officers, who in their view are doing the best they can under extremely adverse conditions. When off duty and out of uniform, officers may hear derogatory remarks from neighbors as well as strangers.

With increasing reports of police brutality or misconduct, citizen pressures for review boards and investigations have increased. The result is that the police officer must be extremely cautious, maybe overly so, in action.

Behavior that police may think correct and appropriate may lead to hearings, disciplinary action, and citizen complaints, and so are avoided.

Thus, many factors are at work which can shape officers' views that police work, difficult and often dangerous, is unappreciated and, worse, unimportant. If no one else cares, why should they?

THE PROBLEM OF PUBLIC SUPPORT SERVICES

Due to economic "crunches," individuals, families, schools, and businesses are required to do more with less money. So are the police. Often this may mean using equipment which is inferior. It may also mean using the same number or fewer officers to meet an increased level of criminal activity. Less obvious is the lack of clerical support. Officers must fill out many forms, an activity which prevents them from being in the field, where they could be doing more important and more satisfying work. As inaccurate as TV cop shows may be, scenes of officers presenting their paperwork seem accurate.

Other factors also weigh heavily on police officers. While not directly affecting their self-esteem as police officers, these additional factors can affect officers' feelings about themselves as persons. Most importantly, they are sources of stress which can dramatically increase the likelihood of burnout.

THE PROBLEM OF PEOPLE INTERACTIONS

The nature of police work requires officers to deal with people, usually under adverse circumstances. When things are going well, the police are seldom, if ever, called. So they often see people at their worst. They invariably encounter people when emotional intensity is high. People kicking, screaming, drunk, angry, frightened, or the victims of such people; the grief of a parent whose child is lost or dead; the rage of a married couple engaged in an argument; the battered, bleeding carnage seen in automobile accidents; the feelings of sorrow and anger surrounding a case of child abuse; an elderly citizen confused, dazed, or helpless after a mugging.

It is impossible not to be touched and affected by such scenes, yet officers are expected to remain calm and in control. They are to be a parent figure to kids on their beat, marriage counselors to families in trouble; above all, they are to remain calm while the world around them may be falling apart. It seems too much to ask of any human being, but it is continually asked of law enforcement people. A woman who is raped, a child who is beaten, an elderly citizen who is robbed must all touch the affection officers feel for their own spouses, children, and parents. There are constant reminders of what can happen to them, adding to an already intense emotional state which the officer must deal with in a calm, detached, logical way.

THE PROBLEM OF EMOTIONAL INSULATION

Emotional insulation refers to the processes that officers use to minimize the emotionally arousing effects of exposure to high-intensity situations. Officers often mask or, as we will see later, even deny their emotions in order to maintain control and avoid being constantly aroused, a very unpleasant and unhealthy situation. Thus, to avoid this unpleasant state of affairs, police officers begin to discuss accident victims in terms such as "the body showed . . ." or "the suspect was bleeding." They unconsciously dehumanize the experience, unconsciously ignore the pain and emotion surrounding them. The same process is seen in physicians, psychologists, and nurses who have to deal with emotionally arousing events. The result is shutting off or insulation of the officer from the intense emotional situations inherent in police work.

Emotional insulation is a helpful and, perhaps, necessary defense mechanism. However, it is not easily turned off when officers go home. This same mechanism can prevent them from noticing and responding to the emotional needs of their families. The same detachment which is so helpful in the field can keep officer's and their family members from experiencing closeness to one another. Relatives of burned-out police officers report that they are made to feel they are not trusted or as if they were being interrogated.

THE PROBLEM OF EMOTIONAL ISOLATION

Emotional isolation refers to the process by which officers keep the negative aspects of their work from family members. Often, this reluctance to share helps prevent the officers from reliving the negative experience. Another reason is to protect family members from what has been seen, heard, and felt. So officers keep their fear, anger, frustration, and embarrassment to themselves. The goal is noble, but the price is high. The reluctance to share feelings from work often spreads into a reluctance to share feelings in general. This can increase the distance between the officer and family members. Research suggests that police officers suffering from high levels of stress are twice as likely to report feeling distant from their children. Their children are much more likely to go to their mothers for emotional support. Officers suffering from high levels of burnout also report that they don't think that their wives understand police work and how stressful their work is.

A by-product of emotional insulation and isolation is that officers may begin to spend more and more time with other officers and do their sharing with them. However, even this is not totally satisfactory. An unwritten "machismo" code makes it difficult for officers to express feelings of fear, hurt, embarrassment, or inadequacy. Instead, talk may become negative and cynical, with complaints about lack of citizen support, disdain of "deviant" citizens, comments on how offenders deserve what they got, and slurs on minority persons and people from lower socioeconomic levels.

Since contacts with co-workers may be the most (and in some cases only) satisfying ones, there is pressure to adopt and express similar values. Differences of opinion disappear, and "right" and "wrong" become clearer and more rigidly defined. This is often reflected in family life, where decisions about what's best, what's appropriate, what's right or wrong may be made unilaterally by the officer without much discussion or openness to change. This can do little but increase isolation in the family.

THE PROBLEM OF TIME DEMANDS

Police work, perhaps as no other, places incredible demands on an officer's time. First of all, there is shift work. After several weeks or months of working on a particular shift and getting their body accustomed to the routine, police officers must change to another shift. It has been shown that daytime sleep is different from and less satisfying than nighttime sleep. This, coupled with constantly shifting sleep patterns, can affect a person's natural body rhythms and lower the efficiency with which the body functions.

Added to the effects of sleep disruption is the problem of meals. Often, on-duty officers cannot eat a normal meal. Many workers may sit and eat a nutritionally sound meal in a relatively relaxed and unhurried manner. With some conversation, often humorous and pleasant, meals can be a real help in stress reduction. For police officers it is different. Often they must grab a bite of nutritionally marginal fast food, and gulp it down. They must eat when they can. Often it is under less than pleasant and relaxing circumstances. The negative effects of this practice on health and the ability to handle stress are clear.

Most people can count on not having to work on major holidays and being able to spend those days with friends and family. Police officers draw duty on Christmas, New Year's, Thanksgiving, and other holidays. The effects of such scheduling can lead to a loss of morale for many officers and to serious family problems.

Other time pressures revolve around overtime during emergencies and courtroom testimony. Emergencies can't be predicted. Although courtroom appearances are scheduled, this is done without regard to what shift an officer may be working. If either attorney wants to postpone a case or go on vacation, the case will be postponed. The officer must be there or dismissal is likely, and the work leading to the arrest will have been wasted.

THE PROBLEM OF A SATISFYING
PERSONAL LIFE

Another important factor leading to burnout in police officers is difficulty in their personal lives. Emotional insulation and isolation serve to create distance between the officer and family members and to reduce meaningful communication. Rotating shift work makes it very difficult to plan family activities very far ahead of time. Planning a picnic, attending a birthday party or a little league game, taken for granted by many people, can become very "iffy" and "chancy" events in the family of a police officer.

As mentioned before, police officers are "on duty" twenty-four hours a day, and in many cases they must carry their guns with them even when off duty. This makes it very difficult simply to relax and watch a ball game or go to dinner or watch a movie.

Thus, even though they can take off their uniforms, it is more difficult for them to take off their weapons and their attitude that they must remain cautious, vigilant, and on duty at all times. Also, their emotional detachment, useful on the job, becomes a part of their lives and can't be taken off with the uniform at the end of a shift.

When officers try to relax and get away from their work, others won't always let them. At parties, when others find out their occupation, police officers may be confronted with conversations about a ticket that was "unfairly" given, questions about why drug abuse is so high and "nothing" is being done about it, or questions about police work which raise issues officers are trying to forget. Police often don't want others to know what they do for a living, so they avoid these types of conversations. This adds to the stresses already present in an officer's personal life and makes it even more likely that social activities will involve only co-workers. Other officers will understand.

THE PROBLEM OF PHYSICAL ROLE CONFLICTS

When they are screened and subsequently graduated from a police academy or its equivalent, police officers are among the most physically fit of all Americans. However, after some time on the job, officers become more susceptible than most Americans to premature death, heart disease, coronary risk, digestive disorders, and lower-back pain. What happens to cause this dramatic turnabout? Ironically, the nature of police work is sedentary. Studies suggest that sixty-five to seventy-five percent of police work is sedentary. Long hours in a patrol car, filling out reports, taking statements from witnesses, and other such activities can fill an officer's day. Extended periods of time are characterized by inactivity. In spite of this inactivity, when the work shift is over, the officer may be physically and emotionally tired and want to sit around and relax. Police officers have been found to lead a less active life than the general population. Sedentary work and an inactive life style result in a lower state of physical fitness than among the general population. A body which becomes inactive is less able to handle stress. The many stresses of police work and personal life continue, and there is an accumulation of the stress effects. The result is increased susceptibility to various illnesses and health problems.

Not all police work is sedentary, however. Occasionally there are situations which require a burst of activity where strength or physical endurance is needed. Examples are foot chases and physical struggles. In these cases, the body, ill-prepared by inactivity, is unable to handle these sudden activities and is more susceptible to injuries.

THE PROBLEM OF STATUS

The perceived status of police officers is closely related to their levels of self-esteem and can contribute to burnout. We've seen that circumstances can lead officers to believe they are doing a job that very few people appreciate and that they aren't doing the job very well. Studies suggest that few officers believe they are doing a job which enjoys a good reputation. In fact, less than half of the general population believes that police work is a high-status profession. A part of the problem is that a greater percentage of the public thinks police work is a less prestigious occupation than police officers do! They lose a sense of personal competence, which can be compounded by personal and family difficulties.

What can be done? Changing jobs isn't so easy. The longer officers stay in the profession, the less able they feel to do anything else for a living. They feel locked into their profession, one which enjoys little status. Promotions are very difficult to come by in police departments since there are relatively few upper-level jobs. Most police officers begin and end their careers on regular patrol. Some may become sergeants, detectives, lieutenants, captains, or even chiefs, but most will not. Even specialized, more interesting and challenging assignments are very limited.

When promotions are given out, many officers feel they are distributed unfairly. Objective criteria are thought to be less important than personalities in the promotion process. The few opportunities for advancement in the organization may thus be seen as unattainable or beyond the officer's control. Transfer to another police department is possible, but the same difficulties are likely to be encountered in the new department. Such factors can only serve to lower morale.

SYMPTOMS OF POLICE BURNOUT

PHYSICAL

As in many other professions, fatigue is an early sign of burnout. The police officer, even though not physically active for several days, comes home tired. A day or even a weekend off is not enough to relieve this fatigue. Difficulty in falling asleep and in getting a good night's sleep accompanies this type of fatigue.

A generally poor level of physical conditioning is another early sign of burnout. Inactivity on the job and as a life style in general suggests a person who is less likely to be able to handle stresses which may occur at work or at home.

With a lowered level of physical conditioning, officers are prone to many physical illnesses. Among these are digestive disorders such as ulcers. In addition, there is an increased risk of coronary problems and heart disease. Problems with the area of the lower back are also common to police work, probably due to prolonged periods of sitting combined with bursts of vigorous activity.

As far as these symptoms are reflective of a lowered level of physical condition, they may be early signs that the more complex phenomenon of burnout is beginning.

INTELLECTUAL

One of the common signs of police burnout is a negative attitude toward the job. Problems with supervisors, shortages of equipment, overtime, or court-room testimony which were previously easy to handle now become frequent topics of complaint. Job-related complaints increase in frequency. Whatever was rewarding about the job seems not to be enough to balance the increasing attention paid to its negative aspects.

Following closely on the heels of negative attitudes toward the job is an attitude of cynicism. Suggestions from supervisors may be dismissed with comments such as "that makes no sense," "we've tried that before," or "the sarge is sure bucking for that promotion." The cynicism may also be directed toward the public. Criminals may more often be seen as "deserving" of what they've got, whereas previously they may have been seen as victims of difficult circumstances. This cynicism may also appear at home, where the officer may become more demanding and less appreciative of the spouse.

Burned-out officers may also demonstrate inaccurate judgment of public appreciation. They may think that no one appreciates police work. This inaccurate judgment may soon be followed by increased incidents of aggression toward the public. Verbal interchanges with citizens can become curt and more sarcastic and may even lead to the unnecessary use of force on occasion. It is more difficult to be "nice" and forgiving, even when dealing with citizen complaints and minor violations of the law.

Finally, an increased sense of unionism may be found in the burnout process. As ideals of protecting and serving recede, they are replaced by more attention to details of contracts, fringe benefits, and other administrative items. In order to help achieve these goals, incidences of "blue flu" may increase: The actual job of police work no longer being rewarding enough, officers may fail to report for duty in order to gain more concessions.

EMOTIONAL

The most common emotional symptoms of police burnout are anger and frustration which cannot be effectively expressed. Lack of public support, unfavorable court decisions, taunts from strangers, invitations to "take off the badge and fight," and arguments at home all lead to anger and frustration. They all can result in increased emotional levels which can last for extended periods of time, showing up in losses of temper and feelings of suspicion and distrust of the public and of family members.

Difficulty in handling the problems at work and at home can lead to feelings of helplessness and inadequacy. This may lead to depression, characterized by sleep disturbances, eating disturbances, and generalized feelings of pessimism at work and at home. Often, in cases of depression, there is the loss of something important. For police officers this loss may include the dream of protecting and serving, the support of the public, and the love and closeness of family.

SOCIAL

The emotional insulation and isolation previously described result in officers who have difficulty in maintaining satisfying interpersonal relationships. The mistrust and cynicism carry over into their personal lives. Officers feel alone and closed off from those closest to them, their spouses and family. They want to spare their families from the negative parts of their job and in so doing close off other important areas of communication. The control of emotions which is necessary on the job begins to take over the officer's entire life. Children of burned-out cops are known to go to their mothers much more frequently for emotional support. Wives of burned-out policemen report that conversations with their husbands are less pleasant than they used to be and that their husbands have become colder and don't seem to love them as much, if at all. Divorce rates for police officers have been estimated to be from two to four times the national average.

As things get worse at home, officers spend less and less time there. They spend more time with fellow officers, who understand their work better. However, a reluctance to share fear, anger, or inadequacy with colleagues makes the relationships with co-workers more superficial and less satisfying than they could be. Another possibility is that as things get worse at home, the officer may choose to spend time alone rather than with family or friends. The net result is similar—a lack of satisfying interpersonal relationships.

SPIRITUAL

The main spiritual symptom of burnout in police officers seems to be alcoholism. The dream of protecting and serving is falling apart; so is the officer's marriage and family life. Even relationships with colleagues are not what they might be. As a result, police may turn to drinking as a way to escape the stresses and pressures of job and family life. Other officers are experiencing the same difficulties. Drinking, initially to relax after an often frustrating day, can become a routine part of the day. The alcoholism rate for police officers is two to three times the national rate.

For some officers, even drinking can't help them to escape from the frustrations and pressures they feel. They believe they can't do anything about the increasing crime rates or the decreasing happiness levels at home. Feeling hopeless, they turn to suicide as a final way out. The suicide rate for police officers is estimated at two to six times the norm for other occupations.

We have written much about officers who feel they are doing a job which is meaningless, unimportant, and not appreciated by the public. Because transfers to other departments aren't especially promising, they may feel bound to stay in a job without much chance of getting to the top or getting out. The result is police officers who feel trapped and simply go through the motions in order to survive and qualify for a pension.

CURES FOR POLICE BURNOUT

PHYSICAL

One major problem in preventing burnout is learning to cope with stress. There are several current methods which seem popular. Among these are deep muscle relaxation, biofeedback, and transcendental meditation. All result in a lowering of tension levels and restore the body to a more normal state. Once learned, these techniques may be practiced in a patrol car or at a desk in an inconspicuous manner. Another remedy is to get sufficient rest.

Another way to help cope with stress is to increase the level of physical conditioning. A physically fit body is much more able to handle stress effectively. The lack of physical fitness prevalent among police officers shows up in three major areas:

Flexibility. Exercises which improve flexibility can decrease the likelihood of lower-back problems. Yoga or stretching routines or sit-ups would be especially helpful and take only a short time each day. (A general exercise program appears in Chapter 15 of Part Two). While on the job, trying to keep the back straight when standing can reduce spinal curvature and lower back injuries. Stand instead of sitting whenever possible. If standing for prolonged periods, attempt to keep one knee bent, possibly on a step or rail. When sitting, try to have at least one knee higher than the level of the hips. This can be done in patrol cars by moving the seat forward and placing the knees on the dash and straightening the back. When leaving a car, swivel on the seat and try to place both feet on the ground, bending over to get out of the car. When sleeping, try to sleep on your side, with knees slightly drawn up. This helps to straighten the spine. Avoid sleeping on the stomach or back. A pillow placed under the knees can help straighten the spine if one has to sleep on the back.

Muscular strength. Weight lifting is one way to build muscular strength. Caution must be given to lifting weights properly in order to maximize the benefits and eliminate the possibility of injury. Push-ups and pull-ups are also good strength builders. Isometric exercises can be performed while riding in a car or sitting at a desk and can add to strength and muscle tone. This is an area in which police officers can insist that the city provide facilities for such training. It is possible that memberships in local health clubs or the Y.M.C.A. could be arranged by the city for all officers.

Endurance. Any sport or activity that involves running or walking is helpful. Swimming, bike riding, basketball, golf, tennis, racquetball, walking, and jogging are all excellent. Jumping rope is an especially good activity for endurance and requires very little room. All of these activities are good for the heart and lungs. Challenge the firefighters, Jaycees, Chamber of Commerce, local radio DJs, or recreational center teams to games. Such "pigs versus the rest of the world" events can serve to lessen the negative expectations the public has voiced about police officers.

Another way to help prevent physical symptoms of burnout is to follow a nutritious eating plan. It would be easy to carry nutritious foods in a patrol car or keep them in an office desk or refrigerator. A diet especially good for officers in high-stress situations would include the folowing provisos:

1. keep consumption of refined white sugar, coffee, tea, and cola to a minimum
2. avoid factory-added chemicals by consuming more natural foods
3. reduce the number of different foods per meal by selecting only three items—for instance, whole wheat bread, cheese, and lettuce
4. limit alcoholic drinks to two per working day

This approach will save energy ordinarily used in digestion for other physical activities. Supplement this diet by carrying snacks of fresh fruit and vegetables and nuts on the job. Drink fruit juices, milk, or water instead of coffee or soft drinks. If eating nutritious food is impractical while on duty, try to make up for this by eating better when off duty. While these suggestions may seem a bit far-fetched, they will help reduce stress, reduce fatigue, and maintain high energy levels. Whenever possible, try to eat slowly and in an unhurried manner.

EMOTIONAL

The emotional symptoms of burnout can be devastating. Yet there are many possibilities which may reduce or eliminate these problems. First of all, groups composed of police officers and run by a well-trained leader, can be of unlimited help. The problems of emotional isolation and insulation can only be countered by the honest, direct expression of emotions. Anger, fear, frustration, and embarrassment should be expressed. Encounter groups are specifically designed for this purpose. If sharing feelings is at first too difficult, individual counseling sessions might be pursued. Seeing a counselor doesn't mean an officer is crazy or sick. It simply means that the pressures of the job are so great that additional ways to handle this pressure are needed. Some police departments have a psychologist on staff, and others will provide one through insurance payments. All that is needed is for an officer to take the first step and seek assistance.

Another very promising activity would be to engage in marriage and family counseling. Frustrations of husbands, wives, and children can be expressed in counseling sessions and constructive methods of communication adopted. The fact that major police departments recognize the benefits of this type of counseling and encourage and support it should help other officers to seek such assistance.

Another way to help reduce the emotional effects of burnout is to learn effective ways of communication. Whenever dealing with accidents, quarrels, shootings, or deaths, or whenever emotions are intense, special ways of communicating are helpful. These communication techniques can be learned in courses taught at universities, community colleges, or free universities. Police departments can also arrange to have such courses offered to their personnel. The investment of time and energy is well worth it.

Finally, engaging in some type of volunteer work might prove beneficial. The dream of protecting and serving, of helping others, might be blocked. By volunteering, an officer can get involved in doing something helpful and useful, can experience success at it, and ultimately regain some lost self-esteem. Being a Big Brother or Big Sister, a Partner, a coach in Little League or the Police Athletic League, and tutoring students are common opportunities. Many more exist.

SOCIAL

When experiencing cynicism toward certain groups or the public in general, spending time with the disliked group can help to remove stereotypes and negative feelings toward these people and groups. There are numerous possibilities, all having in common encounters between conflicting parties.

Try to establish some public relations type of activity. Perhaps a police officer of the month, based on criteria selected by officers themselves, would be one such activity. Another might be to have a column in a local paper to which officers could contribute articles representing their point of view and answers to questions submitted by readers.

To deal with problems of misunderstandings between officers and family members we would suggest groups for families which explain the nature of police work and the unusual stresses and strains inherent in this profession. Often the emotional isolation we have described prevents the officer from doing this explaining. Again, larger police departments have attempted such groups and report positive results. Also helpful are groups for the spouses of police officers which allow them to share their frustrations, anger, fear, and loneliness. Such groups can help families to express the emotions which they find difficult to express directly to the police officer.

A baby-sitting group composed of officers' families might be helpful. Such a group would know each other and the particular idiosyncrasies of its members. It would enable couples to get out more frequently, at less cost, and perhaps somehow beat some of the limitations of shift work such as not being able to plan ahead. Another suggestion would be "shift-specific" parties which would help insure a fairly constant group of people with temporarily similar schedules. A pleasant party can do a lot towards recharging tired and stressed people.

For some family problems, vacations can do a lot to get away from stress and recharge the family batteries. In some cases, enforced vacations or leaves of absence must be taken. It would be more desirable if these times away from work were voluntary, but for economic or personal reasons some officers won't take time off until it is too late. Several short vacations may be better than one long vacation. Even getting out of town for a day or two can prove beneficial.

SPIRITUAL

Spiritual symptoms, in our terminology, describe a loss of meaning in one's job and in one's life. To counteract this we would suggest that officers compare their work to that of their counterparts in totalitarian states, such as the Soviet Union. This should help make it clear that they do in fact provide a useful and meaningful function in our democratic society. The fact that they work for people and not against them should emerge from such a comparison.

We would also strongly suggest occasional follow-up contact with citizens they encounter in cases. A short call to someone they've helped will do much to remove the notion that nothing they do has any effect. Keeping a log or journal of cases may aid in jogging the memory for positive, helpful things they have done. Such a journal may also provide an outlet for writing. Speaking to or instructing young officers who are just entering police work can also help officers get back in touch with their motivations for entering the profession and restore meaning to their lives.

BURNOUT AND THE HEALERS

7. Physicians

*"Three faces wears the doctor: when first sought
An Angel's; and a god's the cure half-wrought;
But when, the cure complete, he seeks his fee,
The Devil looks less terrible than he."*

—Anonymous

Of all the professions, none is held in higher esteem than medicine. The skill of physicians in prolonging life is held in awe by many and in great respect by most. So great is this respect that physicians' opinions on nonmedical matters are also treated with great respect. The income of physicians matches the respect they receive—they are the highest paid of all professionals. The gratification of helping someone back to health is as powerful as money for many physicians. Parents still dream of their children becoming doctors.

Despite all these positive factors, burnout among physicians is on the increase. What happens to turn the most respected of professions into a cycle of tension and unhappiness? What causes physicians to lose interest in the practice of medicine, their patients, and their families? What causes them to burn out?

WHAT WENT WRONG IN THE HOSPITAL?

THE PROBLEM OF TIME PRESSURES

Surveys of physicians' and their spouses' dissatisfaction with the profession of medicine point to one major factor—time pressures. Physicians simply see too many patients. In an attempt to build a successful practice, patients are never turned away. The treatment of the ill is a strong obligation to physicians, and this also makes it difficult to say no to a prospective patient. Many physicians work sixty to eighty hours per week, with sixteen-hour days not uncommon. The physician's day does not end upon leaving the office, as many physicians are on call during evening and early morning hours. Emergencies don't respect the clock or a doctor's sleep schedule. Thus, interruptions in the middle of the night are frequent and regular sleep is often difficult to obtain. This only adds to the chronic fatigue that many physicians feel.

A spinoff of overwork is the complaint of both physicians and their spouses that they have no leisure time. They don't have the opportunity to spend time with relatives and friends. They don't have much time that they can spend with each other. These are the two most commonly mentioned dissatisfactions with the medical profession. They are a sign that the physician is on the road to burnout.

THE PROBLEM OF ENVIRONMENTAL STRESSES

These factors relate to the nature of the environment in which physicians must work. Most importantly, they are continually confronted by persons who are suffering from illness, injury, and disease. Their patients are scared, in pain, confused, and depressed. Spending time with such persons lead to parallel reactions in physicians. They begin to mirror similar emotions, but experience them for longer periods of times. This is a great drain on their energy and contributes to their chronic fatigue. It is also one of the causes of the emotional insulation discussed in the section on symptoms.

The physiological stress of practicing medicine is often ignored. It can be devastating. For example, the mean heart rate for physicians while performing surgery may be as high as 120 beats per minute and may rise as high as 150. The strain implied by such statistics is difficult to imagine. It is as if one were to engage in vigorous physical activity for an hour or two without stopping while concentrating on some extremely technical subject. It is no wonder that such practices can lead to physical and emotional exhaustion.

Recent societal trends have also dictated that nonmedical factors also add stress to the physician's working environment. Insurance rates for protection against malpractice suits have risen dramatically since the mid-seventies. Combined with the fear of possible malpractice suits, additional pressures are created for physicians. The prices of equipment, medication, office space, office help, and many other necessities have also risen dramatically. This has forced the physician to worry more about making ends meet, adding pressure to an already pressure-filled job.

THE PROBLEM OF VALUES CONFLICTS

Physicians come to the practice of medicine with many values. Once they get involved in their practices, the realities of the world come into conflict with their ideals. The result is values conflicts which hasten the process of burnout.

Perhaps the most profound conflict revolves around the desire to relieve pain and suffering. This is undoubtedly a major value for most physicians. They are sensitive to it, and it defines the profession for many. The reality, however, is that for many patients the pain and suffering can't be stopped. During medical school, diagnosis and treatment are taught under the assumption that they will cure or help the patient. When the diagnosis can't be made clearly or the suggested treatment works slowly or not at all, the physicians are stuck in the middle. They want to help, but they have done all they can. Too often the result is that they begin to have doubts about their competence and ability as physicians.

A second values conflict centers around altruism and business. The prevailing value for many physicians is, again, wanting to help others. However, this soon runs directly into the business realities of medicine. All the costs are rising steadily; physicians are forced to charge higher fees and to see more patients in order to meet them. They also find it difficult to miss work since bills and costs are constant but money only comes in when patients are seen. Malpractice has been a topic of increasing importance in medicine. Some physicians have become "gun-shy" and choose not to prescribe certain procedures or treatments because they run a higher risk of malpractice suits and such suits would be bad for business. The altruistic and moral values of physicians come into conflict with business and legal realities. The result is often a lowered sense of self-esteem and self-worth for the physician.

Another conflict centers around the respect that is expected in the medical profession. Persons entering the profession do so with the belief that their work will be respected, that they will be respected, and that their intelligence and dedication will be honored. To some degree this occurs. However, the price is high. Physicians often receive respect for the long hours they work, for the nights they must be on call, and simply for being in the medical profession. But things are changing. Physicians are *expected* to put in long hours; they receive monetary and social rewards for it, true, but they are also expected to do it. If they would choose to spend more time at home and less at the office or hospital, their reputation and business would suffer. So, they receive respect and rewards for hard work but also become trapped by it. No one rewards or honors physicians for slowing down or taking more time off for their own physical and mental health. Respect costs the physician dearly.

Related to this issue of respect is an apparent decline in the prestige of physicians. Patients have become more assertive and demanding about their health. Holistic approaches to health have emphasized the role of the individual in one's own health and have de-emphasized the role of the physician. Medical costs have risen so much that the public has developed hostile and suspicious feelings about the profession. Physicians, the wealthiest and most visible elements in the health care system, have become the chief target of these feelings. The result is that the respect which physicians value so highly is slower in coming. When it does come, the price can be excessive.

THE PROBLEM OF DOCTOR-PATIENT RELATIONSHIPS

The crux of burnout for physicians can be found in the nature of doctor-patient relationships. These relationships are often characterized by overdependency on the part of patients. They come to the office or hospital ready to put themselves totally in the hands of the physician. They expect an omnipotent doctor who knows all and can do all. Although the situation is changing, most patients deny responsibility for their own health care. Rather, they have unlimited expectations of what medicine can and should do for them. This overdependence leads to anger in physicians, who realize they can't be everything to everyone. They realize they can't diagnose and cure all illnesses or diseases, and they resent being put in the position of having to live up to unrealistic expectations. This anger is not easily expressed; it lingers below the surface. The physician thus feels drawn towards someone who needs help and at the same time resents the expectations of this same patient. Such ambivalent feelings are a drain on the physician's energy and lead to the emotional symptoms of burnout.

A second area in which doctor-patient relationships cause problems is that of hostile, aggressive patients. A surprisingly large number of physicians fear violence against themselves and their families from disgruntled patients. The incidence of threats of such violence has risen recently. Patients' unreasonable expectations of unlimited care, in conjunction with rising medical costs, probably contribute to these threats of violence. Suing for malpractice is a common alternative to violence as a means of expressing anger towards a physician. While there undoubtedly have been justified malpractice cases, there just as clearly have been suits which were totally groundless. One patient, for example, went to see a physician and was given the name of several specialists whom he might consult further. The patient selected one of the specialists and then sued the original physician because he, the patient, didn't like the specialist.

THE PROBLEM OF PHYSICIAN SELECTION

Another factor which contributes to physician burnout is the procedures used to select and train physicians. Entrants into medical school are usually students who are interested in the physical sciences and have done well on tests. They are achievement-oriented and tend to be conventional in their values and beliefs. They have the ability to postpone pleasure and to work very hard. Medical school further reinforces these tendencies, and medical students have been described as obsessive-compulsive and perfectionistic. Such hardworking, perfectionistic personalities have difficulty when they experience ambiguous situations. Such situations, where it is unclear as to what is the "right" answer, cause problems for these persons, which lead to feelings of self-doubt and lowered self-esteem. Too often, differential diagnosis of patient complaints is just such an ambiguous situation, and a perfectionistic personality is predisposed to develop negative feelings. Thus, medical schools may play a role in physician burnout by selecting students who are likely to have problems with the ambiguous, unclear situations which physicians face daily.

The training received in medical school also contributes to the production of perfectionistic personalities. There is continuous emphasis on "right" answers and emotional restraint. While we are not questioning the need for excellent training in medical science, we, along with an increasing number of physicians, see the need for a different type of training. In addition to scientific training for physicians, there is a need for training in human relations. There is little if any time given to such matters in many medical schools. Until this changes, physicians will remain ill-prepared to deal with the emotional aspects of medicine and will remain prone to burnout.

THE PROBLEM OF ROLE STRAIN

We have just described how medical schools select and reinforce perfectionistic personalities. The effects of such training naturally lead to what we have called role strain. Being perfectionistic and achievement-oriented, success is a highly desired goal. Physicians translate this desire for success into a need to be maximally competent at all times, both in and out of medicine. In other words, the physician, expected to be perfect in medical school, believes it is necessary to be perfect in all aspects of life. This notion becomes distorted into meaning that the physician can show no sign of weakness. Thus, the physician has to know the answer to every medical question, be able to diagnose every illness, and be able to treat every case successfully. This is, of course, impossible.

The need for maximal competence extends beyond the intellectual abilities required to practice medicine. It extends into the physician's emotional life. Being maximally competent gets translated into being autonomous and self-sufficient. Physicians may find it difficult to express emotions, as this would imply weakness. To admit a need to be loved, to be nurtured and cared for, would be to admit imperfection. To admit that the pressures of medicine are difficult to handle, at times even overwhelming, would be to admit weakness. Thus, physicians are prevented from being fully human by the role they adopt. As mentioned above, playing this role is reinforced by the public, who don't want a doctor they believe is less than omnipotent. The net result is physicians who must deny their feelings and needs, who are not allowed to suffer minor illnesses, who carry their emotions inside of them, and who are prime candidates for burnout.

SYMPTOMS OF PHYSICIAN BURNOUT

PHYSICAL

The physical symptoms of physician burnout are similar to those of members of many other professions. The first sign is chronic fatigue, a tiredness that doesn't disappear with a day off or a weekend out of town. It isn't the tiredness of hard work. Rather it is the tiredness born of emotional struggles fueled by social, intellectual, and spiritual pressures.

With chronic fatigue, the susceptibility to minor ailments and illnesses increases. Thus, headaches and backaches become more frequent, and the physician has difficulty in shaking off the effects of a cold or the flu. Susceptibility to more serious injuries also increases. Along with chronic fatigue comes a tendency to experience more accidents than seems appropriate. A common complaint from the wives of physicians is that their husbands are too tired for sex.

As burnout deepens, the physical signs of anxiety become more prominent. Sweating, increased heart rate, elevated blood pressure, and irritability are experienced. The effect of these symptoms is to increase the fatigue already present and to continue the cycle already described.

Another physical sign of burnout is a deterioration in physical condition. Chronic fatigue and overwork make it difficult to develop and maintain an active conditioning program. Constant use of intellectual faculties to the exclusion of vigorous physical activity leads to a lowered level of physical conditioning. As the body begins to deteriorate, so does the ability to work effectively for extended periods of time. The ability to handle stress is also reduced. The net result is the increased susceptibility to illnesses, ailments, and accidents.

INTELLECTUAL

One of the first intellectual symptoms of burnout is an increase in feelings of self-doubt. All through medical school and training, the young physician has adopted a perfectionistic approach to medicine. Mistakes are intolerable. If a patient is to get well, things must go just right. Once in practice, however, physicians quickly find that they are less than perfect. Not all patients get well and some even die, in spite of a physician's best efforts. In times of stress, the need to be perfect can lead to feelings of inferiority and pessimism, what can be termed self-doubt. Physicians lose confidence, and a fear of failure begins to appear. This causes exaggerated and undeserved anxiety, shame, and guilt. Physicians begin to doubt their own abilities, a doubt fueled by unreasonable expectations of perfection.

Once there is an increase in self-doubt, a second symptom appears: difficulty in making decisions. Plagued by self-doubt and threatened by the increased likelihood of malpractice suits, physicians find it more difficult to make once-routine decisions. Choice of treatment approaches, choice of medication, even choice of examination techniques become a problem for the physician. Which is the best? Even if one is best, is it the safest in terms of legal considerations? Will it offend the patient and thus interfere with treatment? Physicians mull over these questions in their minds and find it increasingly difficult to make such decisions.

Once self-doubt and difficulty in making decisions appear, a negative and cynical attitude soon develops. Suggestions for improvements and changes are met with skepticism. New proposals are met with replies such as "That will never work." Problems which were formerly handled in a calm and efficient manner are now blamed on others. If the right medications or forms are not readily available, aides, nurses, salespersons, or hospital administrators may be blamed. Senior physicians can become the object of scorn and ridicule, with name calling becoming more frequent. "That old grouch" or "that incompetent so-and-so" may be muttered under the breath. This negative, cynical attitude begins to spill over into dealings with patients. Instead of recognizing the pain and suffering of patients, the physician ends up blaming them for their plight. "If they'd only lose some weight" or "if he'd only take better care of himself" are statements that, when made with anger or sarcasm, suggest burnout has affected the intellectual functioning of the physician. Additionally, the physician loses compassion for suffering patients and may believe their illnesses are imagined or exaggerated. Cynicism is often accompanied by suspicion of colleagues and patients. The burned-out physician attributes motivation to persons who are devious and manipulative, motivations which prior to burnout weren't seriously considered. Thus, patients are seen as malingering or whining and colleagues are seen as money-hungry or reaching for glory and fame or playing God. The frustration and anger that the physician experiences are displaced onto others.

Not only does the burned-out physician show cynicism toward patients, but he also relies increasingly on the use of diagnostic categories to describe patients. Mrs. Mary Thomas becomes "the coronary in 412" or "the gall bladder infection." In this way, the patient's pain and suffering can be avoided along with its consequent emotional arousal in the physician. This "dehumanizing" of patients is further manifested in the increased use of statistical descriptions of patients. Blood pressure readings, pulse rates, and temperatures become the focus of the physician's attention. The human qualities of patients, that which makes each of them unique, are lost and put aside in favor of a statistical and mechanical view. Patients become less human, and physicians become more like mechanics.

Another intellectual symptom of burnout is an increased dissatisfaction with the job. When satisfaction with their jobs was low, an interesting pattern emerged. These physicians most keenly felt the absence of leisure time for hobbies and family matters. Among doctors who were more satisfied with their jobs, lack of hospital beds for their patients and changes in the public image of physicians were the most frequent source of dissatisfaction. This suggests that the physician who is burning out (dissatisfied) is primarily concerned with events outside the realm of medicine and may have already begun to separate from the profession.

A final intellectual symptom of burnout is reflected in the physician's attitude towards personal illness and illness in their families. The physician's attitude toward personal illness is often one of denial. The need to be "perfect" and to avoid showing "weakness" is reflected in the denial or over-minimization of symptoms. "It's just a cold" becomes an excuse for not following the same advice which is given to patients. It further reflects a decreased concern for personal health which often results in the more serious physical symptoms already discussed.

When family members become ill, the same process of denial or minimization may occur. Spouses and children may have to become more seriously ill in order to obtain medical attention. At times, the opposite may also occur. The physician may overreact to a minor illness and overtreat the symptoms. In both of these approaches, the needs of the ill family member may go unmet as the physician responds in a stereotyped way, motivated by the need to appear totally competent and to minimize feelings of self-doubt and incompetence.

EMOTIONAL

Emotional symptoms of burnout in physicians are similar to those found in other professions, although they may be more severe. The first of these is emotional insulation. This refers to the process of shutting oneself off from the emotional experiences of an encounter with others. Physicians deal constantly with persons who are suffering, in pain, frightened, depressed, and confused. Continuously dealing with such emotions can cause an emotional drain on physicians. In addition, exposure to people with intense emotions can raise the same emotions in the physician, an unpleasant and disadvantageous prospect. As a result, physicians shut themselves off from many of the emotions of their patients. They tend to concentrate on the physical and more mechanical aspects of human functioning. The section on intellectual symptoms above discusses different examples of how this occurs. What is important to realize here is that emotional insulation is not necessarily bad. It serves a useful purpose in protecting the physician from being in a state of constant emotional arousal which could affect intellectual acuity.

However, when taken to excess, problems become apparent. That emotional factors are important in the development and treatment of illnesses can no longer be denied. Yet, physicians suffering from burnout treat patients as if they were bodies without emotions, as if they were humanoids. Burnout prevents a physician from doing all that can be done for patients.

Emotional insulation can become a habit. When the physician goes home, it becomes difficult to listen to the emotional needs of family members. The same avoidance behavior seen on the job becomes a way of responding at home. Arguments between children or with a spouse are seen as problems to be solved. The fact that there are emotional needs underlying the arguments goes unnoticed in favor of a quick resolution to the argument. Emotional insulation begins to create distance between the physician and family members.

Emotional isolation is a second symptom of emotional burnout. This refers to the keeping of one's emotions, dreams, cares, and worries to oneself. Again, there are seemingly sound reasons for such behavior. The physician would like to spare family and friends from the negative events of the day. The aim is to protect them from the suffering, pain, and even death that is a daily part of the physician's life. This is, perhaps, a noble goal, but the price is too high. Physicians soon become reluctant to share any feelings with their children and spouses. Negative feelings are hidden, and this can soon spread to positive feelings. Just as the Dead Sea analogy suggests, there is no appropriate outlet for the feelings that are kept within. The field of mental health shows the price people pay for not expressing emotions. Physicians, because they are seen as so powerful and important and because their work demands so much competence, are reluctant to express their own needs. To be needy becomes equated with imperfection, something to be dreaded. Thus, to express a need for love, a fear of not knowing exactly what to do or how best to do it, or an admission of being too tired to see a patient become signs of imperfection and weakness. The public and the physician's self-image won't allow such signs of imperfection. Thus, the only recourse for many physicians is to keep such issues to themselves. They cast their patients as less than human, and they themselves become less human. Burnout is beginning to deepen.

Another emotional sign of burnout follows closely on the heels of emotional insulation and isolation. This is a loss of concern for others. As physicians become increasingly insulated and isolated, their emotional lives become less and less satisfying. Since their needs aren't being met in conventional ways, other channels are found. Patients and people don't meet their needs and are placed on the back burner. Instead, increasing attention is paid to business and economic concerns. Buildings, condominiums, and the stock market become the focus of burned-out physicians' lives. While concern over monetary matters in itself is neither good nor bad, and is probably necessary, an almost constant attention to money matters does signal a change in values. People are no longer first; helping and healing are no longer primary. They have been replaced, and that is a sign of burnout.

Emotional signs of burnout include a change in the manner of relating to staff members and colleagues. When a person is a source of problems, that person is avoided. Previously he or she might have been confronted, talked to, and reasoned with. The physician no longer has the emotional energy to deal with such matters and so chooses avoidance instead. Short, to-the-point answers are given to questions. Conversation is minimized and any in-depth relating is absent. The burnout victim goes through the motions of interpersonal relating without really relating at all.

A final emotional symptom of burnout is a plunge into overwork. The physician has spent many years and much energy learning to practice medicine. Further hard work is necessary to build a successful practice. As we have seen, many things can go wrong. The practice of medicine becomes less satisfying than it should be. Family and interpersonal relations begin to suffer. Physicians develop self-doubt and are faced with the burden of admitting human imperfection. All of these factors and others can lead to intense anxiety. A common response to such anxiety is to throw oneself into one's work with renewed vigor. It is as if the physician attempts to remain so busy that there won't be time for anxiety-inducing thoughts. The worries about money, prestige, family, friends, and so forth, are pushed into the back of the mind and are replaced by an increase in the already overcrowded work schedule. That such a strategy is self-defeating is obvious. It only intensifies the already serious problems and deepens the burnout cycle.

SOCIAL

The area which seems to suffer the most in physicians who burn out is that of social relationships. The self-doubt and intellectual defenses of the physician are effective, albeit undesirable, at the office. However, they become habitual and become part of the interpersonal style at home as well. The results are disastrous.

The demand for self-perfection, nurtured since college and medical school, is transferred to family members. They are expected to meet the same standards as the physician. Just as these perfectionistic demands are unreasonable and destructive for the physician, so they are for family members. Spouses and children feel guilty over "not measuring up" and develop anger towards the physician.

Anger of itself is not necessarily bad. However, the physician, already well-practiced in emotional insulation and intellectual defenses, does not deal with the anger effectively, if at all. Just as the emotional needs of patients go unmet as a protective device, so do the emotional needs of family members. The burned-out physician is unresponsive to their emotional needs. Preoccupied with concerns of the practice, kept at arm's length from any emotional expression, the physician becomes a phantom at home, physically present but emotionally absent. Family communications deteriorate, and family members turn elsewhere for emotional support. The physician has nowhere to turn.

An interesting phenomenon can happen in the families of physicians. Unable or unwilling to become involved in the emotional needs of family members, the physician ends up paying attention to family members only when they are ill. The emotional distancing already described prevents much more than routine, mechanical care, but it is attention. This may lead to an overreaction to minor illnesses, an almost hypochondriacal approach, as noted above.

The excessive workload confronting most physicians leads to prolonged absences from home. Most damaging is the absence on holidays, important family days (birthdays, anniversaries), and weekends. The demands of patient care and of building and maintaining a successful practice require an enormous investment of time and energy. As a result, little is left over for family members, and they resent what is perceived as "abandonment" or lack of caring. When combined with demands for perfection by the physician, such a situation can be explosive and damaging to families unequipped to handle such problems. Thus, a general picture begins to emerge. The burned-out physician spends too little time with family members, and when time is available it is not spent in a constructive, nurturing manner.

The spouses of burned-out physicians are in an especially difficult situation. They often have had to work and sacrifice during their mate's education and training. If there are children in the marriage, the physician doesn't have time both to raise the children and to build a practice. This chore falls to the spouse, who must also explain why mom or dad won't be home for a birthday or be able to go to the park as planned. The spouses of burned-out physicians report feeling lonely and neglected. Another very frequent complaint of physicians' spouses is the lack of time to spend with relatives and friends. A satisfactory personal life becomes very difficult to maintain. Many wives report feeling that they are boring to their doctor-husbands. Usually college-educated, bright, and talented, they have had to take a back seat to their husbands' careers. While the physician climbs the ladder of importance and respect, the spouse feels left behind. The talents and dreams which would have resulted in a successful career lie dormant and unfulfilled. This leads to further resentment which does not get heard, accepted, or resolved. Both the physician and spouse have emotional issues begging to be discussed openly and resolved. The fact that fifty to seventy-five percent of marriages involving a physician don't "work" suggests that these issues aren't handled well, if at all.

On top of the difficulties at home, physicians experience additional pressures. They believe they are not understood, that the pressures they face on a daily basis are not comprehended. The demands of the family for attention, advice, direction, love, and tenderness become too much, nothing more than extra pressures with which the physician has to deal. Physicians who are experiencing burnout take the easy way out: they spend more and more time away from home and at work. Overwork becomes an escape. This of course only intensifies the problems, and the cycle deepens.

SPIRITUAL

The dreams of many young persons entering the medical profession are soon shattered for the reasons already discussed. The single goal for which they have been preparing so long no longer provides meaning. Their family lives, once possible sources of meaning, have disintegrated through extended absences, long working hours, and loss of communication. Their lives become empty. With little or no meaning in their lives, physicians turn to extreme measures to ease the pain of a pressure-filled, less-than-rewarding life. The equivalent of some seven medical school graduating classes are lost each year to alcoholism, drug abuse, and suicide, and the problem seems to be increasing.

Alcohol.   The pressures on physicians are severe and have been well documented. It is not surprising that physicians might occasionally take a drink to unwind and relax after an especially tough day. Many persons in many professions do this. However, when physicians begin to realize their lives aren't working, their dreams are not materializing, and all that they have worked for and invested so much time and money in isn't as rewarding as they had hoped, they experience pain of a different type. A vacation can ease the symptoms of stress. The pain of a meaningless life doesn't end and cannot be escaped by a trip to Hawaii. It is a constant companion. The result is that the occasional drink becomes more frequent as the physician attempts to blot out the fear and pain of a life devoid of meaning. Forty percent of those physicians lost to alcohol, drugs, and suicide each year are victims of alcoholism.

There seem to be two major periods when physicians are most susceptible to alcoholism. One is before a successful practice is established, between the ages of thirty and forty. These persons may have had drinking problems as early as medical school or before. The second is after a successful practice has been established for many years, between the ages of fifty and sixty-five. These physicians have spent the time and energy and met the challenges they had to face, only to discover that the prize was not worth the struggle. Their dreams don't match reality, they are disillusioned, and their lives are devoid of meaning. Drinking is one way to escape the pain of these realizations.

Drug abuse. It should come as no surprise that there is a high incidence of drug abuse among physicians. First of all, they have ready access to every imaginable drug. Second, their training has disposed them to view medication as an acceptable, even desirable way to treat discomfort.

In many cases, self-treatment starts the cycle of abuse. Overwork leads to chronic fatigue, and minor physical illnesses often result. Not wanting to miss work or to appear less than perfect, physicians will often treat themselves. A stimulant to get over tiredness and get through a long day; a sedative to help in falling asleep after a tension-filled day; a tranquilizer to calm down after worrying about how bills will be paid—these are just a few examples of how self-treatment can start innocently enough. But when the occasional use of drugs turns to a dependence on them, the spiritual signs of burnout are clear. Only eight states have statutes which require physicians to report colleagues who are misusing medication. Thus, accurate statistics are difficult to come by. Even if there are legal requirements, many physicians are reluctant to report a colleague because of a feeling of comradeship, because it will reflect negatively on the profession, or because it may reflect their own vulnerability. The addiction rate of physicians is estimated to be ten times greater than that in the general population. Other studies suggest a rate of abuse thirty to one hundred times greater than that of the general population. The misuse of mood-altering drugs is twice as likely among physicians as among the general population. These facts cannot easily be attributed solely to the availability of drugs. The pressures and personal pain of life as a physician are more likely the key factors. Further evidence of this is that most physician–drug abusers also have abused alcohol. The pattern of attempting to blot out the pain of loss of meaning is clear. The typical physician-abuser is between thirty-five and forty-five, and Demerol is the most commonly misused drug. The story of Cyril and Stewart Marcus clearly illustrates the degree of spiritual burnout that can be reflected by drug abuse. These twin obstetrician-gynecologists were world-respected authorities on infertility. They taught at a prestigious medical school. By professional standards, they had reached the top. Yet their lives obviously lacked meaning. They were found dead in an apartment, lying in decaying food, human waste, and garbage. The cause of death was barbiturate withdrawal. They were drug addicts.

Suicide. The loss of meaning in the lives of physicians is so devastating partly because of the strength of their dreams. They set as their goal the most prestigious and most revered of professions. Their dedication to achieving this goal is dogged and at times single-minded. Amazing amounts of time, energy, and money are spent in trying to make this dream happen. When it becomes clear that the dream will never come true, the disappointment matches the strength of their hope and their belief in the dream. The realization that such a large part of one's life is gone without having reached one's goal is devastating. For some, even alcohol and drugs aren't enough to ease this pain. For some, the only way to deal with these intolerable circumstances is to avoid them totally. The result is suicide, the clearest sign of a loss of meaning in life.

Early studies suggested that the incidence of suicide among physicians was no different from that of the general population. Recent studies, however, using more sophisticated reporting techniques, suggest that physicians are twice as likely to take their own lives as people in general. It is estimated that the equivalent of one medical school class per year is lost to suicide.

The likelihood of suicide increases with age in the general population. Persons nearing retirement age are three times as likely to take their own lives as persons in the 25-to-34 age group; physicians nearing retirement are *twelve* times as likely to commit suicide as their colleagues in the 25-to-34 age group. Divorced people in general are three times as suicide-prone as married men; divorced physicians are *thirteen* times as likely to commit suicide as their married colleagues. The suicide rate among female physicians is three times that of the general population, and women doctors tend to commit suicide at an earlier age, almost half of them doing so before they reach forty. These figures are a grim testament to the seriousness of burnout among physicians.

CURES FOR PHYSICIAN BURNOUT

PHYSICAL

There are three areas where much may be done to alleviate physical burnout. These are exercise, nutrition, and systematic stress-reduction techniques.

What we suggest here is certainly not novel or revolutionary. We are simply recommending a regular program of mildly strenuous exercise. The two goals of such a program are to increase cardiovascular efficiency and to increase muscle tone. A healthy body is much more able to tolerate the stresses inherent in the practice of medicine. Any exercise or sport is probably acceptable as long as it is mildly strenuous and is done regularly. Physicians can make exercise a *scheduled* part of each working day; many already have. Don't consider it a frill, consider it essential and insist that it be a part of every day. If self-employed, simply schedule two fewer patients a day or exercise during lunch. If employed by a hospital or engaged in group practice, take turns covering for colleagues. If this is impossible, then consider exercising before or after work. We prefer an exercise period during work because it will offer time away from the pressures of the job.

Physicians are in an excellent position to engage in sound nutritional practices. First, they have likely studied nutrition and already know what foods are healthy and unhealthy. Second, they can usually have access to a refrigerator, which means that nutritious fresh foods can be kept on hand at work. Third, they are paid well enough to purchase more nutritious foodstuffs. Just as with exercise, we recommend making nutritious eating a scheduled part of each day. This can be done by making a meal plan for a week at a time and sticking to it. Frequently, including others in such a plan will not only help their nutritional needs but also develop a sense of comradeship which makes it easier to stick to the schedule. Take turns providing the foods for the day. Share the responsibility. It will make it easier to keep to the schedule. Another suggestion is to start making these changes with only one meal per day—lunch, for example. Trying to make too many changes at once decreases the probability of the changes becoming permanent. Strive for consistency, doing something each day.

What we mean by stress reduction is any technique which will relax the body and the mind, taking the person psychologically out of stressful situations. Physical withdrawal from a stressful situation may not be possible, but practice of stress-reduction techniques can effectively do the same thing. Biofeedback, yoga breathing exercises, transcendental meditation, self-hypnosis, and deep muscle relaxation are techniques which all have a relaxing effect on the body and the mind. All can be performed in a relatively short period of time. All can be effective. Make a point of investigating these techniques and choosing one which seems most comfortable. Also, read Chapter 15, in Part Two—it contains suggested meditation techniques which have proven very successful. As with exercise, stress reduction may seem silly, frivolous, and nonessential. Consider, however, that the few minutes each day spent in stress reduction can do much to improve one's level of functioning and one's productivity. A short-term investment of time can yield beneficial long-term benefits.

INTELLECTUAL

One of the causes of physician burnout is the routine nature of much of the work physicians do. Although exciting and interesting cases do come along, for the most part physicians deal with minor aches and illnesses, many of which are self-limiting and require little of the physician's training to treat. One suggestion is for physicians to study their schedules. Try to build variety and eliminate redundancy in the daily schedule. Don't always do the same activities at the same time. Eat lunch at different times on different days. Answer correspondence at different times on different days. Try to devise unique ways of scheduling patients. For example, children could be seen in the mornings one week and adults in the afternoon. Switch during the next week. Or create a mix of adults and children. Take the time and try to build variety into the daily routine. Every little bit helps. Another way to eliminate redundancy is to share workloads, tasks, and responsibilities. This is most easily done in a group practice or in a hospital, but, with some creative thinking, the same can be arranged for private practitioners. Becoming involved in the work of others can help break up a monotonous routine. Ask for and give consultation on interesting or unusual cases. Get together and work cooperatively on bookkeeping matters. Be creative and discover other areas where time can be shared.

Another intellectual activity can also be done in a shared, cooperative manner. Plan and conduct a study of the psychological hazards of medical practice. Sit down with colleagues and decide what are common sources of stress for physicians and what can be done about them. (For help in this area, see Chapter 16 in Part Two, especially the Stressful Habits Test, and the brainstorming technique in Chapter 4.) Consider publishing the results so that other physicians may benefit or consider presenting the results to a meeting of the local or state medical societies.

Another worthwhile intellectual activity is to become involved in establishing or strengthening laws which govern the reporting of impaired physicians. This can begin in the local medical society. Gather facts and figures and study the problem. Contact local legislators and get the process started. Consider what type of program might fit well with such laws. The state of Georgia has a program which seems to work well. A physician who has been reported to be abusing drugs is visited by a team of two physicians who try to convince the doctor to seek treatment. If that proves unsuccessful, the physician is soon visited by another team of two physicians. If they fail, a third team is soon sent to visit the impaired physician. There are other programs, too. Study them and try to implement those which seem to have a good chance of success.

Another approach is to become involved with attempts to change some of the practices of medical schools. One objective might be to increase students' education on the dangers of alcohol and drug abuse in the medical profession. Volunteer to make a presentation to a class or classes at a medical school, or lobby through a local or state medical society to include courses in the medical school curriculum which will deal with such problems.

Another objective might be to change the criteria used by selection committees to choose medical students. The great emphasis placed on ability in the physical sciences is, perhaps, unfortunate. Criteria could include personality factors which would provide some probability of withstanding the psychological stresses of medical practice.

Both the last two suggestions are exercises which will help sharpen intellectual skills that may have become dulled due to burnout. They will also help in the spiritual area of burnout by providing meaning to a physician's life.

Finally, we suggest developing constructive interests outside of medicine. This could include any activity which is intellectually stimulating, such as reading, creative activities, or any of various hobbies. In this way, relaxation can be obtained while one's intellectual facilities are kept at a sharp level.

EMOTIONAL

Our first suggestion to help alleviate the emotional symptoms of burnout is to remove oneself from the sources of stress whenever possible. This can be accomplished in several ways. First of all, use timeouts. These are short periods taken during moments of extreme stress or as soon afterwards as possible. They are not scheduled periods of time; they are to be taken as needed. When events begin to pile up, take a minute or two away from them. Go to the doctors' lounge, the coffee shop, or even a linen closet. With eyes closed, take several deep breaths, inhaling to the count of four, then exhaling to the count of four. With the eyes still closed, think of some pleasant scenes and visualize them in as much detail as possible. As difficult as it may be to take such periods of time away from work, make sure to do so. It can be a lifesaver.

The second way to remove oneself from stressful situations is to schedule rest or relaxation periods. The word *schedule* is important here. Insist on such periods. Make them an integral part of each workday. The time spent in such rest periods will more than be justified by the increase in productivity. Some struggling with administration may be necessary, but it is a small technical problem to arrange coverage for these periods. Physicians who work alone should simply not schedule patients during these periods.

The third way to remove oneself from stressful situations is to schedule mini-vacations. These may be a day or a weekend off. Again, schedule them and don't wait until "there is time" without scheduling. There seldom is "enough" time. Make sure to schedule these mini-vacations at least a month or two ahead of time.

One of the major causes of burnout among physicians is role strain, the maintenance of an independent, autonomous image as one who can handle any situation without any help. What we suggest is to strive for a balance between independence or autonomy and mutual dependence and the need for support. To help clarify what some of these emotional needs are, try the following exercise. List the five most significant people at home, at work, and in the community. Next, list at least two things which, if received from these five people, would make life more pleasant or productive. These may be material things or emotional or behavioral items. Once they are identified, arrange a time to express to each of the five persons what is needed from them. Try to explain these needs in a straightforward manner. Once these needs are expressed, ask the persons what they would like in return. In this way a system of mutual satisfaction and support may be initiated or rekindled.

Another suggestion is to monitor one's emotional states continuously and realistically. This means to keep track of the emotions that are experienced each day for a given period of time. Try and notice if there is a balance between positive and negative emotions. Notice how emotions are expressed. Are they expressed in an appropriate manner or are they held in? Are they expressed explosively or in a nonoffensive manner? Check Chapter 17 of Part Two, especially the Emotional Expression Guide and the Emotions Diary, for help on this activity.

If one works in any type of group setting, a most useful idea is to establish a burnout "lookout." This person's responsibility is to be aware of the symptoms of burnout and to look for them in colleagues. When symptoms are noticed, the lookout notifies other colleagues and the person exhibiting the symptoms. The potential burnout victim is then confronted and problem-solving techniques can be employed. (See Brainstorming in Chapter 18 of Part Two.) Remember, covering up for colleagues showing signs of burnout is not helpful. In fact, it can be most destructive.

Finally, if the emotional symptoms of burnout seem to be lingering or deepening, we strongly suggest counseling of some sort. This will surely fly in the face of the independent, autonomous role which is lived by many physicians. However, we don't see it as a sign of weakness. Declining help is the weakness; having the courage to admit that some help is, on occasion, necessary is wisdom. Group counseling, especially Gestalt or encounter groups, is especially helpful in practicing emotional expression. Counseling does not imply insanity or weakness. It implies humanity. Burnout is a serious enough problem to warrant help. If one waits too long, the problem may be divorce, alcoholism, or suicide. The cost is too high to let pride interfere.

SOCIAL

The major social symptom of burnout is a deterioration in the quality of interpersonal relationships. Our first suggestion therefore centers around improving one's interpersonal relationships. A direct approach would be to enroll in workshops or courses designed to improve communication. A local mental health center, university, or community college is a likely place to find such courses or workshops. The local medical society could easily arrange for a trained facilitator to offer workshops for married couples which focus on effective communication techniques.

The problem of emotional isolation is also a serious one for physicians. An approach which has proven successful in some parts of the country is to utilize the local or regional medical society to organize a group for physicians which is designed to discuss emotional problems common to the participants. If needed, the local mental health center can provide a trained facilitator for such a group. This would help to establish a support group for physicians and eliminate much of the isolation which leads to burnout.

Another major social symptom of burnout is marital difficulties and a less than satisfactory family life. The following suggestions are directed toward diminishing these problems. The easiest solution to implement is a change in the amount of time spent with one's family. Again, to start with, rely on scheduling. Each week plan time that is for the family and not for work. Then stick to the schedule. Allot some time for children, some for the spouse, and some for the family as a whole. The more time allotted, the better it is.

Another simple suggestion is to take one weekend every month (or every two months at the most) and go somewhere with one's spouse. It doesn't have to be a very long trip; one to a neighboring town will suffice. Just go away. Again, scheduling is the best way to begin. If the weekend must wait until there is "time," the time may never come. Work or some other excuse will pop up. So schedule the weekend and stick to the schedule.

Another suggestion is to explore the possibilities of learning to share oneself with family members. This means honest, open communication. It will help broaden one's support network and help to insure that one's emotional needs will be met. This is the time for dropping roles, admitting to spouse and children that medicine is a tough and demanding profession. It is the time to admit to one's family that fear, envy, anger, and other emotions are part of the physician's life. It is the time to admit to one's family that the physician is imperfect, has weaknesses, is a human being.

SPIRITUAL

One suggestion seems so clear as to not need mention. We will mention it anyway. Physicians should avoid treating themselves. Even minor ailments and illnesses, if self-treated, can begin the habit which often leads to alcoholism and drug abuse. So, whenever medical treatment is needed, consult a colleague. Although time-consuming, it makes it more difficult to get into a habit which can have such tragic consequences.

Loss of meaning for physicians often means they believe what they are doing is unimportant and unappreciated. To counter this, give one's obvious talents away to people who need them. Volunteer one day or a half day every few weeks to the poor or underprivileged. Go to an elementary school or high school and teach youngsters about health, VD, physical fitness, or some other topic of interest. Consider speaking to medical school classes about the realities of medical practice which are often not discussed in medical school. If a physician has talents in some nonmedical area, donate these to persons who need them. Consider coaching or teaching art, music, or any other skill that would benefit others. Find meaning in one's life by bringing meaning to the lives of others.

The spouses of physicians often must sacrifice their own lives to help physicians get through school and develop a successful practice. Their talents, dreams, and hopes may disappear. Physicians can encourage their spouses to develop their own identities. In this way, both physician and spouse will have richer lives with more meaning.

Finally, physicians can talk to their patients. Conduct an informal study. Ask patients what life might be like if there were no physicians. Given that most illnesses are minor and self-limiting, ask patients what they would feel like if there was no one to turn to when they were injured or sick. Physicians will quickly find that their mere presence calms patients and gives them a sense of security and well-being. Knowing that one has a personal physician or that a physician is available can do much to alleviate worry and anxiety, helping people to lead more carefree, relaxed lives. Physicians are important, and they need only listen to other human beings to discover just how important.

8. Nurses

*"I think," said Mr. Dooley, "that if th'
Christyan Scientists had some science an' th'
doctors more Christianity, it wudden't make
anny diff'rence which ye called in—if ye
had a good nurse."*
—Finley Peter Dunne ("Mr. Dooley")

Ever since Florence Nightingale founded the nursing profession, it has been honored, praised, and encouraged. Most often, young women have been encouraged to seek out nursing as a career that was proper and useful. Of late, young men have been encouraged too. It is a worthwhile profession. It is worthy of praise. Young people should be encouraged to seek out such praiseworthy and valuable professions.

The problem is that most of the praise has come from our lips and little from our pocketbooks! Another problem is that, for all of the training nurses go through, they have very little real opportunity to use that knowlege. They study for years, but then they are treated only as third-class citizens of the health world.

Unfortunately, nursing is a profession that is the lowest paid and least respected within its own field than any other included in this book. In fact, despite all their training, nurses are the servants of physicians and/or hospitals. Their training for nursing is often wasted on them as their actual jobs become menial and subservient. Is it any wonder that they burn out?

WHAT WENT WRONG AT THE NURSES' STATION?

THE PROBLEM OF DISILLUSIONMENT

A major cause of burnout among nurses is disillusionment. Nurses enter their profession with a dream. They want to help people, to heal the sick and injured, to make life and death more comfortable, and in general to do good for humanity. However, what they find is that they must submit themselves to political decisions made by administrators and physicians who are concerned about cost effectiveness and the mass production of health care. Instead of caring for sick people, much of a nurse's time is spent in managerial and supervisory tasks with aides and ancillary workers. They keep track of supply inventories instead of patients. In school, student nurses are often taught by idealistic faculty members, many of whom have very little experience in hospital settings. The ideals taught in school are often unrelated to the "real world" of health care. When they finally reach a health care setting, nurses find that, instead of spending time with patients, they spend their time filling out forms, dealing with complaints from subordinates, evaluating the performance of aides and other helpers, and any number of other tasks which keep the nurse away from patients.

A special case of disillusionment is seen in young, inexperienced nurses. They may possess what has been termed a "rescue fantasy" or "savior complex." Fresh out of nursing school, they have feelings bordering on omnipotence, believing what they have learned in school will enable them to cure or help any case they encounter. When, as so often happens, a patient leaves the hospital not cured or not even improved, negative feelings about their competence and worth as nurses develop. Disillusionment increases and burnout is more likely.

THE PROBLEM OF HELPLESSNESS

A second major cause of burnout are feelings of helplessness. In general, nurses are faced with situations which defy solutions. In some cases, nurses have complained about having little or no input into creating policies and procedures which they have to follow and which directly affect their work. Such decisions are made by physicians and administrators with little appreciation of what nurses have to deal with in their work.

In other instances, nurses observe incidents of poor medical care or even possible malpractice by physicians. A recent survey of 10,000 nurses showed that many had witnessed at least one case of substandard medical care but felt helpless to do anything about it. Whereas physicians can question a nurse's work rather easily, documentation requirements and differences in levels of prestige make it much more difficult for nurses to report substandard practices by physicians. In many hospitals, there may not be a procedure for reporting such incidents. In cases where procedures do exist, nurses have said that once reports are filed, no action is taken, and the paperwork is put away and forgotten.

Finally, nurses may feel especially helpless when it comes to helping patients. Budget constraints prevent the latest and best equipment from being purchased. Administrative tasks limit patient contact. When combined with the fact that medical costs require patients to leave hospitals sooner than they might, nurses can come to believe that there is little or nothing they can do to help patients get well. Feelings of helplessness begin to emerge in all phases of a nurse's job.

THE PROBLEM OF THE WORK SETTING

The health care setting or hospital is itself a source of stress for many nurses. They are confronted by human suffering and misery, and, in many cases, dying and death. Constant exposure to such intense emotional situations raises intense emotions in nurses. Often, they are reminded of their own parents or other family members. Patients, often seemingly neither dead nor alive, with tubes coming out of their bodies, moaning, groaning, and making noises which sound anything but human, can cause feelings of fear, disgust, anger, or pity. Such feelings can be so intense as to be overwhelming. Yet, there are unwritten rules that prevent the nurse from crying or displaying other emotions.

The nurse must be the one who is in control, who can handle whatever situations may arise. The hospital may be in turmoil, but the nurse must exude calmness and the ability to handle any emergency while directing the actions of others. If a patient or family member asks a question the nurse can't answer, unwritten rules make it difficult to say, "I don't know." Nurses may have to resort to hiding behind technical language, knowing they are being dishonest. If a patient is difficult or unreasonable, nurses can't express anger but must continue to provide care. They must ignore the maddening behavior but cannot ignore the patient. If nurses are especially idealistic, they may think it is wrong to have such feelings and may begin to experience guilt, thus compounding the problem.

Nurses have to engage in shift work, periodically having to change their eating, sleeping, and family habits. Research tells us that daytime sleep is not as refreshing or as restful as nighttime sleep. Thus, nurses are often working with less energy than they might. Choice of shift is often not available to them, adding to feelings of helplessness. At times, they may be asked to work double shifts or six-day weeks which increase the stresses and strains inherent in nursing.

THE PROBLEM OF STATUS

Part of the dream that nurses bring to their profession is that their work will be skillful, artful, and effective in helping patients. Further, they expect that this work will be appreciated by the physicians with whom they work. However, in many, many cases, nurses report the opposite. The hard work and long hours that nurses put in go unnoticed. The skill level of nurses are underestimated. Physicians often believe nurses require constant supervision and monitoring.

These types of situations are most likely to occur when a young physician is new to a health care setting. If the nurses there are experienced and self-confident, conflicts can be intensified. At its worst, the situation may lead to intense hostility between nurses and physicians. The effect on the nurses' morale can be devastating. If nurses are young and new to the job, their self-concepts may suffer. For more experienced nurses, the hostility experienced may make the job barely tolerable.

Another factor working to produce lower feelings of status (self-concept) is the relatively low salary nurses are paid. It is difficult to believe one is doing an effective, worthwhile job when the salary does not measure up to the salaries received by other professionals. Nurses may begin to think that their work is unimportant and, consequently, that they are unimportant. Lower salaries get translated into lower status. The strikes by nurses at many hospitals may be seen partly as an attempt to regain some measure of prestige in a job which offers little else in terms of status.

The organization of nursing services may also work to reduce feelings of status. Nursing supervisors may be seen as working for the administration and less for the nurses themselves. Decisions made in conjunction with medical personnel perceived by nurses as "back room" political deals lead to feelings of powerlessness. The message from this situation is that senior nurses and physicians and administrators have the knowledge and the skill needed to make policy, other nurses don't and should limit themselves to their duties on the ward. Even more devastating is that nurses may end up believing that they have nothing to say or contribute since no one appears interested in seeking out their opinions. Again, the feeling is one of doing an unimportant, mechanical job.

THE PROBLEM OF FUNDING

Although not unique to the nursing profession, inadequate funding leads to special strains and stresses. For example, many hospitals and health care settings cannot afford the latest equipment. Knowing this, nurses also know that all that can be done for patients is not being done. The level of care is less, often significantly less, than it could and should be. Although not the fault of nurses, this leads to the belief that the nursing dream is not being realized.

Another way that inadequate funding can affect nurses is in the number of personnel available to work a shift. Double shifts and six-day weeks are reflections of this problem. Also, without sufficient staff, nurses are responsible for far too many patients. This leads to what some have termed "McDonald's nursing." The opposite of one-to-one care, "McDonald's nursing" refers to mass-production medical care whereby most patients are given the same, minimal care, regardless of their individual emotional and psychological needs. Again, knowing that so much more could be done to help relieve suffering and discomfort, yet powerless to add staff that could make such a difference, nurses' dreams begin to fade.

All professionals attempt to keep abreast of the latest developments in their field, and nurses are no exception. To become a better nurse implies continuing education after graduation from nursing school. Many professionals can receive financial assistance for course work and travel to conferences. With limited funding, low salaries, and irregular schedules, such continuing education is difficult for nurses to come by. The result is that many nurses no longer feel they know what they need to know to do a good job. They can begin to develop feelings of inferiority and lack of competence. The part of their dream in which they are skilled, artful healers comes under attack.

SYMPTOMS OF NURSE BURNOUT

How does burnout show up in nurses? What forms does it take? What signs can co-workers, families, and friends look for which would suggest that burnout is occurring? The following symptoms are the most common ones observed among nurses suffering from burnout.

PHYSICAL

The first sign of burnout is fatigue. The nurse will come home tired and wake up tired. Even though the shift may not have been especially hard for several days, the exhaustion is still there. The tiredness seems inappropriate. It isn't the kind of tiredness which will go away with a couple of days of rest or a weekend off. The burned-out nurse wakes up tired, and the thought of going to work only increases this tiredness and fatigue.

Closely following the initial occurrence of fatigue is the onset of minor physical ailments. Colds, flu, headaches, and other assorted aches and pains begin to appear more frequently than in the past and seem more difficult to eliminate. Susceptibility to stress-related illnesses also increases. Perhaps, because of close contact with health care facilities, such minor illnesses may be minimized or ignored. The danger lies not in ignoring a cold but in not becoming aware that it may be a sign of something more serious and dangerous which is just around the corner.

INTELLECTUAL

Burnout also affects the intellectual functioning of nurses. Most common are feelings of helplessness about making any changes in their work situation. They are not asked for their input in policy making, even though the policies will directly affect their jobs. Reports of poor medical practice or even malpractice may go unheard and not be acted upon. Lack of new technology and of adequate personnel make the delivery of high-quality care very difficult. The general feeling for many nurses is one of butting their heads against a brick wall when trying to do a good job and make effective changes. Burned-out nurses seem resigned to a lack of personal power, resigned to a career of submission to the external realities of the profession.

One effect of feelings of helplessness and resignation is stagnation. The friction which arises out of attempted change in an inadquate system soon disappears. Nurses stop trying to make changes and "go through the motions.'' The term "professional autism" has been used to describe nurses who simply go through the motions of their jobs, following established rules and procedures, even if they truly believe something better could be done. Striving for the best possible care is replaced by a "don't make waves" attitude. Side effects of professional autism include a loss of creativity and vision. With little or no hope of making significant changes, there seems to be little motivation to invest time and energy in creative approaches to problem solving. Thus, possible sources of innovation in nursing care are lost. More important, the lack of vision and absence of creativity may spill over into the nurse's private life. Helplessness and lack of creativity come to dominate many major issues in the nurse's personal life. Decisions become increasingly difficult to make and excessive vacillation is common.

Feelings of helplessness and diminished creativity cause changes in the nurse's outlook on the job. Hope is replaced by cynicism. New and more promising ideas are rejected. "We've already tried that and it didn't pan out" is a typical comment from burned-out nurses. If the idea is new, it may be subjected to nit-picking and rejected as unworkable, with little or no thought given to it. Loss of creativity in one team member tends to squelch the creativity of others, and the cycle grows. Again, this may spill over into the personal life of nurses and may result in cynicism about politics, proposed changes in the local school system, or even a new recipe that someone has shared. Cynicism and negativity characterize the entire life of the burned-out nurse.

EMOTIONAL

The major emotional symptom of burned-out nurses is "distancing." This refers to the creation of psychological distance between nurses and their patients. The constant suffering, pain, and misery with which they must deal raises intense emotions in nurses. Being in such a constant state of arousal would be unhealthy and unpleasant, so nurses erect psychological defenses to protect themselves. The same process is seen in physicians, police officers, and other helping professionals. The process is both effective and necessary. Some nurses, trying to lighten an otherwise heavy, oppressive situation, will make jokes. In burnout, however, such joking is not so funny. Humor changes to ridiculing patients and their personalities. Prominent physical characteristics become the source of cruel jokes and sarcasm. No longer is self-defense the issue; rather, there is more of a sense of lashing out, of striking against the factors which are working to destroy the nurse's dream.

Distancing may take various forms. The care and involvement that the nurse originally brought to the job begins to change. Paperwork, formerly a negative part of the job, becomes a haven from the emotional intensity of the ward. Nurses begin to spend more and more time doing administrative and other tasks and choose to spend less and less time with patients. Their openness and commitment has changed to self-preservation.

Distancing can also be reflected in a preoccupation with the technical aspects of care. The readings on the dials of machines and the printouts from various apparatus become the main focus of the nurse's attention instead of the feelings and experiences of the human being who is the patient. Numbers—degrees Fahrenheit or millimeters of pressure—take precedence over the emotional and psychological needs of the patient. Rather than be exposed to the emotions of the patient, the nurse may totally avoid this part of the person and concentrate on the information being transmitted through various machines. The patient may need human contact more than anything, but the nurse suffering from burnout can't give that contact. It is too much of a risk and too much of a drain on emotional resources. The dials, printouts, and numbers are something that can safely be dealt with without the risk of emotional arousal.

Another way of maintaining distance from patients is by referring to them in technical jargon. Mrs. John Doe becomes "the cardiac case" and Ms. Jane Doe becomes "the postoperative infection in 4C." By escaping into jargon, the nurse is able to avoid the humanness of patients and thus emotional vulnerability with its consequent intense arousal. In line with the use of jargon is the use of categorization. Patients are diagnosed and their treatment follows automatically. If they are suffering from A, then treatment A is indicated. If they are suffering from B, treatment B is indicated. "Going by the book" allows escape into a preplanned-treatment approach. Again, the nurse is relieved of having to confront the individual, unique humanness of patients, and dealing with their emotional needs. Patients' fear, pain, despair, and loneliness can be escaped by simply applying the illness A–treatment A formula. Patient fears about a treatment procedure or despair about getting well can be avoided. The nurse need not experience the heightened emotional states which come with such encounters. Escape into categories is simple and effective.

In more serious cases of burnout, the compassion that nurses bring to their work seems to disappear totally. In addition to using sarcasm, they may lose their tempers and even scream at patients. They may be overheard saying that a patient deserves what is happening. Statements such as "he brought it on himself'' or "if she'd lose thirty pounds she wouldn't have so much trouble breathing" are suggestive of serious burnout. Such behaviors can lead to feelings of guilt in nurses, further ensuring the loss of their dream. Instead of feeling good about their work, they end up feeling guilty and depressed, apparently helpless to do anything about it.

SOCIAL

The major social symptom of burnout is a deterioration in the quality of interpersonal relationships. We have seen that distancing is common to burned-out nurses and helps to protect them from the intense emotional arousal which accompanies working with suffering people. The relationship between nurse and patient suffers. Unfortunately, when a nurse takes off the uniform, psychological defenses can't be taken off as easily. When emotions are avoided for eight to ten hours a day on the job, it is quite likely that emotions will be avoided at home also. When burned-out nurses are at home, they don't want to hear about the problems of other family members. A daughter's worry about whether to go out with a certain boy or a son's embarrassment over an acne condition are ignored or avoided. Minor spats between siblings, instead of being handled in a manner respectful to both parties (which requires sensitivity to the emotional needs of both children) may be met with an explosive outburst of temper. The nurse's home becomes an extension of the ward, a place filled with emotions to be avoided. More and more time is spent in noninteractional activities like watching television or just being alone. Family relationships, already strained by shift work, deteriorate further as distancing occurs at home. Exhausted, cynical, and feeling powerless, the burned-out nurse has nothing to give to the family and avoids any activity that will further drain the emotions.

Burnout, then, involves avoidance of emotional interactions with family members. However, there is another side to this problem. The nurse finds it difficult to share emotions with family members. Perhaps the nurse doesn't want to share the many negative aspects of the job which could depress other family members. At any rate, nurses tend to keep their feelings and concerns to themselves. The helplessness, the frustrations, and the irritations of the day don't get expressed. The result is that they come out in an indirect manner such as sarcasm or undeserved temper outbursts. Patterns of noncommunication are established, and family life becomes less and less fulfilling. Family life, which could be a source of energy and inspiration to balance the draining nature of work, becomes instead an additional drain on the burned=out nurse's already impoverished physical and emotional resources. There is little, if any, satisfaction to be gained at work or at home.

Interpersonal relationships suffer at work as well. Communication between burned-out nurses and their co-workers becomes less and less satisfying. Even other nurses, who understand the unique stresses and problems of the profession better than anyone else, are excluded by the burnout victim. Loss of compassion, feelings of hostility toward patients, professional autism, and guilt over these feelings are difficult to express to colleagues. No nurse likes to admit that the noble motivations once held have been given up. Who would admit settling for complacency and comfort? As a result, interactions are often superficial, centering around ward routine or gossip. Chances for meaningful communication, which could lessen the isolation that nurses feel and make the situation less burdensome, pass by unused. The chance to find out that other nurses feel the same way and to feel that there is hope for a better future is missed. With each missed chance, burnout increases and the likelihood of escaping it decreases.

SPIRITUAL

The symptoms we have described as spiritual are quite varied. They do have in common the loss of meaning of a nurse's work. Dreams broken, the job becomes a meaningless, mechanical repetition of routine, dull tasks.

One reflection of a loss of meaning in the nursing profession is the incidence of alcohol and drug abuse. A review of available literature suggests that the problem is serious. Without knowing how to regain meaning in their work and lives, burnout victims resort to substance abuse.

Militant unionism is another reflection of loss of meaning. It is not intended to suggest that striking is wrong or bad. A just salary and decent working conditions are due every worker, including nurses. However, an attitude where the salary, working conditions, and fringe benefits seem to be the sole concerns of union members suggests a loss of many of the ideals with which professionals enter their careers. The meaning of the job, which used to be helping, compassion, and healing, has disappeared. Inability to practice nursing as it should be leaves an emptiness, a feeling of incompetence. To fill this emptiness, to gain a sense of competence, other areas must be investigated. Successes in collective bargaining or gains in salary and vacation days become the signs of power and gauges of competence that come to replace the dedication and idealism that once provided deeper meaning in the nursing profession.

Another reflection of spiritual burnout is related to loss of compassion. At its extreme, we find nurses who actively seek to hurt or inflict pain. Not only do they ignore pain and suffering on the part of patients, they actually seek to add to it. It is as if they are so threatened and devastated by the illness and suffering around them that they come to hate sickness. This is soon extended to hatred of sick persons, who make it impossible to forget illness and to avoid it. This hatred finds expression in the pain that is inflicted in a shot that is given with too much force or a painkiller that is given only after a long delay. The only meaning left for this nurse is to strike out at illness symbolized by patients.

One final symptom of spiritual burnout might be the phenomenon of nurses who could be termed "angels of death." All hope of helping and healing is gone. All the skills, training, and technology are useless. Helplessness is nearly complete. The last chance to remove suffering is by taking life. At least, some shred of meaning can be regained by removal of all pain and suffering, by the extinction of life itself. At this stage, burnout is total.

CURES FOR NURSE BURNOUT

What can be done to alleviate the symptoms of burnout? What steps can be taken to prevent the occurrence or to diminish the likelihood of burnout?

PHYSICAL

Since so many facets of nursing are stress-producing, a real danger exists that the effects of stress may accumulate and result in major or minor illnesses. The first and most important step for nurses is to develop and follow a sensible exercise plan. This doesn't mean training for a marathon race. Rather, a simple, moderately strenuous program of *regular* physical activity is suggested. Success in sticking with an exercise program can be increased by choosing activities that are fun and can be shared with others. If jogging is boring, try to do it with others. If it is still boring, don't jog. Find something else that is more enjoyable. Bicycling, walking, swimming, racquetball are only a few options. If possible, use as many different exercise activities as you can. This will tend to counteract boredom and maintain enjoyment and motivation. The type of activity is less important than *regular* participation. The goal of exercise should be increased cardiovascular efficiency and muscle tone. If these goals can be reached, stressful situations at work and at home will be handled more easily and effectively.

A second step could be careful investigation of current nutritional habits. Most nursing programs include courses in nutrition, yet burned-out nurses report eating at irregular times, eating hurriedly, and eating relatively nonnutritious foods. Since stress is partly a physical phenomenon, the body must have nutritious food to utilize if it is going to function effectively under stress. Fads or fanatical diets are not recommended. Instead, any sensible approach which includes food from all the major food groups in moderate amounts seems reasonable. If additional guidelines like no sugar or no processed white flour or low salt intake seem worthwhile, they may be included in the program. What is important is that a sensible plan be followed regularly. Try to eat with someone else; avoid eating alone. Try to eat slowly and stay relaxed. Nutritional meals are intended to help fight stress, not add to it. In fact, if any meal is interrupted by an emergency at work, insist that that mealtime be reinstated later.

A third general recommendation is to develop and follow some stress-reduction program. There are many different approaches to stress reduction, all with merit. Choose one which is most personally satisfying and seems to fit with your particular life style. Transcendental meditation, deep muscle relaxation, autogenic training, biofeedback, and hatha yoga are all popular methods for reducing stress. All have in common the potential for lowering the physical arousal which accompanies stressful situations. This relaxed state of lowered arousal can be learned and easily produced during stress-filled situations. It should be considered a must.

INTELLECTUAL

Nurses are seldom asked for their opinion, and one result is that they begin to believe they don't have worthwhile ideas to contribute. Another result is that their creativity begins to atrophy form disuse. The following suggestions should be considered a starting point.

One problem facing nurses is a boring routine which may seem the same day in and day out. If this is so, investigate the possibility of switching or sharing responsibilities with nurses on other wards. An occasional change of scenery can do much to alleviate boredom. Seeing new colleagues and co-workers will also help to fight staleness. This can be scheduled as a relatively short-term rotation on other wards and services. Lateral job transfers are another possibility which can add variety to a routine job. Also, try altering the daily schedule. Don't always do paperwork at the same time each day. Don't always eat lunch at the same time. Switch with someone on the shift. Explore these possibilities and think of others. Changes have been made in other hospitals and can be made in all of them.

Another area to investigate is the scheduling of breaks and quiet time. Even five minutes of time to oneself each hour can help dissipate stress. Sit down with others on your shift and work out a plan for small periods of quiet time. Nurses can cover for each other. Short periods away from stress are invaluable. Additionally, working out such a schedule with colleagues may make them more appreciative of the problems other nurses face and vice versa. Find a quiet place on the ward (maybe a linen room) and just go there and relax. Close your eyes and breathe slowly and deeply for several minutes. Have a drink of water and stretch a little. Five minutes away from stress each hour will enable the other fifty-five minutes to be handled more efficiently.

Try to identify what the sources of stress are in the working environment. What are they? When does stress seem to begin? How can you tell? What does it feel like? Decide which of these situations can be changed. Don't dwell on those that are unchangeable. Don't worry about causes of stress once they are identified. Instead spend time and energy thinking of solutions.

Another way to improve the intellectual part of nursing is to look for new aspects of the job. Join professional organizations and attend workshops which deal with timely issues such as burnout, communication, or recent developments. If possible, read professional journals. Try to keep up with recent advances—human, technological, medical, and administrative. Often an article may be the inspiration needed to create changes which can alleviate burnout. Even if no changes come from an article or workshop, the mind is growing and not atrophying. A more knowledgeable nurse is better able to maintain feelings of self-worth. Discuss new learnings with others. Form a discussion group if it seems appropriate. In addition to new learnings, relationship building can occur. Closeness between colleagues can grow with increased sharing of feelings as well as knowledge.

Another possibility is taking a sabbatical or a leave of absence. If burnout is relatively severe, a six-month leave might be appropriate. Although six months may seem lengthy, consider what might happen if the leave were not taken. Quality of care during the six months would likely be below desired levels. Continued stress could deepen burnout, making it even more difficult to overcome. During the six-month period, with burnout becoming more serious, it would also become more difficult to summon the energy needed to take steps and make changes to lessen burnout.

Some changes which could reduce the likelihood of burnout must ultimately be decided upon by the institution where nurses work. However, nurses can take the initiative in suggesting changes. Although their experience may suggest that no one will listen, we encourage trying. Also consider having a staff member designated as a burnout "lookout." This person's task would be to keep an eye on ward or shift personnel. If early signs of burnout appear, suggestions can be made to the person involved. Again, get together with others and brainstorm additional changes which would help in the fight against burnout.

EMOTIONAL

The major emotional symptom of nurses suffering from burnout is excessive "distancing," or psychological detachment from patients. Recent advances in holistic approaches to medicine clearly demonstrate the role of emotional and psychological variables in physical illness. Some view all illness as having psychological components. To the extent that this view is accurate, nursing care which ignores the emotional and and psychological needs of patients is ineffective. Patients are not going to get as well as quickly, and nurses will begin to feel ineffective and see their dreams slipping away. Although not aware of the relationship, nurses, by excessive distancing, are contributing to the destruction of their own dreams.

In order to turn this situation around, distancing needs to be addressed. Instead of ignoring or avoiding patient needs, an attitude of detached concern would seem to be more appropriate and effective. Such an attitude maintains objectivity about patients' needs, giving them recognition without losing the compassion and concern that is so necessary for effective nursing. It is difficult to achieve such a balance, but it can be done. One way would be to take courses in counseling and therapeutic communication. Psychiatrists, psychologists, and other counselors have developed techniques and approaches for mastering detached concern.

Central to these techniques and approaches is the concept of responsibility. It must be realized that the patient "owns" a particular need and that the nurse bears the responsibility for meeting it. The nurse may recognize the need, but it is the nurse's responsibility to see that the need is met. For example, if a patient is very lonely and scared, the nurse can be helpful by acknowledging these feelings and perhaps sharing how those same feelings have affected the nurse personally. Maybe an occasional chat with the patient would help ease the loneliness and fear. However, by making the patient's problem the nurse's, the nurse removes any distance between the professional and the patient. The patient's problem begins to drain the nurse's emotional reserves. Burnout becomes inevitable.

A more sensible and effective approach would be to recognize the patient's needs and discuss possible solutions with the patient, leaving the final choices to the owner of the problem. There is no need to feel guilty if the patient has emotional needs that a nurse can't meet totally. Again, it is a matter of responsibility. Recognizing the need, sharing the recognition with the patient, and leaving the solution to the patient are all components of detached concern. They meet some patient needs and still allow the nurse to maintain enough distance to avoid one of the chief preconditions for burnout.

Another approach which seems fruitful is for nurses to become aware of their own feelings. If angry at a patient, recognize and admit it. Don't deny it and don't dismiss it to tiredness or a bad day. There is certainly nothing wrong or bad about being angry. This does not mean to take anger at a supervisor out on patients, but rather to express anger directly. There is nothing wrong with expressing anger in an appropriate manner. Outside the hospital, people express angry feelings; this is healthy. Why not in the hospital as well? Depending on the condition of the patient different words or a different way of expressing the anger might be chosen, but by all means express it! Serious consequences can result from ignoring one's feelings. Admit them. Own them. Once they are owned, analyze their source. If a patient is demanding and this causes angry feelings, make sure everything reasonable has been done; if it has, relax and accept the fact that nurses can't be everything to all patients. Admit that the best has been done. That is all anyone can do, even a nurse.

SOCIAL

What seems obvious from the symptoms in this category is that there is a lack of meaningful communication in several spheres of a burnout victim's life. For nurses, one sphere is nurse-patient communication. Instead of fighting to remain calm and in control on the outside, nurses need to learn to express their feelings toward patients in an appropriate manner, especially if the patient's demands are unreasonable or abusive. If they are angry with a patient they should make that known; if they are scared or don't know the answer to a question, they can make it known in an appropriate, nonthreatening manner. Courses in interpersonal communication and assertiveness training might prove especially helpful. Expression of inner feelings can do much to relieve the effects of stress and restore an equilibrium at a lower level of intensity. Evidence suggests that such an open, honest relationship between nurse and patient results in greater well-being for patients. We are suggesting that it results in greater well-being for nurses as well.

Another way to increase communication with patients is to become aligned with patient or consumer groups. The goal of such a strategy would be to become more sensitive to the concerns of patients, not only as an ailing, physical body, but also as consumers and human beings. With hospital costs rising rapidly, patients expect more in the way of services and conveniences. By becoming aware of such concerns, nurses can learn to handle consumer complaints from patients. By becoming involved in patient groups, nurses can restore some of the lost sensitivity to the human needs of patients. By hearing how patients feel frightened, confused, angry, or lonely, nurses might regain some of their lost sensitivity and reestablish meaningful patient contact.

With colleagues, there is a definite need to discuss feelings, especially since other nurses are most likely to share and understand these feelings. As seen above, in cases of burnout there is reluctance for nursing colleagues to share inner feelings with each other. To overcome this reluctance, encounter or therapy type groups might be established. The goals of such groups, facilitated by an experienced group leader, could include building communication skills such as listening and speaking, and discovering that other nurses experience the same frustrations, anger, fears, and guilt. Finding out that one is not alone can be a powerful experience which may lead to increased sharing and exploration and, ultimately, communication.

Further activities with colleagues might include the development of support groups. Potluck socials or occasional parties for ward and shift personnel would go a long way toward building a team closeness and increasing opportunities for meaningful sharing.

If distancing has affected communication between nurse and family, family counseling might be appropriate. The Association for Marriage and Family Therapists can recommend a certified counselor who can help restore meaningful communication between family members. All that is needed is to be aware that communication isn't effective and have a desire to improve it. Seeing a therapist does not imply illness or "craziness." It may just mean that the nurse and family are confronted by highly stressful situations that they could use some help in handling at present.

SPIRITUAL

Spiritual symptoms reflect a loss of meaning in the professional and personal lives of nurses. Consequently, the following suggestions are directed toward restoring that lost meaning.

One idea is to sit down and write out the goals that led the nurse into the profession. Which of these goals are still being met? Which are not? Why not? What changes would have to be made in order for those goals to be met? This is an excellent opportunity for brainstorming with colleagues and can, ideally, lead to meaningful interchanges.

Another suggestion is to keep a journal in which are written as many positive occurrences as can be remembered. Even in serious cases of burnout there are positive things that happen. What are these positive things? What can be done to arrange situations so that positive events are more likely to happen again? What can one do to set up such situations? What can the supervisor or the administration do? It often happens that memory is selective. There seems to be a tendency to remember situations or events that fit in with current attitudes or feelings. If that picture is one of frustration and lack of fulfillment, events that fit that picture will be recalled. More positive events can be overlooked. Thus, we strongly recommend writing down positive events: Any time a patient laughs or feels cared for; any time a favor is done for or by a colleague; any time a patient seems to be getting better; any time a patient expresses emotions and the response is a sensitive, helping one. Write down these and other gratifying occurrences. It will soon become apparent that one is doing a meaningful, worthwhile job. It will also provide a chance to see in what areas one is doing well and the areas in which more could be done. The effects on self-concept should be positive. Once nurses begin to see they are providing a meaningful service, their attitude will also change. When that happens, a cycle can start which leads to more and more helpful behavior which will further reinforce self-concept.

Another very important suggestion is to develop interests outside of work. Nurses suffering from burnout tend to spend more time in work-related activities, often coming in to work early and leaving late. More important, they seem not to have any interests or hobbies which can generate excitement, meaning, and relaxation outside of work. When work, which has become the most—and in many cases, the only—important thing in their lives, goes sour, their lives also go sour. Their work is all they have, and it is not rewarding. However, when there are other sources of growth, excitement, and creativity outside of work, the nurse can get recharged and find an outlet for the energies and emotions which aren't expressed at work. More important, some meaning is restored to a relatively meaningless life. It is remarkable how strong the relationship is between severity of burnout and lack of outside interests.

There are so many possibilities for outside activities that to list them would be impractical. One general suggestion is volunteer work on a *limited* basis. The opportunity to help others will fulfill part of the dream that nurses have. However, we caution against too great an involvement in volunteer work, as it may become a further drain on the already limited emotional resources of the nurse. The opportunities for volunteer work are numerous and varied. Check them out and see if any are especially attractive. Remember, make a limited investment of time and energy.

Hobbies which allow emotional expression, such as music, poetry, painting, pottery, and other related areas, can prove very helpful. Community colleges, adult education classes, and open universities often offer classes in these areas. Take advantage of them.

One final suggestion seems quite clear and is designed to help prevent burnout. While still students, future nurses should be given more time on hospital wards or in health care settings. This would give them exposure to what the profession is really like as opposed to what it *should* be like. It would also expose them to nurses who have a great deal of experience in nursing, unlike many teachers, whose experience is limited. Such a suggestion would do much to bring the dreams of young nurses into line with the realities of the nursing profession.

9. Dentists

"All joys I bless, but I confess
There is one greatest thrill:
What the dentist does when he stops the buzz
and puts away the drill."
—Christopher Morley

Recent news reports in the daily papers and in the broadcast media have indicated that the field of dentistry is in a period of economic decline. Reports are that registrations at dental schools are at an all-time low. Dentists in private practice are being forced out of business. All of this comes at a time when many are just recognizing the pressures under which dentists work and the physical and psychological price they pay for their job selection. If any profession doesn't need more pressure, it is dentistry.

It is a profession in which the physical symptoms seem more severe than in any of the other professions. Certainly, that is confirmed by mortality tables. It is estimated that eighty percent of dentists practicing today will die before the age of sixty-five.

The suicide rate for dentists is among the highest for all professions. Given this new influx of information on the psychological stress dentists face, it is a wonder that there are still persons willing to enter the profession at all and that there are still a few standing who are able to perform their jobs.

WHAT WENT WRONG IN THE DENTIST'S OFFICE?

THE PROBLEM OF PHYSICAL WORKING CONDITIONS

Dentistry is an unusual profession because the ordinary physical demands of the job are among the very demands that contribute to burnout. Dentists stand. Ignoring all the advice to the contrary, dentists have pushed the dentist's chair away from the patient and elected to stand. In fact, the older the dentist, the more likely he or she will not use a chair to sit in while operating. As if that were not enough, the way dentists stand compounds their own problem. Dentists must assume unusual body positions in order to do their work. These strange positions restrict the proper flow of blood to limbs and even to the brain. These positions are held for long periods of time, contributing to their increasingly damaging effects. It must be apparent that constricting bodily positions have a corresponding effect on internal organs. This cramping of internal organs, such as the heart, kidneys, and lungs, coupled with restricted blood flow, is a major factor in the unusually high mortality rates of dentists due to respiratory diseases and circulatory problems.

The position that dentists assume while standing is unbalanced. Much more pressure is placed on one leg than the other. One leg may operate controls while most of the weight is placed on the other. This contributes to the daily musculoskeletal pain experienced by dentists, ultimately, to the early retirement of many dentists.

Further, the small area of the mouth and occasionally poor illumination both contribute to poor vision of the operating field. The strain of close work is made more difficult by the continual readjustments of vision necessary as the dentist peers into the mouth and must then readjust to select instruments, address the assistant, consult X-rays, or any number of other tasks.

These qualities of the working conditions contribute to the daily fatigue and eventual burnout of dentists. Further, overtime is a major factor contributing to their unusually high mortality rates.

THE PROBLEM OF ISOLATION

As if the physical strains of the job of a dentist were not enough, dentists usually work alone. It is this physical and mental isolation which is another major cause of burnout in dentists. Most dentists work in private practice.

They spend their days with frightened patients and, perhaps, an assistant. It is a curious phenomenon of dentists that they report they infrequently have friends or even close colleagues among other dentists. Since they are in private practice, dentists are competitors. That competition may well contribute further to their isolation. It may cause dentists to withdraw more from the opportunity to form friendships with colleagues in an already isolated profession.

THE PROBLEM OF THE NATURE
OF THE JOB

Dentistry, like a number of other occupations explored in this book, turns out to be, upon examination, a profession of repetitious, boring, and unchallenging work. Dentists do much the same thing, patient after patient, hour after hour, day in, and day out. There is little that is challenging. In fact, as we shall see later, when there is a challenge, it can be resented.

It is also sedentary. All the physical pain described above is not from exercise. It is the opposite. Dentists as a group turn out to be among the worst exercisers in the professions! The physical stresses are compounded precisely because it is such a sedentary profession.

It is also stressful because the working environment is a negative one. People do not come cheerfully to the dentist's office. They come filled with fear (not to mention cavities, gum disease, and so forth). Even the routine cleaning of teeth is not viewed with much pleasure.

Since a dentist is self-employed, a high caseload must be maintained in order to have a successful practice (with a few exceptions). So, they see one patient after another, each requiring essentially the same work, each filled with fear. Added to this is the fact that the autonomy of dentists is being steadily eroded by the demands of insurance companies which "legislate" both treatment procedures and fees, and we can see that the job is losing some of its initial appeal. We can understand as well how the job itself can contribute to burnout.

THE PROBLEM OF ECONOMIC PRESSURES

There are many expenses associated with becoming a dentist. Not the least of these are the expenses incurred at dental school. Many dentists go into debt paying the costs of a dental education. Once out of dental school, there are the expenses of setting up a practice. While banks are reasonably free with loans to young professionals who are setting up private practices, the pressures of paying back these loans force young dentists to try to carry unusually high caseloads and to work long hours. They must buy equipment, rent office space, hire assistants, and pay the everyday expenses. Since they are self-employed, time means money. Time for a dentist is the number of patients who can be treated in any given workday. The economic pressures of setting up and maintaining a practice never let up on dentists. There is no such thing as sick pay. If a dentist in private practice is sick, income stops. But expenses continue.

Consider this reasoning when planning a vacation: Work equals money. Vacation equals loss of money. It may be difficult to have a wonderful time at the beach if no money is coming in and, worse, it continues to go out.

The economic pressures for dentists are severe. While it is true that the economic rewards of dentistry are large, they may be eroded by the initial investment of time, money, and psychological commitment as well as the continuing demands of overhead costs. These pressures all add up and contribute to burnout.

THE PROBLEM OF TIME PRESSURES

There are two sorts of time pressures that contribute to burnout in dentists. First, there are the daily pressures of keeping to a schedule. Second, there is the time pressure of making enough money early in one's career so that retirement security is ensured either before or shortly after age forty.

The daily time pressures of scheduling patients are severe. Many dentists carry heavy caseloads (some as many as thirty patients a day), so it is not surprising that a majority of them report that they are always behind schedule. The problem that this creates for dentists is that much of their work is routine and, when it is not, further time pressures are created for them. Emergencies and complications can come to be resented. In fact, if something interesting comes up, it causes conflict for many dentists. It is out of the ordinary, stimulating, maybe even exciting; it is just the cure for the doldrums. But it also demands that the schedule be interrupted. The dentist is conflicted over whether to go ahead and do what is demanded by the job or to try to maintain the good will of other patients and keep to the schedule. Often, such interesting cases are rescheduled even though they may require immediate attention.

Time is money, and when patients miss appointments it is doubly expensive. The loss of income from the patient that didn't come and the loss of income from another patient who might have been scheduled in that time. Distractions by telephone calls, improperly laid out equipment, late X-rays, and an inadequately trained assistant all create stress.

It is not surprising that dentists try to fill their schedules and consequently fall behind, work long hours, miss lunch, work evenings, have no time to exercise, socialize, or relax with the family. That is a made-to-order pattern for burnout.

The second kind of time pressure comes for the aging dentist. Many believe that there is a limited amount of time a dentist can perform the intricate manipulations that are involved in dentistry. Such a concern can cause profound worry over future security and can bring on a crisis that has been building up over time. A fear of the future can cause overwork and constant worry in the present. Mid-life can be a trying time for all of us. It can be especially crucial in the life of a person who believes that it signals the end of his or her productive life as a professional. It is during this time that dentists are especially vulnerable. Even though dentists are at the peak of their careers, it is also the time the risk of suicide is greatest among dentists. The pressures of time appear to many to have finally caught up with them. They have worked too hard for too long to confront a future of declining skills and ability.

THE PROBLEM OF THE JOB AND DENTAL SCHOOL SELECTION PRACTICES

Dental schools select the type of person they think will have the most chance of succeeding as a dentist. The problem is that the person they select may have the very characteristics that lead to burnout. It may also be that the curriculum of the dental schools does nothing to help persons who are dedicated, conscientious, aggressive, and striving for success. Competitive, compulsive people who have a tendency to delay personal gratification need to learn the skills and competencies that would enable them to use those qualities selectively. Such personality characteristics may be entirely appropriate for a business day and entirely inappropriate for social and familial concerns.

There are some who believe that the personality selected for dentistry should be one able to tolerate high levels of frustration and uncertainty. This is in almost direct opposition to the type that dental schools seem to select. It may be that the demands for perfection and permanence encouraged by dental education are an exercise in futility. Patient failures can come to be seen as personal failures by highly demanding, aggressive personalities. Such a point of view is ready-made for burnout. It is practically a given in dentistry that treatment will have to be compromised for many patients. The costs of proper treatment are simply too high for many in our society to bear. Further, some patients, either from fear or ignorance, will not take the dentist's advice and, instead, forego necessary dental work. For a highly perfectionistic personality, one who knows what is "right," this demands a compromise that is difficult to accept. There is a certain built-in futility in dental work that is especially frustrating to perfectionistic personalities.

It may be no accident that dental schools select a particular type of personality to pursue a dental education. First, the faculty consists of dentists who were previously selected for exactly the same characteristics. In addition, dentists are members of the health professions, which as a group engage in the myth that emotions must be controlled by health professionals or they are ineffective. One evidence of this is the new insistence by dental schools that dentistry carries no greater risk of suicide than any other profession. In the face of the research from different points in time and from several different nations, this represents an attempt to deny that real problems exist and to imply that it is somehow a personal problem of individual dentists rather than a problem of the structure of the profession and the preparation of its practitioners. The strains of dentistry are not the fantasy of a few; they are real, dangerous, even deadly strains associated with the profession. Using different methods of arriving at information more favorable to dental educators does not help the dentists who are suffering from the symptoms of burnout. Right now, dentistry doesn't need denial. It needs a serious investigation of the selection practices used by dental educators and a revision of the dental curriculum to include skills, knowledge, and competencies that enable dentists to cope with the real stresses of their professional lives.

THE PROBLEM OF STATUS

The final cause of burnout among dentists is that they are not given the status they deserve in the health professions. Physicians hold a higher standing in the eyes of the public than dentists, regarding them as second-class citizens in the health world. While dentists have worked hard to earn degrees and continue to work hard to provide sound dental care for their patients, this goes largely unnoticed and unappreciated by the general public. As a result, dentists often hold themselves in low esteem.

Given the demands of the work and the lack of appreciation, even hostility, from the public, it is no wonder that dentists are among the professionals most affected by the stresses of their job and primary candidates for burnout.

SYMPTOMS OF DENTIST BURNOUT

PHYSICAL

One half of all dentists who retire do so because of ill health. The younger the dentist is at retirement, the more likely that it is due to ill health. The most often reported problem is diseases of the circulatory system. The second most often reported is diseases of the bone, with back pain mentioned frequently. Coronary disease and hypertension are twenty-five percent more prevalent among dentists than among the population at large.

While these very serious physical symptoms constitute one end result of burnout, there are a host of milder, but still painful, physical symptoms. Dentists suffer from early and chronic fatigue due to the unusual positions they have to assume. Among the symptoms reported by dentists to be most severe for themselves are eyestrain, flat feet, varicose veins, lower back pains, upper respiratory infections, skin allergies, and postural defects. Since dentists stand improperly for long periods of time with their weight unevenly placed, defects of posture turn out to be a common complaint. This improper stance results in uncommon stress in the joints, ligaments, and musculature. It affects the back, particularly in the sacral, lumbar, and cervical vertebrae.

Working too long and without proper conditioning frequently causes muscle spasms, especially in the shoulders and back. And the dentist's reduced resistance increases susceptibility to respiratory, skin, and eye infections.

When fatigued, a dentist may be less careful and cautious with materials and equipment. The result can be X-ray burns or other burns from chemicals used in the operative procedure. The mixing of chemical compounds, if not carefully done, could cause poisoning; the same is true of air pollution from the compounds used with high-speed drills.

Finally, dentists as a group are among the least physically fit professional persons researched. They turn out to be below average on most tests of exercise and above average on none. The exercise they report is trivial. Dentists work in hard physical conditions, with the possibility of poisonous substances coming into contact with their skin and the air they breathe. They are in poor physical condition in a high-stress occupation. The symptoms of physical burnout range from daily fatigue to chronic fatigue to heart disease.

In fact, the list of dentists' maladies is the longest of any occupational group researched for this book. It is apparent that dentistry is a physically demanding job and that little is being done to prepare dentists for even the physical demands of the job they have to do.

INTELLECTUAL

Little has been written about the intellectual burnout of dentists. Certainly, it should be apparent by now that the job is difficult, dull, and disastrous for many who enter it. There is little that is intellectually stimulating in the field of general dentistry. The signs of burnout reveal themselves in a general dislike of the job, and an overriding cynicism about dentistry and life in general. The burned-out dentist is increasingly negative about the patients who require care. Burned-out dentists will begin to complain more and more about how unfair the public is; about how cowardly they are in the face of the drill or needle. Some might even go so far as to be intentionally rough with patients or to inflict unnecessary pain. Before that, they will consciously begin to oppose innovations, to criticize dental education for its unrealistic curriculum, and to cast doubts on the skill and competence of other dentists. New techniques will be ignored, and journals and workshops will be avoided. The intellectually burned-out dentists don't care about new skills, strategies, or techniques. Dentistry has become a job of doing the same old stuff for the same old people in the same old ways.

EMOTIONAL

Emotionally burned-out dentists have many of the same symptoms of burnout as other professionals. The difference is that they have them in greater numbers. Dentists suffer from neurotic disorders in numbers two and one-half times those of other medical practitioners. While much emphasis has been placed on the physical stresses faced by dentists, it is equally true that the emotional stress they face is just as severe. If it is true that dentists can be characterized as highly competitive, then it is equally true that stress is a risk in people with such personality traits.

An early sign of burnout among dentists is irritability at things that once were coped with without complaints. Burned-out dentists will show increasing signs of impatience with family, friends, and patients. Their thinking will become more and more unreasonable as they begin to become defensive about age, skills, strength, and general competence. They will exhibit signs of self-pity, and their approach to life in general and work in particular will evidence less zest. They will become more and more depressed.

SOCIAL

Burned-out dentists have less rewarding contact with family, friends, and clients. Their contact with other dental professionals is virtually nonexistent. Both the process and the product of burnout contribute to marital disharmony for dentists. They work hard and long and have little time left for family and friends. They are reluctant to discuss this and eventually may be incapable of talking with friends and spouse about their problems because they have denied them for so long that they may not be aware of what they are anymore. The typical dentist prone to burnout is a male, in his early forties, with approximately fifteen years experience, married, with 2.5 children (we will leave the mystery of how someone can have half a child up to the statisticians!) and a marriage on the rocks. Burned-out dentists have invested so much in their career that there is little left over for family, friends, or a life outside the dental office. And, as we have indicated above, there is little contact with other dentists which might provide support, enrichment, or a sharing of professional concerns.

SPIRITUAL

The first sign of spiritual burnout is a loss of eagerness to go to work and a lack of anticipation with respect to play. The burned-out dentist expresses little enjoyment of play, work, or, increasingly, life. Like other medical professions, they use their easy access to drugs to escape the developing boredom of the job and abuse other substances such as alcohol, narcotics, and various painkillers.

Most serious is that dentists commit suicide at a far higher rate than the general public or other professionals. It is estimated that the equivalent of one large dental school class a year is lost through suicide. More than a decade ago, a study revealed that dentists committed suicide at more than twice the rate of the general population. A more recent study reaffirmed this, revealing that approximately two percent of dentists' deaths were due to suicide, compared to about one percent of the deaths in the general population. Many years ago in England, a study revealed that of 425 different occupations, dentists were twelfth in the number of suicides as a cause of death. In the same study, they were first among the professionals. This is the most serious symptom of all, of course. Suicide signals the complete loss of meaning in a person's life. For many dentists, for reasons that have been hinted at above, their profession provides insufficient meaning to sustain their lives.

CURES FOR DENTIST BURNOUT

PHYSICAL

There are three central concerns in avoiding or reversing burnout. First, there is nutrition. Second, there is exercise. Third, there is rest and relaxation.

Dentists are in an excellent position to keep nutritious food right in the office. The easiest way to keep strength up is to provide the body with food. It is possible, since there is a refrigerator, to keep fresh fruits and juices right in the office. It is recommended that the dentist's favorite fruits and juices be used to keep energy up throughout the day.

It is most important that lunch not be cut short or cut out. It is an excellent time to call up another dentist in town and suggest a lunch to talk over mutual concerns. This may be the one profession in which it is OK, even advisable, to talk shop during lunch. Dentists appear to be so isolated in their work that talking over dentistry with another dentist at lunch would have positive effects. Experiment with foods at lunch time. Try to find foods that have the best effect on energy in the afternoon and seem to correlate the least with tiredness, drowsiness, and loss of energy. Don't rely on lunch alone to get through the day, but don't skip it either. If a patient absolutely needs an appointment at lunch time, then arrange that day's lunch during the hour before or after the appointment. Take the full lunch hour.

It is probably not advisable to pass up lunch to exercise. Even though exercise is important, it is not so important that lunch can be missed. It is also probably not advisable to have a heavy workout after lunch; before lunch is a better idea. (Maybe it would be possible to have all the dentists in the building or the area gather for a community exercise-lunch one or twice a week.) It is possible and advisable to take a walk after lunch. It is a perfect time to combine exercise and relaxation.

Here is an exercise that is for both the body and the mind. It combines the need for exercise with the need for relaxation. Determine what one's normal walking pace is. Then accelerate the pace until it is a brisk walking pace. While walking, learn to pay more attention to one sense than another. Actually, this is a bit easier than it sounds. It is relatively easy to learn to keep the eyes open but to pay little attention to what is seen. Let the eyes work automatically, and emphasize another sense. For example, walk briskly with the eyes open, but listen carefully to all sounds that come to the ear. Listen for the birds singing, the sounds of the traffic, footfalls on the sidewalk or grass. If possible, walk to a local park or bench. Sit. Allow the sounds of the place to take greatest importance. Close the eyes while sitting, if desired. The brisk walk and the listening and quiet sitting can become a daily routine that is helpful for the body and relaxing for the mind.

Patients missing appointments are a stress for dentists. Here is a way to turn that missed appointment into an exercise time to increase overall physical fitness and especially to emphasize those muscle groups which are most needed by dentists (namely, fingers, wrists, arms, shoulders, neck, and back). One example of a quick exercise program is contained in the back of this book. Here are several exercises that emphasize parts of the body important for dentists.

First, try to learn to rotate a coin back and forth between the fingers like a magician. Second (this is a form of meditation as well), touch the index finger to the thumb, then the middle finger, then the ring finger, then all at once. Start with different fingers. Alter the rotation. All of this increases fine-motor development.

For the wrists, squeeze a rubber ball at least one hundred times a day.

Do five push-ups every hour on the hour for the arms and shoulders.

This next exercise benefits the shoulders. Extend the arms over the head as far as possible and then, keeping the shoulders as straight as possible, push toward the rear with the entire arm. Next, lower the arm straight out from the shoulders and parallel with the floor. Push back as far as possible without pain and hold for a count of five. Feel the relaxation in the shoulders.

Occasionally, rotate the head by bending it forward and rolling it to the right in a complete circle. Repeat in the other direction. Do this slowly. Bend the head as far as possible to the right and then to the left. Rotate it again. This exercise will help you release tension in the neck.

The final suggestion is to sit down when working. Indications are that the use of a stool during a dentist's work can prolong the operator's life by seventeen percent. The dentist's chair is the topic of an excellent article describing stress among dentists in England. This article by E. Paul, entitled "The Elimination of Stress and Fatigue in Operative Dentistry," appeared in the July 1, 1969, issue of the *British Dental Journal*. We recommend it highly for the design of a dentist's office and for the construction of the dentist's and patient's chairs. It is designed specifically to relieve the problems of posture, limb imbalance, and internal constrictions discussed under causes of dentist burnout.

INTELLECTUAL

What seems most important in avoiding or reversing intellectual burnout among dentists is accepting that it is a high-risk profession. Individual dentists can bring the issue to the floor of professional organizations, which can in turn begin to bring pressure on dental schools to make some significant changes in the dental school curriculum. We have provided several specific suggestions that individuals can use to increase the intellectual stimulation in their own lives but can also serve as suggestions to be included in a more enlightened and more humanistic dental education.

First, seek out a course or workshop on body mechanics. An understanding of the pressures placed on the body by the positions assumed by dentists can lead one to the use of a proper dentist's chair and to an exercise program that reduces the chance of the physical deterioration so common to dental practice. Such a course may not be available at a dental school, although it should be, but can be found in departments of physical education at colleges and universities. If one does not live in a town that has such a department, it may be possible to interest the local dentists into sponsoring a workshop for themselves; an expert could come to the local community rather than individual dentists going to a central campus.

Second, seek out information on the occupational stresses that affect dentists in particular. An understanding of these diseases can help one create a personal burnout-prevention program to resist or reverse intellectual burnout. In the same vein, seek out a workshop or weekend encounter in which one can learn that our emotions are not an aspect of ourselves that needs to be feared. Such a workshop can provide the opportunity to learn to accept emotional needs as a valid part of our lives.

Third, seek out a workshop or self-help book that provides information on relaxation. Further, seek to have a professional organization include relaxation workshops, meetings, and talks on this important aspect of dentistry.

And last, encourage the local association to include seminars on techniques for calming frightened patients. It seems clear that calming patients has a beneficial effect on the dentist as well. Research indicates that the dentists' emotional and physiological signs parallel those of their patients. If dentists can learn to calm the fears of patients, they will have taken a big step in reducing their own vulnerability to burnout.

All of these suggestions can apply to dental education. Encourage the professional organizations to bring pressure to bear on dental schools so that such courses become a regular part of the dental curriculum.

EMOTIONAL

The most important recommendation in avoiding and reversing emotional burnout is to seek balance in one's life. Do an analysis of one's life. Look at nutrition, exercise, and rest; social involvements with family, friends, colleagues, and co-workers; intellectual stimulation; and the degree to which the job and life in general are providing meaning to one's existence. If all these factors do not balance, now is the time to build a life style that does provide that balance. If one is working long hours that do not provide the opportunity to build a meaningful contact with family and friends, do something about it. Consider whether income will really suffer that much if the last two appointments of the day are rescheduled to another time. Find a caseload that provides the money necessary but also leaves time for recreation, exercise, social events, and family get-togethers.

We have already indicated that the emotional response of the patient is paralleled by that of the dentist. Learn a way of keeping distraught patients calm. Learn techniques that will reduce discomfort if possible. Learn to give shots in the least painful way. Develop a "chairside" manner that is sympathetic, comforting, and supportive. Learn techniques that can calm patients. Here is one that has worked in other professions. Before doing any dental procedure at all, use this systematic relaxation response with patients. Tell them to close their eyes and lay back on the chair. Have them tense their feet and then relax them. Then, tense the legs, relax. Then the thighs, relax. Then the stomach, relax. Tighten the back and relax it. Tighten the chest and then relax. Tighten the muscles in the neck and then relax them. Now tighten the muscles in the face as tight as possible and then relax. Tighten the muscles in the jaw as much as possible and then relax. Tighten the tongue and then relax. Repeat the exercises for the face twice. If it is at all possible, have an assistant rub the temples of a patient if a shot has to be administered. This is a good supportive and relaxing procedure to use during any operative technique. All during the operative manipulation, have an assistant rub the temples of the patient. Try this. It is a procedure that works for many. Some may not even feel the shot take effect as they enter deep relaxation.

SOCIAL

Plan time with the family. Take a night out with one's spouse that is private and without the kids. Spend one evening with the spouse and the kids that is special for everyone. Try to have a get-together with friends at least once every two weeks.

Take the initiative with fellow dentists in the community and establish a dentists' support group. Take the time once a month to have a meeting at which dentists talk about dental procedures. Provide the opportunity to discuss professional problems. Create an atmosphere in which all feel comfortable to discuss the personal pressure felt in private practice. Discuss new techniques. Provide positive comments about good things heard about fellow dentists. Help one another avoid the self-blame associated with patient failure.

If one is experiencing personal problems or marital discord, seek professional help immediately. Dentistry is a high-stress profession. It might very well be that dentists don't have the time other professionals seem to have before making a trip to a counselor.

SPIRITUAL

If one is to avoid spiritual burnout, the importance of meaning cannot be lost to concerns of economics, time, or status. What counts is that one's own life and work *feel* important. It is necessary that a high level of awareness be kept about the meaning of what one is doing. If it is becoming boring, then do not let it become any more boring. Find out what could make it more exciting and meaningful, and then make that happen.

If suicide is as prevalent as it appears to be among dentists, find out what the signs of suicide are and, if observed in others, express interest and concern. Express a willingness to help in a direct, straightforward way. Here are some signs to look for in oneself and in colleagues; take the time to search out others. First, remember that talk of suicide must be taken seriously. It is not a joke. It is especially serious among dentists. That is a first sign. Take note of any radical change in behavior—positive or negative. Be sensitive to a withdrawal of interest and enthusiasm in people, events, and activities. Finally, be aware of any sudden happiness in a person who has experienced a long period of depressing events. Often this signals that a decision has been make to end it all and that is the cause of relief.

Take time each day to write down the positive things that have happened that day. Do not overlook the small surprises and reliefs which, though small, actually enlighten one's days. Write them down in a way that they are easily remembered and easily retrieved. Take the time to review them each week so that they provide evidence that life contains ups as well as downs and that it holds hope for the future.

Above all, if the symptoms of spiritual burnout begin to appear, don't ignore them. Act on them immediately. In that way, suicide will not claim another victim.

BURNOUT AND THE SAVIORS

10. Clergy

"God loves an idle rainbow no less than the laboring seas."
—Ralph Hodgson

Recently, on a trip across the country, one of the authors encountered a member of the clergy as a fellow passenger. Not only did his dress set him apart from the other passengers, but his behavior was also distinct. He accepted the bumps and minor collisions with the other passengers with more grace and kindness. He spoke to more people and wore a warm smiling face. One was reminded of the informal dictum about the clergy: they are always kind, always cheerful, always helpful—and never angry! If religious people are happy people, then their professional representatives must always manifest the positive side of human existence. It is as if the negative aspects have disappeared. In truth, clergy are encouraged to deny such negativity. How much energy it must take for such professionals to shut off so much of reality for the sake of the "professional image"! It might be well to trace that image to examine the possible bases for burnout.

WHAT WENT WRONG IN THE PULPIT?

THE PROBLEM OF POWER

The "leader of the flock" has the task of the care and the cure of souls. They are the facilitators of growth and healers of the woes which beset the lives of those for whom they have responsibility. They must not only understand human beings but also integrate that understanding with a body of "religious knowledge"—a body of knowledge which, it is assumed, they know better than anyone else. They know it better not only because of training but also because of their "calling." The problem for many is that their calling may take the form of rigid authoritarianism and represents, in the judgment of the authors, one of the major causes of burnout. One's personal biases and prejudices may be believed and set forth as the will of God without an awareness of one's distortions of that will. The professional training of the clergy, by and large, takes place in colleges and seminaries under the auspices of specific religious denominations or groups. To sort out the "divine" from institutional and personal interpretations of knowledge may be a most difficult, if not impossible, task. The applications of such interpretations to caring and curing souls might, therefore, best be done with a tentative and cautious attitude. Failure to come to grips with this flexible, open dynamic of interpretation and practice may invite the setting up of the clergy for burnout. The clergy share this dynamic with professional healers of other desciplines. Obviously, some members of the clergy are aware of this problem. They struggle with the problem of power as they strive to present themselves and their doctrine in ways which maintain their individual faiths but allow the persons they serve to interpret and to seek meaning and understanding in personally important ways. However, they recognize that what they say is often the "last word" on topics of religious concern. This "burden" weighs heavily on persons who are themselves flexible and open thinkers. Easy religious victories in the pulpit are one thing. But recognition that no real dialogue has been established with the people is not so easy to accept and can be a cause of clergy burnout.

Finally, if power corrupts, then consider the power of salvation and what a weapon that can be in molding the lives of the people with whom the clergy come into contact. Some clergy use that weapon freely. Others weary of such power. They weary of their colleagues who misue their power and use religious terms to defend their misuse. They "disarm" themselves and give up the power. Often, that results in a church's dismissing them because, unfortunately, many are drawn to churches because they are authoritarian. Churches do not want flexible leaders. This discovery is a major cause of burnout in the clergy.

THE PROBLEM OF KNOWLEDGE

The clergy acts as "the mouthpiece for God." Its members are charged with the responsibility not only of knowing the "word of God" but of proclaiming it with effectiveness. This is their special mission. This may prove to be too big a burden to bear, for many clergymen interpret this to mean that they must be perfect. They may feel that they have a direct channel to divine resources and that their interpretation of the divine is *the* interpretation. To the question, "Who speaks for God?" it is the clergy who answers, "We do." Such an attitude does not lend itself to open dialogue with others. If people assume a direct telephone hookup to God, it is difficult, if not impossible, for them to entertain other points of view. Their authoritive stance is a major reason the clergy is often cut off from other community resources. The growing antagonism between clergy and psychologists, politicians, journalists, and other professionals may stem, in large part, from the inability of clergy to see their own point of view as *a* point of view rather than *the* point of view. This closed assumption is more apparent in burned-out clergymen who "stay in" the pulpit. They become more and more rigid and less and less tolerant. While those who leave may leave for any number of reasons, it is important to understand that many leave because they were driven out by the intolerance and closed-mindedness of their colleagues, who consider a questioning, open discussion of issues and doctrine to be evidence of lagging faith. Those who leave demonstrate one response to burnout. The clergy who assume such a rigid, closed-minded stance when confronted with an attitude of tentativeness represent another form of burnout. Those who do not view the "proclaiming of the word" as an essentially dialogical process tend to destroy themselves. The danger for the rest of us is that they can damage us as well. The anger, bitterness, fear, and emotional difficulties that are more openly discussed in other professions can be perceived as sinful in the clergy. They might even be perceived as "God's will." In such cases, clouded thinking can be ignored and any objections dismissed as misguided. The deeper the burnout, the more rigidly held the belief. Finally, the danger is that the hostility will turn outward to attack the rest of us. As we have seen, first it affects the open thinkers in the church, then, depending on the number of followers, the larger society.

THE PROBLEM OF BUSINESS

While members of the clergy must care for the "heavenly treasure," they must also be attentive to the "earthen vessels" in which the treasure is received and passed along. They must be concerned about financial, personnel, property, and organizational matters. They must work long hours with budget committees. They must be concerned about the hiring and firing of staff. They must take responsibility for the maintenance of the property in which the congregation is housed. Their share of paperwork increases as they move up in the organizational superstructure. They become a part of the prestige and status hierarchy of the institution. In the end, they may become cogs (however small) in a machine. The very reason they entered the profession in the first place may have been lost. Their profound caring for people has to be sublimated to administrative concerns. The more distance there is between clergy members and the people they entered the profession to serve, the less likely they are to keep the dream alive. Unnurtured, a dream withers and may die. Without a dream, no profession has any purpose. This seems especially dangerous for the clergy.

It is another factor which contributes to burnout. This splitting of the clergy from the dream of service makes them into technocrats in a world of technology. While our technology is powerful and does us much good, it might be worthwhile to consider the dangers of technology applied to the spiritual concerns of the clergy. We have to consider whether a "Madison Avenue" approach to God doesn't distort the search for ultimate meaning. We need to consider if "drive-in" churches, televangelists, and mass production haven't created an imbalance between concern for the spiritual lives of persons and concern for ratings, mass conversion, and more and more money to expand technological approaches to religion. If that is so, then we have a prime example of the effects of burnout in the clergy.

The technological society of the twentieth century is an impressive monument. It may indeed corrupt the purposes of the clergy. In their effort to "take care of business," some clergy may have forgotten that the primary business of the church is the individual soul. That lapse of memory is the most important cause of burnout in the clergy.

THE PROBLEM OF EXPECTATIONS

Finally, it seems to the authors that a contributing factor in clergy burnout is the expectation that they act like members of the clergy all the time. The story at the beginning of this chapter is the portrait of a person wearing a mask—the stereotypical mask of the clergy. It is false. It is a role that is predestined for burnout. Anyone who seeks perfection in life is destined for burnout. In fact, perfection may not even be a worthwhile goal. It certainly happens from time to time, but it may be worthwhile to consider perfection a fleeting moment in the life of a person or an event. Any one who considers failure to be life-damning faces a dreary future and burnout. Clergy are people like the rest of us. They have selected a profession, and in that they are no different from the rest of us. What makes them different is the attitude of many that they aren't like the rest of us. We have denied them the basic human emotions. We have limited their lives to a one-sided shallowness that allows them to be only smiling half-persons. We have, in fact, denied them the right to be human.

There is an episode in the movie "Oh, God! Book II" in which a little girl asks God (George Burns, for those of you who are ignorant of this particular theological point of view) why He allows so much pain, suffering, and evil in the world. He (George) says something on the order of, "The problem is I never learned how to make half of something. I couldn't figure out how to make an up without a down, a right without a left, or a one-sided coin." That is just the problem with our expectations of the clergy. We would have happiness without sadness, joy without tragedy. The problem is that one loses its definition without its opposite. When we insist that the clergy act as if there is no sadness in their own lives, we condemn them to burnout. The one-sided life is not worth living.

SYMPTOMS OF CLERGY BURNOUT

PHYSICAL

One of the authors, who interned at a large general hospital in a great mid-western metropolis, encountered another pastoral counselor who boasted of "touching" in one year all 3,200 beds in that hospital. One might raise the question of how effective such contacts could be. Pushed, short, and per-functory, they could do little but tire out the visitor. The body obviously took quite a beating in the process. Such is the tendency of the clergy, steeped in an orientation which has all too often depreciated the body in deference to the soul. Clergy members have been led away from concern and care for their physical bodies. We label this the "servant syndrome." Fueled by the belief that it is others who count, this syndrome of clergy burnout includes such things as lack of awareness of the body (to say nothing of its well-being), little or no time for physical exercise, poor nutritional habits, and little or no time for rest and relaxation. If there is concern about such factors, it is often accompanied by feelings of guilt. The servants are most effective when they are "suffering servants." That the body is a chief target of such maltreatment is seen in the historical sanction by religious groups of the flagellation of the physical in order that the spiritual may come alive. Overwork (the irrational driving of the body) may, in such light, be viewed as proof of the indwelling of the spirit.

The source of physical burnout for the clergy may stem from this undervaluing of the body or from guilt. Whatever the source, the effects are the same. The body's resistance gradually declines as a result of abuse. Minor illnesses lead to major illness. Consider the possibility that the physical neglect of exercise, nutrition, and rest lead to minor illnesses. Further, since these minor illnesses are not debilitating, the clergy member ignores them as well. Finally, the body collapses and the person is faced with a long-term, serious, and debilitating illness. Finally, the body rests. The remaining problem, of course, is that those clergy who are hospitalized may still experience guilt about having these illnesses and not attending to their "flock"!

INTELLECTUAL

Because so much in the life and work of the clergy is seen to flow from their relationship with the divine, intellectual initiative may be undervalued. The prophetic task is seen to contain no indications for rigorous preparation, analysis, integration, and application with regard to the "truth of God." In such instances scholarly reading is minimized, especially scholarly reading outside the field of specialty. Scholarly writing suffers a similar fate—being inspired is often interpreted to mean that one does not need to record thoughts. Participation in such intellectual opportunities as in-service or continuing education, professional conferences, workshops, and seminars becomes minimal. Intellectual inertia sets in, and clergy members utilize texts as pretexts for repeating the same old communications they developed years ago. Finally, a major sign of burnout is the increasing reluctance to consult sources other than the specific approach from which the clergy come. This increasing intellectual isolation prevents burned-out clergy from discovering sources of help which may exist outside their own profession. It deepens burnout and prevents the clergy from doing its work effectively.

EMOTIONAL

Just as it was said of the village shoemaker who was so absorbed in the mending of the soles of others that he neglected the mending of his own soles, it may be said of the clergy that its members are so absorbed in the curing of the souls that they neglect the curing of their own souls. The martyr complex, held in high esteem historically, might well carry the clergy away from a focus upon its members' own needs. Consequently, their demands for attention and affection, for prominence, go unmet in favor of meeting the needs of others. They truly believe that they are the parson (the person) around whom the world revolves and to whom the world should bow in obeisance.

It is difficult for such parsons (persons) to be aware of their emotional needs or of the available resources for their own emotional sustenance and help. They lose contact with their feelings, especially those feelings which are considered negative by their religious orientation.

Such persons have great difficulty separating themselves from their work, and one often encounters the attitude in them of "I am my work." Their work is seen as the lives of others. Thus, they *are* the lives of others. The devastating result is that their own emotional lives are ignored, and the conditions for burnout are created.

SOCIAL

Service on the part of burned-out clergy is mainly self-service. Though outwardly it appears as service to others (clergy as shepherd), it is basically a need-meeting endeavor for the service giver. The involvement in the community is on the clergyman's terms and schedule. There is little development of I-Thou relationships in which the other person is met as a truly unique and worthwhile person. Persons are looked at in terms of religious criteria and how they meet these criteria. Are they living a "good" life and following the rules of a particular religion? Do they assist in the community? Do they contribute money to the church? This is what Buber meant by an I-It relationship. The church members become instrumental means by which needs of the shepherd for status, prominence, power, and control may be met. Buber's I-Thou relationship, where the unique human needs of each person, their desires, dreams, sorrows, and joys are acknowledged, is not experienced. Emotional wholeness and health could be achieved in this way, But the shepherd treats all the sheep alike. In doing so, the probability of burnout is increased.

Perhaps the most salient aspect of this syndrome is the clergy's symbiotic tie with religious organizations. Sociologists of religion have aptly referred to this phenomenon as a tie with religiosity (the tie with the institutional manifestations of religion which may or may not be religious). The institutional sanctions on who one is and what one does may not be transcended and thus may be mistaken for actual sanctions by God. Success as the shepherd may be judged more by institutional success, such as following rules, than success in the curing of souls.

SPIRITUAL

How can one detect the manifestations of clergy burnout in such a syndrome? First, there is a lack of attentiveness to intensive prayer and meditation. It is common knowledge among parish clergy that when visiting clergy members are present in a worship service, the aspect of the service in which they are asked to participate is the morning prayer. Is this reflective of the aspect of prayer's being the weakest part of the clergy's life? Most clergy express difficulty in maintaining a meaningful prayer life.

Second, there is a lack of examination of the function of religious beliefs and practices in one's life. A good question to ask along this line is that of the degree of change (growth) in one's beliefs and practices. Are the clergy member's beliefs the same as when he or she entered the profession?

Third, there is an absence of personal commitment. What is the meaning and purpose of my life? is a question that gets answered all too often in terms of institutional goals rather than in terms of individual purpose and direction. Meeting the needs of the bishop and running an efficient parish become more important than the clergy's own ideas of what is important and meaningful.

Fourth, there is a lack of commitment to the building of community (in the sense used by Martin Buber) as opposed to the building of organizations. Buber sees the former as based on I-Thou relationships, where the participants are persons of integrity and freedom. The latter are based on I-It relationships in which the participants are determined and manipulated by the role images of the institutions. They are therefore not persons of integrity, nor are they free. Clergy members may be seen as burned-out or not, based on their primary commitment to institutions over people.

CURES FOR CLERGY BURNOUT

How may members of the clergy avoid or relieve burnout? Again, we examine this matter of cures from the standpoint of the five areas of human functioning which seem most affected.

PHYSICAL

Clergy members may become involved in several activities which will deliver them from burnout.

First, they can bring about a more wholesome balance between the spirit and the flesh by carefully assessing the general well-being of their physical bodies. One of the heritages of psychology from historic religion is the mind-body unity. Somewhere in the process of transition this unity has become lost to the clergy. It would behoove the clergy to get in touch again with such rootage.

Second, they can utilize the physical cure for burnout of planning and carrying out a regular regimen of physical exercise. Clergy are often in an excellent position to create their own schedules. With this in mind, plan a regular time every day in which to exercise. The type of exercise is not nearly as important as doing it regularly and consistently. The two goals of such an exercise program are to increase cardiovascular efficiency and to increase muscle tone. If these two goals are met, the clergy will be able to work with more energy and thus accomplish more. Another suggestion is to exercise with parishioners. In this way the exercise will be more fun and the clergy can get to know their parishioners in a different way. Much important work has been accomplished while jogging or playing racquetball.

Third, clergy members can participate in a consistent program of sound nutrition. We don't advocate any specific diet and caution against any fanatical, crash programs. We are less concerned with calories and pounds than we are with nutrition. Plan a sound week's worth of meals and stick to the plan. If weight is a problem, eat a little less and exercise a little more. Most importantly, eat healthy foods. In this way the body will function more efficiently and the quality of work will improve. Again, plan to eat with others and get to know them in ways other than the traditional pastor-parishioner mode. Share the responsibility of where and what to eat. Above all, eat healthy food.

Fourth, members of the clergy need to build in regular periods for rest and relaxation—without guilt! It is so easy to believe that one is needed by everyone that many clergy members overwork themselves. They miss sleep and lose time which should be spent relaxing. Schedule time to rest and relax during each day. Schedule days off. Stick to the schedule. Although it may seem like much time is being wasted, recall that burnout victims usually provide below-standard services and aren't nearly as effectie as they might be. Rest and relaxation will do much to relieve this problem.

Fifth, clergy members can plan and carry out a forty-hour workweek in spite of the irregular demands of their profession. In order to do this they can educate their parishioners to this plan and solidify it by refusing to play the superhuman role.

INTELLECTUAL

Clergy members have many intellectual strategies at hand for minimizing burnout. There is the matter of reading—both professional and nonprofessional material. The offices of the clergy are often referred to as "the study." What an excellent image upon which to lavish such a strategy!

The strategy should include a balance between professional and nonprofessional reading. Try to keep up on trends and interesting questions in the profession. Read what others' ideas are and determine a response or reaction to them. Include reading for pleasure and relaxation. Strive for balance.

Again, there is the intellectual strategy of writing—rigorous writing. Many clergy don't write because they don't believe their ideas are worth writing about. Others feel that they don't have the ability to write. "Don't worry about writing it right, write it down!" is a good rule to counteract such lethargy. The rewards of clarifying and communicating one's ideas through writing are matched by those of a reduced probability of burnout.

Another intellectual strategy is involvement in challenging intellectual endeavors such as workshops, conferences, and seminars. The confrontation of new ideas pushes one into new vistas of growth and keeps the excitement of the profession alive.

EMOTIONAL

In caring for one's own soul, clergy members may utilize these strategies. First, differentiate between selfishness and self-lovingness. For too long, in religious circles, the two have been confused. The prerequisite for service to others is service to self. ("Thou shalt love thy neighbor as *thy-self.*") The strategy of placing one's own name on the list of persons to be loved precedes all other emotional strategies.

Second, be aware of the resources for emotional help, and then utilize them. Such resources may be formal or informal. The clergy member who ignores this strategy is a strong candidate for burnout.

Third, learn to accept manifestations of a wide range of feelings, especially those which are negative. Failure to do this results in those feelings' being projected onto persons who don't deserve them—including oneself (see the example in Chapter 3 of Part Two).

Fourth, learn to separate self from work. Clergy members have a right to get in touch with themselves, just like other helping professionals (see the Burnout Susceptibility Test in Chapter 2 of Part Two).

SOCIAL

The clergy member can well utilize the strategy of deliberately planning for days when one will not use one's car for transportation. By walking, bicycling, or using public transportation, people see things that ordinarily would be missed had they utilized their car. It is good exercise as well as an excellent way of getting to know others and their worlds.

Clergy can also utilize the strategy of broadening their social network. This involves seeking social interaction with persons unlike oneself. To relate to someone else, for example, where religious language has to be disbanded could be a powerful growth-producing relationship.

The development of a "life of dialogue" should be a natural social strategy for the clergy. Usually this means curtailing the "speaking" act in favor of the "hearing" act, for the clergy's tendency is to speak more than to listen.

To help in this endeavor, try slowly counting to five after someone else speaks. This will give time to think of a response and will likely lead to increased speaking on the part of the original speaker.

Another social strategy that clergy members may utilize is that of involvement in social planning, organization, and action. Perhaps there is no better model for this than that of clergy involvement and leadership in the civil rights movement in the United States.

SPIRITUAL

The dictum "physician, heal thyself" may well be applied to the spiritual lives of the clergy. The development of a meaningful prayer and devotional life is a natural strategy for averting clergy burnout. Could it be that the widespread use of meditative strategies by persons of all professions means that they have put to use more effectively that which was indigenous to the clergy?

A second spiritual strategy is that of spending regular and intensive time focusing on how religious beliefs and practices function in one's life. Are such beliefs and practices constructive or destructive? This is a good pivotal question for this strategy.

A third spiritual strategy is that of rekindling one's commitment. In a profession where so much credence is given to high sense of calling, what could be more beneficial than to reexamine the nature and status of that calling? Such an examination is potentially a reservoir of energy and challenge for the clergy.

A final spiritual strategy is building a fellowship with those who care for and cure souls. The clergy should consider the "communication of the good news" through nurturing fellowship as well as through the spoken word. In such fellowship, burnout is minimized. It increases the chance that the shepherd will be whole and the flock cared for.

11. Counselors

"Canst thou not minister to a mind diseas'd,
Pluck from the memory a rooted sorrow, . . .
Cleanse the stuff'd bosom of that perilous stuff
Which weighs upon the heart?"
—William Shakespeare

André Gide, the brilliant French novelist of the first half of the twentieth century, points in *The Counterfeiters* to a phenomenon which may be all too common among humans. It is the phenomenon of a loss of integrity. Gide's characters in the novel are for the most part so involved in what they may *appear* to be (to themselves and others) that they neglect the important task of grasping who they *are*. Hardly a single character is really what he or she seems to be. Could this be the most characteristic description of the counselor in our time? Is the commitment to a life of helping in the human services field also a commitment to becoming so absorbed in appearances, in what one seems or ought to be, that counselors lose a grasp of who they really are? Is burnout inevitable for counselors?

Are counselors mainly of two types—those who burn out and are aware of it and those who burn out and do not know it? With these questions in mind we will examine in this chapter (1) which forces and factors provide the basis for the emergence of burnout (causes), (2) how burnout manifests itself (symptoms), and (3) how burnout might be minimized or eliminated (cures).

WHAT WENT WRONG IN THE CONSULTING ROOM?

The causal factors in burnout are multidimensional, and there is no simple one-to-one relationship between any cause and any effect. These various dimensions are viewed as interdependent, interacting phenomena which form various combinations for a given counselor. There are, therefore, general causal entities for all counselors, and there are also particular entities which have significant impact for a given counselor.

THE PROBLEM OF A SEDENTARY WORKPLACE

The absence of a fully functioning, healthy body may be of primary importance in the production of burnout among counselors. The physical life of a counselor is rather sedentary. One goes to the office, sits at a desk for the entire day, and shuffles papers or talks with clients. There is very little physical activity. Because of a tendency toward overcommitment, one may not be diligent about such things as nutritional needs, exercise, and rest and relaxation. It is all too easy for the counselor to "grab a sandwich" or postpone routine exercise or collapse at home and call it rest. The result is a body which becomes tired, undernourished, and dysfunctional. The psychological image of the counselor as strong—("the helper")—may easily transfer to the physiological realm, and a careful monitoring of the physical functioning of the body may be neglected in favor of the assumption that one is strong physically as well as psychologically. The absence of a physical breakdown is often regarded as evidence of physical well-being. Counselors in such a state may continue to drive the body through extra-long workweeks, missed meals, improper exercise, and insufficient rest and relaxation. Many counselors boast of being "workaholics," interpreting such overcommitment as an indication of dedication.

THE PROBLEM OF THE SUBJECT-OBJECT DICHOTOMY

Crucial in this causal dimension is the tendency for counselors to fall victim to the subject-object dichotomy which is so characteristic of much modern psychological theory. Ours is an age of technology, characterized by a commitment to efficiency (defined as maximum production with minimum effort and time), fragmentation (based on a return to the subject-object split in every aspect of human endeavor), and role definitions which determine one's status, prestige, and sense of identity. How can one truly counsel in an environment of time pressures and distancing required by those assumptions? It appears that one cannot, because from such a framework one is more prone to stand apart, observe, measure, and conclude. Such counselors appear more concerned about distancing than truly meeting another person. Perhaps we need both, but the balance for the burned-out counselor leans more toward distancing than meeting.

Burned-out counselors look to external sources for their work role. "I am a counselor who sees clients for x number of minutes for y number of sessions." Or, "I am a counselor who can stand outside of the client, observe, measure, and diagnose the client." Or, "I am a counselor who performs in accordance with the external guidelines set for me in light of my training, license, or certification." Being "professional" and "ethical" for such persons means conforming to prescribed beliefs, values, and behaviors which are encouched in such professional and ethical guidelines. They do the "job," but they have lost sight of the compassion that led them into the profession.

Where is the person in all of this? Is such a person totally proscribed by such externals? At some point some counselors become aware of this loss and the anger that calls out, unfortunately, even in the helping professions. But the freedom to express anger, hurt, and disappointment are not encouraged openly. Consequently, it gets turned inappropriately toward the client, the self, or the process of counseling. This is a strategy for burnout. It begins in theory and ends in tragedy.

THE PROBLEM OF AUTHENTICITY

One of the authors has spent two and one-half decades working as a counselor in a medical hospital, a state mental hospital, and a community mental health center. From these experiences and from observations of and interactions with counselors in private practice, the evidence seems clear that a significant factor in counselor effectiveness is that the counselor be honest and genuine. Whenever bureaucratic structures prevent such authenticity, the counseling is not only destructive to the client, but to the counselor as well. The destructiveness to the counselor results in burnout. Ultimately, the destructiveness to the client is that they become something to be observed, measured, manipulated, and evaluated. Any change in them is seen as a function of external forces which affect them. And that is how success is measured.

Rules which develop role definitions for counselors nearly always get in the way of authentic relationships. They demand instead that counselors diagnose, objectify, label, and treat clients in approved ways. Such role definitions do not so define a counselor's relationship to a client without at the same time damaging the integrity and ideas of the counselor. It is a pronouncement of death for the counselor, however kindly or sophisticated the communication. One might ask if this is not the reason why professional counselors are encouraged in their training programs to develop the skill of detachment—the skill of "looking away." Unfortunately, looking away turns one's back on the client, situation, and encounter. The result is dishonesty in the consulting room, ineffectual counseling, and counselor burnout.

THE PROBLEM OF THE TRAINING OF COUNSELORS

The literature on counselor effectiveness contains an abundance of evidence that there is a correlation between high levels of emotional functioning on the part of the counselors and their effectiveness. Yet there still appears to be an overbalance, in favor of didactic versus experiential training. We seem more concerned with scientists than with practitioners. Counselors are strong in understanding clients but weak in feeling and sensing with clients. The irony is that in this "emotional" profession, "being emotional" is unacceptable. Highly specialized counselors may face great difficulty in "getting in touch with feelings"—their own as well as those of the client. Such fragmentation may be a major cause of burnout. Are programs for training counselors more concerned about what a counselor knows and can do than about who a counselor is? The evidence seems to point in this direction. Counselor educators may neglect their relationshps with their students in favor of transmitting information about relationships. This aloofness and detachment from their teachers may very well train counselors to be aloof and detached from clients. While it may be workable in the classroom (and this is seriously open to question, given the problem of burnout among teachers), it leaves the counselor with little means of establishing a fulfilling and satisfying relationship with clients—the stuff of which counselor effectiveness seems to be made.

In psychoanalytic psychology much attention is given in the training of analysts to the training analysis. One of its major components is that of identifying and working through any barriers to high-level emotional functioning on the part of the analysand. This is a sound procedure because counselors may know testing, diagnosis, history, and statistics and yet lack personal insight. They are technicians. They have had their idealism used against them as they studied diligently to learn to help others. Academically, they were ready. Emotionally, their training failed them, as they were given little opportunity to explore their own vulnerabilities. It is only a minor exaggeration to say that they were trained to burn out!

THE PROBLEM OF INSTITUTIONAL GOALS, RULES, PROCEDURES

In the conflict between the individual and the social system, it is usually the individual who is the loser. Social systems have powerful influences on what the individual believes, values, feels, and does. Such influences have the potential of making person better (if the system is good) or worse (if the system is bad).

What happens if good counselors get caught up in bad organizational structures? They get swallowed in the hierarchical structure, with its rewards and punishments of status and prestige, with its role definitions of who one is, with its endless flow of caseloads and paperwork, serial numbers and electronic data. The negative sanctions against anyone who challenges the institution are forceful and unrelenting. The result is a host of counselors who do the institution's bidding whether it results in human good or tragedy. Bad organizations may further racism, sexism, elitism, or any number of other isms which are ultimately destructive of persons. Such counselors cast clients into categories. The role definition for many counselors demands more than a forty-hour workweek, case overloads, emergency service overloads, short vacation periods, and a diagnostic labeling system that is terrific for governmental reporting requirements and insurance forms but tells the client or other professionals nothing. All of this offends young idealists (old idealists too!) and causes them to be angry at the agency. The problem is that the agency is too tough an adversary to take on and win. The response is the response of burnout. First they turn their anger outward. Sometimes that anger goes beyond the client to their families and friends. After that it doesn't work. They then turn the anger inward. In the face of all this, one might seriously question if either counselor or client ever approaches honesty in the course of their relationship. When counselors commit themselves to being counselors for the institution, they are burned out. They have lost, for the moment, their definition as a unique, personal, warm, caring, and loving human being—the very characteristics which seem to blend for effectiveness in counseling!

The writers have observed and have received much feedback for counselors-in-training who have gone out in the field of human services. The major learning from such observations and feedback has been that the institutional structures in which they become involved make it highly difficult, if not impossible, to be counselors for persons. Their dreams and hopes, their plans and goals are crushed to bits in the mills of institutional goals, rules, and procedures. It is frightening to believe that the price we pay for order and standardization is burnout. If it is, then a little chaos would not be a dangerous thing!

THE PROBLEM OF THE LOSS OF A SENSE OF MEANING

In light of the preceding sections on burnout, is there any wonder that one could characterize counselors as those who have lost a sense of meaning? Counselors have theoretical orientations, to be sure. They have guidelines for feeling and behaving. They have ethical codes which delineate their value systems. The issue here is whether such orientations, codes, and guidelines spring from within or without the counselor. Deep within every student of counseling is the belief that they can be of help to others. They believe that they can "save" life through their techniques and skills. They believe that someday they will be out from under the dictates of graduate education so that they can, at last, begin to do the good work they feel themselves called to do. Then they run into the institutions which are created to help people with personal psychological problems only to discover that they have entered a "graduate school" of a different sort. The professors there don't control with grades or tests but with jobs and salaries. The young counselor discovers that there is more cruelty in our institutions than anything graduate school ever prepared them for. Rules are more important than people. No one who has ever come up against such institutional thinking can ever again touch, with the same hope and enthusiasm, the dreams of youth. There is a profound loss of innocence in such a discovery. Many never recover. They lose their meaning when they lose their innocence. Their education, their work, the society, and their dreams have all deserted them. Nothing is left for them. Some leave. Some put in their time, bitterly denying the dreams of others. Worst of all, some become convinced that the institutions are right, and they become the willing agents of the goals, rules, and procedures that shattered their idealism. They become the agents of institutions without meaning, counselors without hope.

SYMPTOMS OF COUNSELOR BURNOUT

PHYSICAL

One of the first physical manifestations of counselor burnout is fatigue—the energy reserves have simply run down. Sleep does not refresh. There is no joy in getting out of bed. At work they slump into their chair and try to rest, only to be confronted by the tasks of the day. Lunch time may be extended as work deepens the fatigue day after day. Somehow, building in as many distractions as possible, the physically burned-out counselor makes it through the day, leaves the clinic, drives home rapidly, grabs a beer, and collapses on the sofa. Sometimes he or she stays there until dinner. Other times he or she has to go back to the office for meetings or to meet with emergencies. There seems to be no rest. The routine of working fifty to sixty hours a week exhausts the body. There seems to be no time to eat well, to exercise, or to rest. The problems of clients intrude into private thoughts at night. There seems to be no way to get to sleep. No rest in the day and little sleep at night is an equation that ends in exhaustion.

Another physical symptom of burnout is a marked change in body weight. Usually, it increases (burnout doesn't give us any breaks!) and the body becomes increasingly ill-prepared to deal with stress. Irregular snacks, high sugar intake, and increased coffee drinking all facilitate complications in physical health. Years of inactivity and inattention can weaken the body without serious notice by the counselor.

Accepting increased caseloads and working longer than the forty-hour week cut down on exercise time and may even interfere with pleasant, relaxing lunches. Adding more clients and more hours may be seen as competing successfully with peers, pleasing one's superhuman idealism and one's actual performance. Whatever the case, coupled with the short vacation periods taken by counselors, a gorilla would collapse under the stress—imagine what it does to a sensitive, caring human being!

INTELLECTUAL

Perhaps one of the most dramatic manifestations of counselor burnout is the decrease or loss of interest in what might be called the theoretical side of counseling. Only a few years before, the counselor was an excited, searching, dialoguing student-in-training. Theoretical orientations were challenging entities to be analyzed, critiqued, integrated, and tested. For the burned-out counselor they became excuses, defenses, rationalizations, and blocks used to justify incompetence. New directions are no longer explored. Alternative orientations become threatening. The burned-out counselor has ceased to be an inquiring, questioning, creative and productive thinker. The rules become right, necessary, and rigid.

A related intellectual symptom is the decrease in the sharing, either through writing, speaking, or discussing with colleagues, of ideas relevant to counseling. Concerns such as the current status of counseling, the nature of persons, personal views of counseling, and communication with clients and colleagues have all moved to the bottom of the list of priorities. Intellectual inertia has set in. Burnout has begun.

Still another intellectual symptom of counselor burnout is what might be called the loss of the historical and poetic dimensions of the counseling endeavor. The loss of a sense of origins of the great theories and speculations of counseling signals a loss in caring about one's profession. Concerns about the original meanings of ideas and goals of the helping process, the helper, the "helpee," and the context of the helping process have faded. There is no joy in talk, discussion, argument, or revision. It takes too much time.

The loss of the poetic is the loss of the thrill of counseling, of the invention or discovery of hidden meanings that clarify and enlighten for clients. At the beginning of one's career, the client was somebody special or unique. To trace all the innuendoes within the mosaic of that uniqueness was exciting, even ecstatic. There was no way for the client to be lost in labels or tests or categories. The goal was to uncover, to provide the possibility of life. While similarities with other clients were noted, so were the differences, and the differences were of primary importance. For the burned-out counselor the clients have become standardized. Such a view of clients has far-reaching and serious indications for the planning, treatment, and assessment endeavors in counseling. This absence of the idiosyncratic focus appears as a major indicator of counselor burnout.

EMOTIONAL

Burned-out counselors tend to lack an awareness of their general emotional condition. The assumption of helpers is that they help others. The idea that they might need help too is a bit foreign to them. They become preoccupied with the emotional health of others to the neglect of their own. In fact, it is not difficult to see resentment with feedback about such functioning. Reminders that the counselor might be in need for counseling can be interpreted as dislike, criticism, or jealousy. This seems especially true for counselors who are burned out.

Sometimes there is an intolerance of different points of view in counseling. Such burned-out counselors view clients, colleagues, bosses, even the work setting as fighting against them. This view may express itself in a rather arrogant, elitist stance towards others. Burned-out counselors may present themselves in a superior, know-it-all, conceited way. Their emotional burnout prevents them from entering into an honest exchange of opinion. They must be certain.

A nearly opposite symptom is an inordinate need for affection ("everybody must love me, all the time, and more than they love anyone else"). Most clients tend to put their counselors on pedestals (client evaluations are almost always positive). The manner in which the counselor responds to this tendency may be a tip-off to counselor burnout. Counselors may try to keep clients who are positive around because of the psychological strokes they provide. It might help the counselor for a while, but it isn't especially good for clients.

Another emotional manifestation of counselor burnout is an inability on the part of the counselor to express hostility in a creative, helpful manner. For such counselors, clients, colleagues, friends, and relatives may often become the inappropriate targets of such hostility. The hostility itself often becomes disguised and therefore is not dealt with by the counselor. Such counselors routinely dehumanize clients, compete fiercely with colleagues, and systematically exclude family and friends from their lives.

SOCIAL

The social symptoms of counselor burnout take many forms. One is that of a loss of interest and involvement in relationshps with significant others. From a life of dialogue where others are seen as unique, of inestimable worth, and to be listened to with care, the movement is to a life of monologue where no one counts. Such relationships are characterized by a lot of talk on the part of the counselor, with the expectation of passive listening and acquiesence on the part of the other. Burned-out counselors have a lot of advice for others! These counselors make relationships and other functions into sermons for others. At the other end of the continuum are the counselors who hide out all the time. They miss appointments with clients, and avoid staff meetings, and getting an opinion out of them is like pulling a hippo's tooth.

Another social symptom of counselor burnout is a loss of interest in community. Little or no consideration is given to the matters of identifying understanding, and integrating community persons, resources, and organizations in the counseling process. Burned-out counselors may simply say it isn't their job, hiding behind a narrow but widely held view of counseling. In any case, they aren't of much use in community-building activities. They don't care.

The lack of involvement in the community shows up in another way, too. Burned-out counselors may show a tendency to "socialize" only with others who are negative, beaten down, and/or depressed. It seems as if it might be the other way around—depressed people would more likely seek out happy people. However, it doesn't seem to work out that way. So far as burned-out counselors are concerned, the old maxim holds true: misery loves company. They commit themselves to "the organization" and thus find their existence insulated from any threats by associating with other role players. Taking risks, a sign of a healthy counselor, is almost absent from such people's lives. They do not seek out others. They don't relish new experiences. They don't experiment. They are closed, rigid, and static.

SPIRITUAL

Perhaps the clearest spiritual indication of burnout among counselors is that they do not seem to know who they are, nor do they appear to know what the meaning of their lives is. When this occurs, it is indeed tragic, for there is no other arena in which effectiveness as a counselor is more determined than that of one's knowledge of self and one's sensing of, and commitment to, the essential meaning of life. Burned-out counselors are outer-directed. They are what the professional lore says they are—or what their particular organizational role declares them to be. They have stopped investigating themselves and abdicated the exploration, discovery, and definition of themselves to others. What meaning they had when they entered the profession is lost. Many leave the profession at this point. They are bitter about their clients, their colleagues, the institution, and, most of all, about themselves. Many discover their vigor in other pursuits and, having given up their personal cross of helping, rediscover the richness and fullness of life.

Burned-out counselors have lost their ultimate meaning in the world as well as the ultimate meaning of the world (of nature and of persons) in their lives. All that is left is a concentration upon "showing up at the factory," taking their places on the assembly line, and dying with each passing day.

CURES FOR COUNSELOR BURNOUT

Aware counselors may move away from burnout by the utilization of physiological strategies. Knowing, analyzing, and evaluating how one's physical body functions—both in a general sense and in the specific sense (how the body functions at a given time, in given situations) and noting the areas of strength and weakness may prove effective. One way of doing this is to ask colleagues how they keep fit, what foods seem best, and how and when they rest. It may even be possible to have an ongoing group to discuss physical concerns. Many counselors not only have their bodies checked by regular physical examinations but also seek feedback from their work colleagues, supervisors, friends, and members of their families. They pay careful attention to the feedback they receive.

In addition, counselors may plan and carry out regular physical exercise activities. Regular jogging, swimming, weight lifting, participation in sports, specific exercise regimens, and body-building training all provide avenues through which care and toning of the body may take place for those whose work does not call for a lot of physical activity. One way to combine physical activity with social concerns is to try to get colleagues to join in, form a club or an exercise group to reinforce one another in keeping fit. One might examine the job for indications of how physical exercise could be built in. One of the authors, for example, who worked at a state hospital, always made sure that he was aware of the program component which involved physical activity and participated regularly with colleagues and clients. It might even be a part of therapy.

Counselors can resist burnout by giving their bodies nutritional care. Practically all counselors are aware of the growing number of persons and programs that are resources in the field of nutrition. In many cases, such resources are related formally or informally to the type of service which the counselor offers. In such instances, one may be attentive to the strategy with a minimum of investment and energy. In the face of case overloads and the all-too-common tendencies of counselors to "be of service to others," whatever the cost—both of which may contribute to neglect of nutritional demands, even such a simple one as eating meals regularly—counselors might develop attitudes of dogged determination to make sure that their bodies are fed regularly and properly. Such attitudes have the positive side effect of modeling such important care for the clients with whom one works. It is not impossible for a group of counselors to demand that lunch be at a regular time each day. If emergencies occur during the staff lunch hour, they can be handled the same way emergencies are staffed on weekends. Have a regular roster of counselors who are on call during lunch. If the lunch hour is a particularly heavy appointment time, then change lunches to an earlier time to accommodate for that. Counselors can utilize the physiological strategies of rest and relaxation. Many scholars in the field have identified this as an area of great concern for counselors. Leisure Therapy Workshop findings seem to indicate that burned-out counselors experience difficulty in accepting the need for planning and participation in leisure-time activities and in reconciling these with work activities. A balance between the two appears to be the goal in the minimization and elimination of burnout. Such balance would involve planning and participation in short-term leisure activities at the end of the workday or week as well as routine "removals from the scene" in terms of mental health days or weeks and vacations. Further, it is important that counselors protect the forty-hour workweek. It appears ironic to the writers that in our current "age of leisure" many counselors, if not a majority, work far more than the forty-hour week. A director of a community mental health center program which covers a huge geographical area recently reported that her entire clinical staff spent forty-three hours per week *beyond regular duty hours* on call for emergency services! This director noted that the on-call hours were without pay. We could not have planned a better strategy for burnout. Counselors last about three years. Then they are gone. Some quit the profession. Others try to find another job in another center with a less demanding schedule. They work hard, and the result is that they aren't any good to anybody after a short while. If they had insisted on working a reasonable number of hours a week, then they could have been more effective, lasted longer, and set an example of how not to burn out. As it is, those counselors put in their three years, burn out, and become statistics. The tendency of keeping up with colleagues or getting ahead, along with the organizational concern for accountability, the idealism of being the "perfect helper" makes it easy for counselors to spend many more hours in work activities than they should. Counselors who love themselves and their clients will be better off if they stand firm in the determination to spend no more than forty hours at work per week.

INTELLECTUAL

Counseling involves both theory and practice. Since it is seen as a servive profession, the potential hazard for counselors is that they may become so absorbed in the practice that the theoretical and intellectual aspects of the profession become severely neglected. This is when the counselor becomes stuck in one theoretical orientation. One's mind becomes blocked to variations or alternatives within and without one's orientation. Aware counselors can move away from burnout in this area by being attentive to possible intellectual strategies.

One such strategy is that of reading and thinking. Since there is such a wealth of reading materials, one might well devote time to a reading plan. Such a plan could include (1) surveys of literature so that one might get a glimpse of the several images in given fields, (2) specific materials in one's professional field, (3) specific materials in fields of interest other than one's professional field, and (4) materials from literature, art, and the current world. In the development of such a plan, counselors might be guided by such things as level, variety, challenge, entertainment, and relaxation. The thinking process would enable one to identify old and new vistas of knowlege, to analyze and integrate them, as well as to explore possible indications and applications of these for one's world.

Another intellectual strategy in curing burnout is that of active and regular participation in experiences designed to enhance one's skills, to expand one's understanding, and to assess one's effectiveness as a counselor. Most, if not all, of the agencies in which counselors work provide in-service training opportunities. Professional organizations provide opportunities for participation in meetings, seminars, workshops, and conferences for both agency and private counselors. Outreach education resources of colleges, universities, and institutes make for rich opportunites in the endeavor to develop and expand ideas and skills. What is important about these activities is that they provide the opportunity to get away from work for a time and to learn new things. Both are important ways to relieve or reverse burnout.

A final intellectual strategy is writing, speaking, and presenting one's cases, understandings, and insights. The authors have encountered many counselors who, upon being challenged to write, have expressed pleasant surprise over the possibility of undertaking serious writing projects. It is a formal way of sharing the self with others and a way of keeping intellectual sharpness and a love for the profession itself. Writing does all that. It forces the writer beyond surface understandings. Even when it doesn't, someone who reads the stuff can point out flaws of logic, factual errors, and bad grammar. The writer is enriched either way.

EMOTIONAL

Counselors, being so committed to the healing of others, may easily neglect their own emotional well-being. Periodic assessment of one's emotional well-being is therefore crucial. Counseling effectiveness is largely a result of the counselor's own high-level functioning. High-level functioning on the part of the counselors facilitates high-level functioning on the part of clients. Counselors, therefore, owe both themselves and the clients the responsibility of such assessment. Not only can this be done by the counselor, but it can also be done by others in the helping field. It is so important that, in the absence of built-in checks upon one's emotional status, one should pay or trade another trusted colleague for such service.

Another emotional technique for avoiding counselor burnout is allowing oneself to be emotionally weak or to have emotional limitations. All good counselors are mindful of their limitations. They are aware that clients get well not only because of them, but also *in spite* of them! Accepting this reality, they do not get caught up in having to be gods. A good counselor is aware when help is helpful and when it is not. This sensitivity to the moment can be used in one's own life to look for times when the stresses of the job are becoming too much. Counselors who avoid the serious symptoms of burnout are the ones who are able to call a stop to the pressures for a while.

Some counselors are able to lessen the pressure of the work situation. They do this in two ways: (1) They make sure that they have a support system (composed of persons with whom they do not work) to meet their emotional needs. Persons who give love to the counselors enable them to give love to their clients without demanding an inordinate amount of attention or affection from them. (2) They make sure that their work is not their total world. This does not mean a lack of commitment or loyalty to the job. It means that the job is placed in its proper perspective with the other need-fulfilling networks of relationships to which the counselor has access. Work is a fact of one's life but not all of it.

SOCIAL

Cures for burnout in the social sphere are more difficult to effect, primarily because they involve interaction between the individual and the social system. One may be a good counselor as an individual but be a part (oftimes a loyal part) of a bad institutional or social system. With this multidimensional character of social cures in mind, we suggest the following:

First, spend time getting to know others in your community. It is a good idea to ride a bicycle or walk to work (if possible) and on the other errands in your neighborhood. One's perspective is radically different from a bicycle than from a car. In this same light, leave the car at home and ride public transportation periodically. One might learn much about how others live, what they are talking about, and how they feel. To face the pressures of starting earlier, pushing through long lines, or waiting on delayed vehicles may not only make for more understanding but also for more empathy for those who experience those same pressures on a daily basis. Out of this may come a commitment to the kind of social change which might contribute to the well-being of others in the community.

Second, socialize with persons in addition to those with whom you work. Association exclusively with work colleagues may lead to no more than a confirmation of who and what one is, or what one believes and values, or how one behaves. Socializing with persons who are new and different involves risk-taking, but in the taking of such risks there is a strong possibility of growth and thereby a strong possibility of the minimization and elimination of burnout.

Third, become involved in social planning, organization, and action. Counselors are susceptible to commitments which carry them away from a sense of social responsibility. With the discipline as fragmented and specialized as it is, there is a tendency to view things having sociocultural dimensions as being outside the province of counseling. This is perhaps a contributing factor to the lack of viable preventive programs within the field. As a social planner, the counselor sees the clients affected by organizational bureaucracies and the social system at large. Individual planning is seen within the context of social planning with realistic assessments of how society affects the individual and vice versa. As a social organizer, the counselor not only identifies the community leaders, organizations, and resources, but also lends abilities to the task of bringing about creative coalitions which may be more effective in meeting the needs, interests, and concerns of the population to be serviced. As a social activist, the counselor listens to the needs, interests, and concerns of the persons to be served and, with them, helps develop those strategies and techniques which might prove effective in positive social change. In all of these endeavors,the counselors are tapping their own creative resources, enhancing them through practical endeavors, and hence moving more and more away from burnout.

Fourth, the counselor may relieve or reverse burnout by a careful examination, alone and with others, of the nature of personal relationships. Questions like How do I relate to others? How much do I listen? How much do I speak? What happens to the interaction? may all lead to a discovery of what strengths and weaknesses one has in the creation and facilitation of a "life of dialogue." In such dialogue the "Thous" are never viewed as "Its"—it is the "Its" who burn out.

Fifth, counselors may well eliminate the possibility of burnout by transcending their bureaucracies. Such counselors, while able to identify the worth of organizational structures, are also able to identify their limitations. These counselors never "sell out"—neither do they burn out. They wear the cloak of bureaucratic structure as a "loose garment," never forgetting their commitment to themselves and their clients.

SPIRITUAL

By spiritual is meant those cures which have to do with counselors' having worked through to a clear notion of their purpose in life and of the meaning of their profession. Several avenues are available.

Counselors positively need to spend time alone utilizing whatever strategies are helpful in enabling them to get in touch with the meaning of their lives and the meaning of their work.

Counselor burnout may be relieved or reversed when counselors touch their dreams without apology. In the face of the crushing forces which dare us to dream, we can persist in the task of getting in touch with those goals, hopes, and dreams which provided the fuel of motivation when we first launched upon our career. The technological orientation of our times almost defies this, but it is all the more reason for doing it in the effort to avoid burnout. Certainly, we all know that when dreams die the zest goes out of life. Take some time to sit down and touch base with the dreams. Call it into words and write those words down. Put them in a prominent place and read them from time to time. It might even be a good idea to show them to clients. Have them tell you after a few sessions whether or not the dream is being realized. If they say it is not, then it is time to do something about it. Do it before burnout becomes any worse. Meaning does not have to slip out of our lives. We create it, and we can hold on or create new meaning for ourselves. Here, what it takes is the will.

BURNOUT AND THE MANAGERS

12. Executives

"Perpetual devotion to what a man calls his business, is only to be sustained by perpetual neglect of many other things."
—Robert Louis Stevenson

The American Academy of Family Physicians (AAFP) conducted a survey of 584 corporate executives on such issues as life style and stress on the job. Of six occupational groups studied, executives described their jobs as more stressful than all of the other occupations. In this particular kitchen, the heat is indeed high. Fully eighty-one percent of the executives surveyed viewed their work as stressful. The heat is so high that many have to leave the kitchen. The costs for industry are staggering. It is estimated that the costs due to stress are between $10 and $20 billion a year. This figure does not include any members of the work force except executives. Add to that the costs of other personnel and the problem of burnout becomes an incredible financial problem for American business management.

The climb to the top has always been a struggle. Modern America is no exception. There isn't much room at the top. That is part of the problem. Some view those who make it as champion athletes who have overcome the pressures. That is not quite correct. They have not overcome the pressures, they have learned one of two things. Either they have learned to cope or they have learned not to view the situation as pressure-filled. The latter is most difficult, as we have seen above. Only about twenty percent do not see their jobs as stressful. Whatever the case, it does appear that top executives, as opposed to middle managers, have developed some personal strategy for dealing with the pressures at the top. A 1974 study by the Metropolitan Life Insurance Company discovered that the presidents and vice-presidents of the 500 largest industrial companies were less likely to experience heart attacks than middle managers. In fact, they experienced forty percent fewer heart attacks. There are at least two explanations for this. One, of course, is that the executives at the top are the survivors. They are the ones who have survived middle management because of their ability to cope. They have either inherited some genetic predisposition for a high tolerance for stress or have learned to cope. Another explanation is that top executives have greater psychological protection provided by the companies for which they work. Such protection is usually not provided for middle managers or for executives of smaller organizations.

While some top executives do exhibit this resistance to stress, the problem remains for large numbers of managers in business today. The problem is widespread, costs enormous amounts of money, affects productivity, and is the source of uncounted personal tragedy in the losses to family and friends. Burnout is a major problem for management.

WHAT WENT WRONG IN THE EXECUTIVE SUITE?

THE PROBLEM OF DENIAL

Denial is a strategy that has been tried throughout history. It would not be a bad guess that even in the times before recorded history some creature among the scrubs and grasses of an ancient savannah insisted there was no danger out there. The problem is that they survived. Not enough of them were dinners for whatever lions and tigers and bears might have been out there since their genes made it down through history, and they are still among us. Personally, many executives still deny that they can be affected by burnout. They deny it right up to the day they discover they are drinking too much, have an ulcer, can't think straight, and can't get along with anybody. "It won't happen to me!" Isn't it interesting how people seem to say that just before the Cape buffalo escapes in downtown Chicago to trample the early lunch crowd in its frenzied charge to the salad bar.

The problems of burnout aren't going to go away by being ignored. They can't be managed by pretending it isn't happening. Yet denial seems to be one of our oldest defense strategies.

Obviously, such denial is of little real interest in discussing causes of burnout. The persons who use denial as a strategy soon learn that it doesn't work. The problems still appear. What is of interest is another kind of denial. It is the denial not of a problem for oneself but for others. As incredible as it may seem, there are those who would deny that the problems of burnout and other forms of stress-related dysfunction should be concerns of business, industry, and management. It takes a couple of forms. The first is simply a problem of faulty logic. The second is a philosophical position that has been around for a long time and will be discussed below.

The first position is that executives thrive on pressure. The really good ones are high-powered individuals who need to drive all the time or they aren't actually enjoying life. These go-go personalities get bored when things get slow. These critics of stress management programs and burnout prevention programs believe that hassles stimulate, inspire, motivate, and challenge executives to better performance. Here is the flaw in their logic. They start with the known fact that stress is a part of everyday life. In fact, too little pressure results in boredom. Boredom has the effect of creating burnout. And from that they conclude that stress must be good because too little of it has bad effects. Such dualistic thinking is the Edsel of the human mind. In point of fact, because too little pressure has deleterious effects doesn't mean that a lot is good. What we know is that both have harmful effects. Both can lead to burnout. What we read from time to time is that executives "thrive on stress" or that they are "adrenalin freaks." Such statements are pure silliness. It is extreme thinking that fails to give credit to the persons who have successfully dealt with a challenge. It gives credit to the problem rather than to the solution.

The second kind of thinking might be called "survival of the fittest." It certainly has been called that in the past. That is just what it is—thinking from the past. It is the "old time religion" of the business world. It is the thinking of the "robber baron" capitalists of the nineteenth century. One such attitude is summed up in the old maxim, "If you can't take the heat, get out of the kitchen." Or, as a recent expression had it: if a company has to have a burnout prevention program for its executives, then it has the wrong executives. If people can't take it, then that is just too bad. The tough survive. Solutions to the problem, such as biofeedback or TM, are considered garbage. They might be, but that isn't the issue. What is at issue is a form of denial that might be called "unenlightened self-interests." The "divine right" of kings was most ardently supported by kings. The "survival of the fittest" is most often supported by the current survivors. The denial of human needs, it should come as no surprise, comes from those who aren't feeling the pain. Those who question the importance of programs to reduce stress, help managers cope with pressures, or prevent burnout because of some misinterpretation of Darwin are dangerous to the rest of us. It is they whom management needs to take a long, hard look at to determine if such advice is really helpful. If they can be so far amiss on such a crucial issue of human need, then their business decisions might not be very trustworthy either. Further, we need to recognize that often such advice is not coming from executives themselves but from outside the business world. All of us need to recognize that the belief in the rugged individual, the one who deals with every problem, is always tough, never weak, makes all the right decisions, doesn't need other people, and is a self-made success is nothing more than a myth. That myth is not what made America great. It sounds good on the lips of politicians and it makes good fiction, but the facts simply do not bear it out. The Mountain Men make great myths, but it was the businessman in St. Louis who got rich.

Frankly, what all of us have to face is that it is an attitude born of excess. America is blessed with an "excess," if you will, of talent. What executives must face is that all of them can be replaced. There are any number of middle managers who can replace them. Even tragedies which claim the entire top management of companies do not significantly alter the functioning of such companies. When there is so little room at the top, there is a lot of talent waiting just below the top. Given such talent, it is possible to talk tough and write off a large segment of the management force. It is not so easy when talent is scarce. Human needs remain, whether the environment is one of plenty or scarcity. This is a lesson that has come hard to American management, but that is widely known and practiced today. Still, we have "dinosaurs" who cling to the old-time business philosophy that the only thing that counts is money.

THE PROBLEM OF ORGANIZATIONAL CHARACTERISTICS

The second major source of burnout for executives comes from the characteristics of organizations in America. The way organizations are structured is fascinating. One might never know whether one has "made it" in a large corporation. Consider this phrase. "The president was fired." The president was fired! Well, for goodness sake, who is running the company? The structure of companies now involve higher management, middle management, and even lower management. One might become president of a company and still have superiors. Given the nature of multinationals, holding companies, and corporate structure these days, one might be the president of a movie company owned by an oil company which is actually a company with a name that nobody recognizes which operates all over the world and has a board of directors to whom the president of the movie company is accountable. All of this gets very confusing to those of us who aren't involved. It gets very stressful to those who are. It is important because the primary source of job unhappiness for most executives is a perceived lack of appreciation from those above them. It is difficult for all of us to cope when we don't know where we are. Goals are important, and if we don't know when we have attained them, then it is even more stressful. It is a curious problem.

THE PROBLEM OF IDENTIFICATION

This curious problem might not be such a problem if executives worked in an environment which encouraged them to share personal problems, puzzles, or nags with one another. However, it is still true that most executives work in companies in which emotional concerns, reactions, and sharing are not encouraged. While programs for employees may have been generated, any hint of emotionality makes the executive suspect. It is nonsense, of course, but such an environment still prevails. In an environment which discourages emotional reactions, those reactions have to be kept under cover by executives. Hidden emotional concerns most often take their toll by showing up in some physical form. The symptoms range from mild to severe. But, given the current state of medical knowledge concerning the relationship between pent-up emotions and physical illness, any company that maintains the belief that executives who display emotions are bad executives is a bad company. Please understand, we aren't talking sentiment. Medical evidence is beginning to show that there is a strong relationship between the mind and the body. It has always been so. We took a wrong turn somewhere in medical history which led us down a purely physical path of explanation for illness, but we are now pursuing the relationship between mind and body once again with positive effects. Anger, frustration, joy, happiness, sadness, and guilt can all be expressed and, if the current evidence is correct, then the body is healthier for it. The psychological evidence suggests that in a climate where emotions are accepted and issues are fully discussed out in the open, the decisions that are reached are sounder and better supported by everyone concerned. But in a company in which emotional reactions are discouraged the hostility that builds up can lead to sabotage, low morale, and low productivity.

Another characteristic of our organizations is that they seem to demand that executives identify with the company. Their ego identity is tied up with the company. Loyalty is not a bad thing. It could become a problem, however, if the executive is expected to compromise personal values for organizational values, family values for company values, personal health for a sound balance sheet. In a situation in which the individual is deeply identified with the company, it may be difficult to leave business at the office. The executive may never be "off." Weekends, vacations, and parties must always be business. The lack of separation between home and work never provides a time to forget about work. The pressures never end. The executive may end up with no identity at all. Consider the problems this can cause when the executive's position in the company is threatened. The person's very existence is threatened in such a case.

One of the more pressing problems of ego identification with the company is that an executive may know personally that the next promotion is something that is undesirable. It may take away even more family time. It may demand a move that is not in the best interest of the children. It may demand more of the individual than the person wants to give to the job. Whatever the reasons, the demands of the organization may sometimes exceed the desire of the executive to give. Yet they are caught. On the one hand, they are identified with the company. On the other, they know themselves and their needs. One more cause of burnout in executives is that sometimes the organization views moderation as irresponsible. It may be a perfectly wise decision to turn down a transfer, promotion, or more responsiblity. But the company view is often that the executive is no longer trustworthy. A plant manager may not wish to be a vice-president if it means moving, taking the children out of school, leaving a job that provides great personal satisfaction, or disrupting a pattern of life that is relatively free of stress. It is characteristic of organizations not to respect such personal decisions when they interfere with the needs of the company. Those executives who do so will have taken a step away from company identification toward personal identification.

It is also characteristic of organizations that top executives seem to have better health than middle managers. We have already discussed whether this might not be some form of "natural selection." Many executives, obviously, have learned to cope with the pressures of their job. But what cannot be ignored is that companies take a greater interest in top management than they do in middle or lower management. For example, when organizations begin stress-management or burnout-prevention programs, they are ordinarily aimed at the executive level. Some firms pay as much as $1,500 to $2,000 for major managers to attend workshops aimed at increasing their effectiveness and usefulness to the company. Interestingly, some firms discover that the top management may not find these workshops particularly interesting or helpful. Many of the top managers have already found ways to cope. Some, of course, do profit. But a pattern is beginning to emerge in the problem of burnout. It appears that the problem is more often with middle managers than with top management. Yet the programs to prevent burnout are planned for top management. When some companies discover that top management does not attend or seems not to profit much from stress-management programs, biofeedback, exercise, or burnout prevention, they drop them. One such company discovered that more workers than executives were using its stress-management program, so they discontinued it! That sort of thinking is what is leaving the middle managers without support systems sponsored by the company. They are the ones who are reporting burnout, and they are the ones that the organization provides the least protection for.

No one seriously believes that managers in the world of business, industry, and management can work in a stress-free environment. Part of the cause of burnout is that stress is part of the nature of an executive's job. In the AAFP study mentioned above, over fifty percent of the executives listed deadlines as the major source of stress on the job. Everyone associated with business and industry knows that deadlines are a part of the job. Nearly half listed overwork as the next-highest source of stress for them. One third felt that their superiors were a major source of stress for them. Deadlines, overtime, and getting along with superiors are all parts of the job that can be expected. Such is the nature of the job. In an atmosphere in which an executive faces deadlines, works overtime, and is under pressure from superiors, it is no surprise that many burn out. The daily pressures of a business lunch, late appointments, memos, meetings, and presentations to a board expecting a heroic, charismatic performance takes its toll. Any one of the situations listed above would not be expected to lead to burnout, but taken together, and daily, they add up to a lot of pressure.

The secret is not to deny that the job of an executive is stressful, but to provide individual executives with strategies that actually help them cope with the pressures of the job. Further, it is important that an understanding be reached that, while these pressures are ordinary, they should not be made extraordinary by unnecessary deadlines, demands for extra work, or insensitive superiors. The point is that the job of an executive is tough enough without arbitrary policies that could make it tougher. The insensitivity of corporate organizations to arbitrary beliefs and policy is a major cause of burnout in executives.

THE PROBLEM OF THE EXECUTIVE
LIFE STYLE

While the nature of the organization and the nature of the job are major contributors to burnout, the executives themselves are another contributing factor. The "executive life style" is one which lends itself to burnout. If any group of people in any occupation can be considered "hard-driving," then executives are that group. If it is true that executives are expected to be decisive, dynamic, heroic, charismatic, creative, innovative, and right, then no other group has been more willing to try to fit themselves into these expectations than executives. Given a person of overwhelming ambition who works in a climate in which peers must be considered as competitors for the few top posts, then family, self, and certainly friends must be sacrificed to achievement. It is no wonder, then, that many executives end up being persons who can't do enough work. One executive was lauding transcendental meditation because, after meditating for twenty minutes in the afternoon, he was able to put in several hours more work! Talk about a life style that seems destined for burnout! We have persons who are highly competitive, unable or unwilling to delegate authority, convinced that they are indispensable, and unable to turn down requests for community service. Here is a reasonably clear picture of a hard-driving, ambitious, achievement-oriented executive heading for a top post, given some breaks and the right contacts. It is also a picture of a group of behaviors that are closely associated with heart attacks!

The climb to the top is not easy. There are a number of pressures associated with it. It may have meant climbing past or over or on a friend. It may mean distorting achievements. It may mean minimizing weaknesses. It may mean ignoring family. It may mean ill health. The problem is that when managers reach the "top," there are other pressures associated with staying there. The rising young executive may never have questioned whether getting to the top was worthwhile. Once at the top, there may be no time for such searching personal questions. There are decisions to be made and the constant pressure to be right, to be Solomon. Executives are executives because of the kind of people they are. The kind of people they are can be another cause of their own burnout.

THE FEMALE MANAGER

Females remain a rarity in the executive suite. That's part of the problem. For the women who are there, it is a lonely, isolated attainment. First of all, they must deal with two prejudices: the widely held belief by both men and women that the female executive slept her way to the top, and if she didn't sleep her way to the top, then she is there only because of affirmative action.

Second, in an effort to prove that competence is the reason for promotion, many women executives try to out-drink, out-cuss, and out-tough the males. The result is that heart attacks, ulcers, high blood pressure, and alcoholism are all on the rise among females in managerial positions. In fact, the health profiles of female managers look more like those of males than those of other females. The future doesn't look any better. In fact, it may be worse. The women who are succeeding today are doing so because of sheer talent and a touch of luck. They are pioneers who have demonstrated that success is possible. This signals other women to make the attempt. The problem with that is that once women gain full acceptance into the corporate world, the formula that applies to males will then apply equally to females. That is a formula that says that trying, especially trying unsuccessfully, is a whole lot more stressful than succeeding. There is limited room at the top. Obviously, that means that women, encouraged by the success of present-day female managers, will strive for top positions. Many will be disappointed, and that contributes to burnout for rising young executives more than any other single factor. At present, those who are there who encounter the remark that women can sleep their way to the top may have to be content with Pulitzer-prize-winning Boston *Globe* columnist Ellen Goodman's response, "Hey, if women can sleep their way to the top, then why aren't they there?"[1]

THE PROBLEM OF CHANGING VALUES AND VALUES CONFLICTS

We live in a time in which the old rules of management no longer seem to apply. We are not in the nineteenth century. We aren't even in the 1950s. Obedient workers and to some extent "the man in the gray flannel suit" are images of the past. Modern workers have been no less affected by the demands for social change than college students. There is a strong antiauthoritarian movement that exists in families, communities, government, and business. Any efforts to return to an old "work or be damned" management style are seemingly doomed to failure.

The executives of today are younger and are as much a part of the changing cultural values as other employees. They hold more humanistic values and are, in fact, more sympathetic to expectations of more individual freedom, autonomy, and a healthier, less stressful work environment. They hold similar concerns for themselves. These new management values have

---

[1]Ellen Goodman's words are from *Time*, October 27, 1980, p. 80.

been listed as social equality, changes in the work force, antiauthoritarianism, new expectations and demands at work, the impact of research from the behavioral sciences, the demands for corporate accountability, and the social responsibility of corporations.

While executives hold these values personally, traditional job demands seem not to have changed greatly. Much has been written indicating that profit is no longer the sole goal of business. There is now what might be called corporate social responsiblity as well. While profit may not be the sole goal of business, it is still the primary goal. The new managers have to balance their concerns with profit aginst human needs. It is here, in this sometimes conflicting desire to balance profit with human need, that a stress is created and a cause of burnout can be identified. The manager has to manage not ''workers'' but human beings. Their welfare, future, and physical and psychological health must be considered, too. The conflict of traditional business practices with contemporary values catches the modern executive in between. The stress of having to decide whether to line up on the side of profit or on the side of human need is more stressful for modern managers than it was in the past.

These internal conflicts are matched by an entirely new set of external concerns that plague the executive. These external demands can severely affect business and, to add to the burden, are problems over which the executive has no control. They come from the outside but profoundly affect what goes on within the corporation. Executives face an uncertain future for their companies as well as themselves. They are confronted with uncertainty of energy. Those industries that rely on fossil fuels, American coal, or Arab oil and those that have invested heavily in nuclear power all face the future with little idea of what lies ahead. Inflation seems to have run its course and then wipes out profits during the next quarter. Staggering interest rates dampen the business spirit and fears of a future recession drown it. Given all of this, plus a strong antibusiness climate, unfavorable court decisions, and increasing government regulations, the modern executive has to make decisions in the face of a growing body of unknowns.

THE PROBLEM OF LACK OF OPPORTUNITIES FOR PROFESSIONAL ADVANCEMENT

Many top executives indicate that such pressures are real, but that is what makes the job exciting for them. A problem for many executives is that there are so few top positions. The source of stress that seems most destructive is not success but striving and not succeeding. Trying and not making it seems to be devastating for young managers. The primary candidate for burnout is the rising young executive, the "young turk" at thirty-five who is in the same place at forty. There are problems of success, as indicated above, but the problem of not making it on one's own terms is crushing. Given the executive life style, nothing is as stressful as career stagnation. Comers don't like to be slowed; being stopped is simply unbearable. While coping with the pressures of changing values and external demands, at least the executives at the top have a sense that they can do something. They can make decisions. They might be wrong, but then there are other decisions that can be made. Middle managers carry out the decisions of others. They cannot involve themselves in the policy decisions. They are moved about with little control over their own fate. That is the killing reality. Think of it now as a rising young star might think of it. On the way up there is always the hope that one's fate is eventually going to come into one's own hands. But what happens when another rising star gets the partnership or vice-presidency? These hopes disappear. The sense of personal confidence that has prevailed for so long is now questioned. The positive sense of self is doubted. Certainly, all of that would not be destructive if there were opportunities abounding at the top. The reality is that, once passed over, the opportunity may never present itself again. There may come another vice-presidency, but the presidency may now be out of reach. That is, unless someone else's star fades. Now we are in the terrible situation of building success on the failure of others. Personal achievement cannot help; someone else must stumble, falter, and fall. Again there is the problem of the lack of control over fate. If it is true that trying, rather than achieving, is a primary source of burnout among executives, then, since there are many more trying than achieving, burnout is serious indeed.

THE PROBLEM OF BALANCE

Finally, there is the problem of balance. Executives can be noted for their single-mindedness. They juggle career, family, and personal health and end up bouncing a single ball. Career becomes an all-encompassing passion that burns them up. What follows is a short test of balance. It is a test that can help give executives clues about the amount and the source of stress on the job. Mark each continuum above according to your perception of your job situation. Those marks will provide a profile of the work environment and provide clues to the areas in which some effort is needed to establish balance at work. Obviously, this is not intended to be comprehensive, but simply to give some initial indicators of stress and possible sources of burnout. Take the test. Be honest. See what happens.

I have too much work to do	I am bored because I don't have enough to do
My job is rigidly controlled	My job is ambiguous
I have little conflict	I have lots of role conflict
I have extreme responsibility (especially for people)	I have no responsibility (for people or things)
I work in an environment of negative competition	I work in an environment of no competition
I work in an environment of constant change	I work in an environment of deadening stability
I have too much contact with people (public and/or private)	I am isolated at work

SYMPTOMS OF EXECUTIVE BURNOUT

PHYSICAL

It is apparent that there is a wide range of symptoms that signal burnout. The most dangerous, the seriously debilitating and killing symptoms, have been discussed at length in the journals and newspapers. It is an event when an executive dies of a heart attack or stroke. It is common for persons to die of cancer. It is becoming widely known that modern medicine views these diseases as stress-related. Ulcers are commonly called the executive's disease. These diseases are the end of the line. They cannot be considered signals. What are the symptoms that preceded these life-threatening diseases? It is in the so-called minor symptoms that flags can be recognized in time to do something that could help avoid more dangerous problems.

The most important physical clue that signals something is wrong is a rapid change. Remember, these are physical symptoms that signal stress. They may signal problems in other domains as well. They are most likely accompanied by problems of intellectual, emotional, or spiritual burnout.

There are many changes that can be important signals. Consider the following as only a partial list. Look for changes in sleep patterns. Look for trouble falling asleep when one has never had such problems before. This doesn't mean a single night but more than a week. Look at whether or not one sleeps comfortably throughout the entire night. Check to see if one sleeps a lot more than in the past. Sleep, too much or too little, is one clue to the pressures in life.

Another is food. A sudden loss or gain in appetite can be an indication of stress. So can sudden weight gain or loss.

Interestingly enough, one's complexion can provide clues to stress. Paleness or ruddiness and outbreaks of rashes or blemishes that are highlighted can all signal bodily reactions to stress. Another change that can be noticed is a change in appearance. If one is usually a casual dresser and now dresses formally, that can be a clue to some change in pressure at the job. In fact, what one should look for is any change in personal physical habits. Why all this talk about change? Doesn't one know when one is under pressure? The answer for many is no. Denial and distortion are defenses that are used to prevent the person from "consciously" knowing that he or she is in a situation which is taking a psychological toll. While some people can trick themselves "consciously," there are physical manifestations which do not respond to the trickery. They provide external signs that, if noticed, can act as an early warning system to prevent more serious physical or psychological problems.

The list for such clues is long. It may involve muscular pain, which is a clue that one is holding one's body in tense ways that result in aches without some identifiable source such as tennis or racquetball. Unaccountable muscular weakness, tiredness, or exhaustion out of proportion to any work done are other signs. Chronic back pain can have stress-related causes. Chest pains and problems with breathing are both indicators. Unusual sweating, either at the office or at home, is an early sign.

Any problems with bowel or bladder are early signs that one is under stress. This is such a common response that physicians use the phrase "irritable bowel syndrome" to identify it. These early problems can become more serious and may result in intestinal blockage that eventually require surgery.

Executives seem to have a proneness to allergies. Sometimes the sheer amount of work executives are asked to do can result in a general overall lack of resistance to minor infections, colds, and flu. All of this is important because if the early signs are ignored, the effects become increasingly debilitating. The signs of burnout cannot be ignored in hopes that they will go away. If they are ignored, they just get more severe. The early signs, if accepted, can help the executive seek out a stress-management or burnout-prevention program and hopefully avoid more serious symptoms.

INTELLECTUAL

The intellectual symptoms of burnout strike closer to home for executives. The intellectual symptoms signal a growing loss of ability to do the job. The first sign is growing negativism and cynicism about work and about the world of business. They no longer focus their efforts on making things work; they are more interested in criticizing in philosophical terms the company and its policies. These are not criticisms aimed at improving things; they are often unrealistic and petty. They are actually excuses for real or imagined failures in the job.

The criticism may take the form of blaming some agency outside the company. It might be the economy that is causing the current problems in the office. It might be the steady infringement of government regulations. It might be superiors. Or it might be authority in general. Whatever or whoever is blamed, there is no reference to the self as having any role in the problems being discussed.

Another symptom of intellectual burnout is boredom. The job seems to have no challenge anymore. The executive stops seeking new challenges and begins to avoid opportunities that once could have provided challenges. Meetings are avoided, even dreaded. The result of boredom is that the person is not prepared to deal with problems any longer, since the information to make a decision has not been sought out. Time seems to slip away.

This leads to another symptom of burnout. Burned-out executives seem to have lost the desire for excellence. They are willing to put up with incompetence, accept mediocrity, and tolerate sloppy work where once they would have insisted upon skill, excellence, and high productivity. They may begin to arrive at the office late and in some cases not make it at all. The club might have a higher appeal during working hours than it once did. Burned-out executives, or those facing burnout, now begin to vacillate on decisions. The decisions that require thought are made too quickly. The ones that demand action are delayed. Their reports and presentations contain mistakes and lack information. Executives facing burnout turn increasingly to details. They become nit-pickers who concentrate on detail so that decisions are blocked. They concentrate so much on detail that they lose the ability to concentrate on major issues. They lack organization and exhibit a growing confusion over role and duty within the organization. They have become cynical, bored, poor decision makers, and poor organizers with little concern for excellence. This is intellectual burnout.

EMOTIONAL

The behavioral symptoms of emotional burnout include unnecessary outbursts at colleagues, shouting and stomping around the office in overreaction to some minor mistake, exaggerated overstatements of fact, and the frequent use of words like "always," "never," and "absolutely" in describing the behavior of colleagues or superiors. Behavior becomes more and more impulsive and less and less organized. Executives who are exhibiting emotional signs of burnout may fire off ill-considered letters to newspapers or competitors. They may suddenly decide that the office needs to be redecorated or rearranged. The evaluations of subordinates may radically change from previous evaluations, or they might insist that secretaries be replaced. Another sign could be an inability to stay still. It may involve walking around the office, or it may involve being out of the office a lot on business which had previously been done by others.

The burned-out or burning-out executives' interactions with others worsen. They become more and more irritable. Their irritability reaches into the home as they are less and less able to separate the problems at work from life at home. Burned-out executives are increasingly displeased with others. Nobody can do anything right. As a consequence, they become more and more isolated from subordinates, colleagues, friends, and family.

Finally, their self-confidence, morale, and esteem all plunge. They begin to resort to denial and distortion in an attempt to believe that things don't matter, the job is unimportant, and they really want to do something else. Most people call this depression.

SOCIAL

Withdrawal is a sign that one might see occasionally, but it is the least likely response for an executive. Given the typical executive's life style and "aggressive" approach to life, it is a rare executive who withdraws. The most likely response is to overreact to the stresses of the job. As mentioned above, this results in attacks on subordinates and colleagues. It may also result in attacks on the self. Burning-out executives may drive even harder, work longer hours, and end up lonely, chained to a desk, or doing work that was previously delegated to others. This hyperactivity can be seen as an emotional reaction based on the lack of trust of others. Because of such overreaction to problems at the office, interactions with family and friends deteriorate. Burned-out executives become less and less able to interact socially with others at the office, and this may show up in an inability to conduct a meeting or to attend a meeting without getting into an argument while there.

There is an increased tendency to misjudge people. Executives experiencing burnout are more easily taken in by people who promise more than they can deliver as they desperately seek quick solutions to their crumbling hopes and dreams. The manager may view constructive criticisms as personal attacks and be unable to separate those who wish to help from those who really would relish the collapse of the "boss."

Finally, there is another kind of denial. Overall, executives do not see themselves as having much difficulty at home. Two out of three indicated that they are "very content" at home. But there are problems, especially for burnout victims. In the study by the AAFP, nearly twenty percent of the executives surveyed listed "spouse conflict" as a primary problem at home. An equal percentage listed sexual problems at home. Certainly, any executive experiencing stress at the office and facing additional stress at home in the form of spouse conflict or sexual problems is a more likely candidate for burnout. The stress on the job seems to far outweigh the stress at home. It is more likely that home life is affected by stresses on the job rather than the other way around. Executives who deny their marital problems are setting themselves up for more serious problems resulting in separation or divorce.

SPIRITUAL

While most executives do not report a problem with alcohol or drugs, it can be a real problem for executives facing burnout. If denial is the first ineffective attempt to deal with burnout, alcohol and drugs are the second. There are many such attempts to deal with burnout rather than confront it head-on and accept the fact that some aid from outside is needed. Perhaps a major sign of spiritual burnout is the inability to accept the need for others. Executives turn to any number of things in attempts to deal with burnout before they will seek out a person or persons with whom to discuss the problem. They might, as just mentioned, turn to alcohol or other drugs. Most often, since they are financially well off, there are legal drugs prescribed by a physician, such as tranquilizers. Others might try to deal with problems through casual sexual encounters and move from one partner to another without any real personal satisfaction. What is missing is any real personal meaning in their job, and they seek solutions with nearly everything and everybody before admitting that the problem lies within themselves.

In fact, two out of five executives say that they would do something different with their lives if they had them to live over again. More than fifty percent say that the major reason they would leave their present position is not money or stress, but for another that promises more self-fulfillment.

Loss of meaning is spiritual burnout. The escape into alcohol, drugs, and casual relationships doesn't help. It is entirely possible that spiritual burnout comes because a person enters an occupation without any real examination of the values they have and the values they will be expected to promote once in the occupation. This seems especially true for executives. They seem never to ask themselves whether all the pressures are worthwhile. Executives seem to assume that if they make it to the top, being there will be enough. Will the person have lost so much in the attempt that any personal life will have been sacrificed? It is this apparent failure to ask values questions that seems to result in spiritual burnout for executives. It seems they discover that once there, it is not where they really wanted to be. So they leave the occupation, they leave their family, and they seek a new life. Many find it. It is the waste that concerns us here, and whether or not it is necessary to burn out in order to conduct any real search of personal values worth living for. We think not. The section which follows seeks to provide suggestions for avoiding or reversing the effects of burnout.

CURES FOR EXECUTIVE BURNOUT

PHYSICAL

Let's face it, when people work sixty ot seventy hours a week, the idea of building in some more time for an exercise plan is tough. Still, if one wants to avoid burnout, then a physical burnout-prevention plan is necessary. It is possible, however, that much can be done within working hours. Other aspects of the plan can be integrated into the life style of executives so that the physical burnout-prevention plan is not something tacked on to an already busy schedule.

Here are several suggestions that do not require any special equipment or, for that matter, very much extra time. First, walk whenever possible. Instead of driving to the station to catch the train or bus, walk. If that is not possible, then get off one stop early so that a walk of a block or so is possible.

If executives commute by automobile, select a garage more than a block away so that a short walk is necessary. If there is a garage in the building, use the stairs rather than the elevator. But take every opportunity to walk. The maximum profit from walking can be gained if executives teach themselves to quiet their thoughts during the walk. Don't think about business. The easiest way to start doing that is to count the number of steps between two points. It is hard to plan the day ahead while concentrating on the number of steps or stairs.

Let the body get rid of tension. One way of doing that is to take a stretch at least four times a day. Everyone has a favorite way to stretch. Do what feels good. Here is a good stretch called the Compass Stretch. It involves head, neck, shoulders, arms, back, and legs. A full stretch takes one minute or less. Here is what to do.

1. Stretch the arms toward the ceiling, reach as high as possible, come up on tiptoes, then down.
2. Again raise arms over the head and join hands. Bend at the waist to the north, south, east, and west. Don't bounce, stretch. Then down.
3. Slowly, bend the head and neck north, south, east, and west. Don't bounce, stretch. Then rotate the head slowly to the right in a circle. Then rotate the head slowly to the left in a circle.
4. Hands on hips. Bend to the points of the compass as deeply as possible. Don't bounce, stretch. Rotate at the waist in a complete circle, first to the right and then to the left.
5. Point to the points of the compass with the right leg, as high as possible without pain. Point to the points of the compass with the left leg.
6. Bend over and let the arms hang down for a count of five.
7. Bend over backward and look at the ceiling for a count of five.

Do this four times a day or whenever tension has built up. It takes a lot longer to read than it does to do it!

Start an exercise plan at the office that truly causes deep breathing and cardiovascular exercise. Here is how it can be done. Use the stairs! If executives work in a building with a number of floors (even a two-story building will work), before and after lunch take a walk up and down the stairs. It turns out that walking up a flight of stairs uses more calories than many more strenuous-looking exercises. It causes one to breathe more deeply and gives the cardiovascular system a good workout. If one works on the fifth floor in a ten-story building, before lunch walk up to ten and then down to lunch. After lunch walk up to five and back. If there is time in the morning, walk up to ten and down to five before work. It is good exercise, and it doesn't take that much time.

Finally, use free time at home to do physical work around the house. Mow the lawn, putter in the garden, trim the bushes, and walk everywhere.

Here are some suggestions about eating. They don't involve what sorts of food to eat so much as the manner in which food ought to be eaten. Realize that mealtimes can be relaxing times. Often they are not. If one is to gain control over one's life, mealtimes are a good place to start. First, don't eat so much. Contrary to what all mothers say, it is not necessary to "clean up your plate." Eat what feels comfortable and then stop. Skip seconds. And don't take phone calls.

At the office, limit the number of cups of coffee every day. If possible, substitute something else. Juice is good. Or, crazy as it sounds, plain hot water. If hot water doesn't taste good, add a spoonful of honey. This actually does taste good. It also prevents "coffee anxiety."

Lunch can be a relaxing time if executives assert themselves and insist that it be a time to get rid of tension rather than build up some more. Here are the four commandments for lunch:

1. Don't skip lunch.
2. Don't hurry.
3. Don't talk business.
4. Don't drink alcohol.

If those four commandments are followed, lunch can be a pleasant—and stress-reducing—part of every day.

While many executives claim not to have a problem with alcohol, the "three-martini lunch" has somehow slipped into conventional knowledge. We have already said, "Don't drink at lunch." If other executives put pressure on colleagues to drink, then be polite but firm. If there is some suspicion that drinking at lunch is expected and one's career will suffer if one doesn't go along, buy off the bartender. Order like everyone else and end up with a Shirley Temple. The rule is don't drink. People who drink at lunch and claim that it does not affect their performance are lying to themselves. It is a bad habit to get into and should be avoided. Building on that rule, it is also probably important not to drink at all until the workday is over. When home, another good rule to follow is to measure the alcohol that is put into drinks. There really is a difference between a jigger and a jigger and a half. There is nothing wrong with drinking. There is something wrong with alcohol abuse. Except on special occasions, limit drinks to two a day. Have wine with dinner. Try to avoid heading for the liquor cabinet as soon as the front door closes. Finally, don't drink when depressed.

Last, find some way to rest during the day. Take a catnap each day or, if this is impossible, find some place to sit quietly for five or ten minutes. Skip a coffee break. Make sure that appointments are scheduled with time in between to stretch and to rest. It will pay off in the end. If the suggestions above are followed, physical burnout is much less likely to occur. The business day will still be as long, but it will not be as stressful.

INTELLECTUAL

An intellectual burnout-prevention plan involves first an analysis of one's work and one's life. It has to include an understanding of the demands of the job and of one's personal characteristics and how they can be used to meet work demands. The first step in analysis is to find the level of challenge and change that is comfortable and work to create a situation where that level remains fairly constant. Next, develop an awareness of stress situations at the office in order to be prepared for them. It is important for persons to know their limitations. Take only those jobs which promise a successful conclusion. Finally, know what is intellectually stimulating so that both work and private life have intellectually stimulating aspects to them.

After an analysis, it is important to establish personal goals. The mistake most people make in establishing goals is that they start out setting practical goals without any understanding of a personal code of ethics and values. That is the first step in goal setting. Have a clear idea of a personal system of values. Then set goals according to what one is willing to do and what one is not. Set them so that they are realistic and comfortable. Visualize possible outcomes and plan a strategy for all the outcomes that can be visualized. Finally, set short- and long-term goals.

Goals must include not only career goals but goals for one's life as well. In the setting of goals it is important to remember that one cannot do everything. It means selecting what one has the best chance of doing well. It also means limiting one's involvement in community affairs. A good rule of thumb is to limit oneself to two major activities a year outside of work.

Aside from the general suggestions of analyzing and setting goals, here are some specific recommendations that can become a part of a systematic intellectual burnout-prevention plan. If executives do any thing that is non-productive, it is worrying. Worry is really a useless practice, yet all of us do it. If executives could reduce the amount of worry in their lives, they could also reduce the amount of stress. Here are three steps aimed at helping to reduce worry. First, identify what things are worried about. Write them down, noting how much time one spends or how many times a day one finds oneself worrying about a particular problem. Next. decide whether or not the problem can be changed. Actually, this might be a revelation in itself. For some, the discovery that something can't be changed is enough to prevent them from worrying over it. If it is changeable, design a plan to change it. If it is not and it is still worried over, reduce unproductive worry by writing down one's thoughts in a log or journal when the worry comes into awareness. Finally, concentrate on thinking about solutions rather than causes of the worry. This short plan has worked. It is a quick way to get rid of useless worrying.

The most severe form of stress is the kind that extends over a long period of time. The way to reduce such stress is to break patterns. Don't fall into a rut at work. Plan ways of breaking patterns. There are several ways of doing that. Attend conferences, workshops, or classes, and bring the suggestions back to the office. Change the pace of work in the office. This may be done by varying the assignments of work responsibility. It may even be possible to work out an exchange with someone in another section, department, or industry for a week, quarter, or year. Such changes do not necessarily have to involve moving, but they might. It is also important for executives to do tasks that they actually enjoy and not let them slip away because of other pressures. It is good to plan some enjoyable tasks into each day. Finally, recognize that the opposite of stress is actually moderation. That means that all stress does not have to be avoided. If it comes in controlled doses and can be limited in time, its harmful effects can be avoided.

As sophomoric as it sounds, life goes on. The pressures of the day can be fleeting. No executive is indispensable; dull tasks can be delegated and time given to more enjoyable tasks. It is in doing that which is enjoyable that intellectual burnout can be avoided.

EMOTIONAL

We are often not responsible for what happens to us. We *are* responsible for how we feel about what happens to us. The first step in an emotional burnout-prevention plan is the recognition that we are responsible for our feelings. This is perhaps the most important responsibility of all. It means, ultimately, inner peace. No matter what happens to us, we are ultimately in control of our own lives. We control our feelings. That responsibility allows us to examine irrational beliefs such as "I must succeed" or "I must be liked by everyone." Such beliefs are killers. They are unnecessary. The stresses of the job are real, as we have seen. They do not have to be killers, however.

Every situation can be analyzed and redefined so that it becomes less stressful. It is the emotional understanding that we are responsible for our feelings that frees us to analyze and plan.

Executives are in the position to do something about the emotional climate of the workplace. It is possible, for example, to establish an emotional health program at work. In an emotional health program, either employees or trained professionals can analyze the work environment for stress situations and plan for ways in which they can be made less stressful. Such a plan to identify, change, or prevent stress can make the job a better place to be and a more effective and productive one, too.

Most of the emotional stress that people report comes from an imbalance in their lives. Quick tempers prevent many people from realizing their goals at work and often destroy personal relationships. What these people lack is a more balanced way of responding to stress. Automatic reactions to stress, guilt, shame, and doubt creep into persons' evaluations of themselves. One way to avoid the excesses of a particular way of responding to stress is to role-play, either with friends or alone, the opposite of one's ordinary way of reacting. If one ordinarily responds with haste, then practice waiting for a count of five before responding. If one responds slowly, then practice talking immediately with a planned phrase such as "It seems to me that . . ." Such a phrase, which actually says nothing, gives the speaker time to plan the real response. If one tends to respond with anger, create a system in which some clue is given to the self to keep cool and calm. A suggestion would be to touch the sleeve of one's left arm with the right hand. It serves as a reminder to stay calm. Find a place immediately after the meeting or encounter to get rid of the anger. Remember, one's ordinary response does not have to be eliminated, it just has to be balanced.

Do not be ashamed to take quiet time during the day. Plan times between appointments, before work, after work, before lunch, and/or after lunch to relax quietly. Plan to decompress before going home.

Set some specific rules for what happens when one arrives at home. There is a story of an executive who ran a multimillion-dollar company who sometimes would drive around the block four or five times before he went into the house. He had four teenage children and a wife who met him at the door every night to tell him the problems they had had during the day. It got so that he was afraid to go home at night. After dealing with business problems all day, he had to deal with family problems immediately upon walking through the door at home. Insist that no one in the family greet anyone in the family who works with daily home problems. Insist that fifteen minutes of quiet time be allowed for anyone who works. Come in, and go to a quiet place; after a short time, the family can talk over problems.

Finally, pay attention to internal clues. If one is experiencing internal stress, then take some time off. Take a leave if necessary. But, above all, be good to yourself.

SOCIAL

Social burnout involves co-workers, family, and friends. A social burnout-prevention plan must include all those to be effective. It is often important to share one's thoughts and feelings with a third party. Sometimes that is a friend. Sometimes that is a paid professional. Often, in the business world, it is a group of executives meeting in encounter groups, workshops, or classes. What can be learned in such third-party encounters is that "we are not alone." Many executives share the same pressures and have found many different ways of handling the stresses of their job. Many have not discovered effective ways of coping with stress. In sharing with a third party, executives can discover that they are not all that unique in the pressures that they face and in the actions that work and don't work for them. They also learn that listening to the problems of others can be a way for them to learn new ways of dealing with their own problems.

Certainly, the professional ways work, but the most important way to avoid social burnout is to spend time with people we enjoy. Here is a rule. Whatever the pressures of the job, do not let them interfere with some time to spend with people we like. Do it at least once every two weeks. This does not mean business meetings. It means time at home or "out on the town" with good friends. It is necessary for businesses to meet obligations. It is necessary for individuals to be with friends.

It is equally important to find time to spend with one's family. If busy executives would take thirty minutes a day to spend with their children, they would exceed the national average, for males at least, by three hours a week! How about fifteen minutes a day? Another way to be more involved with the family is to involve the family with work. Find ways of bringing the family to work from time to time so that they are familiar with the job, duties, responsibilities, and stresses of work. Then, all family members could have a better sense of the need for quiet time. It also provides an opportunity for shared time, even during a busy workweek.

At work, a social environment can be established if the executive can plan ways to open up communication with all of the people with whom the office is shared. Bulletins, memos, letters, and talks can all be used to let people in on what is happening in the company. Further, an executive can do much to create a socially supportive work climate. One does not have to have an office party, but it is possible to have potluck dinners or to go out to lunch with the whole office from time to time, just for fun. What that does is create an office in which the people feel that the executive and the company actually care about what happens to them. The result is a climate that is less stressful for everyone.

SPIRITUAL

Meaning, for some reason, seems elusive. It changes from the time we start careers to the middle to the end. The same goals don't seem to last for an entire career. Those who keep discovering and creating meaning in their personal and professional lives are the ones who avoid spiritual burnout.

Personal meaning comes from family, friends, and oneself, from doing what one enjoys with other people who enjoy it too. It is important to remember that recreation and exercise are not necessarily the same thing. Recreation can be involvement in listening to music, going to the theater, playing bridge, or taking a vacation.

Vacations are intended to reduce stress; many times they are stress-producing. There is one factor which will make vacations an important part of any burnout prevention plan: variety. Vary vacations in these five respects:

1. Type. Do not do the same thing every year. Take some vacations that are scenic, some that are educational, some that are nonsensical. Take some for the kids and some for the adults.
2. Length. Don't plan a two-week vacation every year. Take some weekend vacations. Take a day off. Plan for long and short vacations during the year.
3. Frequency. Plan them for different times of the year.
4. Place. Go to different places.
5. Companions. Vary the persons with whom vacations are taken. Avoid people who create stress. If, for example, visiting relatives is not truly relaxing, avoid relatives on vacations.

If these rules are followed, vacations can really be stress-reducing and add meaning to the personal lives of individuals and families.

Another way in which meaning can be added to life is to find a hobby that demands skill, knowledge, and competence, something that takes one's mind away from the everyday concerns of work and family. It should be an activity that fulfills. One of the authors works with wood. It provides a good amount of time during which no one bothers him and also provides presents for lots of his friends. It gives double pleasure. The time spent alone is worthwhile. The pleasure in giving someone something that has been personally created is fulfilling. Many hobbies provide this kind of meaning for persons.

If one has the time, another way of adding meaning to one's personal life is to give time to community service. In helping others one helps oneself. Do not allow this kind of activity to take too much time, but it can be a source of personal satisfaction for many. It can be especially important if things at work are not providing meaning in life and one feels trapped in the job. Community service may be the source of sustenance that makes work tolerable.

One other way to keep meaning in life and in work is to surround oneself with people who enjoy life and can handle stress. Nothing is as depressing as being with people who hate life or who crumple easily under pressure. Seek out other strong lovers of life; that makes life more meaningful for everyone.

Finally, if one's job is not meaningful, then one solution is to leave it. In fact, a good many executives do change jobs. A recent newspaper account indicated that nearly forty percent of corporation presidents came from outside the company. Further, while there is a good bit of moaning and groaning about moving, most executives who have moved to another company have reported that it helped their careers and increased their salaries.

However, it must be noted that changing for career advancement is not the only reason for leaving a job. What we all need to recognize is that it is good to leave a job if it is physically or psychologically harmful. Each of us has to make the decision as to whether we are willing to sacrifice our bodies, psychological health, and families to our career. Some do this only to discover that they have sacrificed the really important aspects of life for an illusion of success. What profit is there in gaining wealth and fame if in the process we lose our friends, family, and health?

Finally, burnout happens to some executives toward the end of their career. Some just hang on. This might be especially true of middle managers who know that they aren't going to advance any higher on the corporate ladder. So, they just hang on until retirement without much enthusiasm. One experiment being conducted in Europe to deal with this particular form of burnout is called decruitment. It is a policy in which managers are offered the chance to accept a lower-status, lower-paying job rather than early retirement or dismissal. Surprisingly enough, many managers snap up the opportunity and move into positions as clerks, security guards, complaint department personnel, statisticians, and so forth. In some companies, all managers are interviewed at age fifty-five to determine if they wish early retirement, or decruitment. A majority interviewed said they would accept decruitment, and those who have taken this route have indicated that it was a wise decision for them.

It is apparent that one does not have to keep one's nose to the grindstone all the time. There are alternatives. It is possible to be a success in life and not kill oneself in the process. These suggestions are aimed at realizing that possibility.

13. Secretaries

*"Skewered through and through with office-pens, and bound hand
and foot with red tape."*

—*Charles Dickens*

The world of work functions not only by the corporate decisions of highly paid, well-trained, and widely honored executives, but also by the labors of armies of skilled technicians, factory workers, and office personnel. Not the least of those who oil the machinery of management and industry are the secretaries. While few of the corporate executive suites are occupied by females, those who prepare the correspondence, greet visitors, file important documents, and often direct a staff which is, in some cases, larger than that of many small businesses, are women. In fact, ninety-nine percent of all secretaries in the United States are female. Fully thirty-five percent of those women are married. It appears that while secretaries are efficient, pleasant, and skilled, they may also find that working as a secretary provides stresses that make the job less enjoyable than it could be and certainly less enjoyable than they assumed it would be.

The reason secretaries burn out and quit their jobs or seek other secretarial jobs are curious. They may not be predictable to those who do not work or have not worked as secretaries. In this chapter, seven have been identified. They account for the rapid changeover in personnel in many offices and indicate one reason why secretaries may not burn out in the manner described for other professions. Primarily, they are able to change jobs if the stresses in one job become too much for them. That is so because the need for secretaries is great and promises to become greater. Second, given that mobility and need, it is entirely possible that secretaries might begin to exercise greater "political" power within offices, especially if they organize in the manner in which other groups have organized. In that case, many of the sources of stress mentioned below might change. For the present, however, secretaries are feeling the stresses of the job they do, and those stresses lead, just as they do for many of the rest of us, to burnout.

WHAT WENT WRONG AT THE OFFICE?

THE PROBLEM OF BOREDOM

There must be a universal image in the business world of the lazy, inefficient, and time-wasting secretary. One envisions secretaries sitting at their desks filing finger nails, talking with one another, taking long breaks and, in some cases, reading. The irony is that all of that may be true. The problem with the image is that most of the rest of us don't know the causes of that behavior. By far the most often reported source of stress for secretaries is boredom. Rather than being lazy and avoiding work, the single most stressing part of the job for secretaries is that they have too little work to do.

Actually, there are two sources of boredom for secretaries. They do have too little work to do. That is to say, there is not a steady flow of work with which to busy themselves during the workday. More about that later. Of more importance than the actual amount of work is the kind of work they are asked to do. The most boring part of the job, secretaries report, is that their work is trivial, routine, and dull. The job of most secretaries is typing and filing, often of the same sort day in and day out. Letters, reports, memos, and forms seem endless. After they are typed, they have to be filed. Secretaries are more likely to leave their present job because of boredom of this sort than for any other single reason. Let the rest of us consider what we might do in a similar situation if we were vibrant and intelligent people asked to do a routine and relatively dull job day after day. Frankly, the myth of the inefficient secretary belongs in a useless information file somewhere. It is a myth born of a relatively few experiences of individual poor performance rather than one which accurately describes the job secretaries actually do. They are, in point of fact, well-trained, skilled, and efficient. That is why they are bored.

THE PROBLEM OF INITIATIVE

Consider a woman who is twenty-seven years old, a college graduate with five years' experience as a secretary, whose responsibilities extend to typing what she is told, filing in a system created by someone else, and making appointments for the boss. Consider further that this is all she is ever going to be able to do in that job. She is stuck. She is stuck in a job that does not allow her to use the intellectual powers she possesses, and she is stuck in a position that offers little in the way of advancement.

Let us ponder for the moment the conditions under which secretaries work. First, there is little advancement in the secretarial field. Let us explode another myth. The myth of the "executive secretary" is much like the myth that the way out of poverty for minorities lies through sports and entertainment. Such roles are not descriptive of the lives of the great majority of persons in the circumstances described. Most secretaries are hired to do a specific job, and that job will remain the same regardless of their personal growth and maturity. They will do the same job year after year unless they leave. They will watch as management trainees enter and rise in the company. They will watch as salespersons move from sales to management. They might watch many people rise in the company as they stay at the same level of status throughout the years. There is no advancement as a secretary.

Second, there is no incentive to improve one's skills or education as a secretary. If a person can do the job, which is often determined before hiring, doing it better and better seems to make no difference. What incentives are there if a person seeks to improve typing skills from seventy words per minute to ninety words per minute? What incentive is there if the secretary streamlines the filing system? What reward is there if the secretary creates a more efficient office arrangement? What support is there in an office when the secretary might want to attend a workshop directed toward improving intraoffice communication? The answers: so long as secretaries do the job they were hired to do, there is little attention paid to incentive programs for them. Why? We are back to the problem of advancement. While incentive programs may be a natural part of many companies, it is almost always tied to improving one's status or earning power within the company. To many if not most managers, such considerations in terms of secretarial assistance are irrelevant.

Third, there is an underlying assumption that the job a secretary does doesn't really call for much intellectual power. In American society there is an unconscious bias that position and talent are somewhat inextricably intertwined. The relationship might be real, but the bias is that it is taken as absolute. We assume that if a person occupies a low-status position, that person must not be very smart. If we assume the person is not very smart, we begin to rely on his or her contributions less and less. In fact, we come to expect that he or she has no contribution to make at all. That is just the case with secretaries. They occupy a low-status position, and their potential as contributing members of the organization goes unrecognized. It has already been discussed above that there is little or no reinforcement for the use of initiative by secretaries. It is now evident why so little value is placed on such incentives in the office. If it is assumed that secretaries have little to contribute to the success of the organization, it follows that there is little reason to spend time and money on incentive programs for them.

That attitude leads to a more difficult problem. It is reported by some secretaries that when they actually take the initiative to make a suggestion, their suggestions are ignored and, in some cases, actively resented. In some offices, this bias is so strong that secretaries are not allowed to make any contribution to the organization. This is probably a problem of power. The boss makes the assumption that the responsibility for running the office lies within an authoritarian structure and suggestions from "underlings" constitute interference rather than help. In those organizations, few options are open to the secretaries. They either build up tolerance, live with increasing hostility, or move on to another job.

Finally, while secretaries may be the people most informed about a situation, event, or problem in an office, they seldom have the decision-making power to do anything about it. While secretaries may be able to improve typing skills, they may not be able to do anything about an office filing system without permission. It is the ultimate recognition of this underlying reality that demonstrates to secretaries day after day that they occupy a position in a company in which they are not expected to use their initiative.

THE PROBLEM OF INTERPERSONAL CONFLICTS

The interpersonal problems secretaries face center around work and home. At work, there are three groups of people who hold the potential for interpersonal difficulties; the boss, co-workers, and customers. So far as secretaries are concerned, it is their supervisors who create the most difficulty at work. If things are going well in the office, the supervisor is probably rewarded and perhaps even promoted. Little of the recognition for efficiency filters down to the secretaries. However, if things are not going well, then the secretaries are often blamed. It is this lack of positive feedback coupled with the idea that the only time secretaries hear anything concerning performance is when something is wrong that contributes to conflicts with bosses. A major complaint is that the negative feedback takes the form of "put-downs." Disguised as humor, supervisors malign dress, work, and attitude. Sometimes the personal life of the secretary may be called into question as a cause affecting work. Whatever the reason, the lack of positive feedback is felt. Whatever the reason, the "put-downs" and criticism drive secretaries away from jobs.

This "management by punishment" approach is a sign of supervisor inefficiency. It is another complaint of secretaries regarding interpersonal problems in the office. Secretaries, reasonably enough, believe that supervisors should be competent to hold the position they hold. A part of that competence extends to interpersonal relationships within the office. It also deals with their ability to give clear, straightforward instructions for the tasks they want secretaries to do. A major complaint of secretaries is that their bosses give insufficient or unclear instructions for jobs. When the secretaries take the complete task to the supervisor, they discover that that is not what the boss wanted. That is frustrating. It is complicated by the problem discussed above. It is seen as the secretary's fault. Certainly, secretaries are the ones who have to do the work over regardless of whose fault it is. But the supervisor's inability to give clear, complete instructions for jobs coupled with a lack of interpersonal communication skills creates a major source of stress for secretaries.

Another source of stress for secretaries is the expectation that they will be expected to provide services outside the regular job description. For example, the "girls in the office" might be expected to have coffee ready in the morning. Or, during the day they might be expected to go out and buy a snack. Or, in some cases they might even be asked to buy presents for the boss's family. Such personal services—helpful and most often appreciated if offered freely—cannot be taken for granted. If they are, they become a source of stress. Some executives have come to expect to be "waited on" by secretaries. This is stressful because the secretary feels that to refuse is to risk losing the job. Such conflicts contribute to interpersonal stresses. If a supervisor lacks an appreciation of the job a secretary does, provides only negative feedback of a personally insulting kind, is unable to provide clear and complete instructions for tasks, and expects personal favors as a part of the job, then a secretary works under stresses which would be unacceptable for any person.

While the supervisor is in the main responsible for the interpersonal climate in an office, co-workers can also be a source of stress. Most often this takes the form of inconsiderate behavior. One person in the office leaves early for lunch, gets back late at the expense of another's lunch hour. A co-worker might not be willing to help on tasks when one person is overloaded. Some persons in the office might seek to gain advantage by complaining to the supervisor about others in the office. In any case, such intraoffice bickering takes a psychological toll on secretaries.

Another problem between secretaries and co-workers is that not all secretaries see the job in the same way. Some have accepted the job the way it is and resent any efforts to change the system. Some have a vested interest in not changing things because they might be exhibiting symptoms of burnout and simply not have the psychic energy to deal enthusiastically with change.

Finally, a cause of interpersonal problems in an office is a lack of effective communication between office workers. This can range from employees' not speaking to one another because of some personal problems between them to a lack of a means of letting everyone in the office know what is going on within the company. It is possible that some office managers actively interfere with the exchange of information among office personnel in order to keep everyone from knowing what is going on. Such effective intraoffice communication might reduce the power of an authoritarian boss. The lack of good communication in an office is reported by secretaries as a source of stress.

The last source of interpersonal stress at work for secretaries comes from having to deal with customers—the "public." It is often the case that secretaries are the most visible representatives of the company. The secretaries are the ones who have to deal with irate and dissatisfied clients. They are the ones who have to take the verbal abuse and directly experience the anger and frustration of hostile consumers. Certainly, they feel resentment when, from their point of view, they have done nothing to a particular customer but are the focal point of the customer's attack.

It is possible that the sources of stress at work from supervisors, co-workers, and customers could be endured if they could all be left behind at the end of the day. Unfortunately, that is not the case for many. It is difficult to separate one's personal life from one's business life. Many secretaries take their jobs home with them, just as executives, police officers, and teachers do. It is this inability to "leave it at the office" that creates added stress at home with friends, spouse, or children. The secretaries find themselves in a double bind. They bring the job home and then are angry because they didn't leave it at the office. It is no different for any person who does not have a place to talk over the concerns of the day with someone else who shares the same work situation. It is only after one has shed the concerns of the job that one can enter into conversations which avoid "shop talk." What can happen, of course, is that a vicious cycle develops whereby pressures at the office create pressures at home which in turn cause more tension at the office which then causes more tension at home and on and on until something explodes. It might explode at work or it might explode at home, but it is fairly certain that unresolved tension in either place affects both.

THE PROBLEM OF INVISIBILITY

One of the authors was talking with a secretary about being ignored in the office. She told this story. Once, when a new member of management was being shown around the office, she was standing between her boss and the new manager. The boss looked right past her to the files and said, "And here are our active files." She was invisible! The two managers looked through her to the files. She wasn't there so far as they were concerned. A major complaint of secretaries is that they are treated as nonpersons.

This story points out the three aspects of treatment that secretaries consider objectionable. First, their invisibility. They are simply ignored when a person of status or prestige is being shown around the office. The "files" might be important enough to be shown to a new manager, but the secretaries aren't important enough to be introduced.

Second, secretaries resent being treated as inferiors. As one secretary phrased it, she was tired of being treated like a clerk and nothing more. It seems that supervisors treat secretaries as inferiors because the supervisors "are up on a high horse because of their title." The separations of pay and status become real in the daily interactions of the office (especially if the boss is a bit inadequate or unsure). Third, some supervisors treat secretaries with disrespect or, as one secretary phrased it, "like dumb broads." One of the authors observed the attitude of invisibility and disrespect in a university setting. An applicant for a position in one of the academic departments was being shown around by the department head before an interview when two faculty members came into the office. Just before going into the office, the two faculty members, the department secretary, the applicant, and the department head all sort of ended up in the same place at the same time. The department head said, "Dr. Smith, I'd like you to meet Dr. Jones and Dr. Brown, two members of the department. Now, let's go into the office." The secretary stood there while everyone exchanged greetings and was simply sidestepped as they went into the office. Such slights are hard to overlook. They play heavily on the minds of secretaries as they consider the pressures of working in an office in which they are considered inferior and, as a consequence, of little worth. Such disrespect is another factor which causes secretaries to leave positions.

In one of our interviews with secretaries, the statement was made that the only choice they had was to work or not to work. But, that is not the case. People who work have rights other than to work or not. A person does not lose rights to personal respect and dignity because they are employed in a service position. Much could be done toward reducing the stress of secretaries if it were recognized that secretaries are neither invisible nor inferior persons.

THE PROBLEM OF FEAST OR FAMINE

Everybody wants it done yesterday. It seems if all offices run on the principle the authors learned in the U.S. Army—hurry up and wait! There seems little to do in the office all morning long and at 4:30 P.M. there is a report that has to be finished before closing time. Every job seems to have a deadline that is always too close. The single most frustrating experience reported by secretaries was the problem of deadlines and the lack of appreciation by supervisors of the stress that causes. It leads to a host of criticism of bosses, since it is viewed as inefficient and inconsiderate. The second most frustrating aspect of the feast-or-famine phenomenon is that it is difficult to work on a project uninterruped. The telephone, visitors, questions from the supervisor, and other tasks all combine to make getting things done on time a frustrating experiment.

Being a secretary seems to involve working in a job that is characterized by peaks and valleys of work but very little that is steady and predictable. There is either too little or too much. The frustrating part is that the too much always seems to be related to deadlines. It is the big, last-minute jobs that create the most stress for secretaries.

Finally, in this vein, secretaries are the persons in the office everyone else assumes they can tell what to do. They are everyone's servant. In fact, another major complaint of secretaries is that there are too many bosses in the office. The consequence is that with many people telling them what to do, they don't know what is really the right thing to do. Combined with the problem of an uneven work flow, interruptions, and deadlines, having no specific person with whom to work creates further pressures for secretaries.

THE PROBLEM OF SEXUAL HARASSMENT

"Boys will be boys" and what is the harm of a little good fun with the "girls in the office"? A little "good fun" can mean anything from telling sexual jokes to fondling to unwelcome sexual advances and finally to demands for sexual favors in order to maintain one's job. In fact, the practice has become so widespread that the Equal Employment Opportunity Commission has issued guidelines which bar sexual harassment in the workplace. While there are no criminal penalties specifically related to sexual harassment, such behavior is considered a form of sex discrimination. In such cases, the costs to the company are severe indeed. In 1979, the Johns-Manville Corporation had to pay damages to a former employee who was dismissed for the refusal to have sex with a company official. The damages: $100,000!

It is estimated that between seventy and eighty percent of working women have been victims of sexual harassment at some point in their working careers. So what is sexual harassment? Equal Employment Opportunities Commission guidelines establish three criteria to determine if an act involves sexual favors, verbal suggestions, sexual advances, and physical conduct of a sexual nature, especially if they are related to hiring, retention, or promotion:

1. if submission is an implicit or an explicit condition of employment;
2. if submission is used as basis of employment.
3. if such conduct interferes with work performance or creates a hostile or offensive workplace.

Under these new guidelines, employers have become more responsible for the acts of its supervisory employees and for the creation of a workplace free from intimidation based on sex. Secretaries report that this practice is a pressure with which they have to deal in their working lives. It is sometimes such a problem that they have to leave one job for another.

THE PROBLEM OF MONEY

While pay is not mentioned as a major cause of stress, it is a factor that affects some secretaries. In a salary survey conducted in 1979, the average salaries ranged from about $7,800 a year to about $16,000 a year depending on whether one is a clerk-typist or an executive secretary. Obviously, there are special circumstances in which individuals make more. However, overall, secretaries are not well paid. If they are unmarried or a single parent, the strain in living on such a salary is apparent. Mostly the problem comes from being trapped in a "go nowhere" job that does not offer the opportunity for greatly increasing salary. Further, secretaries often work for executives who command large salaries. The difference is difficult to tolerate, given the close working relationship and the fact that they both put in the same number of hours a day.

SYMPTOMS OF SECRETARY BURNOUT

PHYSICAL

Being a secretary is a physically demanding job. Most people don't believe that, but typing, for example, places unusual stress on the hands, wrists, arms, shoulders, and back. Such stress slows one down and reduces the productivity that might ordinarily be expected. The aches and pains associated with secretarial work, if not compensated for, can result in an overall loss of vitality and zest for life.

The symptoms of burnout for secretaries are not markedly different from those of other professions. They might suffer from loss of sleep. One area that is reported by secretaries is nightmares. The secretary dreams of being crushed by the keys of a typewriter or faced with reams of illegible shorthand while a nagging supervisor glares down from above.

The stresses on the job are real. In fact, secretaries have an unusually high incidence of disease. A federal study attributed this to demands for productivity, deadlines, and typing a great deal. All of these, as noted above, are sources of stress.

INTELLECTUAL

The symptoms of intellectual stress show up in a lack of desire to continue to do a good job. Some secretaries come to believe that the job they do is not appreciated and thus become careless in tasks in which they once took pride. Mere carelessness gives way for some secretaries to a more negative attitude which results in criticism and blaming of others in the office, from managers to co-workers. It is not uncommon to have a "house cynic" who complains, criticizes, and blames, continually creating a climate in which everyone suffers. Such burned-out secretaries can even become a source of alienation and frustration for others, leading to their burnout as well.

Boredom, one of the major causes of burnout in secretaries, leads to intellectual fatigue. With nothing or only routine and boring tasks to do, clarity of thought and the ability to make rational decisions may become impaired. Boredom can be another cause of sloppy work and apparent carelessness in the office. It is difficult to remain mentally sharp doing dull and trivial tasks. Such tasks as typing routine letters, proofreading, and ordinary filing lend themselves to errors, and a symptom of burnout would be an increasing incidence of such errors.

EMOTIONAL

It is estimated that industry in the United States loses approximately $15 billion a year to stress-related absenteeism. What is important to recognize here is that no job is free of stress; in fact, according to D. Hans Selye, a pioneer in the effects of stress on human beings, it is not stress itself which harms but the response made to it. It is this area of emotional response that accounts for such high absenteeism. The emotional response to stress can be helplessness. It becomes increasingly difficult to face the challenges of work each day. It is simply better to not work. For many, absenteeism becomes so great that they are fired. Many quit. Whatever the case, the financial loss to the company is great.

It should come as no surprise, then, that a symptom of burnout in secretaries is a severe loss of personal worth. First, they are often treated as inferiors. Such a daily diet of personal insult takes its toll. Second, faced with a lack of desire to do well, inability to face the job, and growing dislike of the persons with whom they work, burned-out secretaries begin to direct some of the blame for the loss of enthusiasm toward themselves. The result is that they come to think less and less of their own abilities and personal strengths. They see themselves as less worthy as persons.

SOCIAL

The problem of social burnout takes two unusual forms. First, daily contact with numbers of people results in a constant involvement in superficial relationships. This is so for supervisors, co-workers, and the public. Such a diet of daily superficiality has the effect of training secretaries to treat all of their involvements in such a superficial manner. While on the job one is expected always to be pleasant, courteous, and smiling, deeper relationships require that one move beyond the surface courtesies to more intimate discussions of self, events, and problems. Such opportunities during office hours are necessarily limited, but it is difficult to move from one social environment to another in which the rules of discourse are so different. Many secretaries do not easily make the transition, and their social involvements suffer.

It is also sometimes difficult to overcome the enforced passivity of secretaries toward their employers when they leave the job. While it may not be appropriate in some offices to argue strongly in favor of one's own opinion, it is a necessary part of life outside of work. It is a problem that some secretaries carry their passive behavior from work into their private lives.

Finally, a response of some secretaries to the pressures of office work and the seeming meaninglessness of the job is to place an undue emphasis on social life. The topic of conversation in many offices is going out to bars, parties, and other forms of entertainment. Certainly, there is nothing wrong with an active social life. In fact, it is very important. What we wish to point out here is that a symptom of burnout is an emphasis on social life in which the persons seem to define their lives by the extent to which they go to parties, are entertained, or succeed at superficial interactions in bars. A national publication recently reported that the average length of an encounter in a singles bar was seven seconds! In that extremely short space of time, persons size each other up and determine if they have anything in common to continue the conversation. In such encounters, great weight is placed on external appearance. It is in placing extreme value on success in such ritualized social encounters that one might lose the balance important for the relief social life can provide from stress.

SPIRITUAL

Throughout this book we have used the term *spiritual* to refer to the meaning one gives to life. It is most common when discussing professions to talk about the meaning one finds in the job. For secretaries, who are often denied any decision-making power or real responsibility, it is difficult to attach life meaning to the job itself. However, there are many in our society who take pride in doing well whatever job they have. This is the case with secretaries, too. While career paths may be blocked by lack of opportunity, many secretaries do not lose the desire to do good, efficient work. However, the symptoms of burnout that reveals a loss of meaning in the job is the loss of personal pride in work. If doing a job well loses its meaning, then the job itself is no longer meaningful. It follows that the loss of meaning in one's work is often accompanied by a loss of meaning in one's life.

Characteristics of spiritual burnout for secretaries can take a number of forms. For example, we have already discussed the overemphasis some people place on social concerns. It may be that a person could turn to sex as a way to discover meaning in life. It could take the form of drug and alcohol abuse. Stress is noted to be the leading cause of alcohol and drug abuse in the United States.

Such casual use of sex and drugs might reveal a loss of appreciation for life values. If the body is used in such a casual and abusive way, it is a signal that one has lost meaning and perhaps goals for which to strive. They are symptoms of burnout and become the causative agents for other life distresses. The abuse of drugs can bring about the collapse of the physical body, and sex can create a number of emotional and physical difficulties. For example, a recent survey conducted by *Cosmopolitan* magazine polled 106,000 mostly single, working women between the ages of eighteen and thirty-five. It was revealed that almost one fourth have had abortions. The same survey reported that for single women living alone, eight affairs, usually with married men, was the average. All questions of morality aside, the point we are trying to make is that sexual activity, especially of the casual, "one night stand" variety, may be a signal of a real, profound, and dangerous loss of meaning in a person's life.

CURES FOR SECRETARIAL BURNOUT

PHYSICAL

There are three ways in which physical burnout can be reversed and prevented. First, there is exercise. Given the nature of the job, there are physical activities any secretary can do which will relieve the pressures of work. From time to time, get up and walk around the office. Do not sit beyond the point that sitting becomes uncomfortable. During the typing of a long report or a number of letters, stand up and look out a window, if possible, or do something else for one minute. Then return to the task. Occasionally, take a stretch break. Pay special attention to stretching fingers, flicking the wrist, shaking the arms and shoulders, rolling the head and neck, rolling the eyes, and rotating the back. While all of that may seem a bit strange, it will have the effect of taking the tension off all those parts of the body and making one more effective.

Further, if it is possible, begin to pursue a daily exercise program for strength and flexibility. It is possible to run about a mile a day and exercise during the run. It takes about thirty minutes. Thirty minutes to better physical health? Can the time be spared? Of course!

Finally, suggest to the other secretaries in the office that it might be helpful to give each other a shoulder rub from time to time. It is possible to enroll in classes to learn massage techniques, but they aren't really necessary unless someone is a bit shy about being touched. (That is the person to send to the class!) Or, enroll as a group in massage classes or yoga classes. Any such techniques of relaxation and stretching will make the day less tiring since the body will be more prepared to take the physical stresses of work.

The second major recommendation for resisting or reversing burnout concerns food. Lunch during work is especially important. Here are six don'ts that will make the afternoons better for work.

1. Don't drink alcohol at lunch. Let's face it, folks, alcohol is a depressant and has the effect of dulling our senses and reducing our effectiveness.
2. Don't skip lunch. It is important to eat. It might be worthwhile to skip heavy lunches, but some lunch is important because food provides energy.
3. Don't rush. At least one of the functions of lunch hour is to provide a break. So take that break. And don't rush.
4. Don't always go to lunch with the same people. Not only are new people stimulating, but some variety in lunch companions makes time spent with the regular lunch crowd more enjoyable, too.
5. Don't talk business at lunch. Remember, the whole point is to take a break, seek variety, and *escape* boring talk about work.
6. Don't eat at the same place every day. That's another way to take a break, have variety, and forget about work for a while.

The third recommendation is to take vacations. Plan them to be as hassle-free as possible. Taking vacations is a major way of relieving stress. The sheer pleasure of not having to go to work, the change of physical surroundings, and the freshness of conversation when the vacation is over all act to counteract physical burnout.

INTELLECTUAL

If it is true that secretaries are most often bored with the routine tasks of work, then it is important that they find some way of using their intellectual powers. It is possible that there may be opportunities to use reasoning abilities and creativity at work. It is certainly possible to use those abilities to learn to deal with stress at the office. For example, analyze the pressures under which persons work at the office. Plan a way of dealing with specific stressful situations at work, try them, revise them, and find some that work. If deadlines are a problem, or interruptions, then create a way of dealing with them and keep searching for a solution to them. It may be that there is no solution to those problems. In that case, at least one knows the situation and can decide objectively to tolerate it as a part of the job, take it as evidence that more staff is needed, or simply change jobs.

It is also possible to analyze the pace of the job to discover peaks and valleys at work, and it may be further possible to find a way to smooth out those peaks and valleys so that the job has a more even flow. It is certainly a way to use intellectual talents and abilities and reduce the boredom and routine. Another way to reduce intellectual burnout is to come to the office and take a little time each morning to plan the day. Set goals for each day and make sure to achieve them. It is a source of personal satisfaction which can make the workplace a better place.

Take a book to work every day and read during breaks. It is a way of forgetting work, and it is another way to use the mind.

Do not stop developing skill, competencies, and knowledge. One night of each week could be used as an intellectually stimulating night in which one is enrolled in informal classes to develop more skills, competencies, or knowledge. It is possible that one's goals could be to move from a secretarial job to a job in which there is more opportunity for advancement and prestige. It is possible that one is working to become a senior secretary or executive secretary. In any case, intellectual skills will be enhanced by such further formal training.

One more way of confronting emotional burnout is to create some reason for going home. It is often helpful to have some hobby. For example, gardening, painting, or refinishing old furniture. It should be a hobby that actually refreshes and restores. It can be a real aid in washing away the stresses of the day.

EMOTIONAL

There are three major recommendations for resisting or reversing emotional burnouts. First, a major source of stress for secretaries is intraoffice personal relations. If there are problems in the office, it seems reasonable that the best solution is to resolve them quickly and effectively. Some sort of canned sentence could be used to open up discussion with anyone in the office from the supervisor to peers, provided that a reasonable working relationship exists. The sentence has three parts: ownership, specificity, cause. It goes like this: "I feel _____ when _____ because _____." Fill in the blanks. An actual sentence might go like this: "I feel <u>frustrated</u> when the <u>guys from purchasing keep dropping in to talk during their break</u> because <u>the interruption during the morning slows down the marketing report.</u>" It isn't a miracle worker, but it does leave the ball in the other person's court, so to speak, and offers them the chance to come up with a solution to the problem. In any case, done early in one's job, it signals to the others in the office that problems can be discussed openly and resolved quickly.

Another way to improve intraoffice communication is to act as a person who provides support and encouragement for others in the office when they desire it. It is possible, even for someone with little authority, to provide praise and rewards to others in the office who have done something well. It might even create a climate in which all persons in the office are sensitized to the notion of praising work well done or efforts not ordinarily expected.

The problem of sexual harassment is not easily solved by secretaries alone, but it is possible for one secretary or a group of secretaries to influence company policy. The following procedures can be used to create a less hostile, less manipulative, less undesirable sexual climate at work. Individually or as a group, request that the company do the following things recommended by the Equal Employment Opportunities Commission.

1. Raise the issue affirmatively with supervisory personnel.
2. Inform supervisors that sexual harassment is a serious offense.
3. Make it clear that sexual harassment will not be tolerated.
4. Hold educational programs for employees.
5. Handle complaints quickly and appropriately.
6. Be alert to reprisals.
7. Take action when needed to institute reprimands, transfers, or dismissals.
8. Publish and post prominently the definition of and penalties for sexual harassment.

It is possible, even probable, that the eight steps listed above will end unwanted sexual innuendo and advances in the workplace, making it a more friendly and less stressful place to work.

The second major area in which emotional burnout can be combatted is in the way emotional stress is handled at work. It seems important that one's anger, frustration, even rage at a person or event be dealt with immediately. The key to doing this is to find a place at work where one's rage can be released. That means finding a filing room, restroom, lounge, or some other private place where one can cry, scream, or hit something to release pent-up emotions. It is important to get rid of them at work if you can. Again, it may seem a little silly, but it is important.

In order to deal with the ordinary stresses of the day, make room during the day, during a break or lunch, for "quiet time." This is a time to sit quietly, without the interference of conversation or thoughts about work, a time to just relax and be peaceful with oneself.

A way of handling emotional burnout is to develop a daily routine that might be called a "decompression routine." It is a way of letting the pressure of the job off before one goes home. There are a number of things that might be done to let the air out at the end of the day. Instead of driving home immediately after work, take some time to window-shop or browse through stores. If one travels by bus, then take a later bus and visit a museum or sit at the bus stop and people-watch for a while. It might even be possible to have an early dinner near work and then see a movie or play later on. The important idea here is that the pressures of the day should be left at work, not taken home to roommate, spouse, or children.

SOCIAL

There are three recommendations to help persons develop a social life that reduces burnout. Essentially, it is important to have two social lives. One is personal and not work-related. The other deals with developing the social glue that holds the working place together in a friendly and supportive way. First, it is important that everyone in the workplace have a life outside of work. It is recommended that at least one night each week be devoted to spending some time with friends who do not share the same job or work in the same place. Find ways of seeking out people that are likable, interesting, and different from those on the job.

There are two ways to create a friendly atmosphere at work. One is to take care to spend some social time with people there. Organize a potluck dinner for co-workers and supervisors at least once every three months. It might be worthwhile to organize a night out for everyone in the office at a dinner playhouse once or twice a year. Such efforts will not go unrewarded. They will be appreciated and will provide the foundations for resolving inter-personal difficulties which might arise and also lay the groundwork for favorable responses to suggestions to improve the workplace.

Finally, check to see if it is possible to create an in-house newsletter to communicate with other secretaries and other employees in the office or even in the entire building. Such a newsletter could improve inter- and intraoffice communication and provide another glob of social glue to make work a less stressful place and avoid social burnout.

SPIRITUAL

In order to find meaning in life, one has to take an active part in one's own life. That means that lack of meaning is a personal problem. It doesn't come from other people, it comes from us. It is possible to add meaning to one's life by using talents, skills, and abilities in an active and assertive way.

If the workplace is boring, that does not mean that life itself has to be boring. We do not have to judge outselves by what we do, but we do need to assess who we are. We can hold a boring job and still be a most interesting person. Our talents may not be used on the job, but they most certainly must be used somehow. If our talents are not appreciated at work, we must seek out places in our lives where they are. For example, it is an important part of life to offer service to others, as a volunteer or as a step toward another career. Whatever the case, people have significant roles in professional organizations, social issues organizations, and volunteer social work. Some people drive ambulances in rural areas on weekends or join groups of various kinds for physical fitness or rescue work. Use talents. It is a sure way to avoid burnout.

It is not always necessary to use one's talents publicly. The private use of one's abilities is important, too. Develop writing ability. Write poetry that might be shared with no one. Write in a journal concerning the stresses, joys, and even ordinary happenings in one's life. It provides a record of growth and change. It may even be possible to write for publication in journals such as *Today's Secretary* or company newsletters and other publications. All of these efforts have the effect of adding meaning and joy to one's life even in the face of a boring and routine job.

It is not absolutely necessary to accept that one's job is boring and routine. It may be possible to negotiate more and more autonomy and decision-making power. Take a look at the places in one's work where no one else seems to know what to do, and move in that direction. Let's give an example of that. One of the authors was an enlisted man in the U.S. Army. Once, when he was a private first class (a very low rank), he was alone in the administrative office of a unit headquarters. The phone rang and the person on the other end requested permission to take an army car to pick up some supplies. No one else was in the office, so he gave permission. They requested his name and he told them. A minute or so later the phone rang again and the motor pool asked for him by name and demanded to know if he had given permission for the car to be released. He said he had. From that day on, every car that left the unit left by his permission! People simply assumed that he had the authority to say who could and who could not take an official car off base. It even extended to persons with the rank of major (a reasonably high rank). The point is that no one else was doing that particular job; it was vacant, so he filled it. There may be such jobs in any office if they are examined for that particular purpose. People who assume authority can gain more and more of it as others come to see them as people who can, and do, make decisions. Then, the workplace might be more stimulating.

The last recommendation is that if all of the recommendations above don't seem to help, seek out another job where one's talents can be more appreciated. We have already noted that the demand for secretaries is growing and that gives them the power to be more selective and demanding of a job.

BURNOUT AND THE MESSENGERS

14. Journalists

"Burke said there were Three Estates in Parliament; but, in the Reporters' Gallery yonder, there sat a Fourth Estate more important far than they all."
—*Thomas Carlyle*

Historically, journalists have been portrayed as hard-driving, whiskey-drinking, cigarette-puffing cynics whose hard exterior covers a heart of gold. From *The Front Page* to *The Big Story* to *Lou Grant,* the journalist's single-minded pursuit of a story, usually with an idealistic motive, occasionally with a self-serving motive, takes precedence over courtship, family, and personal health. Every now and then, there is an episode in which a journalist is shown for whom the booze, smoke, and pace have been too much. They are the hacks of journalism who, while they might have once been idealistic and dedicated, are now content to report the commonplace, the stereotype, and the expected. They have no energy to follow up on a complicated lead or to track down an eyewitness. They no longer have the drive to expose the corrupt or protect the innocent. All of that takes idealism, commitment, and dedication, sentiments that have long since been given up by the cynical journalist. The "older but wiser" veterans may still be hard-drinking and hard-smoking, but no longer are such journalists hard-driving and committed to their field. They are burned-out.

WHAT WENT WRONG IN THE
NEWS ROOM?

THE PROBLEM OF THE JOURNALIST'S VIEW
OF HUMAN NATURE

It seems that journalists work in a field in which they are exposed to the worst of the worst of human nature day after day. They can come to hold a view of human nature that is essentially negative. Journalists report on people at their worst. They must cover wars, executions, rapes, murders, child abuse, parent abuse, and any number of other human tragedies. They witness agony, social aberrations, and injustice on practically every assignment. In fact, rarely do journalists cover news that presents humanity in a favorable light. Certainly, we can all remember "human interest" stories that showed the comical, unusual, and sometimes decent events of human lives. We probably remember such stories because of their rarity. However, it is much more characteristic of journalists to dwell on problems. It is this continual exposure to human tragedy, both to the victims and to the criminal, the selfish, or the inconsiderate, that causes journalists to come to doubt the worth of humanity and the worth of their role in protecting freedom and insuring that the average person is not overwhelmed by the powerful. Once that ideal is lost, a journalist becomes a likely target for burnout.

THE PROBLEM OF LACK OF APPRECIATION

All of us want to be appreciated. We all like praise. Most of all, we want praise that is deserved. Worst of all is to work hard, extend ourselves, do more than is asked, and be ignored. Journalists are no different from the rest of us. They work hard and want their work appreciated. Yet they are in a profession in which such appreciation is most difficult to come by. Their employers seem to provide feedback to them only if the job they do is not acceptable. Their employers have little sympathy for them if they are not doing the job. The journalist who is not doing well is simply replaced. A major source of frustration among journalists is that they are not only not appreciated by their employers but that any signs of stress are treated as signs of weakness and signs of unfitness for the job. The assumption among many employers is that the hard-drinking, hard-smoking, and hard-driving image from book, movies, and television actually makes the best journalist. Given such as assumption, there is little that is done to alleviate the stresses under which journalists work. If the journalist is a tough cookie, then appreciation isn't necessary. The problem is, of course, that journalists aren't any tougher than the rest of us. Just like everybody else, they need appreciation and praise. Their employers aren't meeting these needs, and that is one cause of burnout.

The second source from which journalists do not receive praise or appreciation is the public. As mentioned above, much of journalistic work is done anonymously. It is difficult to praise those we do not know. Even when a journalist has a byline or is identified in broadcast journalism, little praise flows from the public. When it does, it seems reserved for a few. The anchor on the evening news may become a celebrity, but consider this question for a moment: Who is your weekend newscaster? Tough question, isn't it? For every star in journalism, there are thousands of unknowns who are not recognized and appreciated.

Finally, there is the public assumption that journalists who do expose corruption and other forms of wrongdoing are not motivated by pure altruism. Despite the social good that a story might do, if it attacks a popular public figure, reveals scandal, or challenges socially accepted traditions, the journalist is not appreciated but personally vilified. For all the social good an investigative journalist might do, our society simply does not appreciate the job of a "muckraker." It comes to this: when journalists do their job best, we like them least.

THE PROBLEM OF THE NATURE
OF THE JOB

Journalists do not work at a leisurely pace. They are, perhaps as in no other profession, pressured by deadlines. And the deadlines never stop. One story can be finished only to be succeeded by another that has to be done immediately. It is difficult to take much satisfaction from tasks when there are so many to do at one time and so little time to relish personal accomplishment. As soon as one story is completed, the journalist may have to rush off to complete another story and may never see or read the final version of either!

An interesting problem for print journalists is the increasing use of computers to set up stories, make corrections, and finalize copy. One frustration is to have a power failure wipe out all their work. As publishers become more and more enamored with technology, journalists become increasingly distant from the final product. They have little personal satisfaction when a story is completed because they have little idea of how the final copy will read.

Another major source of dissatisfaction among journalists is that in the organizations for which they work there are no clear lines of authority or of communication. New journalists are often in the dark about what the expectations of the job are and to whom they are directly responsible. Further, a major complaint is that organizations suffer from a lack of professional management talent. The outcome of that misorganization is that journalists' jobs are threatened by the folding of a newspaper (awful pun) or by frequent changes in the management team. Under such conditions it is difficult to feel secure in the job, to determine what routes and skills will be most beneficial in promotions, and so fourth.

While management competency is a major source of dissatisfaction among journalists, concerns about the job itself are also sources of stress. Salary, job security, and job availability are all major concerns. Further, while salary and job security are important, once a journalist has a job, the work that is demanded is often boring and lacking in real challenge. The image of the reporter helping the police solve an important murder case makes a good movie, but it exists more in the minds of scriptwriters than in the daily lives of journalists. The "big story" is rare. Most journalists spend their time at the football game, the flower show, the bickering school board meeting, the preprogrammed political speech, and the routine human tragedies that make up the daily news. Despite the Hollywood image, much of journalism consists of long, boring hours spent doing routine and unrewarding tasks.

As difficult as that is, many young journalists could put up with it if there appeared to be an opportunity to move up in the organization. It becomes a major source of burnout when journalists discover that there is little opportunity for promotion and personal growth. As in most organizations, there is little room at the top, and in this case, the top positions are often held by nonjournalists. And personal growth is stunted because there is so little time.

Finally, there is little privacy in journalism. Ordinarily, journalists do not have private offices in which they can get away from other persons for a while. They are in plain view much of the time, confronted by noise and the hustle and bustle of a modern news room. Consider a job in which the activities are boring most of the time, there is little opportunity to avoid such boring tasks, the pay is low, the job is insecure, the working conditions are poor, the chain of command is uncertain, and tight deadlines are inescapable. The result: journalists burn out.

THE PROBLEM OF THE LACK
OF RESPONSIBILITY

There are two sources of burnout associated with responsibility. First, not enough individual responsibility is given to journalists by their employers. Second, too much personal responsibility must be assumed for the quality of their work. In a sense, it is a paradox. While individual journalists enter the profession with strong personal obligations to maintain exceedingly high quality and standards of accuracy, their employers allow them very little autonomy. Their assignments, the time they may spend on them, and even the ultimate form or use of the fruits of their labors are controlled. While most persons outside journalism assume that the journalist is a sort of lone wolf out looking for any hot scoop, the actual job is highly controlled, and that is a source of burnout for journalists.

The second source of burnout associated with responsibility is that journalists seek to adhere to self-imposed standards of excellence and accuracy that are unrealistically high. No work is every good enough. Further, it is the journalists with just such high personal standards that stand the best chance of burning out. It is one of the characteristics of journalists that they are never off work. It is for this reason that the pressures can gain such intensity. While most of us can put in our time and then go home to forget about work for a while, a journalist is always on duty. If a newsworthy event happens and a journalist is there, that journalist is expected to stop whatever he or she is doing and start collecting information for a story. The sense of never being off duty is another stress for journalists which contributes to burnout.

THE PROBLEM OF THE EFFECTS
ON FAMILY

The major impact of a journalist's job on family is that the job comes first. Long hours interrupt normal family functions. Dinners planned in advance have to be cancelled at the last minute. Vacations may have to be postponed because of a journalist's involvement in an ongoing story. The effect on the family is severe, and many families are not able to adjust. Given a choice between job and family, a journalist is placed in a terrible bind. Long before such a choice is made necessary, journalists must face deteriorating personal relationships, lack of support at home, and the recognition that many significant family events are being missed. All of that takes a toll.

Finally, journalists are aware that stories unpopular with the community may be a journalistic duty but that spouses and children are often the ones who have to accept the abuse of neighbors or classmates. An unpopular story can bring threats of physical harm to family members and harassment in public places such as supermarkets and school. While the family suffers these indignities, the journalist suffers the pressures of trying to maintain standards of journalistic responsibility and trying to keep the family safe.

SYMPTOMS OF JOURNALIST BURNOUT

PHYSICAL

The physical symptoms of burnout for journalists are much the same as for other professions. They can begin with headaches or with tired, irritated eyes. The journalist may feel tired, fatigued, even exhausted all the time. It becomes increasingly difficult to get up to go to work. It is a tiredness that is compounded by the common response of insomnia. The journalist is tired at work and unable to sleep at home. It all begins to add up and take its toll. The physical symptoms begin to appear as an increased susceptibility to illnesses. Common colds and flu become more frequent. The final stages of physical burnout can involve more serious illnesses such as ulcers, respiratory infections, strokes, and heart attacks.

Such susceptibility is compounded by the lack of exercise in the journalist's schedule and by the necessity of missing lunch or eating on the run. Given a poor diet, lack of exercise, and improper rest, the journalist loses the physical ability to respond quickly and simply cannot muster the energy to do good journalistic work. Physical burnout is just that—lack of energy. It is no surprise that energy is lacking in persons who do no exercise and rest and eat poorly.

INTELLECTUAL

The first sign of intellectual burnout is a tendency to blame others for personal problems or for problems encountered at work. The end result of such blaming is a pessimistic and cynical outlook on the possibility of change. The burned-out journalist has lost faith in society, government, business, and the public as well as in the power of journalism to have an effect on the great institutions of our time.

The burned-out journalist is quick to criticize the young, idealistic new persons on the staff who are still willing to dig deep into a story to reveal its motivations and corruptions; he or she is content to be a hack, characterized by cliches and stereotypes. Burned-out journalists simply go through the motions and report the surface information. They are too cynical to believe that digging deep and revealing something important is really going to make any difference in the society on which they have given up.

EMOTIONAL

Emotional burnout in journalists begins by refusing to confront the sources of stress at work and by continuing to work in a situation that repeatedly hardens the feelings of journalists toward others. They become less sympathetic to persons involved in situations of human suffering and tragedy. They become curt with the victims they have to interview. They care less about what happens to the persons in their stories. They become more and more mechanical in their treatment of human dilemmas. In fact, burned-out journalists take on many of the stereotypical characteristics of the journalists of fiction. They become tough, hard, and cynical and in the process refuse to accept their own human feelings and the feelings of the persons about whom they report. Such an attitude prevents journalists from looking at themselves and at the effect their job and their attitude of toughness is having on their lives.

SOCIAL

Journalists' family problems are worsened by their refusal to talk about what is happening on the job. They have become increasingly isolated from their own feelings and do not want to share their fears and doubts with family members. This initial lack of willingness to share thoughts and feelings about the job leads to a general reluctance to share anything at all with the spouse and other family members.

Ultimately, the unwillingness to share extends to friends, and the journalist has created the situation in which burnout is inevitable. Isolated from family, friends, and colleagues, they have nowhere or no one to turn to for help in arresting the signs of burnout that can no longer be denied.

SPIRITUAL

The work of a burned-out journalist can be called "one long, gray line" of bland, uneventful prose. This flatness of writing or speaking reveals the lack of zest in the journalist's work. The job has lost its meaning. Far more important is the increasing use of alcohol and drugs to dull the pain associated with the loss of meaning. Most important is the loss of faith in humanity. It is bad enough to lose faith in one's profession, but the spiritual burnout of journalists involves even more than that. These people have lost faith in the effects of journalism on public policy or on private habits and have taken the next step in doubting humanity's ability to solve the kinds of problems they report on every day. Lacking faith in self, profession, and people, the journalist is left with the choices of putting in time without any zest or of leving the profession. They are totally burned out.

CURES FOR JOURNALIST BURNOUT

PHYSICAL

The problem for journalists is time. They have little time to do anything about their physical condition because they do not have extra time in which to exercise. They do not eat well because sometimes their schedule does not allow them to stop to eat properly. They might not get enough rest if sleep is interrupted because of an assignment and they are not able to get back to sleep before the next workday.

It is a problem. But it is a problem of conception, not of fact. What has happened to journalists has happened to most of us. The schedule has taken charge of them rather than the other way around. So the first recommendation in reversing or resisting burnout is to take charge of the schedule.

Exercise, rest, and nutrition are the central ingredients in a physical stress-reduction plan. And, despite all the protest to the contrary, people do have time to give to all of them—*if* they take charge of their time.

If one is to have the strength and energy to do the job, one has to be in good physical condition. The first step is to exercise. If it is possible, have the owners set a room aside in the building for the purpose of exercise. It is possible to have a physical exercise plan that can be done daily in less than thirty minutes which will tone and maintain the body.(See Chapter 1 in Part Two for one such plan.) If journalists would adopt the thirty-minute plan at the office, they would have more strength and energy.

It is important to rest. Make a rule. If you have to interrupt sleep to do something related to work, take an equal amount of time off the next day to rest (sleep). Make that arrangement with employers. If one's job involves forty hours a week, stick pretty close to forty hours a week. Make another rule. If it is known that one will have to do overtime, find some time during regular hours to rest. Find a quiet place at work to sit quietly and rest or, even better, go home and take a nap. If it is one's desire to be a better journalist, then these are not silly recommendations. They are recommendations that will, in the long run, make one a better journalist, because those journalists who follow such advice will run less risk of burning out. It is not a weakness to acknowledge one's physical limitations. We all need rest. Some of us don't take it and keep on driving. It is equally true that some of us die early!

Sometimes we have to rush through lunch or dinner because an emergency comes up. The best way to maintain a good diet is to make sure that you don't have to depend on fast-food restaurants in crisis situations. What that implies is that it is possible to keep nutritious food in the car or in one's desk. Set a limit on the number of cups of coffee one drinks a day. At other times, drink citrus juices or other fruit drinks. Many such drinks come in single-serving cans that are conveniently stored in the office or car. It is possible to carry dried fruit or some other healthy snack that one likes. If journalists would take care of their food, they would have the energy to tackle long and arduous assignments and increase the likelihood of success. If journalists don't tire out, they can be there when the story breaks. In addition, they will be fresher and more alert.

INTELLECTUAL

Here are several recommendations to avoid intellectual burnout. First, do not wait to be given responsibility at work. Assume responsibility in an area which is being neglected. Develop a specialty and develop stories in that specialty whether or not they are assigned. Submit them for publication. If one is accepted, that is an opening that can be exploited for more and more work that is challenging and of personal interest. If personal growth is important, make time for personal growth projects. It may be impossible to attend classes in journalism or in some area of specialty, but it is not impossible to carry out self-improvement projects under the supervision of another expert. Do those in the time that can be arranged. Discuss the possibility of employers' sponsoring workshops right in the building where journalists work, aimed at skill improvement and other journalistic requirements.

Take some time to learn to express oneself in another medium. If one is asked to go on an assignment and a photographer is not available, start to learn how to take pictures. If one has a variety of talents, one has a greater chance of avoiding boring, unchallenging work. As a journalist increases skills, the organization comes up with more and more challenging assignments.

Finally, try to create the opportunity to speak at a journalism school or workshops to let others in on the pressures and realities of journalism work. It is a way of organizing one's own thoughts and another way to avoid intellectual burnout.

EMOTIONAL

If it is true that a large part of the emotional drain on journalists is due to the problem of seeing human nature at its worst, make a rule that for every ten stories done on human tragedy, one will be written on human goodness or even magnificence. Take the time to seek out human beings who are acting unselfishly, who sacrifice for the good of many, and who represent the best of humanity. If journalists can do that, humanity can present itself to them in a better light, and it will be easier to keep faith in the human ability to solve our problems.

Another source of dissatisfaction among journalists is lack of appreciation. In order to avoid burnout associated with this, produce work in some other area than usual. If one is in print journalism, develop a piece for the Sunday supplement. If one is in broadcast journalism, write a series for the local newspaper. If it is possible, take an editorial stand on an issue and seek to have it published. The important idea is to reach outside the ordinary confines of work to do something that is different and so gain not only a personal sense of achievement but also the attention of employers and colleagues.

It is also possible for a journalist to create the opportunity for several colleagues to gather and discuss similar problems and to form a support group for one another. This permits everyone to share common problems and seek solutions together.

Analyze sources of stress at work and, if possible, avoid them. If it is not possible to avoid the stress-producing aspects of the job, realize that they are conditions of work and accept them instead of wasting time trying to change them. Invest energy in changing things that can be changed.

Finally, analyze one's personal standards of work and if they are unrealistic (too high, for example), work at ways to eliminate them by developing more reasonable, workable standards. Talk this over with other journalists to help decide on such a reasonable level of quality.

SOCIAL

There are three aspects to helping reverse or avoid burnout: family, friends, and colleagues. Of these, family is the most important. The family is the primary relationship in one's life. It is most sad that persons neglect their families in favor of jobs or other activities. The payoff is not nearly as great as the emotional and social satisfaction that we get from a happy home life. In order to avoid family disputes based on a misunderstanding of what journalists do, it might be possible to involve the family in one's work. For example, have lunch with one's spouse at least once a week. And once a year, invite the children to tour the office. The important idea here is to put energy into the marriage and the family. Another idea is to have family members read and comment on work projects and to offer suggestions for improvement and nonprofessional insights.

Colleagues understand work-related problems better than anyone else. Provide opportunities for sharing more, both professionally and personally, with colleagues. Don't assume every assignment has to be individual. Create opportunities to team up with another person in the organization to complete an assignment. Brainstorm different assignments with colleagues to learn new, innovative, and creative ways of handling the assignment. Create time to exercise with colleagues at the office. Start a "praise-help club" with colleagues. One way to do that is to give other people on the staff praise for work which is really well done. In that way, an individual in an office can create an atmosphere in which it is accepted, and later expected, that praise will be given for excellent work. It will also increase the chances of getting deserved praise for one's own work.

Develop a relationship with friends that acts as a support. If there are troublesome aspects of the job, share them with friends. Be willing to serve as a sounding board for their professional concerns as well. Don't pass up a chance to be with friends. Be an active agent in setting up potluck suppers, picnics, or parties. Seek out a variety of activities that are enjoyed with friends and make a special plan for some activity with family and friends at least once every six months.

SPIRITUAL

Spiritual burnout comes when the meaning goes out of work. It is hard to keep meaning in work if the reasons for entering it are lost. Take the time to restate the reasons for becoming a journalist. Do not be ashamed of idealism or concerns over a free press or over the role of the press in a democracy. Consider what one might be doing as a journalist in a nation in which the press was not free. In essence, touch base from time to time with the positive side of being a journalist. It might even be possible to develop a personal code of ethics. Keep track of the time when the code has been tested and maintained. Keep a daily journal of the joys, pleasures, and successes that have been experienced. Read it at the end of each week so that life presents the good things along with the negative.

Lastly, plan a specific amount of time in which all of the assignments one takes are about human strength, dignity, heroics, achievements, joy, and happiness. Perhaps it can be a year-long assignment, perhaps only a few months long. But plan some time like that. It will contribute to the meaning one has in life and act to prevent burnout.

II

ACTIVITIES

In Part One, we identified five aspects of human functioning which are affected by burnout (physical, intellectual, emotional, social, and spiritual). In Part Two, we offer specific activities designed to relieve or prevent burnout that are suitable for persons in any profession. To derive the maximum benefit from this part of the book, determine which area or areas of functioning are most in need of improvement. To help with this determination, take the Burnout Susceptibility Test in Chapter 16. Then, turn to the sections identified by the test for activities which will deal specifically with that aspect of burnout.

Although each of the activities is valuable, some may be more appealing than others. Start with those that appeal to you most. Try as many as you like and find the ones which work best. Repeat them as often as necessary. If an activity seems difficult, don't dismiss it. It may seem difficult because it deals with an area in which the most change is needed.

Although it may seem time-consuming, working on these activities is well worth the effort. The time and energy devoted to the activities in the short run will save time and increase productivity in the long run. We urge you to give them a try. Good luck!

15. Physical

GENERAL FITNESS TEST

The simple test below can give a quick measure of general fitness. It can also provide information about which area of fitness most needs improvement. It is a first step in becoming more physically fit. There are four parts to the General Fitness Test. First, there is a measure provided for flexibility and strength. Second, the oxygen system is tested. The oxygen system is more important for endurance over long periods of time. Third, there is a test for the "quick energy" system. Quick energy is useful for bursts of activities that take less than ten seconds. Fourth, there is a test for high-intensity effort. This test measures energy available for exercises which take from one to three minutes. The measures of strength and flexibility, together with the tests of the oxygen system (endurance), quick energy (under ten seconds), and high intensity (one to three minutes) provide an overall assessment of general fitness, a quick measure of one's fitness for work and play.

1. *Flexibility and Strength*
   There are three simple tests for flexibility and strength: push-ups, touching the toes, and the sit-and-reach and stand-and-reach tests.
   A. Push-ups. Lie on the stomach, with hands shoulder-width apart and toes

touching the floor. Keeping the body as straight as possible, push until the arms are fully extended. Then lower the body to the floor. Do as many push-ups as possible in two minutes.

B. Touch the toes. While the exact amount of flexibility one should possess is not known, a general measure is the ability to touch the toes without bending the knees. Stretch but do not bounce.

C. Sit or stand and reach.[1] A slightly more difficult method of measuring flexibility is the sit-and-reach or stand-and-reach test. It is more difficult because it calls more muscles into play and because it requires some equipment in order to be administered. This test involves the flexibility of the back, buttocks, upper legs, and lower legs. Buy an inexpensive yardstick and cut it off at 24 inches or mark a 24 inch stick in ¼-inch increments. For the sit-and-reach test, tape or attach in any way the 24-inch ruler to a box or stool approximately 12 inches in height with 12 inches extending from the edge of the stool (see diagram). Place the feet against the box, sit up, and extend the arms as far as possible, without bouncing, along the ruler. For the stand-and-reach test, place the 24-inch ruler along the side of the box or stool with 12 inches alongside the box and 12 inches extending above. Bend over as if to touch the toes and extend the arms as far as possible, without bouncing, along the ruler.

Scoring

Push-ups

Guidelines for Strength Using Push-Ups[2] (Number of Repetitions)

| | AGE 15-25 | | 26-35 | | 35+ | |
Classification	Male	Female*	Male	Female*	Male	Female*
Minimum	8	8	7	7	3	3
Fair	15	15	12	12	8	8
Good	25	25	20	20	15	15
Excellent	40	40	30	30	20	20

*Push-ups performed using a stool about 10 inches high.

Flexibility

The ability to touch the toes without bending the knees or bouncing is all that's needed to pass this test.

Sit or stand and reach

The higher the number on the ruler, the great the flexibility.

2. *The Oxygen System*

Walk or jog comfortably for 12 minutes. This provides a good measure of the oxygen system.

[1]Adapted from Edward L. Fox and Donald K. Mathews, *Interval Training,* New York: Holt, Rinehart & Winston, 1974, p. 243.

[2]Adapted from Fox & Mathews, pp. 241-2.

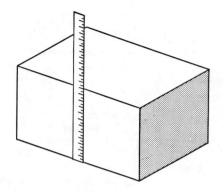

Guidelines for 12-Minute Test of the Oxygen System[3] (in Miles)

Classification	AGE UNDER 30		30-39		40-49		50+	
	Male	Female	Male	Female	Male	Female	Male	Female
Very Poor	−1	−.95	−.95	−.85	−.85	−.75	−.80	−.65
Poor	1.0–	.95–	.95–	.85–	.85–	.75–	.80–	.65–
	1.24	1.14	1.14	1.04	1.04	.94	.99	.84
Fair	1.25–	1.15–	1.15–	1.05–	1.05–	.95–	1.0–	.85–
	1.49	1.39	1.39	1.24	1.29	1.14	1.24	1.04
Good	1.50–	1.40–	1.40–	1.25–	1.30–	1.15–	1.25–	1.05–
	1.74	1.64	1.64	1.54	1.54	1.44	1.49	1.34
Excellent	1.74+	1.64+	1.64+	1.54+	1.54+	1.44+	1.49+	1.34+

3. *The Quick-Energy System*
   The quick-energy system may be measured by running the 50-yard dash with a 15-yard running start.

Guidelines for the 50-Yard Dash for Males[4] (in Seconds)

Classification	Age 15-20	20-30	30-40	40-50	50+
Poor	7.1+	7.8+	9.0+	10.8+	13.0+
Fair	7.1-6.8	7.8-7.5	9.0-8.6	10.8-10.3	13.0-12.4
Good	6.7-6.5	7.4-7.1	8.5-8.1	10.2-9.7	12.3-11.6
Excellent	−6.5	−7.1	−8.1	−9.7	−11.6

[3]Adapted from Fox & Mathews, pp. 254–5.
[4]Adapted from Fox & Mathews, p. 262.

Guidelines for the 50-Yard Dash for Females[5] (in Seconds)

Classification	Age 15–20	20–30	30–40	40–50	50+
Poor	9.1+	10.0+	11.5+	13.8+	16.5+
Fair	9.1–8.4	10.0–9.2	11.5–10.6	13.8–12.7	16.5–15.2
Good	8.3–7.9	9.1–8.7	10.5–10.0	12.6–12.0	15.1–14.4
Excellent	–7.9	–8.7	–10.0	–12.0	–14.4

4. *High Intensity Efforts.*

Lie on the back with knees bent and do the number of sit-ups that are comfortable in two minutes.

Sit-ups. Sit-ups are performed by lying on the back with the knees bent and the legs at less than a 90-degree angle. Another person may hold the feet or they may be placed under a chair or sofa. Hands are locked behind the head. Lie flat on the back and come to a sitting position. Do as many sit-ups as possible in two minutes without over exertion.

Scoring

Sit-ups

Guidelines for Strength Using Sit-Ups[6] (Number of Repetitions)

Classification	AGE 15–25		26–35		35+	
	Male	Female	Male	Female	Male	Female
Minimum	10	5	8	4	5	2
Fair	25	15	20	10	15	5
Good	50	20	40	15	30	10
Excellent	80	30	70	20	50	15

BENEFITS

While the General Fitness Test provides a measure of general fitness, it also provides recommendations for what might be done to improve general fitness. If one is weak in any of the areas, a program can be devised to improve that area. The classifications give a general indication of where one should be for one's gender and age. That information can become the goal for regaining or maintaining overall physical condition.

[5]Adapted from Fox & Mathews, p. 262.
[6]Adapted from Fox & Mathews, pp. 241-2.

GOOD MORNING, AMERICA
A MORNING EXERCISE PROGRAM
TIME: 15 MINUTES

(Note: These exercises may be used as preactivity warm-ups for sporting events; they may also be used as postactivity cool-downs as well. Such a pre- and postactivity schedule will help to reduce injuries during play and also reduce muscle soreness after play.) These exercises will provide flexibility and strength for the upper and lower body. They take approximately 15 minutes and are helpful in controlling weight and maintaining muscle tone.

INSTRUCTIONS FOR EXERCISE

1. These are stretching exercises. Therefore, all bouncing should be avoided.
2. Exercise for stretch, not pain.
3. Each exercise should be done with 10 repetitions. (Increase to 20 if desired.)
4. For preactivity, use 10 repetitions. (Increase gradually to 20 if desired.)
5. For postactivity, use 10 repetitions.
6. If a muscle or joint has been injured or is very inflexible, use more repetitions for that area.
7. All exercises should be done with rhythm, slowly and under control.

EXERCISES

1. *Neck Rotation*
   Gently lean head to the left as far as possible without pain. Then lean head as far as possible to the right without pain. Then tilt the head straight back until looking directly at the ceiling. Then tilt the head forward until the chin is on the chest and stretch it forward and down. Then rotate the head to the left in a circle until it returns to the original head-down, chin-on-chest position. Last, rotate the head to the right in a circle until it returns to the original head-down, chin-on-chest position. This series counts as one repetition. Repeat ten times.
2. *Side Bending*
   Spread the feet about shoulder-width apart. With arms at the sides, bend to the side and slide the left arm down the left leg. Repeat on the right side. Repeat 10 times for each side.
3. *Trunk Rotation*
   With the feet about shoulder-width apart, place hands on hips. Bend at the waist as far left as possible. Then bend to the right. Then bend backwards as far as possible and look at the ceiling. Then bend forward at the waist as far as possible. Then rotate at the waist to the left in a circle until back at the original position. Last, rotate to the right at the waist in a circle until back at the original position. This series counts as one repetition. Repeat ten times.

4. *Groin Stretch*
   a. Sit with the legs straight out and the fists between the knees. Push the knees together for a count of two. Repeat ten times.
   b. Sit with the soles of the feet touching, with elbows inside knees and hands clasped. Push knees against elbows for a count of two. Relax, then pull heels closer to groin. When heels are close to groin, push down with elbows for a count of two. Repeat ten times.

5. *Knee/Leg Stretch*
   Lie flat on the floor on the back. Bring the right knee as close to the chest as possible on the right side. Then as close as possible to the left shoulder. Then try to touch the chin to the knee. Next, bring the left knee as close as possible to the chest on the left side. Then as close as possible to the right shoulder. Then try to touch the chin to the knee. As much as possible, keep the back and the leg not being used flat on the floor. Repeat ten times with each leg.

6. *Hip Flexibility*
   Lie in a prone position, with the stomach flat on the floor. Keeping the knees together, raise the right leg so that the knee is flexed at a 90-degree angle (straight up). Now raise the thigh off the floor until tightness is felt in front of the hip. *Do not* rotate the hip. Return thigh to floor. Now repeat with the other leg. Keep knee bent and tucked inward at all times. Do this exercise slowly. Do not over-extend the back. Repeat ten times with each leg.

7. *Quadriceps*
   Lie flat on the stomach with the knees close together. Bend the knee and bring the right leg as close to the thigh as possible. With the right hand, pull down on the ankle for a count of two. Return to straight position. Then bend the left knee and bring the leg as close as possible to the thigh. With the left hand, pull down on the ankle for a count of two. Return to straight position. Repeat ten times with each leg.

8. *Straight Leg Raises*
   Lie on the back. Raise the right leg, with knees straight and ankle pulled toward you, straight up. Lower to flat position. Raise the left leg, knee straight and ankle pulled toward you, straight up. As much as possible, keep the back and the leg not in use flat on the floor. Repeat ten times with each leg.

9. *Lower Leg Extensions*
   Lie flat on the back and lift the right leg with the knee slightly bent. Grasp the leg underneath the knee and stabilize the thigh in this position. Then raise the left leg straight up, as straight as possible. Return to the flat position. Do the same with the left leg. Repeat ten times with each leg.

10. *Sit-ups*
    Lie flat on the back with the knees bent and heels about 12 inches from the buttocks. Hands are clasped behind the head. Come to a sitting position with the head as close as possible to the knees. Return to lying position. Repeat ten times.

11. *Leg Stretch.*
    Stand facing a support, a foot or two away. Lean forward and grasp the support, bending the right leg slightly and keeping the left leg straight with its heel on the

floor. Lean slowly toward the support by bending elbows and forward leg until tightness is felt in the rear leg. Do this first with toes pointed in, then with toes pointed out, and finally with toes pointed straight ahead. Alternate legs. Repeat ten times with each leg.

12. *More Leg Stretch*
Stand as in exercise 11. Lean slowly, moving hips forward, toward the support by bending elbows and front leg until tightness is felt in the rear leg. Do this first with toes pointed in, then with toes pointed out, and finally with toes pointed straight ahead. Alternate legs. Repeat ten times with each leg.

13. *Ankle Stretch*
Stand facing and grasping a support, with the right leg slightly bent and the left leg straight with the toes of rear foot on a surface. Put gradual pressure down and forward by bending the front knee. Do this first with toes pointed in, then with toes pointed out, and finally with toes pointed straight ahead. Alternate ankles. Repeat ten times with each ankle.

14. *More Ankle Stretch*
Standing with slight support, roll to outside edge of both feet at the same time. Then roll to the inside edge of both feet. Repeat ten times with each ankle.

15. *Push-ups*
Lie on the stomach with legs together, hands about shoulder-width apart, and toes touching the floor. Keeping the body as straight as possible, push with the hands and arms until the arms are fully extended. Lower to original position. Repeat ten times.

HEALTH WALK-RUN

Here is the design for a health walk-run that can be established in one's own neighborhood or suggested to the local recreation department to have built in parks. The health walk-run is approximately one mile long, with ten exercise stations built along the way. It takes approximately twenty to thirty minutes to complete, depending on the speed of the participant. Each station features a different exercise. The advantage of the health walk-run is that it provides an excellent starting place in exercising for a person who has not exercised for a long time. Further, it allows the person to establish his or her own pace. It is possible to start out walking and gradually increase the pace to a rapid run between each station.

The health walk-run is designed in the following way:

The starting point may be anywhere. It might be the front steps or the corner of the block. From the starting point, walk or run approximately 200 yards to Station 1.

Station 1. Touch the toes—Bend at the waist and stretch, don't bounce, as far as possible. Try to touch the toes with the fingers. Ten times is good, but initially do the number that feels comfortable.

Walk or run approximately 150 yards to station 2.

Station 2. Waist bend—Place the hands on the buttocks and bend at the waist, with the head looking up, until the body is parallel to the ground. Ten times is good.

Walk or run approximately 150 yards to station 3.

Station 3. Jumping jacks—Start with the feet together and the hands at the sides. Jump, moving both feet approximately shoulder-width apart, and clap the hands over the head. Twenty times is good.

Walk or run approximately 150 yards to station 4.

Station 4. Push-ups—Lie on the stomach with the hands shoulder-width apart at the shoulders and the toes touching the ground. Keeping the body as straight as possible, push until the arms are fully extended. Try to do this rapidly. Ten is very good.

Walk or run approximately 150 yards to station 5.

Station 5. Windmill toe-touch—Stand with the feet more than shoulder-width apart and the arms extended at shoulder level parallel to the ground. Bend at the waist and touch the left foot with the fingers of the right hand. Continue by alternating hands and feet. Ten times on each side is good.

Walk or run approximately 150 yards to station 6.

Station 6. Upper-back stretch—Stand with the feet slightly apart and the arms bent at the elbow and at shoulder level. Push the elbows back as far as possible. Hold this position for a count of five and then release. Ten times is good.

Walk or run approximately 150 yards to station 7.

Station 7. Arm push—Find a tree or a wall and push as hard as possible against it with the palms flat against the tree. Hold this position for a count of five. Ten times is good.

Walk or run approximately 150 yards to station 8.

> *Station 8. Behind-the-head clasp—Stand with the feet slightly apart and place the hands behind the head. Curl the fingers of both hands and lock them together like an S. Pull as hard as possible with both arms but do not break the lock. Hold this for a count of five. Ten times is good.*

Walk or run approximately 150 yards to station 9.

> *Station 9. Sit-ups—Lie on the back with the knees bent and the legs at less than a 90-degree angle. Hands are locked behind the head. Lie flat on the back and come to a sitting position. Ten times is good.*

Walk or run approximately 150 yards to station 10.

> *Station 10. Spine stretch—Get down on all fours with the back slightly humped. Bend the elbows and move the chest down toward the ground while straightening the back. Ten times is good.*

Walk or run approximately 160 yards to the end of the health walk-run.

It is possible to design a health walk-run so that it begins and ends in the same place. Obviously, that place can be one's own front door!

SLEEP AND REST CHARTING

Using the twenty-four-hour clock (24 is midnight, 12 is noon, 6 is 6:00 A.M. and 18 is 6:00 P.M.), indicate the hours of sleep in any given twenty-four-hour period in one color and the periods of rest in a different color. After the periods of rest and sleep have been colored in, look at the chart to see the pattern it reveals. Respond to these questions.

1. Do I sleep at least six hours a day? (At least six hours a day is needed by most of us. Occasionally, there is a rare person who really does not need this amount of sleep. Notice, we said a *rare* person.)
2. Are there periods of rest and relaxation indicated? If not, plan in at least two rest periods during the day that balance out the sleep cycle. For example, sometime during the workday, find time to rest—instead of a traditional coffee break, perhaps. Another time to rest is after work and before any social engagements.

   Remember, these exercises are planned to help people avoid or arrest physical burnout. If they appear silly, consider that the people who do not sleep

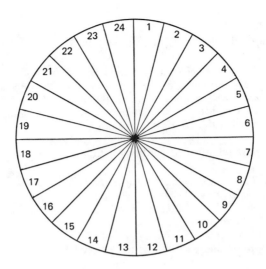

and rest properly are the ones who are reporting physical burnout and a lack of sufficient energy to do their jobs. Charting can make these people more aware of their need for sleep and rest.

RELAXING THE BODY AND MIND

Relaxation isn't tough. It does require a little time. That is why so many people think it is tough to relax. If you take the time, relaxation is easy. In fact, here are three "relaxation techniques" that are simple, arranged from the easiest to the most complex (which isn't very complex).

1. Sit and relax. Sit in a comfortable chair, close the eyes, don't talk to anybody, think of anything but nothing in particular and stay there for five minutes! Too tough? Try the next one.
2. Talke a warm bath! Stay in it for fifteen minutes. Especially before bedtime.
3. Here is a seven-step system that is a "relaxation technique."
   a. Sit or lie down in a comfortable place.
   b. Close the eyes.
   c. Become aware of breathing. Concentrate on the intake of breath. Breathe in through the nose to a count of four. Exhale through the mouth to a count of four.
   d. Continue to concentrate on breathing. Now, picture in the mind a mountain meadow. Hear the rushing water. Picture the wild flowers. Feel the breeze against the face. Hear the sounds of birds, bees, wind. Immerse the mind totally in the experience of the meadow.

e. With every intruding thought, repeat this phrase: "I am thinking of a mountain meadow."
f. Do this for ten minutes.
g. Set a timer so that time is not a problem.

MEDITATION

When all the hullabaloo is cut away, essentially what remains is that there are two forms of meditation. In nontechnical language, they are opening-up meditation and shutting-down meditation. There are five systems of opening-up meditation and seven systems of shutting-down meditation. Despite all the claims of the various systems, no system of meditation can demonstrate that it is superior to other systems. It turns out to be a highly personal matter. It may demand some experimentation, but what works best for individuals is probably the best indicator of what system of meditation should be used. Below, all five systems of opening-up meditation are explained, and examples of all seven systems of shutting-down meditation are given.

OPENING UP

Opening up consists of emphasizing the five senses of the body: seeing, hearing, touching, tasting, and smelling. Here is how they apply to meditation. Anything may be used to emphasize the senses. For the purpose of this example, an orange will be used to demonstrate all five systems of opening-up meditation. While it may seem silly, remember, the purpose of this is to relax the physical body and the mind, as the reader will soon realize. Ten minutes is the time to practice each meditation. Explore each one to see which works best. Obviously, such emphasizing of the senses could be done on a walk in the park or around the block or at work in the morning.

1. Seeing. Take an orange and closely examine the outer skin. Look closely at the color and texture. Peel the orange and look closely at the edge of the peel. Look at the inside of the peel. Look closely at the wedges. Break open a wedge and look at the meat of the orange. Examine the small pieces carefully. It is even permissible to use a magnifying glass.
2. Hearing. Squeeze an orange. Is there a sound? Peel the orange. Listen. Bend the peel and listen to the sounds. What sound is it? Close the eyes and break a wedge in half. What sound is there? Rub the fingers along the outside of the peel. Is there a sound? Rub the fingers along the inside of the peel. What difference is there?

3. Touching. Close the eyes and rub the fingers along the outside of an unpeeled orange. Feel the texture. Rub the orange all over. Spend five minutes examining the orange with the fingers before peeling it. Peel the orange slowly, feeling each piece. Break the orange into wedges and explore each wedge. Feel the inside of the peel. Examine the edges.
4. Tasting. Close the eyes and place a wedge of orange in the mouth. Bite slowly into the wedge. Bite a piece of the peel. Taste the pulp. How many different tastes are there in an orange?
5. Smelling. Sniff an unpeeled orange. Peel the orange and smell the inside of the peel. Smell a wedge of orange. Bend an orange peel and smell the acid as it explodes from the peel. Smell the pulp. Smell a squeezed wedge. How many different smells are there in an orange?

Obviously, the exercise with an orange is nonsense. It has no special meaning. There is nothing inherently mystical about it. There is no hidden meaning. There is no secret learning to be gained from it. The point is that in extending the senses one forgets about present problems and is able to relax. By allowing in more than the ordinary amount of information for a single sense, other thoughts are blocked. That is why it is called meditation. It must be patently apparent that if one can extend the senses to examine an orange, those senses can be used in an even more extensive way during a walk in the woods. Or, they could be used on a city block on the way to work or during lunch. It is a handy, quick, and efficient way to meditate. It will even work with the orange!

SHUTTING DOWN

Another way to block the thoughts is to shut them out by concentrating on something else. That "something else" can be anything else. Certainly, many of the systems of meditation take many years to perfect. But what we must realize is that those systems are not being used merely to relax but to explore deeper and deeper meanings of life and of one's own personal nature. While in some systems an entirely new method of cognition is being developed, the procedures advocated below are suggested purely and simply as a way to relax and counter the stresses that can build up and lead to burnout. There are seven classes of shutting-down meditation that include most, if not all, popular systems of meditation. They will be listed with some examples of how they have been used in the past. For each system, an easily learned method of meditation will be provided.

1. Breathing. Breathing is an exercise that is taught in many disciplines. Each of us knows that anxiety, fear, and stress are signaled by shallow breathing. One way

to counteract each of them is to practice deep breathing on purpose during an anxious moment or during a period of stress. Here is a simple breathing meditation. Breathe normally with the exception that the eyes are closed and as much concentration as possible is centered on the nose and mouth. Without much effort, begin to inhale through the nose and exhale through the mouth. A variation is to breathe first through the right nostril (use a finger to block the other nostril; later this won't be necessary) and exhale through the mouth and then breathe through the left nostril and exhale through the mouth. See if this exercise works in blocking out thoughts.

2. Focusing on a point. Primarily, this is the meditation that most people make fun of. It is the "contemplate the navel" meditation! The point of focus can be a flame, a mandala (a complex figure, sometimes with hidden meanings), or some other object such as a cross or a Star of David. Focusing on a point is one of the exercises taught in the Lamaze method of childbirth. All one has to do is set up some object, sit down, and stare at it. If intruding thoughts present themselves, redouble the staring. It is recommended that initially a flame be used. It seems this is the point that is easiest for many beginners to stare at.

3. Sounds. Sounds may be internal or external. The system of transcendental meditation (TM) is famous for its "secret" special words that its practitioners use to help them refocus in that system of meditation. Often in systems that use an internal sound, the sound is imbued with special meaning. The systems that use an external sound might ordinarily be called chants. The most famous of these are the Gregorian chants. Yes, those monks were meditating when they marched around the monasteries chanting. In the East, a popular chant of meditation is the sound *OM*. It is a pleasant sensation, and one that many find easily drives away any interfering thoughts. Sit quietly (if a group wants to meditate together, this is an especially good one) and say the sound *OM*. Stretch out the sound like this—OMMMMMMMMMMMMMMMMMMMMMMMM. Allow the sound to vibrate all through the head. Hold the sound for as long as possible. Take a deep breath and then repeat the sound again. Over and over for about ten minutes.

4. Visualization. This system uses images to block out thoughts. It can be the picture of a loved one, a pleasant scene, or a religious figure. Such visualizations may be of Buddha, Jesus Christ, or the Virgin Mary. Here is one visualization that works for many people. Build a wall of bricks, one brick at a time. Envision the piece of ground on which it is to be built, level the ground, place the first row of bricks, and, brick by brick, build the wall. If thoughts present themselves, build the wall faster.

5. Movement. Movement meditations will be recognized in Sufi dancing (whirling dervishes), worry stones and beads, and the Rosary. Here is a movement meditation that requires no equipment. Place the hands on a table top with the fingers spread out. Tap the little finger of each hand on the table top. Then the ring finger and so on down to the thumb. As you do that, count to five, one count for each finger. This one is virtually guaranteed to drive away any thoughts.

6. Devotional practices. The meditations that involve devotional practices are familiar to us as prayer (Hail Mary, Our Father), Sufi stories, parables, and problems to be solved (koans). If one is a religious person, any number of

devotional practices can be obtained at one's house of worship. A more secular practice that would be highly similar would be quietly reciting "Desiderata" or a favorite poem over and over.

7. Methodless meditation. Some people, it turns out, are "natural" meditators. They do not have any particular system but seem to be able to stop thoughts through a number of ordinary daily practices that are not specially performed during the day but whenever they seem necessary. Here are several examples of methodless meditation that are common. Musical instruments provide a combination of sounds and movement meditation that allows many hours of relaxation to people who are practitioners. Simply listening to music is another form of using sound as meditation.

Many forms of athletic endeavor can be viewed as movement meditation, as can dancing. Writing can be seen as a form of meditation. In fact, there is little that is absorbing that is not a form of meditation for persons who concentrate so much on the task that time and distractions are forgotten.

SUMMARY

Any of these twelve systems of meditation holds out the promise of relaxation and tension reduction. Try them to see which one or ones work best. Then, use the one that does work best daily for ten to twenty minutes. It is also possible to take two- or three-minute mini-breaks to ease the pressures of the moment. While hard evidence is difficult to come by, many have suggested that persons who are able to take such mini-breaks are more efficient and productive.

DECOMPRESSION ROUTINE

This Decompression Routine is designed to help people who work and commute to build a part of their burnout prevention into their travel. It is a way to relieve the stress of the day and to help avoid the stresses that immediately confront many of us as we walk through the doors of our homes. It is meant to be done daily. It is meant to become a regular part of one's life so that other members of the family expect it to be followed. It is, as the title suggests, a routine.

Step 1. At the end of the workday, take three to five minutes before leaving the workplace. Sit quietly, breathe deeply. Inhale through the nose to a count of four and exhale through the mouth to a count of four. Just sit quietly, breathing for three to five minutes before leaving to catch a train or bus or to drive home.

Step 2. If at all possible, try to find several different ways home. If privileged to live in a scenic area, try to find a number of different routes home so that alternative routes can be explored each evening. Make the drive home as pleasant as possible and try to avoid the mad rush that is observed in so many commuters.

Step 3. Try to find a scenic place on the route home. Stop there and take a little time to walk, relax, or meditate. One way of "meditating" is to accentuate one of the senses. For example, while walking, keeping the eyes open but not paying much attention to sight, listen carefully to sounds of birds whistling, trees moaning in the wind, snow crunching under shoes, the wind in the leaves, even the sounds of traffic. Try it. It is a relaxing experience.

Step 4. If driving, after the car is parked, do not go into the house right away. Sit and let the song on the radio finish. Or, take a little time to think over the coming evening and plan it quietly in the mind. If a member of a car pool, don't go into the house right away. Take some time and walk around the block before going in. If a train or bus commuter, do the same. If at all possible, do not be met at the station. Walk home.

Step 5. Insist on a rule that the first fifteen minutes after any person who works arrives home that they will not be asked questions or told any crises of the day. The first fifteen minutes is quiet time. It is a time to change clothes, fiddle around, whatever. But until those fifteen minutes are up, no problems, no crises and no gossip should be shared. Too many of us are confronted at the door every evening with the "terrors" of the day. Insist that time be given to collect thoughts and get a sense of "being home" before any new stresses are suffered.

ENERGIZING EXERCISES

Here is an energizing exercise that can be used to stimulate the body into higher energy. Sometimes, especially in the afternoons for many of us, energy declines and we may become drowsy and ineffective in our tasks. This exercise, which can be done in less than two minutes, actually does arouse the body and the alertness which is needed to work efficiently.

Body slapping. This exercise is best done privately or in a group of people all energizing together. (Otherwise, an uninformed observer may think you're crazy!) The point is to firmly but gently slap most portions of the body. Begin by bending at the waist and slapping the left leg up to the thigh. Then slap the right leg from the bottom to the top. Next, straighten up and slap the stomach and chest. Slap the left arm and then the right. Slap the back with both hands as thoroughly as possible. Slap the face, firmly but gently, all over. Finally, tap the scalp with the finger tips. The result should be a tingling sensation all over the body and an increased alertness. Remember, the point is not to hurt but to stimulate.

SITTING FOR HEALTH

Consider for a moment the amount of time all of us spend sitting. For many of the professions discussed in this book, sitting occupies a majority of the working day. Personally examine the number of hours spent in a chair or automobile on the job in an average working day. _____ Next, estimate the number of hours spent in a chair at home in an average day. _____ Add them up. It's remarkable, isn't it!

Now, select the chair (or whatever you sit on at work—car seat, stool) and rate its "sitability" on the test below. Rate one's favorite chair at home in the second column.

Use a scale from 1 to 5 to rate the chairs, 1 being poor fit and 5 the best fit.

	On the job	At home
1. The small of the back is supported.	———	———
2. The seat fully supports the upper legs without pressing into the lower legs.	———	———
3. The seat height allows the legs to rest comfortably on the floor.	———	———
4. There is space between the front legs of the chair.	———	———
5. The chair feels firm.	———	———
6. The seat's front edge is rounded and smooth.	———	———
7. The front of the seat is slightly higher than the rear of the seat.	———	———
8. There is a slight angle (105°) between the chair seat and its back.	———	———
9. The chair provides arm support.	———	———
10. Overall the chair is comfortable.	———	———

Total the score for the chair at the office. If the score isn't at least 35 points, then get a chair that does provide the qualities on this test. The same is true for the home chair. Everyone deserves at least a comfortable chair![7]

SOME COMMON-SENSE, NONFANATICAL INFORMATION ON NUTRITION[8]

The human body requires roughly forty nutrients to grow and stay healthy. The substances that provide the nutrients can be classified as proteins, fats, carbohydrates, vitamins, minerals, water, and fiber.

The proteins function in the maintenance, growth, and repair of the body. While there is controversy among nutritionists regarding the amount and source of protein, there is no controversy regarding how important it is to us. Protein requirements vary according to our health. For example, the greatest amount is needed when the body is building new tissue. More protein is needed when the body is pregnant, mending broken bones, recovering from surgery, fighting infections, or healing burns. Approximately ten percent of the total calorie intake, or about thirty to fifty grams of protein a day, with about two-thirds coming from vegetable sources, is considered to be sufficient for greater vitality and extended longevity.

The main role of carbohydrates is to provide energy for the body. They also act to enable the body to produce some of the B-complex vitamins. Starch is the most important carbohydrate form. Starch is nature's way of storing energy. Complex carbohydrates such as starches are found mainly in plants and provide roughage to help in the elimination of solid waste.

Fats are a concentrated source of energy. Those not used will be deposited and act as insulation for vital organs. Obviously, too much fat, not used as energy, becomes, as the physicists tell us, energy in another form, matter. Too much matter makes fat people! It is estimated that roughly twenty to forty percent of the total diet should be fats. Of that, roughly twenty percent should be unsaturated fats. The fats most of us recognize are butter, oils, and the fat in meats, but fat is also abundant in eggs, milk, nuts, and whole-grain cereals. Unsaturated fats are liquid at room temperature whereas saturated fats are

[7]Adapted from Loretta Jean Engelhardt, "Wellness models for self-regulation, nutrition, and self-discovery." Published project in lieu of dissertation, University of Northern Colorado, 1980.
[8]Adapted from Loretta Jean Engelhardt, "Wellness models for self-regulation, nutrition, and self-discovery." Published project in lieu of dissertation, University of Northern Colorado, 1980.

solid. An important quality of fats is that they carry the fat-soluble vitamins such as A, D, E, and K into the body and help to absorb them.

One substance that is vital to human life does not provide energy but acts to transform foods into energy. These are the vitamins. They are crucial for the growth and maintenance of the body.

Minerals aid in the development of skeletal and soft tissues and the regulation of the body. The regular functions of the body include such vital ones as heartbeat, circulation, oxygen flow from the lungs to the tissues, and blood clotting. The minerals needed in large amounts are sodium, calcium, potassium, magnesium, phosphorus, and sulfur. Others, needed in smaller amounts, include iron, zinc, cobalt, copper, manganese, and iodine. Usually these minerals are provided by any well-balanced diet.

Water is our most important food substance. In fact, our bodies consist of seventy-five percent water. A loss of only ten percent can result in death. Each of us needs to take in about two quarts of water a day—about eight large glasses. Luckily, water composes about ninety percent of the vegetables and eighty percent of the fruits. Meat, poultry, and fish are roughly seventy percent water. So, the absolute amount of fluid we take in is balanced among the many foods we eat. Still, water is a terrific source of fluid!

Fiber is useful in the retention of water and aids in the normal functioning of the intestines. Fiber comes in the carbohydrates we take in. Salad greens, wheat bran, celery, and apple skins are excellent sources of fiber. Sufficient fiber is consumed if fresh vegetables and fruits are eaten each day.

A NOTE ON HOW TO EAT

The best advice is to get up from the table before a button pops off. If one feels light yet satisfied, a proper amount has been eaten. If the body is bloated, stuffed, and tired following a meal, too much was eaten. The signs of improper or excessive eating are burping and gas (from eating too fast), heartburn, indigestion, and diarrhea (food is not being assimilated by the body, from stress or overeating). Mealtime is best a time of calm, quiet, and companionship. Strive to make it that and don't eat too much.

SOME SUGGESTIONS

Below are some activities to help determine if the foods in one's diet are actually contributing to physical health. This is a nonfanatical, common-sense approach that allows people to eat what they like but also ensures that they

Keeping a Food Log[9]

Food	Day of Week	Time of Day	Where	Ate Alone?	Protein	Carbohydrates	Fat	Reason for Eating	Feeling of Satisfaction	Energy Level

have a balanced, healthy diet that actually makes them feel better and gives them more energy to do the things they want to do in life.

ANALYZING THE FOOD LOG[10]

Using our food log, divide the circle into slices representing the proportion of proteins, carbohydrate, and fat eaten in an average day.

[9]Adapted from Loretta Jean Engelhardt, "Wellness models for self-regulation, nutrition, and self-discovery." Published project in lieu of dissertation. University of Northern Colorado, 1980.
[10]*Ibid.*

Recommended daily intake   *My percentage of daily intake.*
   10% Protein   _____ % Protein
40–50% Carbohydrate   _____ % Carbohydrate
20–40% Fat   _____ % Fat

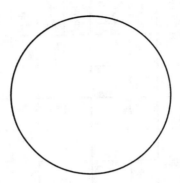

    How do your proportions of protein, carbohydrate, and fat compare with the recommended daily intake amounts of these nutrients? What do you need that you don't presently have for healthy eating?

NUTRITIONAL GOAL SETTING[11]

List your nutritional habits with which you are satisfied.

    List the three nutritional goals for healthy living you can work towards beginning today.

  1. _____
  2. _____
  3. _____

[11]*Ibid.*

16. Intellectual

THE BURNOUT SUSCEPTIBILITY TEST

The following test has proven useful in helping persons become aware of their susceptibility to burnout. Simply answer each of the seventy-five questions Strongly Agree, Mildly Agree, Mildly Disagree, or Strongly Disagree. These answers are weighted as follows: Strongly Agree = 3. Mildly Agree = 2. Mildly Disagree = 1. Strongly Disagree = 0. Total the number of points and fill in the Burnout Thermometer up to that "temperature" for your susceptibility to burnout. Each of the five areas of human functioning are represented in this test. Thus, by examining the pattern of one's responses, it is possible to find if one or more areas are in special need of activities to remedy the existing state of burnout. For example, if the score in the physical area is relatively high, special attention might be paid to finding activities aimed at restoring physical well-being.

The Test

	Score
Physical	

1. I usually feel fatigued and worn-out. _____
2. I seldom get a full night's sleep. _____
3. If awakened, it's difficult to fall asleep again. _____
4. I exercise less than twice a week. _____
5. I ride elevators and escalators rather than climb stairs. _____
6. Most people would consider me a worrier. _____
7. I don't have a burnout prevention plan. _____
8. I seldom eat raw fruits or vegetables. _____
9. I often eat sugar and refined foods. _____
10. I am overweight. _____
11. I add salt to my food without tasting it. _____
12. I drink more than four cups of coffee or tea a day. _____
13. I drink more than four soft drinks a day. _____
14. I eat until I feel stuffed. _____
15. I smoke more than ten cigarettes a day. _____

Intellectual

16. I seldom introduce an innovation into my work. _____
17. I seldom read a journal or book in my profession. _____
18. I do not have a plan for intellectual relaxation. _____
19. I seldom read anything besides a newspaper. _____
20. I don't have a hobby. _____
21. I don't express my feelings in any medium—art, music, dance, writing, etc. _____
22. I don't enjoy solving complex problems. _____
23. I don't know who represents me in Congress. _____
24. I don't keep abreast of current events. _____
25. I seldom attend a workshop or professional meeting in my field. _____
26. Two opposite opinions cannot both be correct. _____
27. I don't know what parts of my job cause me stress. _____
28. I can only think of one or two ways to combat stress at work. _____
29. I think daydreaming is a waste of time. _____
30. Problems at work have only one "best" answer. _____

Emotional

31. I am uncertain of my beliefs. _____
32. I am unhappy much of the time. _____
33. I seldom compliment others. _____
34. I do not approve of anger. _____
35. I strike back if my feelings are hurt. _____
36. I don't see much that is funny. _____
37. I have sexual problems. _____
38. I seldom cry and do not believe it is proper. _____

(Continued)

The Test (Continued)

Emotional (cont.)

39. I am overworked because I can't say no. _____
40. I often find fault with myself. _____
41. I have no colleagues at work with whom I share important feelings. _____
42. I have no one to turn to if I have a personal problem. _____
43. I have few interests outside my job. _____
44. I am embarrassed by compliments. _____
45. I often find fault with others. _____

Social

46. I don't have any close friends. _____
47. I seldom meet anyone I would like to know better. _____
48. My relationships with family members are less than satisfactory. _____
49. It is better not to become involved if I see a crime being committed. _____
50. I am not liked by most people. _____
51. I seldom go out with my family. _____
52. I think drinking and driving is acceptable. _____
53. I don't know my neighbors and don't care to. _____
54. I make no efforts to conserve energy. _____
55. I seldom have social relations with my co-workers. _____
56. I seldom participate in community affairs. _____
57. There are no causes or concerns to which I would contribute money or time. _____
58. I think voting is a waste of time. _____
59. I am uncomfortable in most social interactions. _____
60. I am generally dissatisfied with my interactions with others. _____

Spiritual

61. The future does not look promising to me. _____
62. I don't think my work is important. _____
63. I dislike being alone. _____
64. I feel little obligation for the lives of others. _____
65. I doubt that I can be a success. _____
66. I often take sleeping pills or tranquilizers. _____
67. I have more than two alcoholic drinks a day. _____
68. I drink when I am depressed or nervous. _____
69. I drink at lunch. _____
70. I seldom like to do anything unless it is planned. _____
71. I don't see much that is positive about life. _____
72. I don't do my job especially well. _____
73. I refuse to waste my time helping others. _____
74. It is impossible to change the system. _____
75. I no longer enjoy my work. _____

Total _____

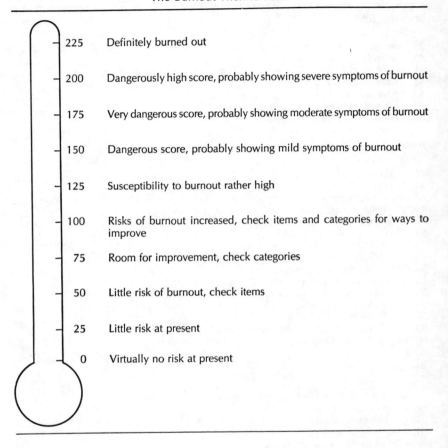

225	Definitely burned out
200	Dangerously high score, probably showing severe symptoms of burnout
175	Very dangerous score, probably showing moderate symptoms of burnout
150	Dangerous score, probably showing mild symptoms of burnout
125	Susceptibility to burnout rather high
100	Risks of burnout increased, check items and categories for ways to improve
75	Room for improvement, check categories
50	Little risk of burnout, check items
25	Little risk at present
0	Virtually no risk at present

BOARD FOR ORGANIZATION
OF THOUGHTS

This activity has been developed from ideas originally contributed by Abraham Maslow, one of the great psychologists of modern times. Maslow believed that for persons to achieve their full potential they first had to have certain needs met or overcome. These needs were arranged in a hierarchy. A diagram of Maslow's hierarchy of needs look like a pyramid with the basic needs at the bottom and the higher needs on top.

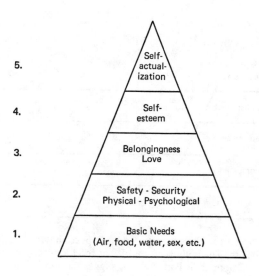

DIRECTION FOR USING THE BOOT

We have taken Maslow's list of needs and translated them into more specific daily activities. For Maslow's Basic Needs we have used Physical Health; for Security we have used Risk-competence; for Belongingness we have used Friendship-closeness; for Self-esteem we have used Accomplishment; and for Self-actualization we have used Creation-innovation. See the BOOT diagram for how they are arranged.

Each morning set aside five minutes to plan the day according to the BOOT principles. Plan some concrete activity which will meet each of the needs listed in the BOOT diagram. We will make some suggestions and encourage the development of others by you.

A variety of concrete suggestions would greatly enhance the actualiza tion process. Simply use the BOOT diagram to list the concrete activities which will be done to meet the need. Do this every morning. Every afternoon before you go home, check to see if the activities have been accomplished. If not, select some way to meet the unmet need after work.

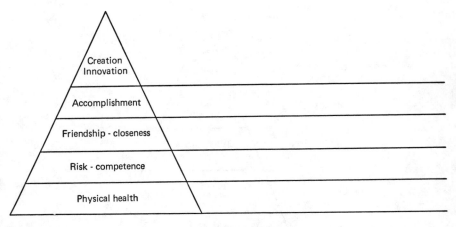

List the chosen activities next to the basic need they will satisfy.

1. Physical health. The body needs nutritious food, oxygen, water, rest, and relaxation. See Chapter 1 of Part Two for suggestions about meeting these needs.
2. Risk-competence. In order to feel safe and secure, a person may withdraw. However, this approach will develop a timid person who is only safe when avoiding new experiences. The only way to feel safe and secure is to develop competence, and this can be done only by taking risks. By risking and confronting new situations, a person can gain feelings of self-competence and feel safe and secure. So, take risks. Try to confront honestly persons at work with whom you don't agree. Don't be an automatic yes-sayer. Tell the boss or supervisor if you think an idea is a bad one. Do things you've never done before at home or in the community. Seek out novelty and avoid repetition and habit. Meet someone new or spend some time getting to know better someone you don't especially like.
3. Friendship-closeness. Identify people you like. (See the Stressful Habits Test in this chapter or the Relationship Squares in Chapter 4 of Part Two.) Plan to spend some time every day with a person you like at work, from the community, or in your family.
4. Accomplishment. This suggests we need to feel good about ourselves. One way to do this is to become more aware of our strengths and accomplishments. See the instructions for writing a journal in Chapter 5 of Part Two. List accomplishments and reread them at the end of each day. Plan some activity that will be completed in every working day.
5. Creation-innovation. This highest need can be met by refusing to allow the job to become routine and boring. Every day, list some creative or innovative activity that you will engage in. It may mean changing a form letter, rearranging the furniture in the office, exploring new markets, cutting costs, writing for publication, or inventing a workshop for people in your profession. Whatever it is, large or small, do not let a day go by on which something innovative or creative is not done.

STRESSFUL HABITS TEST

The lack of awareness of those attitudes, feelings, and behaviors which prove dysfunctional to a person is a crucial causal factor in burnout. There is a need for persons not only to monitor regularly these attitudes, feelings, and behaviors, but also to have some means whereby this might be done.

The Stressful Habits Test is designed to provide a means for enhancing one's awareness of the stressful habits which are contributors to burnout.

DIRECTIONS

To complete this test, find a quiet place. Think back on the last few days. Think back on what happened at work, at home, and in the community.

When did you feel under stress? _____
Where did it happen? _____
Who else was there? _____
What were the circumstances surrounding the event? _____
_____
_____
_____

In the exercise that follows, there are twelve squares in the identification sheet. If stress was experienced around a certain person at home, find the square in which the categories of people and home intersect (square 2). Place the person's name in square 2. If the stressful event happened in the living room, write living room in square 5. In this way, any stress experience can be analyzed with respect to the persons, places, and events surrounding the experience.

By reading down the columns, one can analyze stressful experiences at work, at home, and in the community. By reading across the rows one can analyze stressful events with respect to the people involved and look for trends in this area. Or, one can analyze stressful experiences according to places and look for trends in this area. One of the main goals of this exercise is to increase one's awareness of stress-inducing factors. Once this is accomplished, thought may be given to changing something which will lead to decreased stress.

Stressful Habits Test

	Work	Home	Community
People (family, friends, colleagues, boss, clients, etc.)	1.	2.	3.
Places (room, office, lounge, etc.)	4.	5.	6.
Events (more accidental: meetings, dinners, social events, awards, etc.)	7.	8.	9.
Tasks (more intentional: lawn, dishes, deadlines, fund raisers, political activities, etc.)	10.	11.	12.

THE CREATIVE WRITING WHEEL

This activity is designed to provide intellectual stimulation and relaxation at the same time. It is an activity that can be done alone or as a game with the entire family.

INSTRUCTIONS FOR MAKING THE WHEEL

Cut a 6″ diameter wheel from cardboard of the sort used in cereal boxes. Fill in the wheel with the categories below as shown in the sample wheel. If you like, cut out our example and glue it to the cardboard. All the elements for a creative story are now present. The categories and topics are:

Person	Place	Event	Feeling	Type	Gender
Client	Home	Sports	Anger	Children	Male
Colleague	Work	Meetings	Joy	Mystery	Female
Children	Community	Dinner in	Awe	Sci-Fi	
Spouse	School	Dinner out	Fear	Romance	
Friend	Theater	Games	Love	Comedy	
Supervisor	Restaurant	Birthday	Compassion	Tragedy	
Supervisee	House of Worship	Anniversary	Frustration	Horror	
Stranger	Outdoors	Wedding	Sadness	Western	

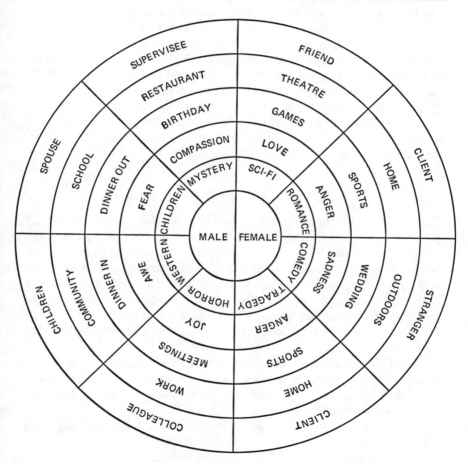

Cut a hole in the center of the cardboard wheel so that a pointer may be inserted that is long enough to reach from the center to the edge of the wheel. Make it so that it spins freely.

INSTRUCTIONS FOR WRITING

Spin the pointer six times. The first spin selects a person from the outer circle to be the major character in the story. Another spin will determine the setting for the story. The third spin will provide an event around which the story can be written. The fourth spin provides the major emotion of the story. The fifth spin tells you what type of story to write. And the last spin gives the gender of the major character. For example, the spins might provide the words Stranger, Theater, Sports, Anger, Mystery, and Male. Once these are revealed, write a story of at least 500 words (two pages, typed, double-spaced) using all six of these elements. The order of the elements does not matter; you can combine male and stranger, for example. Often the stories get wild since you'll come up with unique combinations of persons and events. Do remember that you don't have to show anyone your story if you're doing it alone—please yourself. In a group, let your imaginations run wild and have fun. You may be very surprised with what you come up with!

FANTASY

Find a comfortable spot and sit in a relaxed manner. Close your eyes and say your name to yourself three times. Think of one of your favorite places and imagine yourself there—alone. Then, in fantasy, start walking and as you look across the way you see an old man with white hair standing on top of an outcropping of rock. He has a calendar, a book, and a pen in his hands. You keep walking and as you approach the old man, he calls you by name and tells you that you may ask him three questions: One question may be about your job. One question may be about any significant relationship. One may be about yourself.

Ask the questions one at a time. Pause after each question long enough for the old man to answer. After he has answered the last question, turn slowly and walk away. Return to your original comfortable spot, and when you are ready, open your eyes.

Take a pad and pencil and record the questions and answers. Take about fifteen minutes to think about where you went in the fantasy, how the old man looked, what you asked, and what his answers were.

ANALOGIES
Avoiding Stereotyped Thinking

This is a Jungian technique to help persons break out of and avoid stereotypical thinking and simultaneously develop creative power. Follow the steps below for any problem or concept you want to develop. You will be amazed at the number of different ideas that are generated and the new insights gained by using this simple technique.

This technique is especially good for helping to find relationships between things that may have been unknown. Try to use this approach at least once a week to keep intellectual and creative powers sharply honed. It isn't necessary to use this technique only on work-related problems. For fun, take any concept and explore it. This is a fun activity to do with the family in a collaborative manner. Joint poems, songs, or drawings can do much to draw family members closer together.

1. Choose a concept or an idea or an object. For example, " a rock." You may also choose a problem which exists at work, such as "no one seems to care about the customers."
2. Construct or generate *as many analogies as possible*. An analogy is formed by comparing any one thing, idea, feeling, place, event, and so forth with something else. It is easiest when using a sentence with the word "like" for comparison. For example:

A rock is like . . .

    1. cement
    2. cheese
    3. a ball
    4. a planet
      .
      .
      .
   30. . . . .

The same techniques may be used with a problem at work. For example,

No one caring for clients is like

    1. . . . .
    2. . . . .
    3. . . . .
    4. . . . .
      .
      .
   30. . . . .

3. Next, go back over each analogy and think of as many reasons as possible why the analogy seems to be appropriate. For example:

A rock is like ...

1. Cement because it is hard and sometimes smooth ... (think of more)
2. Cheese because it has holes, is hard like stale cheese, can get soft when heated ... (think of more)
3. A ball because it can fit in one's hand, it can be thrown or hit ... (think of more).

4. At this point, it is often beneficial to find some medium to combine, refine, and express the ideas generated above. Possible media are:

poetry
song
dance or movement
prose (an article or story)
drama
drawing
(think of others)

5. Now construct analogies which follow this format:

If I were a rock, it would be like ...
If I were cheese, it would be like ...
If I were cement, it would be like ...
If I were a ball, it would be like ...
If I were a planet, it would be like ...

Again, use any of the media generated to express these ideas.

6. Finally, try and think of concepts, ideas, or objects or people that are unlike or opposite to the one under consideration. For example: A rock is like *cement* but not like *marshmallows*. List the reasons for the dissimilarity.
7. At this point, consider the many ideas generated to determine if any of them provide novel solutions, insights, product ideas, techniques, or strategies which have been overlooked in the past.

THE DECISION SCALE

Decisions are often complicated by the fact that we don't keep records of the positive and negative aspects of the decision. This exercise provides a strategy to keep track of the positives and negatives and suggests that a simple frequency count would aid in the decision. It is important to count the positive gains to self and others as well as the approval and disapproval of self and others in making any decision. The Decision Scale provides for four parameters to be used in helping to make a decision: gains to the self, gains to others, and approval of others.

These scales should be completed for each possibility for any decision that has to be made. Here is a sample.

My Transportation Problem

Possibility 1: Buying a new car. (Other possibilities might be: buying a used car, having the old car repaired, not having a car.)

SELF	
Gains	*Losses*
Positive expectations	*Negative expectations*
1. Better-looking	1. Money
2. Less problems	2. Anxiety of driving
3. Gas mileage	3. Might get a lemon
4. More comfort	
+4	−3

OTHER	
Gains	*Losses*
1. Friends can borrow a better car	
2. More comfort	
+2	−0

SELF	
Approval	*Disapproval*
1. Smaller car is better ecologically	1. Too materialistic
	2. Manipulated by ads
	3. Anxiety due to payments
+1	−3

(Continued)

My Transportation Problem (*Continued*)

OTHERS

Approval	Disapproval
1. More affluent	1. Jealous
2. Work hard	2. Spendthrift
3. Conscientious	3. Show off
+3	−3
+10 Total in favor	−9 Total against

According to this example, buying a new car has about the same number of positive and negative attributes to it. This might suggest that another possibility be explored. For each possibility, all four scales would be completed and a total rating determined. Then, to make the best decision, the scores of all possibilities would be compared.

SURVEY OF FLEXIBLE THINKING

Most of us who live in the Western world have been educated to think primarily in an *either/or* fashion rather than a *both/and* fashion. Many aspects of reality can best be grasped by looking at a word or statement which refers to an idea, concept, event, or person in both positive and negative ways. Often we view ideas, concepts, etc., in one way or the other without taking the time and effort to view opposing points of view. If we examine both the positive and negative aspects of words and statements, we are in a better position to make a judgment about them. Even better is to look to see if the concepts, positions, or what have you are actually different. This exercise asks you to stretch the words and idea with which you are familiar.

There are two columns of words following that represent opposites. Use these instructions for this activity.

1. List three positive aspects for each word in column 1.
2. List three positive aspects for the opposite word in column 2.
3. In a sentence, indicate the difference between the two words.
4. In a sentence, indicate how there is *no difference* between the two words!

Column 1	Column 2
1. Religion	1. Secularism
2. Physican	2. Witch doctors
3. Death penalty	3. Minimum sentence
4. Peace	4. War
5. Capitalism	5. Communism
6. Teacher	6. Propagandist
7. Abortion	7. Right to life
8. Homosexuals	8. Heterosexuals
9. Police	9. Criminals
10. Counselors	10. Manipulators
11. Politics	11. Anarchy
12. ERA	12. Woman's place in the home
13. SALT	13. Nuclear superiority
14. God	14. Satan
15. Premarital sex	16. Chastity

LOGICAL REASONING

Logical reasoning is a prerequisite for coping with the problems of burnout. In order to understand the many variables contributing to burnout, a person must have the ability to think in logical ways. The problem with many aspects of burnout is that their sources are not concrete. They are often not single-cause phenomena at all, but combinations of causes and interrelationships that require combinative logic and propositional thinking in order to understand them. This test is specifically designed to identify the sort of thinking needed to diagnose and understand such multicausal problems. Write out your answers on a separate piece of paper and then check them against the answer sheet on pages 295–96.

One way to improve one's score is to look over the questions missed on this test and figure out why they were answered in a way other than the keyed response. Another is to complete the activities in this section, espeically those that call for analogies, decision making, and flexible thinking.

LOGICAL REASONING TEST*

INSTRUCTIONS

1. For most of the questions on this test you will need only to place a cross in the space on the answer sheet like this (X). For a few of the questions, you will be asked to give two or three answers. Instructions for answering these questions will be given when they appear in the test.
2. Several questions refer to diagrams and you should examine these diagrams closely before answering these questions.
3. If you have to change an answer, erase it completely and mark the new choice.
4. Try to answer all questions; if you are not sure of an answer, then choose the one that you think is most apt to be right.
5. Think carefully before you answer each question.

*   *   *

1. In the diagram below, the line XYZ represents a wall, and a tennis ball is hit onto the wall so that it always hits at Y. Angle 1 equals angle 6, angle 2 equals angle 5, and angle 3 equals angle 4. If a ball bounces from Y to B it must have been hit from: (a) A (b) B (c) C (d) D (e) E

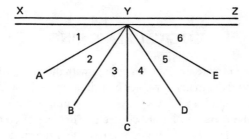

Here is a new diagram similar to the first one. Study it carefully and *use it to answer questions 2 and 3.*

*From Gilbert M. Burney, "The Construction and Validation of an Objective Formal Reasoning Instrument," D.Ed. dissertation, University of Northern Colorado, 1974.

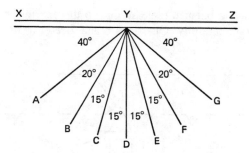

2. If a ball is hit accurately from B to Y on the wall, it will bounce to: (a) A (b) E (c) C (d) F (e) G

3. If a ball bounces from Y to A it must have been hit from: (a) A (b) E (c) C (d) F (e) G

4. In the diagram below, a ball is hit from A to a point Y on the wall. The angle the new path of the ball makes with CY is: (a) 50° (b) 75° (c) 65° (d) 40° (e) 25°

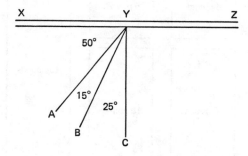

5. A tennis ball is hit from somewhere in the section marked "Right-Hand Side" in the diagram below. The ball hits the wall at Y and bounces to C. The size of the angle, from XZ, at which the ball must be hit is: (a) 25° (b) 40° (c) 65° (d) 60° (e) 25°

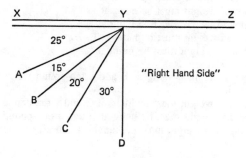

Suppose you have a balance scale similar to the one in the diagram below. Study the diagram carefully. Questions 6 and 7 refer to it.

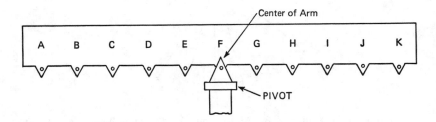

Weights which can be used:

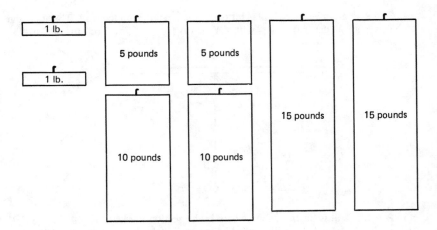

6. A five-pound weight is hung at D. To balance the arm again:
   (a) a one-pound weight must be hung at A.
   (b) a ten-pound weight must be hung at J.
   (c) a five-pound weight must be hung at H.
   (d) a ten-pound weight must be hung at E.
   (e) a five-pound weight must be hung at K.
   (f) is impossible.
7. A five-pound weight is hung at E and a ten-pound weight at C. To balance the arm again:
   (a) a five-pound weight must be hung at G and a ten-pound weight at J.
   (b) a ten-pound weight must be hung at H and a one-pound weight at K.
   (c) a fifteen-pound weight must be hung at I and a one-pound weight at H.

(d) a ten-pound weight must be hung at I and a five-pound weight at G.
(e) is impossible.
(f) a five-pound weight must be hung at I and a five-pound weight at G.

Questions 8 to 10 are called syllogisms. Each syllogism consists of two premises and a conclusion. You are to determine whether each argument is valid or not. Example:

> P_1: No one-year-old babies can walk.
> P_2: Paul is a one-year-old baby.
>   _____ C: Therefore, Paul cannot walk.

This is a valid argument.

8. P_1: Not all Rs are Ts.
     P_2: All Ts are Ms.
     _____ C: Therefore, Some Rs may not be Ms.
     (a) Valid (b) Invalid
9. P_1: All coal is white.
     P_2: All white coal produces red smoke when burning.
     _____ C: Therefore when coal burns, the smoke is gray.
     (a) Valid (b) Invalid
10. P_1: When John gets angry at [Bill], he [yells].
     P_2: John is not angry at [Bill].
     _____ C: Therefore John will not [yell].
     (a) Valid (b) Invalid

The diagram below represents two open-top containers with water in them. There is a length of hose connecting them that will allow water to pass from one container to the other. Container B has a larger diameter than container A. Use the diagram to answer questions 11 and 12.

11. Container A and container B are moved down the same distance. The water levels in the containers will:
     (a) stay at the original height above the table.
     (b) change so that the level in A is above the original height above the table and the level in B is below.
     (c) change so that the level in B is above the original height above the table and the level in A is below.
     (d) change so that the levels in A and B are the same distance above the original height above the table.
     (e) change so that the levels in A and B are the same distance below the original height above the table.

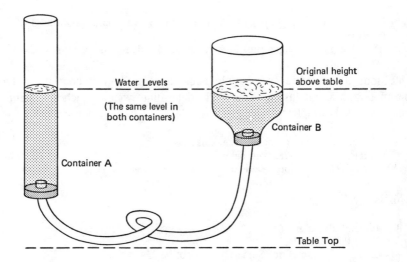

Water Levels

(The same level in
both containers)

Original height
above table

Container B

Container A

Table Top

12. Container A and container B are moved up the same distance. The water levels in the containers will:
   (a) stay at the original height above the table.
   (b) change so that the levels in A and B are the same distance below the original height above the table.
   (c) change so that the level in A is above the original height above the table and the level in B is below.
   (d) change so that the levels in A and B are the same distance above the original height above the table.
   (e) change so that the level in B is above the original height above the table and the level in A is below.

The apparatus pictured below can be used to throw shadows onto a screen. The rings pictured can be placed at points D, E, or F or anywhere along a line through D, E, and F between the light and the screen. The shadows that are referred to in the questions are the circular shadows of the rings only, not the ring stands. The distances of D, E, and F from the screen are indicated at the left and the distances of D, E, and F from the light are indicated in the center of the apparatus. Study the diagram carefully and use it to answer questions 13 and 14.

292

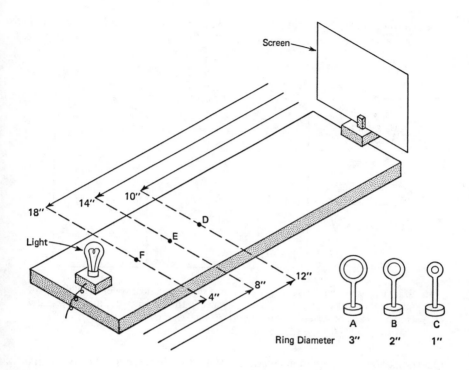

13. Ring A is placed at D and its shadow allowed to fall onto the screen and the size of the shadow is measured. Ring A is removed and ring B is placed at D and the size of its shadow on the screen is measured. The two shadows formed:
    (a) will be of equal size.
    (b) will be of unequal size, the shadow of A being larger than the shadow of B.
    (c) will be of unequal size, the shadow of B being larger than the shadow of A.
    (d) will be of unequal size, the shadow of A being smaller than the shadow of B.

14. Ring B is placed at D and its shadow allowed to fall onto the screen and the size of the shadow is measured. Ring B is removed and ring C is placed at D and the size of its shadow on the screen is measured. The two shadows formed:
    (a) will be of equal size.
    (b) will be of unequal size, the shadow of B being larger than the shadow of C.
    (c) will be of unequal size, the shadow of C being larger than the shadow of B.
    (d) will be of unequal size, the shadow of B being smaller than the shadow of C.

The diagram below represents two glasses, a small one and a large one, and two jars, a small one and a large one. Use this diagram for problem 15.

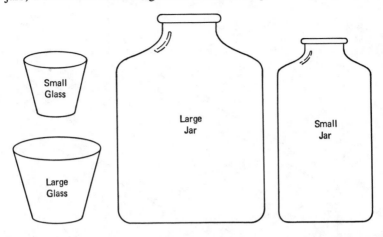

15. If it takes six large glasses of water or nine small glasses of water to fill the small jar, and it takes eight large glasses of water to fill the large jar, then how many small glasses of water does it take to fill the large jar?
    (a) 10 (b) 15 (c) 11 (d) 16 (e) 12

Questions 16 to 21 are verbal analogies. Verbal analogies consist of two pairs of words with each pair having the same relationship. "*In* is to *out* as *up* is to *down*" is an example of an analogy. The common relationship between *in* and *out* and *up* and *down* is that they are opposites. Order of the pair of words is also important. "*Peel* is to *banana* as *paint* is to *house*" is correct, while "*peel* is to *banana* as *house* is to *paint*" is incorrect. In the following questions you are to choose two or three words that will best complete each analogy.

Example:

(a) tire		(e) anchor	
(b) motor	*is to* car *as*	(f) deck	*is to* ship
(c) highway		(g) captain	
(d) map		(h) ocean	

In this example, the best choices to complete the analogy are *highway* and *ocean,* resulting in the analogy "*Highway* is to *car* as *ocean* is to *ship.*" In this case "operates on" is the common relationship: a car operates on a highway and a ship operates on the ocean. On the answer sheet, the above question would be answered as shown.

Example, c,h

Be careful to mark all required answers for each question on your answer sheet. Some questions require two answers and some require three.

16.
task *is to*
(a) attempt
(b) completion
(c) work
(d) question
as
(e) problem
(f) chemical
(g) man
(h) answer
is to
solution

17.
light bulb *is to*
(a) switch
(b) wire
(c) socket
(d) electricity
as
(e) engine
(f) canoe
(g) motor
(h) steam
is to
(i) boat
(j) engine
(k) tractor
(l) paddle

18.
(a) walk
(b) toe
(c) knee
(d) foot
is to body
as
wheel
is to
(e) roll
(f) machine
(g) bicycle
(h) spokes

19.
(a) cow
(b) horse
(c) sheep
(d) foot
is to flock
as
(e) soldier
(f) swarm
(g) pack
(h) litter
is to
(i) bee
(j) pig
(k) regiment
(l) wolf

20.
(a) brain
(b) eye
(c) hat
(d) ear
is to head
as
(e) spring
(f) blanket
(g) caster
(h) pillow
is to
(i) bedpost
(j) ticking
(k) bed
(l) summer

21.
(a) music
(b) house
(c) bench
(d) tuner
is to piano
as
(e) chair
(f) leg
(g) eat
(h) furniture
is to table

LOGICAL REASONING TEST
ANSWER SHEET

1. d
2. d
3. e

4. d
5. d
6. c
7. d
8. a
9. b
10. b
11. e
12. d
13. b
14. b
15. e
16. b, e
17. d, f, l
18. d, g
19. c, e, k
20. c, f, k
21. c, e

In order to be counted as correct, questions 16 to 21 must be answered exactly as they are listed in the answer sheet.

Rating.   Formal 15–21. Able to solve complex problems. Transitional 10–14 With practice, able to solve complex problems. Concrete or below 0–9 Not likely to be able to solve complex problems.

CREATIVITY

A common symptom of burnout is the loss of sharpness of intellectual functioning. This is reflected in diminished use of the intellectual skills involved in creativity. When burnout deepens, stereotyped, habitual modes of thinking predominate, and the chances of finding novel solutions to problems is decreased. This activity is designed to test one's ability to think flexibly and creatively. Take the test and follow the instructions for scoring and interpretation at the end of the test.

If your level of creativity is lower than you like, try the analogies, brainstorming, creative writing, and fantasy activities contained elsewhere in Part Two of this book. There are many books available which offer problems to test and develop creative thinking. Here are a couple we think are especially good.

1. Eugene Raudsepp, *Creative Growth Games,* Jove Publications, 1977.
2. James F. Fixx, *Games for the Super-intelligent,* Popular Library, 1972.

CREATIVITY TEST[2]

Most people speak of creativity without knowing quite what it means. Is it just the capacity to paint an original picture or write a poem? Far from it. Creativity is a basic characteristic built into all human beings and almost completely absent in animals. It involves seeing novel relationships between things, and as such it is closely related to intelligence. It involves converting the random, the mediocre, or the dull into something with form, style, and originality. It is relatively easy to measure, and psychologists have recently devised tests to do this.

Interest in measuring creativity in an objective way only started in earnest after launch of the first Sputnik. Staggered by the apparent lead which the USSR had gained in space technology, the US began to realize the great need for selecting the most creative scientists and technologists. The focus of interest shifted from what had once been considered to be the essence of creativity—artistic appreciation, skill, and endeavor—towards the problem-solving nature of the creative process. Special psychological tests of great sophistication are now employed to study this, and the following questionnaire should be taken as establishing a guideline only. Nevertheless, if you tackle it carefully, thoughtfully and honestly, it could help you to an appreciation of your own creative potential. The first section deals with creative thinking itself.

SECTION 1: CREATIVITY TESTS

The first section is divided into eight "do-it-yourself" tests. You should allow yourself two minutes, and two minutes only, for each test, so have a watch with a second hand at your side. Do each test independently, and do *not* refer to the scoring code and analysis until you have completed all eight tests. Give yourself a break between the tests—the break can be as long as you like, but a quarter of an hour is perhaps the ideal. This means that to do this test properly

[2]Christopher Evans, *Understanding Yourself,* A & W Visual Library, New York, 1977, pp. 65–67.

you will have to set a few hours aside without interruption. You could, of course, spread it over a few evenings, but remember *do not refer* to the analysis and *do not start* the second section until you have completed all eight tests.

Mark your answers on a separate sheet.

It is important that you keep strictly to the time limit of *two minutes* for each question.

Test 1. Start off with any word, idea or image then write down the next thing that comes to mind, then the next associated with the second, and so on. Let your mind roam freely: it does not matter about making sense.

Test 2. How many things could this picture represent?

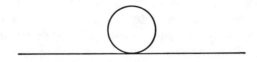

Test 3. Write down as many names of trees as you can.

Test 4. Look at the diagram steadily. How many times does your perspective change in the two minutes?

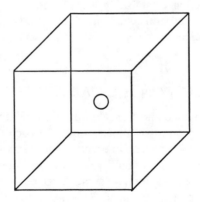

Test 5. Name as many objects as you can that are white, soft and edible.

Test 6. How many uses can you think of for a piece of brown paper?

Test 7. Write down as many words as you can beginning with the letter I.

Test 8. Take away two matches from the pattern and leave two complete squares and no spare matches.

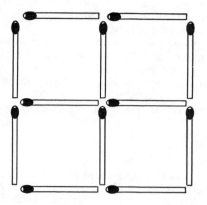

SECTION 2: MULTIPLE CHOICES

This is a more straightforward multiple choice questionnaire, and it simply deals with creativity in everyday life. Complete the questionnaire and then refer to the end for the analysis of sections 1 and 2.

1. If you get the chance to do something you have never done before, do you
   a. Turn it down?
   b. Hesitate between interest and apprehension?
   c. Take it eagerly?
2. You visit a friend's house and notice that the furniture is not arranged conveniently or comfortably. Would you
   a. Say nothing?
   b. Figure out roughly how you might change it?
   c. Make suggestions and draw up a plan?
3. Do you find you question things that most people seem to take for granted?
   a. Rarely
   b. Often
   c. Sometimes
4. When you see a competition for dreaming up slogans, do you
   a. Turn the page quickly?
   b. Consider it idly for a couple of minutes?
   c. Really try to work something out, and perhaps send it in?
5. When you read something interesting, do you
   a. File it in your mind for future use?
   b. Forget it soon afterwards?
   c. Follow it up by trying to find out more about the topic?

6. You have to look after a child for an afternoon and he complains of being bored. Would you
    a. Think of some activities that you know will keep him happy and busy?
    b. Tell him to stop bothering you and to play by himself?
    c. Make suggestions for activities to him?
7. When you go in for "do-it-yourself" or when you cook, do you
    a. Improvise rather than follow the instructions or recipe exactly?
    b. Always stick to the instructions?
    c. Only try variations after you have followed the recipe or instructions a couple of times?
8. Do you have ideas about how improvements could be made at work?
    a. Often
    b. Occasionally
    c. Not really
9. If you answered *a* or *b* to question 8, do you
    a. Not bother to tell anyone else your ideas?
    b. Tell them to someone else, but not work out the details?
    c. Draw up a plan, get your facts and figures right, then present it to your boss?
10. How do you feel if you see a movie with a strange ending, leaving you uncertain about what actually happened?
    a. Uneasy, wanting it to be clear.
    b. Intrigued, and interested in thinking it out for yourself.
    c. Puzzled, but not worried.
11. When friends come to you with problems, do you
    a. Listen sympathetically?
    b. Think of what you would do in their situation, but say little?
    c. Make constructive suggestions?
12. Which is true for you?
    a. I like a peaceful life with a dependable routine.
    b. I like lots of change and excitement in my life.
    c. I like a certain amount of excitement in my life, but not too much.
13. When a change takes place in your life, like leaving home, taking a new job, getting married, or getting divorced, do you
    a. Feel frightened about the unknown future?
    b. See the positive possibilities in the new situation?
    c. Alternate between fear and excitement?
14. If you inherited your parents' home, would you
    a. Keep it as they did, because it would feel somehow wrong to change it?
    b. Change it to suit your own personality and day-to-day convenience?
    c. Make some changes, but keep some things to remind you of them?
15. Do you find that unconventional sexual experimenting between two people who care for each other is
    a. Disgusting?
    b. Pleasureable?
    c. Possibly fun?

16. How would you choose to spend a birthday or special anniversary?
    a. Going out to a favorite restaurant.
    b. Quietly at home.
    c. Going somewhere new.
17. You get stuck on some practical task (making a dress or building a patio, for example) and nothing seems to be going right. Would you be more likely to
    a. Give up in disgust?
    b. Keep doggedly on the same lines as before?
    c. Think of a new way around the problems?
18. When you read about the problems of world poverty, do you
    a. Feel that nothing can be done and that human beings have to put up with harsh conditions?
    b. Get angry and upset, but feel helpless?
    c. Make some effort, even if it is only sending a little money to a charity?
19. You are on the brink of a love affair that would bring you the disapproval of your friends and associates. Would you
    a. Go ahead joyfully?
    b. Go ahead, but take care to conceal your activities?
    c. Regretfully back out?
20. Which are you more afraid of?
    a. Boredom
    b. Loneliness
    c. Uncertainty

SCORES

Total your scores to find your analysis below. The scores here refer to section 2 of the questionnaire only. For a discussion of your results on the tests in section 1, refer to the analysis which follows.

1. a. 0 b. 1 c. 2	11. a. 0 b. 1 c. 2
2. a. 0 b. 1 c. 2	12. a. 0 b. 2 c. 1
3. a. 0 b. 2 c. 1	13. a. 0 b. 2 c. 1
4. a. 0 b. 1 c. 2	14. a. 0 b. 2 c. 1
5. a. 1 b. 0 c. 2	15. a. 0 b. 2 c. 1
6. a. 2 b. 0 c. 1	16. a. 1 b. 0 c. 2
7. a. 2 b. 0 c. 1	17. a. 0 b. 1 c. 2
8. a. 2 b. 1 c. 0	18. a. 0 b. 1 c. 2
9. a. 0 b. 1 c. 2	19. a. 2 b. 1 c. 0
10. a. 0 b. 2 c. 1	20. a. 2 b. 1 c. 0

ANALYSIS

SECTION 1: CREATIVITY TESTS

The essence of creativity is, of course, originality, and trying to find ways of scoring such an elusive concept has been a major problem confronting psychologists working in this area. After research, it was found that when people are faced with a problem situation, whether simple or complex, the number of possible responses or solutions to the problem they were able to come up with was a good indication of their creativity. In other words, the more ideas people produce relevant to a particular situation, the more original they tend to be

Test 1. Score one point for every association you were able to come up with in the two minutes. A score of 10 or less indicates generally low creativity; 11–20, average creativity; over 20, high creativity.

Test 2. Count one for each answer you were able to come up with. 0–5 indicates low creativity; 6–10, average; over 10, high creativity.

Test 3. Count one for each answer you were able to come up with. 0–7 indicates low creativity; 8–15, average; above 15, high.

Test 4. On the whole, the more this Necker cube fluctuates, the more flexible your perception. If it changed one, two, or three times, this indicates low flexibility, hence low creativity; four or five times, average; more than five times, high flexibility.

Test 5. Count one for each answer. 0–5 indicates low creativity: 6–10, average; above 10, high.

Test 6. Count one for each answer. In this case you should try to assess the originality of your answers by working out how many types of response you gave. Wrapping would be one type of response; if you suggested wrapping several kinds of objects, that is less original than suggesting one thing to be wrapped and then going on to other uses, such as making it into a blind, for example. Take two bonus points for each truly different use. 0–5 indicates low creativity; 6–10, average; over 10, high.

Test 7. Count one for each answer. 0–5 indicates low creativity; 6–10, average; above 10, high.

Test 8. The instructions did not say that the two squares had to be the same size! Did you get stuck on this one, or were you able to switch to a new way of seeing the problem? If you got it right, you score in the high-creativity group.

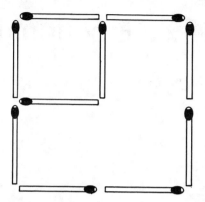

If you picked up between 2 and 4 high creativity scores in the eight tests, this is a good average score, 4 to 6 indicates a high level of creativity, and 7 or 8 an especially high level.

SECTION 2

Here we are concerned with your potential for creativity in everyday life. The factors contributing to a high score can be summed up in the following seven questions:

1. How open are you to new experiences?
2. What kind of need do you feel for stimulation from the environment?
3. How much are you prepared to tolerate uncertainty or ambiguity?
4. How adventurous are you?
5. How quick are you at perceiving the nature of problems?
6. How flexible are you in your thought processes?
7. How free are you from fear of authority?

You will have ended up with a score between 0 and 40. A score under 10 indicates a low level of creativity; from 11 to 20, an average level; 21 to 30, a generally high level; and 31 to 40, an exceedingly high level of creativity.

17. Emotional

SUGGESTED TIMEOUT PROCEDURES

Persons in the process of burnout often report a sense of being overwhelmed with requests, problems, and the concerns of others. Their sense of time is that they have no time for themselves. Periodic, built-in blocks of time for the individual may contribute to the prevention of the minimization of burnout. Timeouts (about fifteen minutes) are suggested as regular parts of one's daily schedule.

SOME WAYS TO PLAN TIMEOUTS

1. Study your daily schedule and identify the times when a fifteen-minute break would be most helpful to you.
2. Develop a plan for one or two timeouts per day and discuss the plan with your supervisor, spouse, colleagues, or appropriate friends. Explain the rationale to them.
3. Carefully monitor the timeouts to determine their effectiveness. Make changes accordingly, using steps 1 and 2 above.

4. Once the timeouts have been scheduled, try to determine the place where you can be alone to meditate, relax, think, or "just be alone" best.
5. Some considerations which may help in the dtermination of the effectiveness of the timeouts are:
   a. What place is best for my being alone?
   b. What do I do, think, or feel during a timeout?
   c. What seems to contribute to my effective functioning?
   d. Are the timeouts scheduled well?
   e. Do I need a timeout when I come home?
   f. How do I function after timeouts?
   g. How does my boss, spouse, colleague, or friend feel about my timeout?

SELECT A FUN EXPERIENCE

One of the recent findings in clinical psychology is that persons who become depressed tend not to engage in activities that may simply be called fun. They tend not to do as many fun things as nondepressed persons. Depression is even treated by having persons make an effort to engage in activities they consider fun. This often results in lessening the severity of depression. Our thoughts suggest taking these findings a step further. By engaging in fun activities, the depression which accompanies burnout may be avoided. Certainly, much of the spiritual burnout, centering around a lack of meaning in life, can be avoided.

To use SAFE, simply read down the list of activities and decide how much fun each is.

0 = No fun
1 = Some fun
2 = Lots of fun

Once all items are rated, select some of the 1- or 2-rated ones to engage in. Try to do at least one each day. If possible, do more than one. Once a week, sit down and plan which events you will do on which days of the week. Remember, do at least one a day.

We have selected ten categories of activities and placed ten activities in each category. This by no means exhausts all possible activities. Feel free to add activities to each category. Feel free to add categories we didn't list. Write them in, rate them, and do them!

SAFE (Selecting a Fun Experience)

Nature

_____ Backpacking
_____ Walking outdoors
_____ Going to the ocean
_____ Mountain climbing
_____ Camping
_____ Studying animals in their natural habitat
_____ Observing natural beauty
_____ Taking a nature walk, observing flowers, plants, and animals
_____ Going on a picnic
_____ Canoeing/rafting

Money

_____ Eating in an expensive restaurant
_____ Dressing up
_____ Buying something expensive especially for yourself
_____ Contributing money to a favorite cause or charity
_____ Betting money on games of chance
_____ Buying something special for someone else
_____ Having your hair styled or a manicure
_____ Attending sales, auctions, flea markets, garage sales
_____ Buying something special for your home or car
_____ Buying a sculpture or painting

Sports

_____ Discussing sports with a friend
_____ Lifting weights
_____ Going on a fishing trip
_____ Going on a hunting trip (with a camera!)
_____ Going to a shooting range
_____ Playing a team sport
_____ Taking a bicycle ride or trip
_____ Going horseback riding
_____ Walking or jogging for exercise
_____ Playing your favorite individual sport

Recreation

_____ Fishing
_____ Hunting

_____ Going to a sporting event
_____ Going on a vacation
_____ Going out to drink with friends
_____ Going to a party
_____ Throwing a party
_____ Playing table games
_____ Riding recreational vehicles
_____ Fixing something mechanical

Community involvement

_____ Being active in church affairs
_____ Reading your local newspaper
_____ Writing a letter to the editor of the local newspaper
_____ Being politically active (working in a campaign, attending city council meetings)
_____ Coaching a youth sports team
_____ Recycling paper and metal products
_____ Visiting sick and infirm people, being a hospital volunteer
_____ Engaging in activities with a service club (Lions, Rotary, etc.)
_____ Volunteering your services to community agencies (Boys Club, tutoring)
_____ Working in a women's shelter

Intellectual

_____ Reading
_____ Writing
_____ Attending speeches, lectures, workshops, classes, conferences
_____ Performing or practicing music
_____ Writing music
_____ Working on riddles, puzzles, problems
_____ Meditating
_____ Discussing religion, philosophy, politics, etc., with others
_____ Keeping a journal
_____ Visiting the local library

Cultural

_____ Attending a live musical event
_____ Attending a play
_____ Listening to recorded music
_____ Visiting a museum
_____ Attending a dance
_____ Attending a discussion or lecture about the arts

_____ Reading about famous artists, musicians, etc.
_____ Making a presentation to others about a famous person in the arts
_____ Writing poetry
_____ Painting, sculpting, or drawing

Hobbies

_____ Building models
_____ Working with wood
_____ Working with antiques
_____ Gardening
_____ Singing in a group
_____ Taking photographs
_____ Cooking
_____ Making wine or beer
_____ Remodeling an old car
_____ Working on a collection

Relaxation

_____ Taking a hot bath or shower
_____ Doing biofeedback
_____ Going barefoot
_____ Taking a sun bath
_____ Taking a nap
_____ Daydreaming, creating a fantasy
_____ Sleeping late in the morning
_____ Making love
_____ Having a bull session
_____ Spending some time alone

Growth

_____ Meeting new people
_____ Giving and receiving massages and back rubs
_____ Participating in an encounter group
_____ Reading a self-help book
_____ Practicing yoga, meditation, relaxation
_____ Taking a risk, doing something you have never done before
_____ Doing something you did as a child
_____ Meeting someone from another culture
_____ Going to a foreign film
_____ Doing something you disliked as a child

A DREAM JOURNAL

Dreams provide a way to examine emotions that many in our culture do not use. However, keeping a dream journal is not too difficult, and analyzing one's dreams does not require special skills for the purposes included here.

HOW TO KEEP A DREAM JOURNAL

1. Keep a pad and a pencil beside the bed. (Or a tape recorder.)
2. If you have trouble remembering dreams, do any (or all) of the following:
   a. Before you go to sleep, say out loud to yourself, "I will remember my dreams in the morning."
   b. Before you go to sleep, decide on specific things to dream about. Or make up a dream before going to sleep.
   c. Set the alarm for an arbitrary time to "catch" yourself dreaming.
   d. Wake up gradually to allow images to emerge just before you are fully awake.
3. Record your dreams immediately. If you wake up from a dream, don't wait until morning to write it down. First thing in the morning, before you get out of bed, write down any dreams you remember.
4. Record even parts of dreams. Don't leave them out just because you don't remember the entire dream or don't remember the ending.

WHAT TO DO WITH THE DREAM JOURNAL

1. Do not concern yourself with hidden meanings or the "real" meaning of the dream.
2. Ask yourself, "What does this dream mean to me?" Accept that it may not mean anything.
3. Ask yourself, "Is there any event in my life right now that this dream may be about?"
4. Can you use the dream as a basis for some creative writing and thus explore emotions further?

THE ASSERTIVENESS SCHEDULE[1]

How assertive are you? Do you bow to social pressures and constantly do the bidding of others? Do you speak your mind and stick up for your rights? Or are you somewhere in between?

[1]Spencer A. Rathus, "A 30 - item schedule for assessing assertive Behavior" *Behavior Therapy*, 1973, 398–406.

Find out how assertive you are by taking the following self-report test of assertive behavior. Then turn to the end of this chapter to find out how to determine your score and to compare your results with the scores of 1,400 students from thirty-five college and university campuses across the United States.

Directions. Indicate how descriptive each item is of you by using this code:

> 3 = *very much like me*
> 2 = *rather like me*
> 1 = *slightly like me*
> −1 = *slightly unlike me*
> −2 = *rather unlike me*
> −3 = *very unlike me*

_____1. Most people seem to be more aggressive and assertive than I am.*

_____2. I have hesitated to make or accept dates because of "shyness."*

_____3. When the food served at a restaurant is not done to my satisfaction, I complain about it to the waiter or waitress.

_____4. I am careful to avoid hurting other people's feelings, even when I feel that I have been injured.*

_____5. If a salesman has gone to considerable trouble to show me merchandise that is not quite suitable, I have a difficult time saying "No."*

_____6. When I am asked to do something, I insist upon knowing why.

_____7. There are times when I look for a good, vigorous argument.

_____8. I strive to get ahead as well as most people in my position.

_____9. To be honest, people often take advantage of me.*

_____10. I enjoy starting conversations with new acquaintances and strangers.

_____11. I often don't know what to say to attractive persons of the opposite sex.*

_____12. I will hesitate to make phone calls to business establishments and institutions.*

_____13. I would rather apply for a job or for admission to college by writing letters than by going through with personal interviews.*

_____14. I find it embarrassing to return merchandise.*

_____15. If a close and respected relative were annoying me, I would smother my feelings rather than express my annoyance.*

_____16. I have avoided asking questions for fear of sounding stupid.*

_____17. During an argument I am sometimes afraid that I will get so upset that I will shake all over.*

_____18. If a famed and respected lecturer makes a comment that I think is incorrect, I will have the audience hear my point of view as well.

_____19. I avoid arguing over prices with clerks and salesmen.*

_____20. When I have done something important or worthwhile, I manage to let others know about it.

_____21. I am open and frank about my feelings.

_____22. If someone has been spreading false and bad stories about me, I see him (her) as soon as possible and "have a talk" about it.

_____23. I often have a hard time saying "No."*

_____24. I tend to bottle up my emotions rather than make a scene.*

_____25. I complain about poor service in a restaurant and elsewhere.

_____26. When I am given a compliment, I sometimes just don't know what to say.*

_____27. If a couple near me in a theater or at a lecture were conversing rather loudly, I would ask them to be quiet or to take their conversation elsewhere.

_____28. Anyone attempting to push ahead of me in a line is in for a good battle.

_____29. I am quick to express an opinion.

_____30. There are times when I just can't say anything.*

SCORING THE ASSERTIVENESS SCHEDULE

Tabulate your score as follows: Change the signs of all items followed by an asterisk (*). Then add the thirty item scores. For example, if the response to an asterisked item was 2, place a minus sign (−) before the 2. If the response to an asterisked item was −3, change the minus sign to a plus sign (+) by adding a vertical stroke.

Scores on this test can vary from +90 to −90. The table below will show you how your score compared with those of 764 college women and 637 college men from thirty-five campuses all across the United States. For example, if you are a woman and your score was 26, it exceeded that of 80 percent of the women in the sample. A score of 15 for a male exceeds that of 55 to 60 percent of the men in the sample.

The results of this test should only be used as a rough approximation of your level of assertiveness. If your score is lower than you think is appro-

Women's scores	Percentile	Men's scores
55	99	65
48	97	54
45	95	48
37	90	40
31	85	33
26	80	30
23	75	26
19	70	24
17	65	19
14	60	17
11	55	14
8	50	11
6	45	8
2	40	6
−1	35	3
−4	30	1
−8	25	−3
−13	20	−7
−17	15	−11
−24	10	−15
−34	5	−24
−39	3	−30
−48	1	−41

priate, several steps may be taken. Courses in assertiveness training are numerous and easy to find. There are also many useful self-help books which deal with assertiveness and how to improve it.

CLIENT HARDNESS SCALE

One of the symptoms of burnout found in almost every profession is a change in attitude toward clients or the people to whom service is given. The desire to help changes to one of indifference and even anger towards people. This exercise is designed to obtain information about your attitudes toward those you are supposed to help or serve. The information comes from three sources: yourself, colleagues, and those you are supposed to help. This should give a picture of whether your views are shared by your co-workers and those who are to be helped or served. The questions sample the following attitudes toward the persons to be helped.

Persons to be helped are:

1. seen as competent and able to run their own lives
2. cared about rather than treated mechanically
3. listened to carefully as opposed to just "heard"
4. helped to clarify their own needs rather than having some other's values imposed on them
5. exposed to the real feelings of the helper rather than an impersonal, nonsharing attitude
6. related to as individuals rather than members of some group (ethnic, gender, socioeconomic, diagnostic, etc.)
7. relating to a person who feels and understands their feelings and doesn't try to ignore or escape these feelings.

HOW TO RESPOND TO THE SCALE

Answer the questions in Section 1 by assigning a rating of from 1 to 5 for each question.

Section 1: Personal (answer these questions yourself)

1. I believe that the people I am supposed to help and serve are competent, able, and responsible for their own lives.

1	2	3	4	5
Don't believe it at all		Believe to some extent		Deeply believe

2. I honestly care about the persons I am supposed to help and serve.

1	2	3	4	5
Don't care at all		Care to some extent		Deeply care

3. I listen carefully and with interest to the persons I am supposed to help.

1	2	3	4	5
Fake listening, have no interest		Listen with moderate interest		Listen carefully with interest

4. I don't impose my values on the persons I am supposed to help or serve. Rather, I help them to clarify what their real needs are.

1	2	3	4	5
Impose my wishes, don't help clarify		Impose my values to some extent		Do not impose values, do help clarify

5. I try not to conceal my own feelings from those persons I am supposed to help or serve.

1	2	3	4	5
Conceal my feelings		Am moderately open about my feelings		Am totally open, conceal no feelings

6. I believe in relating to the persons I am supposed to help or serve as individuals rather than as members of a group.

1	2	3	4	5
Relate to persons chiefly as members of some group		Relate to persons as individuals to some extent		Relate to persons primarily as individuals

7. When the persons I am supposed to help or serve share and talk about their feelings or are experiencing emotions, I understand and accept their behavior.

1	2	3	4	5
I neither understand nor encourage such behavior		I understand and encourage to some extent		I understand and encourage

Section 2: Colleagues

Have two or more colleagues answer the following questions.

1. In my opinion _____ honestly believes that the persons he/she is supposed to help or serve are competent, able, and responsible for their own lives.

1	2	3	4	5
Doesn't believe at all		Believes to some extent		Believes deeply

2. _____ honestly cares about the persons he/she is supposed to help or serve.

1	2	3	4	5
Doesn't care at all		Cares to some extent		Cares deeply

3. _____ listens carefully and with interest to the persons he/she is supposed to help or serve.

1	2	3	4	5
Doesn't listen or care at all		Listens with interest		Listens and cares deeply

4. _____ doesn't impose his/her values on the persons he/she is supposed to help or serve. Rather, he/she helps them to clarify what their real needs are.

1	2	3	4	5
Imposes own values, offers little clarification		Imposes values to some extent		Does not impose values, does clarify

5. _____ tries not to conceal his/her own feelings.

1	2	3	4	5
Conceals all feelings		Is moderately open about feelings		Is quite open, conceals no feelings

6. _____ believes in relating to the persons he/she is supposed to help or serve as individuals rather than as members of a group.

1	2	3	4	5
Relates to persons chiefly as members of a group		Relates to persons as individuals to some extent		Relates to persons as individuals

7. When the person _____ is supposed to help or serve shares and talks about personal feelings or is experiencing strong emotions, _____ understands and accepts these feelings.

1	2	3	4	5
Neither under-stands nor encourages such behavior		Understands and encourages to some extent		Understands and encourages

Section 3: Persons helped or served

Have the persons helped or served answer the following questions.

1. In my opinion _____ honestly believes that I am able, competent, and responsible for my own life.

1	2	3	4	5
Doesn't believe at all		Believes to some extent		Believes deeply

2. _____ honestly cares about me.

1	2	3	4	5
Doesn't care at all		Cares to some extent		Cares deeply

3. _____ listens carefully and with interest to me.

1	2	3	4	5
Doesn't listen or display interest		Listens with moderate interest		Listens carefully with interest

4. _____ doesn't impose his/her values on me. Rather, he/she helps me to clarify what my real needs are.

1	2	3	4	5
Imposes values, offers little clarification		Imposes values to some extent		Does not impose values, does clarify

5. _____ tries not to conceal his/her own feelings from me.

1	2	3	4	5
Conceals all feelings		Conceals feelings to some extent		Conceals no feelings

6. _____ relates to me as an individual rather than as a member of a group.

1	2	3	4	5
Relates to me primarily as a member of a group		Relates to me as an individual to some extent		Relates to me primarily as an individual

7. When I share and talk about my feelings, _____ understands and accepts them.

1	2	3	4	5
Neither understands nor encourages such behavior		Understands and encourages to some extent		Understands and encourages

WHAT TO DO WITH THE RATINGS

Once you, your colleagues, and the persons to be helped or served have finished the ratings, you have valuable information in your hands. First, check the personal ratings. Does it suggest a less-than-optimal attitude toward those to be helped or served? Does it suggest any of the symptoms of burnout?

Next, check what others have said about your attitudes. Do their responses match up with your views? If you show symptoms of burnout, are they noticed by others? If so, talk to them about it. Valuable suggestions may result from such talks. If your own analysis suggests burnout but the others' analyses don't, discuss that with them.

Remember, this is not a scientifically valid test. It is offered as a guide, to help develop some awareness of attitudes and to generate food for thought and investigation.

EMOTIONS DIARY

Emotions are very much a vital part of us but are often difficult to identify and express clearly. The blocking of the awareness of many of the feelings one may have suggests the need for special attempts to become more alert to these feelings, to make some sense out of them and to see how their meaning and function fit into one's total life pattern.

The Emotions Diary is an activity which will enable one to keep a daily accounting of emotions felt and expressed, to determine both positive and negative aspects of these emotions, and to consider steps toward an effective integration of those emotions.

KEEPING AN EMOTIONS DIARY

1. Get a book in which you can easily record the emotions you have felt and expressed during the day—toward yourself, toward others, and toward the world in general. Note, if possible, the time you felt or expressed each emotion.
2. After recording the emotions, categorize them. Spend some time analyzing them, noting the positive and negative aspects.
3. Divide a page into two columns. List the emotions, dividing them roughly into happy or sad.
4. Count the emotions in each column to determine if you are feeling and expressing an imbalance of emotions (many more in one column than the other).
5. If there is an obvious imbalance, consider possible changes or directions in which you will alter your emotional expressions. If there is an imbalance toward the happy side, (it is possible that sad emotions are being blocked, and vice versa.)

EMOTIONAL ANALYSIS

In conjunction with the Emotional Diary, Emotional Analysis will prove to be a helpful exercise. The goal of Emotional Analysis is to beome aware of the meaning of one's emotions. In order to do this, one has to analyze emotions from the inside and attempt to discover the values and beliefs that underlie them. Once this has been done, one can look for specific behaviors that are influenced by the values and beliefs.

DIRECTIONS FOR EMOTIONAL ANALYSIS

1. Pick any emotional response you have to a situation, person, or event—crying, laughing, liking or disliking a character in a movie, anger at someone at work. Any emotion is suitable for analysis.
2. Ask the question, "Why did I feel that way in particular?"
3. When you have answered number 2, ask the question, "Why is that?"
4. By repeating these "Why" questions, values and beliefs will become apparent.
5. Once the values and beliefs are discovered, think of specific examples of behavior which are influenced by the values and beliefs.

EXAMPLE

Here is an example to clarify this process. The steps are the same as those listed above.

1. I liked the character of Dirty Harry in the movie *The Enforcer*.
2. Why did I feel this way? Because he was able to handle almost any situation and because he helped people in trouble.
3. Why did these ideas make me like him? Because I believe it is important and good for people to be able to handle themselves in most situations. I also believe it is good and important to help people if they really need it.
4. (Another "why" question may be asked here, but the values and beliefs are already apparent.)
5. What are specific examples of my behavior that are influenced by these values and beliefs?
   a. I read a lot so that I will know enough to teach classes well and answer questions posed by students.
   b. I exercise regularly and follow a nutritional plan so that I will be physically able to perform well at work and in recreational activities such as tennis, backpacking, and so forth.
   c. When I see a larger child picking on a smaller one, I usually attempt to stop the fight.
   d. I spend a good amount of time counseling others.
   e. ....
   f. ....

The example revolves around an emotional response to a movie. It could just as easily revolve around an emotional response at work or home. By completing the analysis, one becomes aware of the meaning of specific emotional responses and can better understand why one behaves in certain ways. When applied to the work or home situation, insights can be gained which will help heighten awareness of one's feelings, determining what they mean, and planning any changes which seem desirable.

EMOTIONAL EXPRESSION GUIDE

Persons can express their emotions in many different ways. The different modes of expression may include direct or indirect, verbal or nonverbal, sudden or gradual. This exercise is designed to explain various modes of emotional expression. Examination of the total range of all one's emotional expressions can provide an idea of the degree of intensity and balance of these ways of expression. This information can then be evaluated with respect to one's personal goals, one's professional guidelines, and one's social needs and expectancies.

The EEG will help in such an examination. Here are the steps to follow.

1. List the emotions which you have experienced during a given day or week in the table below.
2. Fill in, in the appropriate spaces, the person to whom the emotion was expressed, the time of day it was expressed (morning, afternoon, evening), where it was expressed, the degree to which it was expressed (little, moderate, much), and why it was expressed.
3. When you have completed this table, study it and see what patterns develop. Use it to help plan any changes in emotional expression which might be helpful. For example, if mostly positive emotions are expressed, consider obtaining a balance by increasing the expression of negative emotions.

Table for Emotional Expression Guide

	Feeling	Who	When	Where	How much	Why
1	Anger	Wife	Morning	Home (kitchen)	Lots	Toast was burned
2						
3						
4						
5						
6						
7						
8						
9						
10						

THE FEAR SCALE

One of the manifestations of burnout is fear and a sense of threat to one's being. It may be that these go unrecognized. Persons most likely to suffer burnout are those who deny their fears and threats. The persons most likely to reduce burnout are those who are aware of real threats and who develop specific ways of dealing with them.

The Fear Scale is an activity which will assist one in becoming more aware of major threats and help plan how to deal with them more effectively.

THE FEAR SCALE

1. List three major threats (fears) you have experienced in your lifetime.

   _____

   _____

   _____

2. List three major threats (fears) that you are experiencing in the present.

   _____

   _____

   _____

3. List three major threats (fears) that you have about the future.

   _____

   _____

   _____

4. Analyze steps 1 through 3 on the basis of the following questions.
   a. How did you deal with the threats in question 1? List those actions which were effective and those which were not.

   Effective   Ineffective

   _____   _____

   _____   _____

   _____   _____

   b. How are you dealing with the threats in question 2? List those actions which are effective and those which are not.

   Effective   Ineffective

   _____   _____

   _____   _____

   _____   _____

   c. How do you plan to deal with the threats (fears) in question 3? How will your plan differ from what you did or are doing? How will it be similar?

   Similarities   Differences

   _____   _____

   _____   _____

   _____   _____

SELF-CONCEPT STRENGTHENERS

Self-concept is obviously a problem for persons suffering from the symptoms of burnout. It is a problem for many of us even if we are not particularly burned out. This short series of activities is designed to provide evidence that persons are more competent and successful than they often believe. These activities may be eye-openers. Try them. Stretch yourself. If you can't think of a way to complete the activity, that is a clue to something to work on in your life.

1. List three things that you do well.
   a.
   b.
   c.
2. List three things that you don't do well that would be helpful to improve.
   a.
   b.
   c.

Once this is done, decide on a way to provide evidence that you are improving in these areas. Figure out a way to measure your skill level and don't measure it again for one week. Then measure it against the first measurement. Keep using the first measure as a way to measure change.

3. List three aspects of your life where you can assume leadership.
   a.
   b.
   c.
4. List three times during the next month to talk about something important to you.
   a.
   b.
   c.
5. List three things that are important to you that could be used to decorate your place of work. (Do not use photographs).
   a.
   b.
   c.
6. List three ways you can have a voice in decisions which directly affect you.
   a.
   b.
   c.
7. List three persons (family members, friends, or colleagues) to invite to lunch at least once a month.
   a.
   b.
   c.
8. List three persons (family members, friends, or colleagues) to invite to your job every few months to learn more about what you do.
   a.
   b.
   c.

9. List three ways you can gauge your success or improvement *without* comparing yourself to others.
   a.
   b.
   c.
10. List three successes you have had in the past week. (Do this activity once a week).
    a.
    b.
    c.
    If you can't think of three, then this is an area in which to begin work immediately.

18. Social

FAMILY MEETING

Communication sometimes breaks down in a family simply because no time is specifically set aside to communicate. This can be cured by holding regular family meetings even when there is nothing crucial to discuss or solve. The time might be used for nothing more than chatting with one another, but that is time well spent.

Here are some simple instructions for conducting a family meeting.

1. Set a regular time of the week to hold the meeting. This may be Sunday afternoon or an evening when everyone can be present.
2. Set a time limit. One hour is usually sufficient.
3. Establish the ground rules. Here are some suggestions. Have a rotating "chairman" conduct the meeting. Do not allow interruptions. Let each person have their full say. (You might try having persons stand when they talk. No one else can talk until they sit down). One vote per person. Start each meeting with a round of praise for all the good things they have done for each other during the week. Allow each member to say something positive about each other family member. Set the family schedule for the week.
4. Establish an agenda each week.

5. Use the family meeting to resolve family disputes. (See "Brainstorming" elsewhere in this chapter.)

Here is a sample agenda for a family meeting.

1. Round of praise among members
2. Allocation of time to persons who want to talk
3. Consideration of new rules in the family
4. Family problems (statements of concern)
5. Likes and dislikes (changing the rules)
6. Family schedule for next week
7. Budget matters (allowances, clothing, toys)
8. Final sharing

SOCIAL FACILITATION SCHEDULE

This activity is one that has for years proven its worth. It involves sitting down and making decisions. What is important is to not put off doing the exercise because it seems silly or time-consuming. It is a serious activity of great potential value. Although following the suggestions takes time, consider this: Persons who suffer from burnout have probably not engaged in such activities. Their professional lives are not working and are not productive and have not been for a long time. If they had taken the time early enough, burnout could have been avoided and their professional lives enhanced. It is a simple matter of trade-off. Invest a little time now and avoid the wasting of an entire career in the future. Short-term expenditure of time can prevent long-term losses. That is what this exercise is about.

INSTRUCTIONS

Sit down and relax. Make the following decisions right now. Don't delay. Do it now!

1. What day or evening of the week can you give to your children? _____ _____ Take that day or evening and spend it with the children. This may be done with other families.
2. What day or evening of the week can you give to your spouse? _____ This means that the two of you will be together and alone.
3. What weekend during the next three months can you and your spouse go off together and get away from the children? _____

4. What weekend during the next six months can your family take a mini-vacation? _____
5. What day or evening in the next two weeks can you get together with adult friends without the children? _____
6. What day or evening in the next three months can you get together with a mix of colleagues and noncolleagues for a party? _____

For all of the six items above, get out a calendar and decide right now on the days or evenings for each of them. Don't put the calendar down until you have selected the time to be spent with family and friends. If something comes up that makes spending time as planned impossible, immediately find another day to substitute for it.

SOCIAL SHARING OF SELF SCALE

Read each item on the scale and mark the level of sharing with the person(s) indicated on the answer sheet following the scale. The answer sheet contains the instructions for how to answer each question.

SELF

1. What I think and feel are my strengths and weaknesses.
2. What I think and feel about my likes and dislikes.
3. What I really think and feel about sex.
4. What I consider to be attractive in the opposite sex.
5. What I consider to be attractive in my own sex.
6. What I think and feel about my personality.
7. What has occurred positively and negatively in my past.
8. What I think and feel about my body.
9. What I think and feel about being emotional.
10. What I think and feel about my intelligence.

OTHERS

1. What I think and feel about my colleagues.
2. What I think and feel about my family.
3. What I think and feel about my friends.
4. What I think and feel about the people I am committed to serve.
5. What I think and feel about people of another race.
6. What I think and feel about older people.

7. What I think and feel about homosexuals.
8. What I think and feel about persons of a different religion.
9. What I think and feel about people on welfare.
10. What I think and feel about foreigners.

PLAY

1. What I think and feel about being a spectator.
2. What I think and feel about competition.
3. What I think and feel about planning regular times for play.
4. What I think and feel about winning.
5. What I think and feel about losing.
6. What I think and feel about playing with kids.
7. What I think and feel about playing with my spouse/lover.
8. What I think and feel about being a participant.
9. What I think and feel about my ability in sports.
10. What kinds of play bring joy or bore me.

WORK

1. What I think and feel about my salary.
2. What I think and feel about my boss or supervisor(s).
3. What I think and feel about the stresses at work.
4. What I think and feel about my challenges at work.
5. What I think and feel about my ambitions and goals.
6. What I think and feel about my strengths and weakness at work.
7. What I think and feel about my choice of career.
8. What I think and feel about my successes at work.
9. What I think and feel about my failures in my career.
10. What satisfies me about my work.

VALUES

1. What my political convictions are.
2. What my religious convictions are.
3. What I think and feel about drugs.
4. What I think and feel about alcohol.
5. What I think and feel about gambling.
6. What I think and feel about nationalism.
7. What I think and feel about the environment.
8. What I think and feel about the economy.
9. What I think and feel about deprecating humor.
10. What my philosophy of life is.

SCORING SHEET

Use the following guidelines to answer the questions in the Social Sharing of Self Scale. For each of the person(s) listed below, indicate in the proper column the degree to which you have shared yourself with those persons.

0 = you have shared nothing of this with the person(s)

X = you have deliberately lied and misrepresented yourself to the person(s) (scored as a −1)

1 = you have shared yourself in vague, general terms with the person(s).

2 = you have shared yourself completely with the other person(s).

| | FAMILY | | FRIENDS | | COLLEAGUES | | CLIENTS | |
	Spouse	Children	Male	Female	Male	Female	Male	Female
SELF								
1.								
2.								
3.								
4.								
5.								
6.								
7.								
8.								
9.								
10.								
OTHERS								
1.								
2.								
3.								
4.								
5.								

(Continued)

	FAMILY		FRIENDS		COLLEAGUES		CLIENTS	
	Spouse	*Children*	*Male*	*Female*	*Male*	*Female*	*Male*	*Female*
6.								
7.								
8.								
9.								
10.								
PLAY								
1.								
2.								
3.								
4.								
5.								
6.								
7.								
8.								
9.								
10.								
WORK								
1.								
2.								
3.								
4.								
5.								
6.								
7.								

(Continued)

| | FAMILY | | FRIENDS | | COLLEAGUES | | CLIENTS | |
	Spouse	Children	Male	Female	Male	Female	Male	Female
8.								
9.								
10.								
VALUES								
1.								
2.								
3.								
4.								
5.								
6.								
7.								
8.								
9.								
10.								
TOTALS								

WHAT TO DO WITH THE SCORES

Total the numbers in each column (spouse, children, friends, colleagues, and clients). This will give you an indication of how much self-disclosure one achieves with important persons in one's life. By adding scores across the five horizontal categories, an indication can be obtained of how much one discloses in these five areas. Once these scores are obtained, think about what they might mean. Decide if more self-disclosure would be beneficial and, if so, what can be done to bring this about. Family meetings, the Relationship Squares, and the Social Facilitation Schedule are all exercises which may be helpful in increasing self-disclosure.

COMMUNICATIONS ASSUMPTIONS TEST

Here is a test that will provide an indication of your communication skills by determining your communication assumptions. It is a forced-choice test. Select the choice that most fits your belief. If neither choice fits what you believe exactly, select the one which comes closest. The scoring sheet follows the test.

Once the CAT is scored, look at the results. If the score in the blocking column seems high, think about why this is so. Check the items which suggest blocking of effective communication. Can you think of actual examples in your communicating when this block might have occurred? Try and think of alternative ways in which the situation might have been handled.

TEST OF COMMUNICATION SKILLS

1. a. If the other person is wrong or mistaken, interrupting them is the best way to prevent further mistakes.
   b. Listening until a person is finished, even if they are wrong or mistaken, is the best way to prevent further mistakes.
2. a. It is best to be direct and open in communication.
   b. It is best to find the best strategy to use to influence or persuade another person.
3. a. It is best to hide and disguise feelings.
   b. It is best to understand and confront feelings.
4. a. It is best to help another person when it is clear that he or she is wrong or mistaken.
   b. It is best to let people solve their own problems even when it is clear that they are wrong or mistaken.
5. a. In meetings, it is best to focus on your own behavior, opinions, beliefs.
   b. In meetings, it is best to focus on the behavior, opinions, or beliefs of the other person.
6. a. It is best to stay with and work through difficult problems.
   b. It is best to put off difficult problems until later.
7. a. It is best to take a risk and confront personal problems within a group
   b. It is best to let someone else take the risk and to act as a mediator.
8. a. It is best to talk directly to the person over whom a problem exists.
   b. It is best to talk about the problem to others rather than to the person over whom the problem exists.
9. a. It is best to waive the rules if an impasse is reached.
   b. It is best to stick to the rules when an impasse is reached
10. a. It is best to recognize and agree openly that different points of view can be legitimate, honest, and worthwhile.
    b. It is best to recognize that even if other points of view are legitimate, honest, and worthwhile they cannot be agreed to openly.

11. a. It is best to gain everything possible if one has the power or votes.
    b. It is best to compromise or reach a consensus.
12. a. It is best to be courteous rather than confront mistakes or inaccurate statements.
    b. It is best to confront mistakes and inaccuracies openly and honestly.
13. a. It is best to show an interest in the attitudes, research, and opinions of others.
    b. It is best to show disinterest in the attitudes, research, and opinions of others.
14. a. It is best to use confrontation as the primary relationship style.
    b. It is best to compromise.
15. a. It is best to express honest feelings.
    b. It is best to try to make the other person defensive in order to get your own way.
16. a. It is best to give an expected answer.
    b. It is best to take a risk and express honest feelings.
17. a. It is best to act on the most current statistical information when dealing with persons.
    b. It is best to treat people as individuals.
18. a. It is best to promote the interests of the institution.
    b. It is best to promote the interests of individuals.
19. a. It is most efficient to negotiate and collaborate.
    b. It is most efficient to use power if it is available.
20. a. It is best not to talk rather than express hostile feelings.
    b. It is best to express hostile feelings.
21. a. It is best to recognize ethnic differences.
    b. It is best to treat everyone the same.
22. a. It is best to tolerate some mistakes.
    b. It is best to insist on perfection.
23. a. It is best to understand that people are all the same.
    b. It is best to understand that people are different.
24. a. It is best to understand that skin color is unimportant in interpersonal relationships in America.
    b. It is best to understand that skin color is important in interpersonal relationships in America.
25. a. It is best to create interdependence.
    b. It is best to create independence.

STYLE OF CONFLICT TEST

This simple test is designed to give persons insight into their style of resolving differences with other persons. In every profession we have studied, communication with clients, colleagues, and family members is disrupted during burnout. A person's particular style of resolving conflict can cause additional strains on communications which are already less than effective. By taking

Scoring Sheet

	Blocking	Facilitating
1	a	b
2	b	a
3	a	b
4	a	b
5	b	a
6	b	a
7	b	a
8	b	a
9	b	a
10	b	a
11	a	b
12	a	b
13	b	a
14	a	b
15	b	a
16	a	b
17	a	b
18	a	b
19	b	a
20	a	b
21	b	a
22	b	a
23	a	b
24	a	b
25	b	a
Total		

this test and thinking about the results, increased awareness of one's conflict-resolution style should emerge. This knowledge can then be applied to adopting a more effective style, if necessary. One's style may also be compared with other persons' styles to see where possible conflicts arise and whether another style may prove more beneficial and balanced.

The test below is what is called a forced-choice test. That means that there are two statements and you must pick the one that best or most typically describes how you would respond. There are twenty-five forced choice statements in the test. If neither choice describes your style very well, pick the one that comes closest. Following the test, a score sheet and instructions are provided for you to take a look at your responses to the test. It may provide some insight into your typical style.

STYLE OF CONFLICT TEST

1. a. I avoid controversy.
   b. It is more important that the other person be happy.
2. a. I always think there is a middle ground.
   b. It is important that everyone's wishes be met.
3. a. I logically show that my position is best.
   b. I always respect the other person's wishes.
4. a. If it is really important, the other person's wishes should be respected.
   b. I compromise.
5. a. It is important to satisfy everyone.
   b. Many times I'll just let someone else take the responsibility.
6. a. I actually tend to consider the other person's wishes first.
   b. Open discussion is the best way to handle problems.
7. a. It is best to solve problems immediately.
   b. I work it out so I lose a little and gain a little.
8. a. It is best to get issues out in the open immediately.
   b. I try to put off making a decision until all the facts are in.
9. a. I am firm in getting what I want.
   b. I avoid useless problems.
10. a. I let others take the lead in solving problems.
    b. I talk about the things we agree on.
11. a. Compromise is the best solution.
    b. It is better to work things out so everyone is satisfied.
12. a. I am firm in getting what I want.
    b. It is more important to stay friends than it is to confront issues.
13. a. I try to find a compromise.
    b. It is more important that the other person be satisfied
14. a. It is important to involve others in the solution.
    b. I avoid unpleasantness.
15. a. There is no point in creating unnecessary tension.
    b. I work for what I want.
16. a. It is important to think things over before making a decision.
    b. I'll give a little if the other person will.
17. a. It is important to work for what I want.
    b. It is important to get issues out in the open immediately.
18. a. Worrying about differences is not worth the effort.
    b. I attempt to get what I want.
19. a. I am firm about what I want.
    b. I usually try to find a way to get some of what I want.
20. a. It is better to get everyone's concerns out in the open.
    b. I let the other person have their way so they won't be mad.
21. a. I don't like to hurt the other person's feelings.
    b. I try to get the other person to see the logic of my position.
22. a. I try not to bring up things that will hurt a relationship.
    b. I try to work things out so that I get some of what I want and the other persons get some of what they want

23. a. It is best to get everyone's ideas on the problem.
    b. I work for my position.
24. a. I think there is always a middle ground.
    b. I am firm about what I want.
25. a. I think it is best to avoid controversy.
    b. I'll give up some of my points to win others.

Scoring the Style of Conflict Test

Circle your answers in the columns below. Then total the columns.

Competitive	Cooperative	Compromising	Soothing	Avoiding
3A	2B	2A	1B	1A
9A	5A	4B	3B	5B
12A	6B	7B	4A	8B
15B	7A	11A	6A	9B
17A	8A	13A	10B	10A
18B	11B	16B	12B	14B
19A	14A	19B	13B	15A
21B	17B	22B	20B	16A
23B	20A	24A	21A	18A
24B	23A	25B	22A	25A

Totals

This test is meant to provide information regarding one's style of conflict. Here are some questions to help you analyze the results.

1. How accurate does it seem to you? What were the surprises?
2. Share your score with someone else. What do they think?
3. What pattern does one's spouse have? Is it compatible?
4. What about a boss or colleague?
5. What could you do to get a better balance in the scores?

SOCIOGRAMS

The target sociogram is a way of becoming aware of, analyzing, and understanding patterns of communication and interaction among groups. Any dimension of interpersonal interaction may be the focus of sociograms. In this exercise we suggest that communications, support, and power be studied among family, colleagues, and friends.

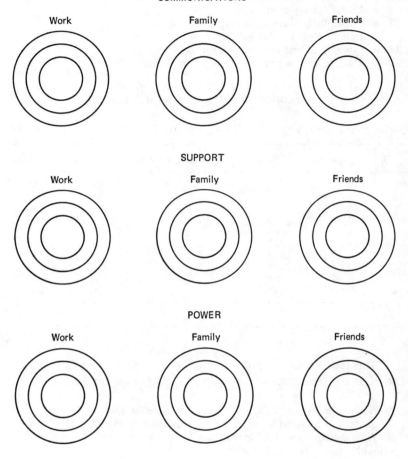

COMMUNICATIONS

Work　　　　　　Family　　　　　　Friends

SUPPORT

Work　　　　　　Family　　　　　　Friends

POWER

Work　　　　　　Family　　　　　　Friends

INSTRUCTIONS FOR THE COMMUNICATIONS SOCIOGRAM

1. Work
   a. Draw three concentric circles on an 8½″ x 11″ sheet of paper (see examples above).
   b. Write your initials in the center of the first circle.
   c. The innermost circle represents the area of greatest trust. Write the initials of those people at work with whom you would communicate most freely or openly in this inner circle.

d. The middle circle represents the area of moderate trust. Write the initials of those colleagues with whom you would communicate with moderate ease within this circle.

e. The outer circle represents the area of least trust. Write the initials of those colleagues with whom you would communicate least freely within this circle.

2. Family
Repeat steps a through d above, substituting family members for colleagues.

3. Friends
Repeat steps a through d above, substituting friends for colleagues.

INSTRUCTIONS FOR THE SUPPORT SOCIOGRAM

1. Family (nuclear or extended)
   a. Draw three concentric circles on an 8½" x 11" sheet of paper. Mark the center circle with your initials.
   b. The innermost circle represents the area of greatest support given to you. Write the initials of the family members who give you the greatest support within this circle.
   c. The middle circle represents the area of moderate support. Write the initials of the family members who give you moderate support within this circle.
   d. The outer circle represents the area of least support. Write the initials of the family member who gives you the least support within this circle.

2. Work
Repeat steps a through d, substituting colleagues for family members.

3. Friends
Repeat steps a through d, substituting friends for family members.

INSTRUCTIONS FOR THE POWER SOCIOGRAMS

1. Friends
   a. Draw three concentric circles on an 8½" x 11" sheet of paper.
   b. The innermost circle represents the area of greatest power. Write the initials of the person in your circle of friends, including yourself, who exerts the greatest power.
   c. The middle circle represents the area of moderate power. Write the initials of the person in your circle of friends, including yourself, who exerts moderate power.
   d. The outer circle represents the area of least power. Write the initials of the person in your circle of friends, including yourself, who exerts the least power.
   e. Where did you fall in this sociogram?

2. Family
   Repeat steps a through e, substituting family members for friends.
3. Work
   Repeat steps a through e, substituting colleagues for friends.

After you have drawn the sociograms, the following questions will facilitate your analysis and understanding.

1. Did the sociograms reveal new information for you? What?
2. What is the relationship between the sociograms? Are support and communication similar or different? Are communication and power similar or different?
3. What suggestions for improving social interaction comes out of the sociograms?
4. With respect to power, did you discover that your need for power was not being met? How might you meet this need?
5. What seems to be the roles of power, communication, and support in the creation or the elimination of burnout? (Be specific and concrete in making applications to yourself, your family, and your work colleagues.)

BRAINSTORMING

The following suggestions may be used any time a problem exists at work or at home. The goal of brainstorming is to generate as many ideas or solutions as possible under the assumption that initial ideas and solutions may not be the best. Initial ideas are often the result of habitual, stereotyped thinking patterns and hence relatively uncreative. If this is so, the greater the number of possible solutions, the greater should be the chances of finding the most effective ones.

RULES FOR BRAINSTORMING

Phase I.

1. Select and define a problem which needs to be solved. If there is no clear-cut, commonly agreed-upon problem to discuss, skip to step 2 and brainstorm what problems need to be addressed.
2. All ideas, solutions, or suggestions are acceptable. Suspend *all* evaluation or criticism during the first phase of brainstorming. Write down all suggestions so that they are available to all participants.
3. Encourage seemingly wild and far-fetched ideas. Have fun.
4. Encourage participants to modify ideas already presented. This is referred to as "piggybacking."
5. When an agreed-upon period of time has passed, the second phase may begin.

Phase II.

6. Discuss all the items generated in phase I. Now is the time to become critical. Try to cover the strong points and weak points of each idea.
7. Select one or two of the better ideas to try.
8. Plan how these ideas will be implemented. Discuss what needs to be done or changed to implement them.
9. Decide when and how to evaluate the ideas for effectiveness once they have been put into practice. Decide how judgments of success or failure will be made *before* any changes are implemented.

GROUP RESPONSE TEST

One of the intellectual symptoms of burnout is stereotyping. The labeling and categorization of persons may have undeniable social consequences as well. It may be that certain groups are the recipients of discriminating practices based more on the stereotyped image of them than on their reality. This activity is designed to facilitate your checking out the degree to which your responses and reactions may give rise to stereotypical thinking.

You are to look at each word on the following list and immediately write the first word or words which come to mind. After you have completed this, use the questions to increase your analysis and understanding.

Write the word or words which immediately come to mind for each of the following groups.

Police _____   _____
Lawyers _____   _____
Counselors _____   _____
Supervisors _____   _____
Patients _____   _____
Clergy _____   _____
Nurses _____   _____
Clients _____   _____
Blue-collar workers _____   _____
Christians _____   _____
Physicians _____   _____
Homosexuals _____   _____
Jews _____   _____
Secretaries _____   _____
Students _____   _____
Arabs _____   _____
Blacks _____   _____

Males _____   _____
Teachers _____   _____
Females _____   _____
Hispanics _____   _____

Now that you have responded to the words above, react to these questions.

1. What trends do you see among your responses and reactions?
2.· Which groups received your most positive responses?
3. Which groups received your most negative reactions?
4. What values are indicated in your responses and reactions?
5. How do these values affect or influence other behavior in your daily interactions with others? (Give specific examples.)

RELATIONSHIP SQUARES

This is a technique to help define those persons in families, at work, and among friends who actually contribute to social health and those who seem to contribute to social inadequacy. It is a simple, straightforward technique which demands only that the respondent answer the questions "honestly." Honestly, in this sense, means quick, first-impression answers. There is no trick. It is a simple technique to help determine those persons with whom we really want to spend time and those with whom we really don't.

WORK

	Good	*Bad*
Males	1. 2. 3. 4. 5.	1. 2. 3. 4. 5.
Females	1. 2. 3. 4. 5.	1. 2. 3. 4. 5.

List in the appropriate box those people at work who make you feel good about yourself when you are around them. List in the appropriate box those people at work who make you feel bad about yourself when you are around them.

When you are finished, you will have a list of people in the "good" column who are the persons in your social life who are natural "antidotes" to burnout. The persons in the "bad" column are persons who are contributing to your burnout. Contacts with the persons in the "good" column should be increased and contacts with persons in the "bad" column should be decreased or changed in some way.

FAMILY

	Good	Bad
Males	1. 2. 3. 4. 5.	1. 2. 3. 4. 5.
Females	1. 2. 3. 4. 5.	1. 2. 3. 4. 5.

List in the appropriate box those people in your extended family (brothers, sisters, uncles, aunts, etc.) who make you feel good about yourself when you are around them. List in the appropriate box those people in your extended family who make you feel bad about yourself when you are around them. The persons in the "good" column are the ones who help you avoid burnout, and more time should be spent with them. The persons in the "bad" column are persons who are contributing to your burnout. Change something about the relationships with these persons or limit contact with them.

List in the appropriate box those friends who make you feel good about yourself when you are around them. List in the appropriate box those friends who make you feel bad about yourself when you are around them. If there are friends who appear in the "bad" column, those friends are contributing to your burnout; contact should be reduced or eliminated with those friends in favor of the ones who appear in the "good" column.

	Good	Bad
Males	1. 2. 3. 4. 5.	1. 2. 3. 4. 5.
Females	1. 2. 3. 4. 5.	1. 2. 3. 4. 5.

This exercise relies on the "gut" impressions that fly across one's mind when first asked the questions. The more consideration given to the task, the less effective it becomes. However, if those first impressions are trusted, in each of the areas assessed a large step will have been taken to avoid burnout.

BLOCK PARTY KIT

At several different places in this book we have suggested socializing as a remedy for certain symptoms of burnout. One way to do this is to have a block party. In addition to the fun of the party, planning for the party and carrying it out can do much to build effective communications between people.

BLOCK PARTY KIT

1. Here is a suggested form for invitations to a planning meeting for a block party.
   Hi. I'm _____ and I live at _____. I'm trying to plan a party for the people who live on our block. I would like to invite you to my home on _____ at _____o'clock to plan this party. Please let me know by telephone if you can come to help us plan the party. My number is _____.
2. Meet at someone's house to assign committees for the following areas of responsibility:
   a. Permit. This may have to be obtained from the local police department or city agency responsible for streets.
   b. Food and drink.

c. PR or advertising, to inform the rest of the block.
d. Child care.
e. Recreation. Many recreation departments provide party kits which include games such as volleyball, frisbees, horseshoes, badminton, and board games.
f. Clean-up. One quick, fun way to do this is to have everyone line up abreast, stretching across the block. Usually one sweep down the block will result in everything's being picked up. If there are enough people, organize them into "waves." This certainly will clean the block. It might even be cleaner after the party than before!

   Provide plastic trash bags for the cleaners.
3. Select a committee to plan the next party. Consider expanding the party to include other blocks.

19. Spiritual

A PERSONAL JOURNAL

At several places throughout this book we have suggested the idea of keeping a journal. The purpose of a journal is basically to increase people's awareness of the positive and negative events that occur in their lives. When the stresses of the day pile up, it is easy to forget the moments of joy and tenderness that may have occurred. For various reasons, victims of burnout seem to remember more of the negative events and fewer of the positive ones. Our belief is that by increasing one's awareness of positive events—in fact, of all significant events—one can more easily come to the conclusion that there is some meaning in life, something which makes life worthwhile. In this way, future burnout can be made less likely and current burnout can be minimized.

SUGGESTIONS FOR WRITING
THE JOURNAL

1. *Don't* buy a small, bound book. Get some type of book that is large (8½" x 11") and that will lie flat on a table. Make sure it is not too flimsy and can be kept, reread, and stored.
2. Use a multicolored pen set.
3. Do not use paper with lines.

4. Do not write in straight lines. Do not write page after page. Write in circles. Draw pictures. Express emotions and events in quick, insightful thoughts.
5. Try not to write sentences. Instead write down thoughts, feelings, phrases, ideas, and words.
6. *Don't* write it right, write it down. This means don't worry about grammatically perfect sentences. No one will read this (unless you show it to them). It is more important to get your ideas down than it is to edit before recording significant events in your life.
7. A journal is not a diary. You do not have to record every detail of your day. This is a journal of significant events, thoughts, feelings, and ideas.
8. Write down events, feelings, and thoughts as they happen. Memory can be tricky.
9. Try to find time to read through the journal at the end of the day.
10. Review the journal at the end of each week.

WHAT TO WRITE IN THE JOURNAL

In general, write down any event which leads to genuine emotions—happiness, joy, contentment, sadness, fear, anger. Some suggestions are:

Any success at work, even if "small"
Anything done well
Joyous, happy moments
Good places you've gone
Inspirational moments
Kindnesses extended to others
Kindnesses extended by others
Works of art or music you liked
Any altruistic act you have done
Any passages from books or movies you have liked
Enjoyable moments with adults
Enjoyable moments with children
Tender moments with spouse
Especially cute or meaningful comments of children
Good places to eat
Any moment of true emotion, positive or negative

STAGES OF SPIRITUAL STRESS TEST

The process of spiritual burnout appears to develop gradually. Several stages can be delineated which appear to move from lesser to greater severity. A progression of five stages seems apparent. This test serves to identify the stage at which a person involved in burnout is. After checking the items, turn to the end of the test for scoring instructions and interpretations.

Check each item if it is true for you.

_____ 1. I don't believe I am a likely victim of burnout.
_____ 2. Most of my colleagues don't really care about the people they are supposed to help or serve.
_____ 3. If I would just work a little harder, I would be more effective in my job.
_____ 4. Nobody really listens when I complain.
_____ 5. My superiors really know more about how my job should be done than I do.
_____ 6. I have not experienced any of the symptoms of burnout.
_____ 7. The organization I work for doesn't really care about the people it is supposed to help or serve.
_____ 8. If I would get more advanced training, I would be able to do my job much better.
_____ 9. Just going to work makes me tired.
_____ 10. It's impossible to change the system.
_____ 11. Burnout is not really a problem for me in my job.
_____ 12. My clients' problems are mostly due to their own weaknesses.
_____ 13. By doing the jobs that no one else likes to do, I can gain status.
_____ 14. Nobody cares about the job my profession does.
_____ 15. A comfortable retirement is my major goal.
_____ 16. I am sufficiently aware of the causes of burnout that it won't happen to me.
_____ 17. My family doesn't understand what I go through at work.
_____ 18. I could do more to convince my colleagues how competent I really am.
_____ 19. No matter how hard I work, it doesn't make any difference.
_____ 20. I derive no pleasure from work; I do it mostly for the money.
_____ 21. People in my profession don't appreciate how good things really are.
_____ 22. My immediate supervisor prevents me from doing my job as effectively as I might.
_____ 23. My clients are often the only ones who really know about my good work.
_____ 24. This job is just impossible.
_____ 25. Burnout happens to people who are weak.

SCORING

Assign one point for each item checked and record the items checked in the boxes below. Total each column to determine the stages most characteristic of your burnout. If no columns show significant differences from any other column but the total score is 15 or more, consider that a high resignation score.

Denial	Blaming, Resentment	Overcompensation	Depression	Resignation
1.	2.	3.	4.	5.
6.	7.	8.	9.	10.
11.	12.	13.	14.	15.
16.	17.	18.	19.	20.
21.	22.	23.	24.	25.

HOW TO USE THE RESULTS OF THE SSST

The categories explained below represent five stages of spiritual burnout.

1. **Denial.** This stage is characterized by a lack of awareness of one's susceptibility to burnout. This appears very frequently among graduate students and young professionals.
2. **Blaming, Resentment.** This is the stage at which anger, often misplaced, becomes more frequent. It is not identified as emerging from within the individual; usually outside forces (colleagues, bosses, clients, and significant others) are blamed or resented.
3. **Overcompensation.** The major characteristic of this stage is a feeling of incompetence coupled with an increased striving to do more and better work. Such striving is believed to eliminate the feeling of incompetence.
4. **Depression.** This stage is characterized by feelings of helplessness, hopelessness, and fatigue.
5. **Resignation.** This stage is characterized by capitulation to the status quo. Changes which before were seen as merely impractical are now viewed as undesirable.

Once the scores are recorded, one should have a profile of where one stands in each stage. The next step would be to look for cures which are appropriate to each stage (see next paragraph). Thus, if a person is characterized by the stage of denial, this person might look in two places. First, find the chapter related to his or her profession. Look under "Cures" for the sections devoted to emotional and spiritual suggestions to relieve burnout. These sections will give specific suggestions for dealing with these aspects of burnout. Second, look at the relevant chapters in Part Two of this book for general activities that are helpful to members of any profession. By following such suggestions, the process of spiritual burnout may be relieved or reversed.

GENERAL GUIDELINES FOR USING THE
SSST

1. The responses to these questions should be thought of as signals. These signals suggest that if things go on as they are, without changes being made, the process of burnout becomes more likely and can deepen.
2. The more items that one checks, the deeper one is into the stages of burnout. The higher the score on the test, the more imperative it is that one begin to make changes which will counter the burnout process.
3. Although a person's burnout may not follow the stages exactly, they can be helpful in alerting one about what may be coming next. The test can offer hints about what behaviors and attitudes to look for in the near future. In this way, corrective steps may be taken before one is deeply burned out.
4. The test may reveal a person's style of being. Much has been written about the "high-IQ whiner." By checking one's responses to items in stages 2 and 3, one can discover if that "diagnosis" is appropriate for oneself.
5. Each of the stages is related to the following general areas of functioning discussed throughout the book.

Denial: Emotional, Spiritual
Blaming, Resentment: Emotional, Spiritual
Overcompensation: Social, Intellectual
Depression: Spiritual
Resignation: Spiritual

GOAL ASSESSMENT SURVEY

Many persons do not take or make the opportunity to reexamine and reformulate their major life purposes or the goals which they set for themselves when they were young. This exercise is an activity in which you may focus on such purposes and goals. It will assist you in exploring the question of whether your many activities seem to have direction and purpose.

You may want to do the following specific activities all at once or on a one-a-day or one-a-week basis. Whatever strategy you decide on, make sure that all are completed.

Here are the activities.

1. Write what you believe your spouse would say you have contributed to the marriage.
2. Write your boss's next evaluation of your performance.
3. Write what you'd like to be said of you at your retirement.
4. Write the inscription for your retirement plaque.

5. Write your own epitaph.
6. Write your own eulogy (100 words at the most).

Once all of these are completed, reexamine for the following:

1. What trends or common threads emerge?
2. What do they say about what you regard as your significant purposes in life?
3. Are you getting what is important to you through your activities?
4. What major and minor changes do you wish to make in your life based on the information gained from this activity?

If it is at all possible, it would be a significant contribution to this activity if you had someone important in your life read your specific responses to the six activities and then answer the four reexamination questions for you (without knowledge of your answers to them). Then, discuss similarities and differences between your answers. This last suggestion will provide a measure of how you see yourself and how you are perceived by others.

A FAMILY TREE

The concern for origins can be more than a fad stimulated by the popular television movie *Roots*. It can provide a real sense of obligation to history and to the future. It can provide a sense of commitment to living up to standards thay may have slipped away in the daily struggles of keeping up and keeping ahead. It can provide a sense of pride to one's family and to oneself.

Here are some guidelines to help establish a family tree. This provides an opportunity to pass on to others in the family a sense of history that can be maintained in their lives as well. It may even serve as a stimulus to contact members of the family who have remained isolated for many years.

For the purposes of this family tree, include only the persons who are directly related. Do not include those related by marriage. For one's spouse, use the instructions below to complete a separate family tree for each member of his or her family, if desired.

For each family tree being investigated, collect the following information for every relative to be mentioned.

1. Name
2. Date of birth
3. Date of death (if appropriate)

4. Profession(s)
5. Professional contribution and length of time spent at each profession
6. Gifts between you and the person (material and nonmaterial)
7. Most memorable characteristic of the person
8. Ways in which the person was most like you
9. Ways in which the person was least like you
10. Things that can be learned from the person's life (mistakes, strong points, etc.)

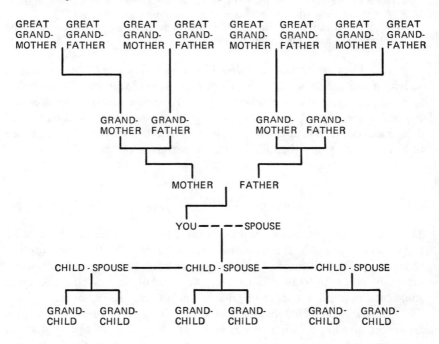

A PERSONAL CREED

Sometimes it is difficult to know if we are violating our own values at work or in our daily living. It is difficult because many of us have not taken the time to set down what our values are. This exercise asks that you do just that.

In the categories listed, follow the instructions for creating your own personal creed.

1. Develop your thoughts for at least the following categories.

WHAT I BELIEVE ABOUT:
Human beings
Self
Children
Work
Education
Religion
Money
Relationships
The universe
Nature
Love

2. Write it out. Use only one sentence for each topic.
3. The sentence should describe, as fully as possible and as clearly as possible, what you believe.
4. Work on each statement until it is a tightly knit statement of your belief.
5. Have the creed typed or hand-lettered and display it in a prominent place.
6. Read it regularly.
7. Check periodically to see if you are living up to your beliefs. If not, sit down and decide what needs to be changed in order for you to start living in accordance with your own self-chosen statement of beliefs.
8. Each year set aside a day to revise your creed in light of any changes in your beliefs.

A LETTER TO YOUR CHILDREN

Many persons have indicated that coming to grips with death is one of the major ways of coming to grips with life. Once one has made a personal peace with death, life takes on more significance and meaning. One way to confront death is to accept the option that you may not be alive to see your children grow into adults. That means that you will not be around to provide guidance throughout their formative years. The chances to teach will not present themselves gradually. How can you tell them the beliefs you hold most dear if you are not going to be there? One way is to write them a letter as if you were going to die. Tell them the things in life that you count most precious. Here is a format to use in writing such a letter. (See the Personal Creed in this chapter as well.)

>　Dear _____,
>　　　I am writing this letter to you in case I should die before I get to tell you the things about life and living that I believe. It is important to me to have you know these things even if I am not here to tell them to you in person. This is a part of what it means to me to be a mother/father. It is

something I want to leave to you. These are the values I have tried to live by, and I believe they are important enough to leave them to you in the hope that you will consider them as a basis for your life as well.

This is what I would like you to know about ———
(Suggested topics)
Marriage
Work/Career
Friendship
Religion
Money
Life
Sex
Politics
Family
Love

Write this letter even if you do not anticipate dying. Put it in a safe place. Consider adding to it or altering it as you grow older and learn more about yourself. Be sure to include it among the papers that will be discovered on your death. It can be among the most important gifts a parent can leave behind for a child.

ATTITUDES TOWARD DEATH

Imagine that you have been told that you have only ten days to live. Answer the following questions.

1. What would you plan to do?
2. Where would you go?
3. With whom would you choose to spend your time?
4. What major things would you say to your loved ones? (See "A Letter to Your Children" in this section.)
5. What tasks would you consider necessary to complete?

Now that these questions have been answered, what information have you gained about living since you are not going to die?!

SUICIDE INFORMATION TEST

Complete the following test to assess your knowledge of suicide. Then read the information below to inform yourself further so that you can be helpful in case a family member, friend, or colleague considers suicide.

Select either True or False for each of the items in the test.

T F *1. Suicide occurs without warning.*
T F *2. If you think of suicide, you will probably do it.*
T F *3. It is bad to talk to a depressed person about suicide.*
T F *4. If a person is serious about suicide, you can't stop them.*
T F *5. Few people who attempt suicide have sought help.*
T F *6. Suicide occurs at the depths of depression.*
T F *7. Suicide occurs mostly among the poor.*
T F *8. Suicide is cowardly.*
T F *9. Suicide is just a way to get attention.*
T F 10. Attempting suicide is a sign that a person is crazy.
T F 11. If a person is talked out of suicide, he or she won't try again.
T F 12. Only a person seeking attention fails at suicide.
T F 13. Suicide is an impulsive act.
T F 14. If someone talks about suicide, there is little chance he or she will actually do it.
T F 15. Suicides don't care about their families.

In fact, all of the statements above are false. Many are common misconceptions about suicide. If we are to help others, we must know what is a misconception and what is true. Here are some facts about suicide associated with the statements above.

1. A majority of persons give verbal indication of their suicide months before their attempt. Nearly half have seen a mental health worker in the week preceding their attempt.
2. Thoughts of suicide are common.
3. There is no indication that people commit suicide because of a discussion with someone about it.
4. This is patently and obviously false. People are often talked out of suicide.
5. See 1 above.
6. Many people appear to show signs of new vitality just before a suicide.
7. Suicide occurs among all socioeconomic groups.
8. The great majority of successful suicides have made prior attempts. About ten out of every hundred people who attempt suicide will succeed within two years.
9. It may be a form of escape, but many persons have rational reasons for suicide, An elderly person may seek it as a means of relieving his or her children of financial burdens, or it may be a reasonable way to confront a hopeless, lingering terminal illness.
10. Few potential suicides show signs of losing touch with reality.
11. See 9 above.
12. See 9 above.
13. See 1 above.
14. See 1 above.
15. Many suicides take great pains to leave their affairs in order. It is not uncommon for suicide notes to leave detailed instructions for survivors.

WHAT TO DO IF A COLLEAGUE, FRIEND, OR FAMILY MEMBER IS CONTEMPLATING SUICIDE

It is apparent from the literature on burnout that many of the professions are susceptible to an increased likelihood of suicide. Even if the reader actually knows of no one who has attempted suicide, persons at work, in the community, or in the home may be considering it. If so, some basic notions of how to deal with potential suicides may prove useful.

1. In light of the information above, take talk of suicide seriously.
2. Encourage the person to seek professional help.
3. If the person won't seek professional help, try to engage him or her in conversation about the suicidal thoughts. Ask why. The person may have had no one to talk over their problems with. Simply expressing them may help.
4. Engage the person in discussing possibilities other than suicide.
5. If you have to leave the person alone, obtain a promise that he or she won't do anything before seeing you again.
6. Try to have the person tell you what he or she plan to do. If the response is very specific, the likelihood of suicide is great. Seek other help immediately.
7. If the person has pills or weapons, attempt to have him or her give them to you.
8. Try to get the person to go with you to a professional.

Some behaviors to avoid:

1. Do not deny or minimize the suicidal person's problems.
2. Do not suggest that the person is crazy.
3. Do not suggest that the person is somehow inadequate because he or she is considering suicide.
4. Do not insist that the person see parents, spouse, children, or religious advisers.

DRUG COUNTING

This exercise is designed to help persons become aware of the all-too-common reaction of substance abuse. Since availability of drugs is one of the main factors contributing to their misuse, completing this simple exercise will increase awareness of the possibilities of substance abuse.

Go to your medicine cabinet or wherever drugs are kept. Count all of the different medications, both prescription and nonprescription. This includes aspirin, cold medicines, and any other drugs which are ingested.

How many are there? _____

If there are more than five, stop and think.

How often do I take medicines? _____

If they are taken only during illnesses, what does that suggest? Is too-frequent illness a sign of burnout?

Which of the drugs listed could you really do without.

_____	_____
_____	_____
_____	_____
_____	_____

For example, it is commonly accepted by the medical profession that medications for the common cold do little to actually help (considering that no infection such as strep throat or tonsilitis is involved). Consider throwing those medications away and not replacing them.

What else can be done in place of ingesting drugs?

Brainstorm possible alternatives. (See "Brainstorming" in Chapter 4 in Part Two.)

_____	_____	_____
_____	_____	_____
_____	_____	_____
_____	_____	_____

Are there tranquilizers in the medicine cabinet? Yes _____ *No* _____

Certainly, tranquilizers can be effective. But, consider that many in the medical profession and allied health professions hold that tranquilizers are among the most pernicious drugs. It might be far better to throw away the tranquilizer drugs and consider other available alternatives. (For example, meditation and relaxation techniques. Even the exercise plan suggested in Chapter 1 of Part Two may be an alternative.)

Brainstorm other options.

_____	_____	_____
_____	_____	_____
_____	_____	_____
_____	_____	_____

Remember, the three main goals of this exercise are (1) to become aware of the number of drugs you have, (2) to become aware of your drug-taking habits, and (3) to generate possible alternatives to drug taking.

ALCOHOL TEST

These questions ask you to assess your drinking behavior. In the space provided, check whether the question is True or False for you.

ALCOHOL TEST

T F   *1. I do most of my drinking alone.*
T F   *2. I need an early morning drink.*
T F   *3. Drinking is causing problems in my family relationships.*
T F   *4. I am frequently absent from work because of drinking.*
T F   *5. Drinking alleviates my feelings of inadequacy.*
T F   *6. If I stop drinking I get the shakes.*
T F   *7. I pay less attention to my spouse/loved one because of drinking.*
T F   *8. My reputation is suffering because of drinking.*
T F   *9. I have experienced blackouts (loss of memory) after drinking.*
T F   *10. My business is suffering because of my drinking.*
T F   *11. I lose sexual potency after drinking.*
T F   *12. I have bodily complaints after drinking.*
T F   *13. I have trouble limiting the amount I drink.*
T F   *14. I drink at lunch.*
T F   *15. My moods change markedly when I drink.*
T F   *16. When I drink I have trouble sleeping.*
T F   *17. I am more impulsive after I drink.*
T F   *18. I have less self-control when I drink.*
T F   *19. I drink in social situations to relieve anxiety.*
T F   *20. I am harder to get along with when I drink.*

If you answered "true" to 5 of these questions you may be a problem drinker; 10, you are probably a potential alcoholic; more than 10, you have a clear problem.

Bibliography

A B A Banking Journal. "EEOC says: 'Sexual harassment of workers is no joking matter.'" May 1980, pp. 24–26.

Administrative Management. "Heading for a breakdown." November 1978, pp. 13–14.

Alexander, D.A. and Haldane, J.D. "Medical education: a student perspective." *Medical Education,* 1979, pp. 336–341.

Altschull, J. Herbert. "The press and police: news flow and ideology." *Journal of Police Science and Administration,* 1975, pp. 425–433.

Bardo, Pamela. "The pain of teacher burnout: a case history." *Phi Delta Kappan,* December 1979, pp. 252–254.

Barrand, John. "Masochism, masturbation and matriarchy." *Australian Family Physician,* June 1979, pp. 663–667.

Baxter, John E. "Job stress won't go away, learn to cope!" *Iron Age,* December 10, 1979, pp. 24–26.

Bower, Ward. "A survival guide for associates." *Barrister,* Winter 1979, pp. 17–19.

Brodsky, Carroll M. "Long-term work stress in teachers and prison guards." *Journal of Occupational Medicine,* February 1977, pp. 133–138.

Broussard, Randy. "Using Relaxation for COPD." *American Journal of Nursing,* November 1979, p. 1962.

Brown, Robert U. "The stress of the press." *Editor and Publisher,* September 18, 1977, p. 32.

Business Week. "Executive's guide to living with stress." August 23, 1976, pp. 75–80.

——. "Executive stress may not be all bad." April 30, 1979, p. 96.

——. "Stress has no gender." November 15, 1976, pp. 73–76.

Carlson, Gary B. "A human systems approach to coping with future shock." *Personnel Journal,* August 1974, pp. 618–622.

Clary, Thomas C. and Clary, Erica W. "Managing stress before it manages you." *Governmental Finance,* February 1977, pp. 22–29.

Collingwood, Thomas R. "Police stress and physical activity." *The Police Chief,* February 1980, pp. 25–27.

Connelly, John C. "The Alcoholic Physician." *The Journal of the Kansas Medical Society,* November 1978, pp. 601–604.

Cooper, Cary L.; Mallinger, Mark; and Kahn, Richard. "Identifying sources of occupational stress among dentists." *Journal of Occupational Psychology,* 1978, pp. 227–234.

Cousins, Norman. "Stress." *Journal of the American Medical Association,* August 3, 1979, p. 459.

Daley, Michael R. "Preventing worker burnout in child welfare." *Child Welfare,* July/August 1979, pp. 443–450.

Davidson, Virginia M. "Coping styles of women medical students." *Journal of Medical Education,* November 1978, pp. 902–907.

Degenaro, Raymond T. "Sources of stress within a police organization." *The Police Chief,* February 1980, pp. 22–24.

Deutsch, Cynthia. "When outside stresses infiltrate a marriage." *Parents,* January 1980, p. 20.

Dinkmeyer, Don, and Dinkmeyer, Don, Jr. "Holistic approaches to health." *Elementary School Guidance and Counseling,* December 1979, pp. 108–112.

Dudley, Donald L., and Welke, Elton. "Change: it could kill you." *The Sunday Denver Post,* October 23, 1977, pp. 14–15.

Dutton, LaVerne M., et al. "Stress levels of ambulance paramedics and fire fighters." *Journal of Occupational Medicine,* February 1978, pp. 111–115.

Emener, William G., Jr. "Professional burnout: rehabilitation's hidden handicap." *Journal of Rehabilitation,* January/February/March 1979, pp. 55–58.

Evans, Christopher. *Understanding Yourself.* New York: A & W Publishers, Inc., 1977.

Executive Fitness Newsletter. "How to live with stress? Listen to the expert—yourself." December 31, 1977.

———. "Learn how to handle stress—ask your secretary." July 1, 1978.

Feinberg, Mortimer R. "What makes you mad?" *Restaurant Business,* April 1, 1979, p. 66.

Fischer-Kowalski, Marina; Leitner, Fritz; and Steinert, Heinz. "Status management and interactional conflict of the police." *International Journal of Criminology and Penology,* 1976, pp. 161–175.

Forrest, William R. "Stresses and self-destructive behaviors of dentists." *Dental Clinics of North America,* July 1978, pp. 361–371.

Fox, Edward, and Matthews, Donald. *Interval Training.* New York: Holt, Rinehart & Winston, 1974.

Fretz, Donald R. "The family effect." *The Judges' Journal,* Summer 1979, p. 33.

Freudenberger, Herbert J. "Burn-out: occupational hazard of the child care worker." *Child Care Quarterly,* Summer 1977, pp. 90–99.

———. "The staff burn-out syndrome in alternative institutions." *Psychotherapy: Theory, Research, and Practice,* Spring 1975, pp. 73–82.

Friggens, Paul. "The indispensable man is only a modern myth." *Nation's Business,* May 1979, pp. 63–66.

Garte, Sumner H., and Rosenblum, Mark L. "Lighting fires in burned-out counselors." *Personnel and Guidance Journal,* November 1978, pp. 158–160.

Gavney, Robert; Calderwood, John; and Knowles, Lyle. "Attitude of patrol officers and wives toward a four-day workweek." *The Police Chief,* February 1979, pp. 33–35.

Gill, James J. "Burnout: a growing threat in ministry." *Human Development,* Summer 1980, pp. 21–27.

Ginsburg, Sigmund G. "The problem of the burned out executive." *Personnel Journal,* August 1974, pp. 598–600.

Grant, Michael J. "Role conflicts of sergeants as first-line supervisors." *The Police Chief,* February 1979, pp. 30–32.

Greeley (Colorado) *Tribune.* "Stress filled jobs causing 'burnout.'" December 20, 1979, p. 44.

Green, David. "Unsafe at any speed?" *Dental Management,* May 1975, pp. 27–38.

Gross, Solomon. "Police isolation: its sources and effects." *The Police Chief,* February 1980, pp. 38–42.

Gruber, Charles A. "The relationship of stress to the practice of police work." *The Police Chief,* February 1980, pp. 16-19.

Guda, Harry E. "Depressed Physicians" (Letter to the Editor). *Journal of the American Medical Association,* August 17, 1979, p. 616.

Hageman, Mary Jan; Kennedy, Robert B.; and Price, Norman. "Coping with stress." *The Police Chief,* February 1979, pp. 27-28.

Hall, Richard C.W.; Stickney, Sondra K.; and Popkin, Michael K. "Physician Drug Abuser." *Journal of Nervous and Mental Disease,* 1978, pp. 787-793.

Hendrickson, Barbara. "Principals: your job is a hazard to your health." *The Executive Educator,* March 1979, pp. 22-24.

Henry, Sarah. "Alcohol and drugs: the doctor's own prescription." *Canadian Medical Association Journal,* April 21, 1979, p. 889.

Houpt, Jeffrey L., et al. "The role of psychiatric and behavioral factors in the practice of medicine." *American Journal of Psychiatry,* January 1980, pp. 37-47.

Houston, Allen. "Courses help wives cope with police husbands." *Greeley* (Colorado) *Tribune,* January 31, 1980, p. 18.

Howard, John H., et al. "Stress in the job and career of a dentist." *Journal of the American Dental Association,* September 1979, pp. 630-636.

Hunter, Madeline. "Counterirritants to . . . teaching." *Instructor,* August 1977, pp. 120-123.

Intellect. "Coping with stress effective." July 1977, pp. 13-14.

International Management. "Decruitment: a solution for burned-out executives." April 1978, pp. 44-46.

Jenkins, Gladys Gardner. "For parents particularly (II)." *Childhood Education,* January 1979, pp. 157-159.

Jenkins, John A. "Picket." *Student Lawyer,* January 1979, pp. 20-23.

Journal of Accountancy. "Family health under stress!" November 1979, p. 40.

————. "How to break the worry cycle." October 1979, p. 36.

Kales, Joyce D.; Martin, Enos D.; and Soldatos, Constantin R. "Emotional problems of physicians and their families." *Pennsylvania Medicine,* December 1978, pp. 14-16.

Kassover, Jodi. "The burned-out counselor." Speech delivered at the University of Northern Colorado, July 12, 1978.

Kimes, J. D. "Handling stress in the accounting profession." *Management Accounting,* September 1977, pp. 17-23.

Kimmel, Karlheinz. "The expectations of the dentist." *International Dental Journal,* 1974, pp. 356-360.

Kobasa, Suzanne C.; Hilker, Robert R.J.; and Maddi, Salvatore R. "Who stays healthy under stress?" *Journal of Occupational Medicine,* September 1979, pp. 595-598.

Kremer, Bruce J., and Owne, William A. "Stress in the life of the counselor." *The School Counselor,* September 1979, pp. 40-46.

Kyriacou, Chris, and Sutcliffe, John. "Teacher stress: a review." *Educational Review,* 1977, pp. 299-306.

――――. "Teacher stress: prevalence, sources and symptoms." *British Journal of Educational Psychology,* 1978, pp. 159-167.

Lee, Margaret M. "Stress: how to cool it." *Today's Secretary,* January 1980, pp. 24-27.

Looney, John G., et al. "Psychiatrists' transition from training to career: stress and mastery." *American Journal of Psychiatry,* January 1980, pp. 33-36.

Mademoiselle. "What stress can do to your body." October 1979, p. 80.

Manuso, James S. "Executive stress management." *Personnel Administrator,* November 1979, pp. 23-26.

Maslach, Christina. "Burned-out." *Human Behavior,* September 1976, pp. 17-21.

――――. "The client role in staff burn-out." *Journal of Social Issues,* 1978, pp. 111-124.

Maslach, Christina, and Jackson, Susan E. "Lawyer burn-out." *Barrister,* Spring 1978, p. 8.

――――. "Burned-out cops and their families." *Psychology Today,* May 1979, pp. 59-62.

Maslach, Christina, and Pines, Ayala. "The burn-out syndrome in the day-care setting." *Child Care Quarterly,* Summer 1977, pp. 100-113.

Mattingly, Martha A. "Sources of stress and burn-out in professional child care work." *Child Care Quarterly,* Summer 1977, pp. 127-137.

――――. "Stress and burn-out in child care." *Child Care Quarterly,* Summer 1977, pp. 88-89.

Mawardi, Betty Hosmer. "Satisfactions, dissatisfactions, and causes of stress in medical practice." *Journal of the American Medical Association,* April 6, 1979, pp. 1483-1486.

Maynard, Peter E., and Maynard, Nancy W. "Preventing police family stress through couples communication training." *The Police Chief,* February 1980, pp. 30-31.

McCafferty, William B., et al. "The stress of coaching." *Physician and Sports Medicine,* February 1978, pp. 66-71.

McGuire, Patrick. "Burned out on job? There are ways to bounce back." *Denver Post,* January 17, 1979, p. 37.

McGuire, Willard H. "Teacher burnout." *Today's Education,* November-December 1979, p. 5.

Megarry, Robert. "Temptations of the bench." *Alberta Law Review,* 1978, pp. 406–416.

Mirkin, Gabe. "How to cope with job stress." *Nation's Business,* January 1979, pp. 69–72.

Moe, Dorothy. "Teacher burnout: a prescription." *Today's Education,* November-December 1979, pp. 35–36.

Morris, Carolyn L. "Relaxation therapy in a clinic." *American Journal of Nursing,* November 1979, pp. 1958–1959.

Murray, Robin M. "The health of doctors: a review." *Journal of the Royal College of Physicians,* October 1978, pp. 403–415.

Nadelson, Carol C.; Notman, Malkah T.; and Lowenstein, Penny. "The practice patterns, life styles, and stresses of women and men entering medicine: a follow-up study of Harvard medical school graduates from 1967 to 1977. " *Journal of American Medical Women's Association.* November 1979, pp. 400–406.

National Institute of Mental Health, U.S. Department of Health and Human Services. *Plain Talk about Stress.* Rockville, Maryland, 1980.

Nation's Business. "A simple, cost-free, and comfortable way to combat job tension." December 1976, pp. 29–31.

Nealy, Donna Perry. "Police stress... way of life on the job." *Greeley* (Colorado) *Tribune,* December 5, 1979, p. 12.

Nelson, Elof G.; and Henry, William F. "Psychosocial factors seen as problems by family practice residents and their spouses." *Journal of Family Practice,* 1978, pp. 581–590.

Nelson, Sarah B. "Some dynamics of medical marriages." *Journal of the Royal College of General Practitioners,* October 1978, pp. 585–586.

Odiorne, George S. "Executive under siege: strategies for survival." *Management Review,* April 1978, pp. 7–12.

O'Flynn-Comiskey, Alice I. "The type A individual." *American Journal of Nursing,* November 1979, pp. 1956–1958.

O'Rear, Joyce M., and Hope, Kerry. "Coping with stress: getting the message across." *Personnel and Guidance Journal,* June 1979, pp. 556–557.

Paul, E. "The elimination of stress and fatigue in operative dentistry." *British Dental Journal,* July 1, 1969, pp. 37–41.

Pelligrino, John F. "Managing stress ... a challenge for American business." *Mortgage Banker,* July 1979, pp. 12-20.

————. "Stress: how to manage it." *Mortgage Banker,* August 1979, pp. 7-12.

Pines, Ayala, and Maslach, Christina. "Characteristics of staff burnout in mental health settings." *Hospital and Community Psychiatry,* April 1978, pp. 233-237.

Psychology Today. "Taking stress in stride." October 1979, pp. 35-36.

Rathus, Spencer. "A 30-item schedule for assessing assertive behavior." *Behavior Therapy,* 1973, pp. 388-406.

Reed, Michael J. "Stress in live-in child care." *Child Care Quarterly,* Summer 1977, pp. 114-119.

Reed, Phil, and Patty, Mike. "Stress: a common reason for child-beating." *Rocky Mountain News,* May 28, 1979, p. 4.

Reed, Sally. "What you can do to prevent teacher burnout." *National Elementary Principal,* March 1979, pp. 67-70.

Rosch, Paul J. "Stress and illness." *Journal of the American Medical Association,* August 3, 1979, pp. 427-428.

Rose, K. Daniel, and Rosow, Irving. "Physicians who kill themselves." *Archives of General Psychiatry,* December 1973, pp. 800-805.

Rose-Clapp, Margery. "Burnout syndrome: who ministers to the overworked minister?" *Denver Post,* December 16, 1979, p. 98.

Rubenstein, Carin. "Survey report on how Americans view vacations." *Psychology Today,* May 1980, pp. 62-76.

Rupp, Carla Marie. "Press stresses aired at ANPA encounter." *Editor and Publisher,* April 30, 1977, p. 15.

Russek, Henry I. "Emotional stress and coronary heart disease in American physicians, dentists, and lawyers." *American Journal of the Medical Sciences,* 1962, pp. 716-726.

Russell, John A. "Athletes, businessmen share tension." *Automotive News,* September 24, 1979, p. 24.

Salter, Leonard M. "In defense of the legal profession: hath not a lawyer hands, organs, senses, affections, passions?" *Commercial Law Journal,* April 1980, pp. 142-143.

Saper, Marshall B. "Police wives: the hidden resource." *The Police Chief,* February 1980, pp. 28-29.

Savings and Loan News. "Coping techniques minimize stress." May 1979, pp. 102-103.

Scrivens, Robert. "The big click." *Today's Education,* November/December 1979, pp. 34-35.

Seiderman, Stanley. "Combatting staff burn-out." *Day Care and Early Education,* Summer 1978, pp. 6–9.

Shortt, S.E.D. "Psychiatric illness in physicians." *Canadian Medical Association Journal,* August 4, 1979, pp. 283–288.

Shubin, Seymour. "Burnout: the professional hazard you face in nursing." *Nursing78,* July 1978, pp. 22–27.

————. "Rx for stress—your stress." *Nursing79,* January 1979, pp. 53–55.

Singleton, Gary W., and Teahan, John. "Effects of job-related stress on the physical and psychological adjustment of police officers." *Journal of Police Science and Administration,* 1978, pp. 355–361.

Slater, Shirley. "Creative coping: teaching students to cope with crises." *Forecast for Home Economics,* May/June 1976, p. 49.

Smith, Marcy J.T.; and Selye, Hans. "Reducing the negative effects of stress." *American Journal of Nursing,* November 1979, pp. 1953–1955.

Smith, Reginald L. "Those people aren't people anymore..." *Hospital Topics,* November/December 1979, pp. 14–15.

Solicitors' journal. "Unpopularity and criticism of lawyers." July 27, 1979, pp. 499–501.

Sparks, Dennis. "A teacher center tackles the issue." *Today's Education,* November/December 1979, pp. 37–39.

Sparks, Dennis, and Ingram, Marjorie J. "Stress prevention and management: a workshop approach." *Personnel and Guidance Journal,* November 1979, pp. 197–200.

Speich, Pamela L. "Taking a psychosocial stress 'pulse.'" *Journal of Emergency Nursing,* August 1979, pp. 43–47.

Storlie, Frances J. "Burnout: the elaboration of a concept." *American Journal of Nursing,* December 1979, pp. 2108–2111.

Stratton, John G. "Police stress and the criminal investigator." *The Police Chief,* February 1979, pp. 22–26.

Student, Kurt R. "Changing values and management stress." *Personnel,* January/February 1977, pp. 48–55.

————. "Personnel's newest challenge: helping to cope with greater stress." *Personnel Administrator,* November 1978, pp. 20–24.

Suinn, Richard M. "How to break the vicious cycle of stress." *Psychology Today,* December 1976, pp. 59–60.

Sullivan, Ruth Christ. "The burn-out syndrome." *Journal of Autism and Developmental Disorders,* 1979, pp. 111–126.

Sutton, Beverly. "Consideration of career time in child care work: observations on child care work experiences." *Child Care Quarterly,* Summer 1977, pp. 121–125.

Switzer, Lucigrace. "Gelusil, jogging, and gin: how executive educators deal with stress." *The Executive Educator,* January 1979, pp. 27–29.

Time. "Help! Teacher can't teach!" June 16, 1980, pp. 54–63.

Today's Secretary. "Salary survey: 1979." March 1979, p. 32.

Training and Development Journal. "10 ways to cope with pressure." July 1978, pp. 69–71.

Truell, George. "Where have all the achievers gone?" *Personnel,* November/December 1973, pp. 37–40.

USA Today. "Causes of emotional distress." April 1979, p. 16.

———. "When work isn't fun anymore." October 1979, pp. 7–9.

Van Auken, Steven. "Youth counselor burnout." *Personnel and Guidance Journal,* October 1979, pp. 143–144.

Walsh, Debbie. "Classroom stress and teacher burnout." *Phi Delta Kappan,* December 1979, p. 253.

Warnath, Charles F., and Shelton, John L. "The ultimate disappointment: the burned-out counselor." *Personnel and Guidance Journal,* December 1976, pp. 172–175.

White, Jane See. "'Underload' causes boredom, frustration." *Greeley* (Colorado) *Tribune,* December 8, 1979, p. 11.

Willee, A. W. "How to avoid the occupational hazards of dentistry." *Australian Dental Journal,* August 1967, pp. 348–359.

Williams, Andrea. "Teaching gifted students how to deal with stress." *Gifted Child Quarterly,* Spring 1979, pp. 136–141.

Zotti, Ed. "Ten questions to ask yourself before you become a lawyer." *Student Lawyer,* December 1978, pp. 32–33.

Index

367

369

Public attitudes (*cont.*)
    toward police, 96-97, 101-2, 103, 104, 108
    toward principals, 45-46
    toward teachers, 17, 19

Reading, 55, 144, 174, 189
Relationship squares activity, 340-42
Relaxation techniques, 32, 86, 88, 89, 105, 125-26, 143, 159-60, 262-66
Religious institutions, 167-68
Respiratory infections, 49, 156, 243
Responsibility, burnout and, 44-45, 60-61, 145-46, 165-66, 242
Rest, 32, 67, 86, 128, 173, 188, 245
Retirement, 124, 217-18
Role conflict, 42, 95, 101, 128
Routinism, 50-51, 52, 57-58, 87, 143-44, 206, 220, 244
Running, 67

SAFE activity, 305-8
Salaries (*see under each job or professional category*)
Sarcasm, 117, 139
Secretary burnout:
    causes of, 219-28
    cures for, 231-37
    symptoms of, 228-31
Self-blame, 44-45, 52
Self-concept strengtheners activity, 321-23
Self-doubt, 116, 120
Self-esteem, loss of, 28, 74, 75, 94, 101-2, 135-36, 207
Self-knowledge, 37, 39-40, 68, 128, 175, 189-90, 247, 326-30
Sexual activity, 231
Sexual harassment, 227
Sitting for health activity, 268-69
Sleep problems, 49, 63, 183, 205, 228, 243
Social burnout prevention activities, 324-43
Social facilitation schedule activity, 325-26
Social sharing of self scale, 326-30
Sociograms, 335-38
Spiritual burnout prevention activities, 349-56
Spiritual stress stages test, 345-48
SQ, student survival and, 62
Status, lack of, 135-36, 225-26 (*see also* Public attitudes)
Stereotyped thinking, 283-84
Stereotyping, group response test and, 339-40
Stress:
    accidents and, 64
    complexion and, 205
    identification of sources of, 54, 126, 144
    management of, 234-35
    reduction, 34, 37, 48, 53, 105, 127-28, 213
Stressful habits test, 279-80
Stretching exercises, 86, 105, 210, 231

Strokes, 204, 243
Student burnout:
    causes of, 59-63
    cures for, 66-70
    symptoms of, 63-66
Student-teacher ratio, 20, 22
Students:
    changing attitudes of, 21
    contacts with principals, 47
    disruptive, 18-19
    energy restoring techniques for, 33
    participation in educational decisions, 23
    physical assaults against teachers, 16
Style of conflict test, 332-35
Subject-object dichotomy, 178-79
Suicide:
    of college students, 66, 70
    of dentists, 150, 154, 155, 158-59, 163
    knowledge test, 352-54
    of physicians, 124
    prevention methods, 354
    of youth, 59
Support groups, 38, 91

Teacher burnout:
    causes of, 16-29
    cures for, 29-40
    symptoms of, 25-29
Temper, 27, 139, 140, 207, 214
Time pressures:
    dentists and, 153-54
    journalists and, 240-41
    physicians and, 126
Timeouts, 33, 127-28, 304-5
Tiredness (*see* Fatigue)

Ulcers, 26, 204, 243

Vacations, 16, 28, 36, 40, 108, 153, 216, 232, 242
Values, 68, 73-74, 112-13, 201-2
Victims of crimes, police and, 97-98
Vocabulary changes (*see* Language changes)
Volunteer work, 107, 149

Walking, 67, 159-60, 175, 190-91, 209-10
Warm baths and showers, 32, 54
Weekends, 130
Weight maintenance, 32, 53, 183, 205
Withdrawal, 12, 65
Word conditions (*see under each job or professional category*)
Work hours (*see under job or professional category*)
Worries, identification of, 212-13
Writing, 170, 174, 236
    and creative writing wheel, 280-81
    (*see also* Journals)

Youth (*see* Student burnout)